1986

The Vatican and Italian Fascism,
1929–32

i

THE VATICAN AND ITALIAN FASCISM, 1929–32

A study in conflict

JOHN F. POLLARD

Senior Lecturer in Italian History,
Cambridgeshire College of Arts and Technology

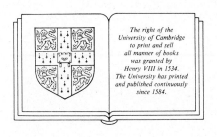

The right of the
University of Cambridge
to print and sell
all manner of books
was granted by
Henry VIII in 1534.
The University has printed
and published continuously
since 1584.

CAMBRIDGE UNIVERSITY PRESS

Cambridge

London   New York   New Rochelle

Melbourne   Sydney

Published by the Press Syndicate of the University of Cambridge
The Pitt Building, Trumpington Street, Cambridge CB2 1RP
32 East 57th Street, New York, NY 10022, USA
10 Stamford Road, Oakleigh, Melbourne 3166, Australia

First published 1985

Printed in Great Britain by the University Press, Cambridge

Library of Congress catalogue card number: 85–5889

British Library cataloguing in publication data
Pollard, John F.
The Vatican and Italian Fascism, 1929–32: a
study in conflict
1. Italy–Foreign relations–Vatican City
2. Vatican City–Foreign relations–Italy
I. Title
327.45045'634   DG499.V3

ISBN 0 521 26870 2

To Martin

Contents

Acknowledgements

This study was originally written as a doctoral thesis for the Department of Italian Studies of the University of Reading. I should therefore like to thank Professor Stuart Woolf for his help and encouragement at the beginning of the project. I am deeply indebted to my supervisor Dr Paul Corner without whose patience, kindness and unstinting professional advice and assistance this project would not have been completed.

I am grateful to the following who gave me so much advice and assistance in Rome: Prof. Claudio Pavone, Prof. Pietro Scoppola, Prof. Lionello Carocci, Prof. Vincenzo Saba, the late Prof. Federico Alessandrini, Dott. Consigliere Federico Tomassi and the late Prof. Angelo Jervolino. I feel bound to make a special mention of Prof. Sebastiano Fadda, whose friendship and hospitality made working in Rome an enjoyable as well as a productive experience.

My research would not have been possible without a year's paid study leave and other financial assistance granted by Cambridgeshire College of Arts and Technology. I am grateful for this and for the encouragement of Charles Dodd, the College Staff Development Officer.

Like all those engaged in research, I am indebted to the staff of a number of archives and libraries, but unfortunately space does not permit me to mention them all here. I am particularly indebted to Dr Paola Carucci and her colleagues for guiding me through the complexities of the Archivo Centrale dello Stato in Rome. I should also like to thank Dott. Romanelli of the library of Azione Cattolica Italiana, Padre Martini of the archives and library of La Civilta Cattolica and the staff of the Istituto Luigi Sturzo whose kindness and sense of humour made their library the most congenial place to work in Rome. My thanks are also due to Clarissa Campbell-Orr, Noel Currer Briggs, Peter Hebblethwaite, Paul McHugh and Donald Pirie for reading various drafts.

Finally I would like to thank my sister Veronica for typing the last draft.

Cambridge   J. F. P.
September 1984

Abbreviations

ABBREVIATIONS USED IN THE TEXT

ABBREVIATIONS USED IN THE FOOTNOTES

ARCHIVAL SOURCES

A.C.C.   Archivio della Civiltà Cattolica (Archive of the Jesuit Order)
A.C.S.   Archivio Centrale dello Stato (Central State Archive), Rome

Ministry of the Interior
C.P.C.   Casellario Politico Centrale (File of Political Suspects)
D.G.P.S.   Direzione Generale della Pubblica Sicurezza (Police H.Q.)
M.P.P.   Materia Polizia Politica (Political Police Files)
S.C.P.   Segreteria Capo della Polizia (Office of the Chief of Police)

Ministry of Justice
F.C.   Fondo per il Culto (Religious Affairs Department, before 1931)

Miscellaneous
P.C.M.   Presidenza Consiglio dei Ministri (Prime Minister's Office)
S.P.D.   Segreteria Particolare del Duce (Mussolini's Private Office)
A.A.G.   Archivio Amadeo Giannini
P.R.O.,F.O. Public Record Office, Foreign Office Papers

PRINTED SOURCES

Atti	*Atti Parlamentari del Regno d'Italia*, Camera/Senato
D.D.I., 7	*I Documenti Diplomatici Italiani*, *Settima Serie (1922–35)*, Rome 1952–0000
De Felice I	R. De Felice, *Mussolini il rivoluzionario, 1883–1920*, Turin, 1965
De Felice II	R. De Felice, *Mussolini il Fascista*, Vol. I, *La conquista del potere, 1921–25*, Turin, 1966
De Felice III	R. De Felice, *Mussolini il Fascista*, Vol. II, *L'organizzazione dello Stato Fascista, 1925–29*, Turin, 1968
De Felice IV	R. De Felice, *Mussolini il Duce*, Vol. I, *Gli anni del consenso 1929–36*, Turin, 1974
De Vecchi Memorie	Memoirs of C. M. De Vecchi, published posthumously in *Il Tempo*, January–March 1960
Discorsi	*Discorsi di Pio XI*, Vol. II, 1929–33, Turin, 1960
O.O.	*Opera Omnia di Benito Mussolini*, 36 vols., ed. E. and D. Susmel, Florence, 1951–63

PERIODICAL PUBLICATIONS

Bollettino Ufficiale   *Bollettino Ufficiale dell'Azione Cattolica Italiana*

Gazzetta Ufficiale   *Gazzetta Ufficiale del Regno (della Repubblica* after 1946)

CHAPTER 1

Introduction

On 11 February 1929, Pietro Gasparri, Cardinal Secretary of State to Pope Pius XI, and Benito Mussolini, Duce of Fascism and Head of the Italian Government, signed the Treaties of the Lateran, bringing to an end the 'Roman Question', the sixty-year-old dispute between the Papacy and the Kingdom of Italy.

In common with other Church and State disputes in the nineteenth and twentieth centuries, the 'Roman Question' had its origins in an ideological conflict, a conflict between the secularising and modernising tendencies of Liberalism and the resistance to this development on the part of the Catholic Church. Like other European Liberals, the Italian Moderate Liberals led by D'Azeglio and Cavour enacted a series of laws, first in Piedmont and then in the rest of Italy, which wrested control of such matters as education, marriage and censorship from the Church, established freedom of religion for Protestants and Jews, dissolved many of the contemplative religious orders and confiscated a substantial portion of the property of the Church.[1]

But the Church and State dispute in Italy had a dimension that sharply differentiated it from similar disputes elsewhere, for the process of Italian unification necessarily involved the destruction of the Pope's temporal power, that is his sovereignty over the Papal States of central Italy. In September 1870, the last remnant of that sovereignty was extinguished when Italian troops occupied the City of Rome and made it the capital of Italy. Despite all the attempts by Cavour and his successors to find a compromise solution, Pius IX refused to accept the loss of the temporal power. He refused to recognise the Kingdom of Italy and excommunicated its rulers, and his policy was continued, on a formal basis at least, until 1929.

Inevitably, the 'Roman Question' had serious deleterious consequences both for the Church and Italy. Though the Popes quickly learned to live

---

[1] For a full account of the origins and development of the 'Roman Question' see Jemolo, *Chiesa e Stato*, chap. 1, and Binchy, *Church and State*, chap. 1.

without their temporal power, and indeed were eventually thankful to be rid of its burdensome responsibilities, the Church in Italy suffered considerably from its conflict with the State. At the mercy of a political class which was riddled by freemasonry of the continental, anti-clerical variety, the Church was forced to endure periodic outbursts of anti-clerical violence, the imposition of further restrictive anti-clerical legislation and even attempts to introduce divorce.[2] And though there is some evidence of a religious revival in late nineteenth-century Italy (for example, the massive growth of religious orders), in a wider sense the dominance of anti-clerical and secular values in the Liberal era[3] contributed to a progressive 'dechristianisation' of Italian society which was much lamented by Catholic observers.

The 'Roman Question' was equally if not more damaging in its effects upon the development of the new united Italian State. In the diplomatic sphere the 'Roman Question' was more than a momentary embarrassment. It constituted a serious complicating factor in Italy's relations with other Catholic states, particularly Austria, her partner in the Triple Alliance after 1881.[4] The 'Roman Question' also helped to widen the gulf between 'Real' Italy and 'Legal' Italy, that is between the rulers and the ruled. There was some direct papal involvement in the situation of near civil war facing the Government in the South during the 1860s; and in Italy generally, the Church's hostility reinforced the natural diffidence of the peasant masses towards the new State and its ruling class. In addition, the 'Non Expedit' – the papal decree forbidding Catholics to take part in the politics of the Liberal State – deprived Italian public life of the contribution of some of its most talented citizens, and restricted still further the very narrow electorate.

The conflict between Church and State placed an intolerable strain on the consciences of Italian Catholics, making it very difficult to be both an obedient Catholic and a good Italian. In this way, the 'Roman Question' constituted a grave spiritual wound in the Italian Risorgimento.

The resolution of the 'Roman Question' in 1929 was, therefore, a momentous event in the history of Italy and a remarkable achievement for both Pius XI and Mussolini. But this reconciliation or *Conciliazione*, as it is called by Italians, did not inaugurate the long-desired and long-awaited peace between Church and State: on the contrary, in the three years that ran from the signing of the Lateran Pacts until Mussolini's visit to the Pope in February 1932, there was to be more conflict between the Vatican and Fascism than in the preceding seven-year period that had begun with the

[2] Jemolo, *Chiesa e Stato*, chap. 2, pp. 39–45.
[3] The terms 'Liberal Italy' and the 'Liberal era' are here taken to mean the period of Italian history from unification in 1861 to the advent of the Fascism in 1922; they derive from the fact that Italy in this period was ruled by an avowedly 'Liberal' political class.
[4] See Seton-Watson, *Italy from Liberalism to Fascism*, pp. 98–101.

March on Rome or in the one which followed between 1932 and 1939. Relations between the Vatican and the Regime in the period 1929–32 were marked by acrimonious diplomatic disputes, violent polemics between the Catholic and Fascist press and intransigent public statements on the part of both the Pope and Mussolini which culminated in a full-blown crisis in the Spring and Summer of 1931. Eventually a compromise was reached in the Accords of September 1931, which was to provide the basis for a comparatively harmonious relationship, a 'marriage of convenience', that was to last until 1938, when there was a renewal of conflict over Catholic Action and Mussolini's introduction of the Racial Laws.

The object of this study is to consider why it was that the seven preceding years of rapprochement between the Vatican and Fascism, years marked by dramatic changes of policy and substantial sacrifices of position on both sides, not to mention two and a half years of difficult and secret negotiations, were unable to ensure at least a minimum of peace between the two sides in the period 1929–32. Was it largely a question of differing interpretations of the Lateran Pacts – particularly the Concordat – or had the Pacts left unresolved major problems that were to resurface in the three years that followed? Was the conflict in this period due in part at least to the differing and exaggerated expectations for the future being entertained on both sides? Or was the cause of the conflict more serious than any of these problems, namely that the Lateran Pacts were unable to reconcile two fundamentally opposed philosophical systems and satisfy their mutually exclusive claims to the hearts and minds of the young, if not indeed of the whole Italian people?

One is also obliged to ask why it proved possible to resolve the disputes of late 1929 and early 1930 but impossible to prevent the same kind of disputes about the same sorts of problems from developing into a serious crisis in the Spring of 1931. What new factors had emerged in the intervening twelve-month period that would help to account for the bitterness of the crisis of 1931? Finally, it is necessary to consider why it was that the agreement which brought the 1931 crisis to an end was able to ensure for the next seven years a harmony in relations between the Vatican and the Regime that had been so conspicuously lacking in the period 1929–32.

THE PROTAGONISTS: THE CHURCH

It is a matter of fundamental importance to an understanding of the relationship between the Church and Fascism to appreciate that both protagonists were very complicated entities, very much less monolithic and homogeneous than they appear at first sight. Only when the complexity of their internal structures and the nature of their internal tensions are revealed is it possible fully to understand the dynamics of the conflict that developed between them in the period 1929 to 1932.

The Church was in reality a complex of interlocking organisations and forces which operated on various different planes simultaneously. In the first place, the role of the Catholic Church in Italy was, and still is, conditioned by a factor which is missing in every other Catholic country, the physical presence of the Holy See. In consequence, the Catholic Church in Italy speaks with a greater and more direct authority than elsewhere, for its visible head is no mere cardinal primate, but the Bishop of Rome, the Successor of the Prince of the Apostles and the Vicar of Christ himself. As the infallible head of the Church throughout the world, in his dealing with the Italian State, he is able to make use of an immense, international political influence and prestige. The loss of the temporal power in the middle of the nineteenth century did not substantially diminish these assets, and the rise of Catholicism in the New World, especially in the United States of America, actually increased their value.[5]

Relations between the Church and the State in Italy, therefore, have never been and can never be like those in any other country, either in Europe or anywhere else. All Italian governments, whatever their political complexion, must contend with the geographical presence of the Papacy and with the international dimension of that institution. Thus the relationship between the Church and Fascism was not a purely internal, domestic Italian affair, but was also a matter affecting the international standing of both the Vatican and Italy. And, by the same token, as the relationship developed between 1929 and 1932 it was powerfully affected by international issues and events and by the role played by both the Vatican and Italy in those events. Moreover, given the virtually absolute control exercised by the Vatican over the bishops and clergy in Italy, to all intents and purposes the Vatican *was* the Church in Italy, and for this reason, therefore, it is impossible to avoid using these terms interchangeably, as indeed they are used in this book.

Whilst it is clear that the Vatican regarded its relations with Italy as being of paramount importance, if only because Italy was the 'home' and hinterland of the Holy See, Vatican policy towards Italy was not conceived in isolation but formed an integral part of a broader strategy. In the 1920s and 1930s, under the guidance of Pius XI and Cardinal Gasparri, the policy of the Holy See towards secular governments and secular society generally could be summed up as 'Concordats and Catholic Action'. Vatican diplomacy in the reign of Pius XI was directed towards securing cast-iron,

[5] For an account of the role of the Holy See in international affairs in the late nineteenth century and early twentieth century, see Von Aretin, *The Papacy and the Modern World*, Parts 3 and 4, and Holmes, *The Triumph of the Holy See*, chap. 6.

juridical agreements – concordats – as a means of regulating relations between the Church and national governments. During his seventeen-year pontificate, Pius XI signed concordats with seven other states, Bavaria and Lithuania (1924), Poland (1925), Prussia (1929), Baden (1932), Austria and the German Reich (1933), and came close to agreement with three more – Albania, Czechoslavakia and Yugoslavia.[6] For the Vatican Secretariat of State the concordat became a universal panacea, the only guaranteed way of defending the Church's interests in Catholic and non-Catholic countries alike. Thus there was nothing very special or unusual about the Italian Concordat of 1929, except for the fact that whereas all the others had been concluded with more or less democratic regimes, this one had been agreed with a Fascist dictatorship. It remained to be seen whether the Concordat would prove to be as effective a means of defending the Church's interests in a Fascist, totalitarian regime, as it had so far been in liberal, democratic states.

The stress on the efficacy of Catholic Action as the other means of defending the Church's interests and advancing the Christian apostolate in society was another cardinal feature of the reign of Pius XI, earning him the title of 'The Pope of Catholic Action'. It is clear from the many apostolic letters and encyclicals that Pius XI wrote on the subject, and in particular from the major encyclical, *Ubi Arcano Dei* of 1922, that the Pope intended that the conception of Catholic Action, '...the participation of the laity in the Apostolate of the Hierarchy', should be put into practice in all countries with a sizeable Catholic community.[7] Catholic Action was to be the instrument for nothing less than a Christian reconquest of a society corrupted and enslaved by the evils of the modern world.

In his scheme for this Christian reconquest of society Pius XI was not so naive as to neglect the political dimension. But even in Catholic countries he preferred a non-political Catholic Action organisation working *indirectly* to influence politics in a Christian direction rather than an autonomous, avowedly Catholic party exercising *direct* political influence with all the risks that such a policy carried for the Church. He was, therefore, able to view the dissolution of the Catholic P.P.I. in Italy in late 1926 with equanimity, convinced that the Church's interests would soon be secured by a Concordat guaranteeing the continued existence of Catholic Action. Thus, further attacks by the Fascists on Catholic Action after the *Conciliazone*

---

[6] For an analysis of the concordatory policy see Von Aretin, *The Papacy and the Modern World*, pp. 182–8, and Rhodes, *The Vatican in the Age of the Dictators*, chaps. 6, 10, 11 and 12.

[7] The text of *Ubi Arcano Dei* is to be found in Anon., *Pius XI, the Popes and Catholic Action*, along with the texts of apostolic letters to the Archbishops of Breslau and Toledo. According to Hales, *The Catholic Church in the Modern World*, p. 281, in his apostolic letter *Firmissima Constantia* of March 1937, the Pope urged the development of Catholic Action as the answer to anti-clerical persecution in Mexico. The encyclical *Divini Redemptoris* of the same date also advocates the spread of Catholic Action as a cure for Communism.

of 1929 were bound to provoke outraged and intransigent resistance on the part of Pius XI.

Acquiescence in the demise of the P.P.I. implicitly involved acceptance of the demise of Italian democracy. Its passing went unmourned in a Vatican still strongly influenced by traditional Catholic prejudices against the Liberal State whose authoritarian, Fascist successor offered such a promising future to the Church in Italy. But these prejudices were never absolutes, they were never allowed to dominate the Vatican's policy towards other states in the 1920s. The Vatican was happy to do business with democracies, even with the homeland of freemasonry and anticlericalism, the Third French Republic. Indeed, relations between the Vatican and this somewhat errant 'Elder Daughter of the Church' improved out of all recognition in the post-First World War period.

But for reasons which are not entirely clear, Mussolini remained blind to this political pragmatism on the Vatican's part, believing that as a result of the *Conciliazione*, Fascist Italy now enjoyed a 'special relationship' with the Vatican. Only the persistent failure of his attempts to involve the Vatican in schemes to defend or extend Italian interests abroad, coupled with the Vatican's calculated acceptance of the transition from a Catholic monarchy to a secular Republic in Spain, opened his eyes. And this revelation was to have an important influence on the course of the 1931 crisis between the Church and Fascism.

Until very recently the international or diplomatic dimension of the relationship between the Church and Italian Fascism has been largely neglected.[8] Yet it is clearly an important one, and for this reason we shall devote a considerable amount of attention to it and to its ultimate impact on the crisis of 1931.

But the Papacy is not the whole of the Catholic Church, however germane it may be to the peculiar nature of Italian Catholicism. The Church in Italy is also a vast, rambling, capillary organisation, and in the 1920s and 1930s it was a faithful mirror of the regional variety and complexity of Italian society as a whole. The fundamental differences between northern and southern society, in particular, were reflected in the varying levels of social and political consciousness among the bishops, clergy and laity at this time.

Among the bishops and clergy of northern, and to a lesser extent, central Italy there was a strong, lively tradition of awareness and commitment to the economic and social, as well as the purely spiritual, needs of their flocks, especially the poor peasantry. There was also a powerful political consciousness, born of the struggles between 'intransigents' and 'conciliatorists': the 'intransigents' rejecting and boycotting the Liberal

---

[8] See Kent, *The Pope and the Duce.*

State in the wake of unification and the destruction of the Pope's temporal power, and the 'conciliatorists' advocating compromise and reconciliation. In the South and the Islands, apart from a few exceptional areas like Sicily and Calabria, there was little tradition of this sort, the episcopacy and clergy being firmly embedded in the structures of southern backwardness. Furthermore, the southern bishops and parochial clergy were very often indifferent or even hostile to lay initiatives and activities in general and to Catholic Action in particular.

The response of the Italian episcopacy and clergy to the rise of Fascism and to the *Conciliazione* which the Church concluded with it was predictably far from uniform, as was its response to the disputes between the Church and Fascism as they developed between 1929 and 1932.

Beyond the Papacy and the ecclesiastical hierarchy of bishops and clergy there was a third dimension to Italian Catholicism, and one which is very central to our theme – the Catholic movement. The term 'Catholic movement' itself covers a number of distinct but connected organisations and forces, united ultimately by a common religious faith and obedience to the Pope. The Italian Catholic movement of clergy and laity originally developed as a manifestation of the Church's felt need to defend itself against the anti-clerical, Liberal State in the mid- and late nineteenth century. In this endeavour, a combative Catholic press and other organisations, like the Società della Gioventù Cattolica Italiana, the male Catholic youth organisation, were born,[9] and the 'Non Expedit', the Vatican's ban on Catholic participation in Italian politics, reinforced the process whereby Catholics obedient to the Holy See withdrew into a kind of 'ghetto' to escape the contaminating influences of Liberal Italy.

The development of the Italian Catholic movement received a further impetus from Pope Leo XIII's encyclical *Rerum Novarum* of 1891 which stressed the duty of Catholics, clergy and laity alike, to assist actively in the moral and material improvement of the conditions of the working masses. By the end of the nineteenth century, the Catholic movement had created a vast network of banks, mutual benefit societies, peasant co-operatives, industrial trade unions, recreational and cultural associations not to mention a flourishing press, in whose organisation the parochial clergy of northern and central Italy were deeply and directly involved.

But as an American historian of the Italian Catholic movement has pointed out: 'It is always a mistake to write of Catholics, in Italy, or elsewhere, as a bloc. Within the general limits of obedience to the Holy See there is room for all but the most radical differences.'[10] This was especially true of Italian Catholics in the first decade of this century, for

---

[9] For the early history of the Italian Catholic movement see Candeloro, *Il Movimento Cattolico in Italia*; De Rosa, *Il Movimento cattolica in Italia*; and Webster, *The Cross and the Fasces*.   [10] Webster, *The Cross and the Fasces*, p. 20.

within the limits of that obedience, and under the common banner of the Catholic movement, some very divergent currents of thought, on economic, social and political matters, managed to co-exist.

Though an 'intransigent' faction continued to exercise an ever-declining influence within the Opera dei Congressi, the official umbrella organisation of the Catholic movement, the conciliatorist/intransigent battles were largely a thing of the past, and new doctrinal and factional differences emerged to take the place of the old. Apart from the Integristi, whose essential object was to combat the spread of 'Modernism' and whose consequent favour in the Vatican during the pontificate of St Pius X also gave them some influence in the Catholic movement,[11] the two most important groups for the history of the Catholic movement, and what is more important for this study of Church and State relations in the Fascist period, were the factions known as the Clerico-Moderates and the Christian Democrats.

The Clerico-Moderates were very much a product of the new political possibilities that opened up for Italian Catholics between the beginning of the twentieth century and the outbreak of the First World War, a period known as the 'Giolittian Era' because of the political dominance of Giovanni Giolitti.[12] They were 'clericals' in as much as being 'obedient' Catholics; a major plank in their platform was the defence of the interests of the Church and the recovery of the privileges and property which it had lost in Italy during the Risorgimento. Ultimately, their aim was the reconciliation of the Church and the Italian State through a mutually satisfactory solution of the 'Roman Question'. They were 'moderates', in the Italian sense of the word, in that they were conservatives in economic and political matters: as representatives of the Catholic landowning aristocracy and mercantile bourgeoisie, the Clerico-Moderates shared the economic and political interests of the Liberal ruling class.[13] The Clerico-Moderates played a dominant role in the Catholic movement in Giolittian Italy, controlling the majority of its banks, the bulk of its newspapers, and after its establishment in 1904, its political arm the Unione Elettorale. After the First World War, the majority of the Clerico-Moderates adhered to the new Catholic political force – the P.P.I., but when yet another star appeared on the political horizon the Clerico-Moderates followed many of

---

[11] As Webster, ibid., p. 21, points out the influence of the Integristi was effectively destroyed in 1914 when one of their enemies was elected Pope as Benedict XV. For a full account of the Integristi see Poulat, *Catholicisme, Democratie et Socialisme*.

[12] Webster, *The Cross and the Fasces*, chaps. 1 and 2.

[13] And this was clearly seen to be the case by the Liberals. In 1914, A. Capitani d'Arzago, an important Liberal financier and M.P. wrote about the Clerico-Moderates in these terms: '...the Catholics, especially in the city and province of Milan, have shown themselves to be very effective collaborators of the Liberals...For many of them there is no longer any good reason to regard themselves as being different from the Liberals': as quoted in A. Caroleo, *Le Banche Cattoliche*, p. 42.

their Liberal colleagues and rallied to Fascism. As Candeloro describes it, '...the older Clerico–Moderate faction abandoned the P.P.I. and transformed itself into a new Clerico-Fascist group'.[14] In their new guise the Clerico-Moderates carried on their old role as intermediaries between Church and State, forming a bridge between the Vatican and Fascism.

Easily the largest and, in the longer run, by far the most influential faction to emerge inside the Catholic movement at the turn of the century was the Christian Democrats. Owing their original inspiration to the Catholic social teaching enshrined in *Rerum Novarum*, Pope Leo XIII's great encyclical of 1891 on the conditions of the working classes, and further nourished by the ideas of a succession of thinkers like Giuseppe Toniolo, Romolo Murri and Luigi Sturzo, the Christian Democrats advocated a comprehensive and radical programme of economic, social and political reforms. Whilst this is not the place to discuss the politics of the Catholic movement in the Giolittian Era, suffice it to say that after the election of Pope St Pius X in 1903 the Christian Democrats fell out of favour in the Vatican.[15] Though this development was partly due to Murri's dangerously 'modernist' theological tendencies, it also had a great deal to do with the radical nature of the Christian Democratic programme.[16]

Despite this defeat, Christian Democracy took deep root in the Catholic movement, providing the basis for the autonomous, Catholic political party – the P.P.I. – which Don Sturzo was to found in 1919. Christian Democracy was to provide the ideological backbone of Catholic anti-Fascism; for just as the majority of the Clerico-Moderates were to support Fascism, so the majority of Catholics of Christian Democratic beliefs were to oppose it.

This strong, surviving element of Catholic anti-Fascism both inside and outside Catholic Action, as the remnants of the Catholic organisations were renamed in the early 1920s, was a serious, complicating factor in the relationship between the Church and Fascism from 1929 to 1932, playing a central role in the 1931 crisis. As one leading Catholic historian has written of that crisis:

...it is not possible to reconstruct these events purely and simply on the model of a clash between the Church and Fascism, it is also necessary to place them in the

[14] Candeloro, *Il Movimento Cattolico in Italia*, p. 361.
[15] As a direct consequence, the Opera dei Congressi, over which the Christian Democrats had so very recently established a controlling influence, was dissolved by the Pope, and the Catholic movement was re-organised into three separate bodies – the Unione Economica-Sociale to co-ordinate the work of Catholic financial institutions, co-operatives and trade unions; the Unione Elettorale to direct the Catholic electorate after the first relaxation of the 'Non Expedit' and the Unione Popolare to supervise Catholic sporting, recreational and cultural activities. A marked feature of the new structure was the increased control by the bishops and the Vatican over the lay leadership.
[16] For an account of these developments, see Webster, *The Cross and the Fasces*, chap. 1, and for fuller treatment see De Rosa, *Il Movimento cattolico in Italia*, chaps 11–14.

much broader context of conflict between the Catholic leadership and 'rank and file' on the one hand, and of a conflict between the Fascist leadership and 'rank and file' on the other.[17]

And this was more particularly true on the Catholic side.

THE PROTAGONISTS: ITALIAN FASCISM

This tension between the leadership and the 'rank and file' was also characteristic, though to a lesser extent, of the other protagonist in this story – Italian Fascism. By 1929 the Fascist Regime had virtually completed its development as a highly centralised, one-party, police state, under the personal dictatorship of Mussolini as Duce of Fascism and Head of the Italian Government.[18] And though as an essential part of this process Mussolini had defeated the unruly, intransigent and 'revolutionary' elements in the Fascist Party, and had reduced that organisation to a subordinate role in the structure of the Regime, the Party continued to harbour some remarkably varied and independent currents and factions.[19] Fascist anti-clericalism did not itself constitute a faction, it hardly needed to because anti-clericalism was the almost instinctive and universal mentality of Fascists of the 'first hour'. Fascist anti-clericalism lost considerable ground inside the Fascist Party in the mid- and late 1920s due to the dominant influence of ex-Nationalists like Alfredo Rocco and Luigi Federzoni in the construction of the Regime. But Fascist anti-clericalism was not entirely vanquished by the success of Mussolini's religious policy. As will become very evident, the Fascist anti-clericals were to show their teeth on several occasions between 1929 and 1932. A recent historian of Fascist Italy, writing of the influence exerted on Fascism by such institutions as the Crown, the Army and the Church, and by big business and other interests, has declared: 'In fact the history of the period 1925–29 is in large part a history of the process by which Mussolini eliminated the resistance of the Fascist movement to measures by which he achieved a stable entente with these institutions.'[20] It needs to be stressed, however, that as far as the Church was concerned, Mussolini had by no means eliminated the resistance of the Fascist movement to its influence by 1929. As we shall see, that resistance was to continue for some years to come.

Just as the Vatican's overall strategy towards national governments influenced its relations with Fascist Italy, so Fascist Italy's wider foreign

---

[17] Scoppola and Traniello (eds.), *I Cattolici tra Fascismo e Democrazia*, Introduction, pp. 14–15.
[18] For a concise account of this process see A. Aquarone, 'The Rise of the Fascist State', in Sarti (ed.), *The Axe Within*, pp. 101–15.
[19] De Felice, *Intervista sul Fascismo*, pp. 27–30.
[20] Lyttelton, *The Seizure of Power*, p. 268.

policy interest influenced its relations with the Vatican. Italian foreign policy in this period was still modest and largely unaggressive. Only after Mussolini's return to the Ministry of Foreign Affairs in July 1932, and, more importantly, after Hitler's accession to power in Germany in January 1933, did Fascist foreign policy begin to move in the aggressive, expansionist direction that was to be its hallmark in the 1930s. Until then, Italy's foreign policy aspirations and ambitions, and the opportunities for achieving them were limited by a sort of international 'immobilism', Italy's room for diplomatic manoeuvre being restricted by the virtually unchallenged dominance of the League of Nations and of European affairs by Britain and France.[21]

Even so, Fascist Italy had essential interests in Austria and Yugoslavia which were in large part determined by its treatment of the German and Slav minorities in the north-eastern territories around Trento and Trieste ceded to Italy by the Treaty of Versailles. In addition, despite the constraints of the international situation, Fascist Italy already nursed imperialistic designs in the Mediterranean and in the Middle East. In all of these areas of Italian interest the role of the Vatican was potentially crucial, offering, or so it seemed to Mussolini, the possibility of diplomatic and moral support. Thus the failure of the Vatican to live up to Mussolini's expectations in this regard was an important contributory factor to the worsening of relations between the Church and the Fascist Regime between 1929 and 1932.

There were two other major preoccupations of the Fascist Regime in this period that were to have a significant bearing on its relations with the Church. The first involved the continuing efforts being made to realise the dream of the 'Totalitarian State'. Though the process of 'fascistising' the constitutional and political structures of the Italian State had been virtually completed, Fascism was far from achieving total control of the spheres of education and the economy. Certainly, in 1929, the 'fascistisation' of education and youth was not yet a reality.[22] As will be seen, in part at least these efforts were prompted by the enormous gains which the Church had made in the educational field by means of the Concordat of 1929, and by further protection afforded to Catholic youth organisations by that agreement. Given Pius XI's unyielding commitment to the defence of the Church's rights in the fields of youth and education, the continuation of the process of 'fascistisation' in these areas in the three years under consideration was bound to lead to conflict.

As far as the field of labour relations was concerned, the Regime had already created the mechanisms of repression and control over the working classes – the destruction of the Socialist and Catholic trade unions, the

---

[21] For a broad outline of Italian Fascist foreign policy in this period see Lowe and Marzari, *Italian Foreign Policy 1870–1940*, chaps. 9 and 10.
[22] See Lyttelton, *The Seizure of Power*, pp. 402–15.

establishment of the monopoly of Fascist trade unionism and the passing of the labour legislation outlawing strikes and lockouts. The great 'Charter of Labour', announced with such a triumphant flourish in 1927, was still largely a dead letter in 1929. But the construction of the 'fig-leaf' for this repression – the 'Corporate State' – was still in its early stages; significantly, only one of the corporations provided for by Article 6 of the 'Charter', that for the Professions and the Arts – i.e., the self-employed – had been formed by 1929, the creation of the other corporations being delayed by the world economic crisis in the early 1930s. Whilst it is true that even in its final form – that is after the Law on the Corporations of 1934 and the creation of the Chamber of Fasces and Corporations in 1939 – the 'Corporate State' remained an ineffective façade, nevertheless, in 1929, the completion of the 'Corporate State' was still an important objective of the Regime. The renewal of interest in social and labour questions on the part of Catholic Action in this period, and in particular the intense activities centred on the commemoration of the encyclical *Rerum Novarum* in early 1931, were therefore seen as a serious challenge to the development of Fascist social and labour policy.

For these reasons, it is hardly suprising that one of the Fascist groups that was to put up the most effective resistance to Mussolini's religious policy in this period, and the one which succeeded in shifting the direction of that policy for a time, was gathered around the new party leaders who emerged from the 'Changing of the Guard' of October 1930 – Giovanni Giurati and Carlo Scorza. Unlike the 'doves' of Fascism, Mussolini's brother, Arnaldo, and Giurati's predecessor as Party Secretary, Augusto Turati, Giurati and Scorza placed the integrity of the 'Totalitarian State' above the maintenance of good relations with the Church. In this they were supported by the leaders of the Fascist trade unions, especially by De Marsanich the editor of their mouthpiece, *Il Lavoro Fascista*. The trade union leaders were to become seriously alarmed by what they regarded as the threat which Catholic Action posed to Fascism's monopoly in the labour field. And to a large extent, the fears and anxieties of these Fascist leaders were shared by their followers at a local level.

The other major preoccupation of the Fascist Regime in this period was the impact which the 'Great Depression' had on the Italian economy after 1929. By the end of 1930, the internal economic difficulties which Italy had been suffering since the mid-1920s, which were largely the result of Fascism's own economic policies, were overtaken by the far more serious consequences of the world economic crisis which had been sparked off by the Wall Street 'Crash' of October 1929.[23] The resulting contraction of the Italian economy, with its inevitable corollaries of factory closures,

---

[23] For an analysis of the effects of the 'Great Depression' on Fascist Italy in this period, see De Felice, IV, pp. 58–88.

redundancies and rising unemployment, to mention only some of its effects, provoked widespread social unrest and agitation, and a consequent upsurge in anti-Fascist activity, especially on the part of Catholics. This factor has been almost entirely ignored in other studies of the disputes between the Church and the Regime in the first half of 1931.[24] But it is a factor which cannot and must not be ignored in any comprehensive analysis of the causes of the crisis of 1931, and for this reason considerable attention will be devoted to it in this study.

Over the years, the problem of Church and State relations in the Fascist era has attracted the attention of a number of historians, in both Italy and elsewhere, the most noteworthy being Binchy, Jemolo and Webster, whose works have already been cited, and P. Scoppola, who has contributed an important study using key available documents.[25] In addition, a considerable monograph literature has appeared covering more specialised aspects of the relations between the Church and Fascism, such as the vicissitudes of the various branches of the Catholic movement during the Fascist period,[26] and the impact of the *Conciliazione* on Italy's Protestant denominations.[27] Yet the three most critical years in the development of the relationship between the Church and the Fascist Regime, that is the period from 1929 to 1932, have, as a whole, received less than adequate attention. Historians have tended either to focus attention on the origins and immediate impact of the *Conciliazone*, and/or on the causes and consequences of the crisis of 1931.[28] What has so far been lacking is any attempt to trace and analyse the logical and organic relationship between the two events; no one has yet provided the kind of closely detailed but comprehensive analysis which relations between the Church and the Regime in these three years clearly merit.

The purpose of this work is to do precisely that, to look at all aspects of the relationship between the Church and Fascism in this period, and to place them in the essential contexts of both the Church's overall policy towards secular governments, and the broad development of the Fascist Regime, especially in the economic and foreign policy spheres, in the same period. Only in this way can the origins of the 1931 crisis be properly understood, and the long-term significance of the September Accords

---

[24] The only relevant work which even hints at the contribution which the upsurge of Catholic anti-Fascism made to the 1931 crisis is Webster, *The Cross and the Fasces*, p. 201 n. 3.

[25] Scoppola, *La Chiesa e il Fascimo*.

[26] See, for example, the essays in Scoppola and Traniello (eds.), *I Cattolici tra Fascismo e Democrazia*.

[27] P. Scoppola, 'Il fascismo e le minoranze religiose', in Fontana (ed.), *Il fascismo e le autonomie locali*, pp. 331–95.

[28] For example, Martini, *Studi sulla Questione Romana* and De Felice, III, pp. 399–412, which deals with the *Conciliazione*, and IV, pp. 246–75, which deals with the crisis of 1931.

which resolved that crisis be correctly interpreted. And, of course, the main object of this study must be to investigate the causes and consequences of the 1931 crisis. With that end in view, what is being attempted here is both to document and analyse those factors which require further attention, such as the diplomatic dimension of the relationship between the Vatican and the Regime, the significance of the leadership changes which took place in both camps between the *Conciliazione* of 1929 and the crisis of 1931 and impact of the 'Great Depression', and to carry out a thoroughgoing re-evaluation of prevailing interpretations of the period in the light of new evidence.[29]

The most important of these interpretations concerns the outcome of the 1931 crisis. Whilst there is certainly no consensus in this regard, the view has been taken by a number of authoritative and influential historians that the September Accords which resolved the crisis marked a turning-point in the history of Italian Catholic Action, that they were decisive in shaping the role of that organisation for the rest of the Fascist period.[30] The view is taken here that, in fact, the September Accords affected Catholic Action rather less than appears at first sight, and that the crisis of 1938, followed by the death of Pius XI and the election of Pius XII in 1939, had potentially greater importance for the future of the Catholic movement in Italy.

Nevertheless, regardless of the ultimate significance for Catholic Action of the crisis of 1931, it remains true that the working out of the implications of the Lateran Pacts in the years 1929–32, and in particular the new balance of power which was established between the Church and the Regime by the end of that period, laid down the pattern of relations for virtually the rest of the Fascist period. For this reason alone, these years deserve the closest attention.

[29] For a discussion of the primary source materials used in this study, see Appendix IV.
[30] See Chapter 7, pp. 179–80.

CHAPTER 2

The advent of the 'Conciliazione'

With very few exceptions, historians are now generally agreed that the *Conciliazione* was far from being the work of Mussolini alone, and that the origins of the Lateran Pacts of 1929 reach much further back in Italian history than his coming to power in 1922.[1] By the end of the nineteenth century, a working relationship had been developed between Church and State in Italy, a form of uneasy 'peaceful co-existence', based on the Law of Papal Guarantees of 1871, despite the fact that the Vatican officially rejected that law. The emergence of a common enemy, the Italian working class movement, and the Church's reaction to the development of that movement, greatly eased the tensions between the Church and the Liberal Regime during the Giolittian Era.

The patriotic response of Italian Catholics to the First World War took that process a stage further, and by 1919 so much of the bitterness had gone out of the 'Roman Question' that Italy and the Holy See were able to enter into the first serious, albeit unsuccessful, negotiations for a solution of their sixty-year-old dispute. This dialogue continued under two post-war Prime Ministers, Francesco Nitti and Ivanoe Bonomi, and the progress which they made included agreement on several fundamental points that were to form the basis of the 1929 settlement.

Nevertheless, the final breakthrough was due to the boldly opportunistic policy which Mussolini adopted towards the Church from 1921 onwards. Mussolini's public overtures to the Church, which his Liberal opponents did not dare to make, hamstrung as they were by the masonic, anti-clerical, risorgimental traditions of the Italian ruling class, evoked an enthusiastic response in the Vatican, particularly after the election of Pius XI in 1922. As a result, Mussolini was able to count upon the support of the Vatican in the struggle against Fascism's most formidable adversary, the P.P.I., whose defeat and destruction was essential to his rise to supreme power,

[1] For examples of the dissent of 'Fascist' historians from this view see *Dossier Conciliazione*, ed. Cavaterra, p. xvi, and Tamaro, *Venti anni di Storia*, Vol. II, p. 26.

and after two and a half years of difficult, secret negotiations he was able to claim for himself the glory of having resolved the 'Roman Question'.

CHURCH AND STATE RELATIONS IN THE LIBERAL ERA

The first important step along the difficult road towards a reconciliation between the Church and the Italian State was taken by the Parliament of Liberal Italy in 1871 when it passed the Law of Papal Guarantees.[2] In the difficult circumstances which faced them at the time, the leaders of the Destra Storica – the 'Historic Right', the heirs of Cavour who ruled Italy between 1861 and 1876 – believed that this was the best, if not the only possible solution of the troublesome 'Roman Question'. The Law of Guarantees was essentially based on the proposals which Cavour had made to Pio Nono in the Spring of 1861, proposals which the Pope had come very close to accepting.[3] Whilst the law did not concede any territorial sovereignty to the Holy See, for to have abandoned even an inch of Italian soil would have been an act of political suicide for any Liberal leader at this time, it did grant what amounted to extra-territoriality to the Vatican City and other Vatican possessions in Rome.

The Law also recognised the Pope's *personal* status as a sovereign, with all the honours and privileges attached to that status – including the guarantees and immunities necessary to the free conduct of diplomatic relations with the Catholic powers. In addition, it guaranteed the freedom of conclaves, consistories and general councils of the Church held in Rome, and as compensation for the loss of revenues from the former Papal States it provided for the payment of a generous annual indemnity to the Holy See. But in 1871, in the aftermath of the occupation of Rome by Italian troops the previous September, Pio Nono was even less willing to compromise with the representatives of the Liberal State than he had been in 1861, and this refusal to negotiate then made it possible for him and his successors to denounce the law as an unjust and unilateral act. Thus until his death in 1878, Pio Nono continued to refuse recognition to the Italian State and to issue fulminations and excommunications against its rulers.

Pio Nono's successor, Leo XIII, was equally unwilling to accept the loss of the temporal power and indeed on several occasions sought the diplomatic support of the Catholic powers in his attempts to recover some form of territorial sovereignty;[4] nevertheless, his reign saw the development of a *modus vivendi* between the Church and the Liberal State based on the law itself. Thus the Holy See was quick to denounce any breaches of the law in respect of the immunity of the Vatican City from Italian police jurisdiction, and it jealously guarded the privileges and immunities of both

---

[2] For the text of the Law of Guarantees see Appendix I.
[3] Delzell (ed.), *The Unification of Italy*, p. 87.   [4] See Articles 5 and 7 in Appendix I.

its diplomatic representatives and the representatives of governments accredited to it as laid down in the law.[5]

Furthermore, despite the strength of intransigent opposition to the Liberal State amongst both the lower clergy and the laity involved in the growing Catholic movement, the fact that the Law of Guarantees still permitted the Italian Government a veto over episcopal appointments ensured that the Italian bishops appointed after 1871 were moderate and conciliatory in their attitude to the governmental authorities, with whom they developed a good working relationship. The last quarter of the nineteenth century was not entirely free from outbursts of anti-clerical violence, or from attempts to push further anti-clerical legislation through the Italian Parliament, and on more than one occasion Leo XIII seriously considered leaving Rome;[6] but on the whole Liberals of most hues learned to live with the Church, and even Francesco Crispi, who had condemned the Law of Guarantees as a sell-out to the Church when in opposition, encouraged secret negotiations for a solution of the 'Roman Question' after he became Prime Minister.[7]

The most important factor contributing to a reduction in tension between the Church and the Liberal Regime at the beginning of the twentieth century was the growing strength of the extreme left – Radicals, Republicans, Anarchists and above all a marxist-orientated working class movement. The alarm of the conservative wing of the Italian ruling class at this unwelcome development was clearly manifested in their respressive policies during the End of Century Crisis, and Crispi's flirtations with the Vatican were motivated precisely by a desire to utilise the conservative influence of the Church in the battle against these dangerous forces. The ecclesiastical hierarchy in Italy, including the Vatican, shared these fears, and Leo XIII's encyclical *Rerum Novarum*,[8] whilst genuinely concerned with the appalling conditions of the urban, industrial working classes, was also a reiteration of the Church's condemnation of Socialism.

Even before the nineteenth century had drawn to a close, the Italian ruling class and the Church had begun to co-operate in electoral alliances against the forces of the left at a local level, and this development was taken to its logical conclusion after the election of Pope St Pius X in 1903. 'Papa Sarto' had already learnt the value of these Clerico-Moderate tactics as a means of preventing the anti-clerical left from doing further damage to the Church's interests in local government in his home region of the Veneto. Faced with the first real demonstration of the strength of the working class movement, that is the General Strike of 1904, Pius X ordered

---

[5] See Article 2 in Appendix I. This did not, however, prevent the Italian Government from seizing Palazzo Venezia, the Austrian Embassy to the Holy See, in 1916.
[6] Seton-Watson, *Italy from Liberalism to Fascism*, pp. 222–3.   [7] Ibid., p. 223.
[8] For the text of the encyclical, see *The Papal Encyclicals*, ed. Freemantle, pp. 166–95.

the first relaxation of the 'Non Expedit' at a parliamentary level for the general elections of 1904. In those constituencies where the alternative was a left-wing victory, Catholics were instructed to vote for 'acceptable' Liberal candidates, and in a handful of others Catholics were allowed to stand for the first time.

The policy of supporting the 'Party of Order', i.e., the Liberals, against the forces of the extreme left, was continued at the 1909 general elections and in those of 1913. In the latter elections nothing less than a mobilisation of the Catholic vote *en masse* was sufficient to avoid the danger of a left-wing victory, for the introduction of virtual adult male suffrage in 1911, coupled with Socialist hostility towards Giolitti following the Libyan War, threatened to sweep away the Liberal majority in Parliament. Under the terms of the so-called 'Giolitti–Gentiloni Pact' of 1912, Catholics throughout Italy were instructed by their bishops to vote for Liberal candidates.[9] The Church's support for Giolitti in these crucial elections ensured the continuation of Liberal hegemony in Italy for another six years.[10]

In the short term, Catholic support for the Liberal Regime did much to improve relations between Church and State. Though Giolitti and the Liberals did nothing positive to resolve the 'Roman Question', for it was his policy that Church and State were 'two parallels that should never meet',[11] they did go out of their way to prevent any exacerbation of the dispute, and as their electoral pact with the Catholics required, they opposed legislative measures that were inimical to the Church's interests, like divorce bills.

In the long term, however, the progressive relaxation of the 'Non Expedit' in parliamentary elections was to complicate still further relations between the Vatican and the Italian State. The introduction of Catholics into Italian political life was a carefully controlled experiment, under the close supervision of the local hierarchy and of the Pope himself: both the Catholic electorate and the Catholic M.P.s were subject to the directives of the Unione Elettorale, one of the bodies to emerge from Pius X's fundamental re-organisation of the Italian Catholic movement between 1903 and 1905. Moreover, the vast majority of the Catholic M.P.s elected during the Giolittian period were drawn from the 'Clerico-Moderate' conservative wing of the Catholic movement.

But a handful of the twenty-nine Catholic M.P.s elected in 1913 were Christian Democrats, representing that large section of Catholic opinion

---

[9] For an analysis of the origins and operations of the Unione Elettorale see Bellu, *I Cattolici alle Urne*, chap. 8.

[10] Gentiloni, the President of the Unione Elettorale, claimed that 228 of Giolitti's supporters in the Chamber owed their election to the votes of the Catholics. Seton-Watson, *Italy from Liberalism to Fascism*, p. 388.   [11] As quoted in ibid., p. 280.

which desired radical social, economic and political reforms through the formation of an autonomous, democratic Catholic party, something which Piux X was not prepared to countenance. The leader of the Christian Democrats, the Sicilian priest Luigi Sturzo, was highly critical of the tactics of the Unione Elettorale which he regarded as a cynical manipulation of the Catholic vote for the benefit of Giolitti, 'the minister of the underworld'.[12] This fundamental split in the Catholic ranks, between Christian Democrats and Clerico-Moderates, remained largely obscured during the Intervention Crisis, the war and even the early years of the P.P.I., but when it re-emerged in 1923 and 1924 it did so to the great benefit of Mussolini and Fascism.

THE FIRST WORLD WAR AND THE BIRTH OF THE P.P.I.

The Intervention Crisis and Italy's eventual participation in the First World War took the process of integrating Catholics into Italian political life a stage further. Whilst the balance of opinion inside the Catholic world was probably always on the side of neutrality, (and this is borne out by the largely passive involvement of the Catholic peasant masses), prominent Clerico-Moderate and Christian Democratic figures alike supported intervention, and once the war was declared the bishops urged the faithful to support the Italian Government and the war effort loyally.[13] Almost all the Catholic M.P.s elected in 1913 voted for war in 1915 and for the first time in the history of United Italy two Catholic politicians, the Clerico-Moderates Filippo Meda and Cesare Nava actually accepted government posts. Though the Vatican was quick to point out that they did so on a purely personal basis, their presence in government was inevitably taken to mean the support of the entire Catholic movement for the war.[14]

The Vatican's concern in this matter was prompted less by its formal policy of non-recognition of the Italian State, than by its traditional commitment to non-involvement in international disputes. Nevertheless, the Holy See's natural sympathy for Catholic Austria did not escape the critical eye of the anti-clericals in the interventionist camp, who insisted on interpreting Benedict XV's calls for peace as pro-Alliance propaganda.[15]

Yet despite this, and despite the deliberate exclusion of the Holy See from

---

[12] For an account of Sturzo's hostility to Giolitti, which was based on his experience of the disastrous effects of the policies of the 'minister of the underworld' in his native South, see De Rosa, *Luigi Sturzo*, chap. 10.

[13] An interesting account of Catholic attitudes towards intervention is to be found in Webster, *The Cross and the Fasces*, chap. 4.

[14] See Meda, *I Cattolici Italiani e la Guerra*, p. 56.

[15] See Margiotta-Broglio, *l'Italia e la Santa Sede*, pp. 75–6, where he reproduces an article from *Il Popolo d'Italia* of October 1916 in which Mussolini describes the Vatican as the 'enemy' of Italy on account of its links with the Central Powers.

the Versailles Peace Conference, Benedict did not seek to exploit Italy's weakness, either during the war or afterwards, in order to obtain some remedy for the Vatican's grievances. On the contrary, the assurances by his Cardinal Secretary of State, Pietro Gasparri, that the Holy See had no desire to embarrass the Italian Government and that it looked for a solution of the 'Roman Question' not from 'foreign arms but from the triumph of feelings of justice among the Italian people'[16] prepared the way for the behind-the-scenes negotiations at Versailles between Mons. Cerretti, Nuncio to France, and Vittorio Emmanuele Orlando, the Italian Foreign Minister.[17]

The significant aspect of these talks is not that they failed, but that they revealed just how much ground there was for potential agreement. In particular, certain elements of a settlement emerged, including some sort of sovereignty for the Vatican City, which were to figure in the discussions carried on during Nitti's ministry and were to form the basis of the 1929 settlement.[18]

The other novelty of Benedict XV's reign was the establishment of a Catholic political party. The word 'Catholic' was very carefully avoided by the party leader Sturzo and his followers, because whilst they recognised explicitly the inspiration of Catholic principles and in particular the social teaching contained in *Rerum Novarum* in their largely Christian Democratic programme, they did not wish to be labelled a confessional, clerical party.[19] They were especially anxious that their P.P.I. should not be identified with the Church nor be seen to be the secular instrument of that body.

Thus, though the Party looked to an early satisfactory solution of the 'Roman Question', it placed the problem low down in its list of priorities.[20] This low key approach to the problems of Church and State relations provoked strong criticism from inside the Party, from the integralist right-wing, which at the first party congress at Bologna in 1919 condemned what it regarded as a scandalous lack of concern for the rights and dignity of the Church, which they believed should be the first priority of a 'Catholic' party.[21] This essential ambiguity in the Party's relationship with the Church and the Italian Catholic world generally, also caused problems outside, where the Party was caught in the cross-fire between an intensely

[16] As quoted in Falconi, *The Popes in the Twentieth Century*, p. 128.
[17] For a detailed account of these negotiations, with accompanying documents, see Margiotta-Broglio, *L'Italia e la Santa Sede*, pp. 43–58. See also Orlando, *I Miei Rapporti di Governo con la Santa Sede*, p. 63.
[18] Orlando, *I Miei Rapporti di Governo con la Santa Sede*, pp. 67–71.
[19] De Rosa, *Il Partito popolare*, pp. 8–9.
[20] The question of Church and State relations was covered by just one sentence of the seventh article of the Party Programme: 'Liberty and independence for the Church in the full exercise of its spiritual authority'. As quoted in P. Scoppola, 'L'Affermazione e la crisi del P.P.I.', in Sabbatucci (ed.), *La Crisi Italiana del Primo Dopoguerra*.
[21] The debate is recorded in *Gli Atti dei congressi del P.P.I.*, ed. Malgeri, pp. 58–60.

suspicious anti-clerical press, and the Vatican, which had serious misgivings about the very existence of the P.P.I.

Though Benedict XV had raised no objections to the final abolition of the 'Non Expedit', and despite the impeccably Clerico-Moderate credentials of the 'godparents', there is evidence to suggest that Cardinal Gasparri was extremely unhappy about the P.P.I. and its policies from the moment of its birth.[22] In 1928 Gasparri published a letter to one of the 'godparents', Carlo Santucci, in which he explained that from the beginning he had regarded the P.P.I. as merely '...the least bad of all the parties'.[23] Moreover, the latter demonstrates that Gasparri's main fear was that despite the Party's protestations of 'aconfessionality', the fact that it was led by a priest would identify it in the popular mind with the Church.[24] Gasparri's fear was realised; the masonic, anti-clerical press all too clearly identified the Party and its policies with the Church representing the P.P.I. as a sinister, political emanation of the Vatican.

From the Vatican's point of view the most serious consequence of the emergence of the P.P.I. was that with the enthusiastic, near-unanimous adherence to it of the Catholic unions (which had themselves joined together in an autonomous confederation – the C.I.L. – in 1918), of the press, of the peasant leagues and the bulk of the parochial clergy,[25] the Church had lost control over most of the old Catholic movement. The Holy See could now no longer rely upon the Catholic masses as a lever in its relations with the Italian State, and particularly in its efforts to obtain a restoration of its privileges, property and influence in Italy.

The birth of the P.P.I. was also a blow to the Liberal establishment; if Catholic electoral support had helped to save Giolitti's Liberal majority in 1913, then the P.P.I.'s intransigently independent electoral policy helped to destroy it in 1919, and the Party's equally intransigent parliamentary tactics thereafter made life extremely difficult for the coalition Premiers, Nitti and Giolitti. They, along with Mussolini, were also quick to perceive the Vatican's uneasy relationship with the P.P.I. and to exploit it. For Mussolini this was to provide the key to his success in isolating, dividing and defeating the P.P.I. in the period 1922–5.

The other important prerequisite of Mussolini's successful wooing of the Church was, of course, the change in his 'religious policy' from late 1920 onwards. The brutally anti-clerical stance of the early Fascist movement was very succinctly expressed by its newspaper *Il Popolo d'Italia* in

[22] From the account of the meeting between Sturzo and Gasparri given by De Rosa, *Il Partito Popolare*, p. 12, it would appear that the presence of Carlo Santucci, the retiring President of the Unione Elettorale, was an essential reassurance to the Cardinal of the good behaviour of the new Party.

[23] For the text of the letter, See De Rosa, *I Conservatori Nazionali*, p. 63.

[24] Ibid.

[25] Molony, *The Emergence of Political Catholicism in Italy*, pp. 53–5.

November 1919: ' …there is only one possible revision of the Law of Guarantees and that is its abolition, followed by a firm invitation to his Holiness to quit Rome'.[26]

But, by the Autumn of 1920 Mussolini had seen the light and without abandoning any of his instinctive and lifelong anti-clericalism and atheism, the Fascist leader recognised the critical importance of the Church in Italian politics, as he revealed in a letter to Gabriele D'Annunzio: 'I believe that Catholicism can be used as one of the greatest forces for the expansion of Italy in the World.'[27]

With the same opportunism that had motivated his other shifts to the right, that is the playing down, and eventual abandonment, of both anti-capitalism and republicanism, Mussolini made an overture to the Church in his maiden speech to the Chamber of Deputies in June 1921, when he brazenly declared that ' …Fascism neither practises nor preaches anti-clericalism'.[28] And he followed this with an offer of material aid to the Church in Italy if it would abandon its 'temporalistic dreams'.[29] Henceforth, Mussolini and other Fascist leaders would in public treat the Church with calculated respect, a policy that was to be reinforced after the fusion of the Fascist Party with the Nationalists in 1923,[30] and one which was quickly to pay large dividends in terms of sympathy in the Vatican and support among the conservative elements in the Catholic movement.

The death of Benedict XV and the election of Achille Ratti as Pius XI in February 1922 undoubtedly increased Mussolini's chances of success whilst at the same time diminishing still further sympathy for the P.P.I. inside the Vatican. Ratti was independent-minded, authoritarian and unyielding in argument, qualities which were to manifest themselves in his disputes with the Regime, but probably more important than his temperament was the fact that he almost certainly owed his election to Cardinal Gasparri who went all out for Ratti when he saw his own hopes of succeeding Benedict XV dashed.

Gasparri thus brought to the Chair of St Peter a Pope whose ideas on the major problems facing the Holy See more or less coincided with his own. They shared a strong desire and hope for a setttlement of the 'Roman Question', and Pius XI's appearances to the crowds in St Peter's Square

---

[26] Il Popolo d'Italia, 18 November 1919.

[27] As quoted in Margiotta-Broglio, L'Italia e la Santa Sede, p. 52. He gives a full account of Mussolini's development from violent anti-clerical to opportunistic suitor of the Church on pp. 71–86.

[28] Scoppola, La Chiesa e il Fascimo, pp. 52–4.

[29] Ibid.

[30] The Nationalists had been moving steadily towards a pro-clerical position since before the War, as Webster, The Cross and the Fasces, p. 23, says: 'After 1918 Italian Nationalism broke with its Irredentist "Adriatic" traditions. The "African", openly imperialist aspirations of its leaders, came into prominence; an effort was made then to attract Italian Catholicism.'

(rather than inside St Peter's Basilica, as had been the custom since 1870) after his election and coronation constituted a public declaration that reconciliation with Italy was to be a major objective of his reign. Like Gasparri, Pius XI had a profound fear of Communism. As a result of his three years service as Nuncio to Poland, where he was not only responsible for relations with the resurrected Polish State, but also for the Catholics beyond its eastern borders in Russia, Ratti was spared the *Biennio Rosso*, the period of violent working class militancy between 1918–20 in Italy, on the other hand he experienced at first hand the persecution of religion in the Soviet Union and witnessed the arrival of the Red Army at the gates of Warsaw in August 1920.[31]

In Italy the experience of the *Biennio Rosso* was to have much the same effect on the episcopate and the Vatican, with the added consequence of a drastic deterioration in their relations with the P.P.I. In their alarm at the threat posed by the revolutionary left, the bishops showed little respect for the political autonomy and integrity of Sturzo's party. They were deeply shocked by his refusal to enter into electoral alliances with the variegated forces of the Right in an effort to stem the Socialist tide in the local elections of 1920 and 1921.[32]

The election of Ratti, who unlike his predecessor was unwilling to concede much autonomy to the Catholic masses or their chosen political representatives, merely confirmed an existing trend among the Italian Catholic hierarchy and strengthened Gasparri's policy of distance and detachment from the P.P.I. Pius XI was bound to regard the Party and its Christian Democratic leader with considerable diffidence given his conservatism on so many economic and social issues, a stance which no doubt derived in large part from his wide circle of friends and acquaintances among the Clerico-Moderate bourgeoisie and aristocracy of Milan.[33] During the time he spent as archbishop of that city from September 1921 to February 1922 his closest collaborators were the Caccia-Dominioni brothers – Pietro, who was deeply involved in the world of Catholic banks; Ambrogio, whom he appointed as head of Milanese Catholic Action; and Carlo, whom Pius XI took with him to Rome to fill the important post of papal Maestro di Camera, and who then became the leading spokesman of the Clerico-Fascist interest inside the Vatican.

Instead of an autonomous 'Catholic' political party, Pius XI preferred the kind of Catholic movement which had emerged from the reforms of

---

[31] Ibid., pp. 177–8.

[32] See De Rosa, *Il Partito Popolare*, pp. 72–80. As De Rosa points out, despite all of Sturzo's efforts, the P.P.I. was forced into right-wing electoral alliances in Milan, Naples and Venice due to pressure from the local curias.

[33] Falconi, *The Popes in the Twentieth Century*, pp. 158–60.

his predecessor Pius X in 1905, a network of disciplined Catholic lay organisations operating in various fields but bound together in absolute obedience to the hierarchy and to himself personally. His project for the revitalisation not to say the relaunching of Italian Catholic Action was on the drawingboard early in the new reign – even if its effects were not publicly felt until the appointment of the new national leaders in December 1922 and the promulgation of the new Statutes in 1923. How far the 'March on Rome' affected Pius XI's plans is very difficult to say, but it is extremely unlikely that it altered the underlying principles of his design.

Ever since the foundation of the C.I.L. in 1918 and the P.P.I. in the following year, the Italian Catholic movement had been suffering from a crisis of identity and of confidence. The emergence of C.I.L. had greatly weakened the Unione Economica e Sociale, and the emergence of the Catholic political party, accompanied by the abolition of the 'Non Expedit' had rendered the Unione Elettorale redundant and it was accordingly dissolved. All that effectively remained of the three-branched Catholic movement of 1904 was the Unione Popolare (the nucleus of the Catholic lay apostolate) whose very name caused confusion with the P.P.I. which was in any case diverting the energies and enthusiasm of Italian Catholics away from it.

Under the guidance of Gasparri, the Vatican set about trying to restore the morale and vigour of the rump of the Catholic movement and tried to give it a new identity and purpose. The Unione was officially renamed Azione Cattolica Italiana, with a new programme and an appeal 'to reunite in full harmony of purpose all Italian Catholics irrespective of political differences'.[34] The appointment in June 1920 of Count Giuseppe Dalla Torre, the President of Catholic Action, as the editor of the Vatican organ *L'Osservatore Romano* ensured that henceforth Catholic Action would get maximum coverage in that newspaper, even if it was crowded out of other Catholic papers by reports on the P.P.I. Henceforth that newspaper diminished its coverage of the activities of the P.P.I., and inaugurated a new column devoted to the Unione Popolare later renamed Azione Cattolica.

Despite all these efforts, Catholic Action remained in the doldrums until 1922 when Pius XI embarked on a change in its leadership. In December of that year the Giunta Centrale, or national executive, was reconstituted with the appointment of Mons. Giuseppe Pizzardo, an official of the Vatican Secretariat of State, as General Ecclesiastical Assistant (or representative of the Pope) and Mons. Fernando Roveda as Secretary-General. Both men were of long service and experience in the Catholic movement and possessed the advantage of not being closely associated with the P.P.I.

---

[34] As quoted in ibid.

Similar advantages accrued to Luigi Colombo, the Milanese lawyer and banker whom Pius XI appointed as national President, and a number of other Milanesi whom Pius XI summoned to Rome to take up leading positions in national Catholic Action.[35] The influence of these personal friends of Pius XI, including Fr. Agostino Gemelli, the leading Catholic intellectual and Rector of the Catholic University of Milan, combined with that of leading Jesuits like Padre Enrico Rosa, editor of the authoritative fortnightly *La Civiltà Cattolica*,[36] gave the upper echelons of Catholic Action a distinctly non-*popolare* outlook, even if a large part of the 'base' of the organisation continued to divide its loyalties with the P.P.I.

In September 1923, Pius XI followed his reshuffle at the top of Catholic Action with new Statutes. Catholic Action was re-organised into six major branches – the youth organisation, G.C.I. (male) and G.C.F.I. (female); the adult association, U.D.C.I. (women) and F.I.U.C. (men); and the twin Catholic, university student federations, F.U.C.I.[37] Each of the various branches of the movement had its own organisation, officers and funds at a parochial, diocesan and national level and was represented on the *giunte* or committees of Catholic Action at each of these levels. The outstanding feature of the new organisational set-up was its dependence on the ecclesiastical hierarchy at every level, the *sine qua non* of that docility and obedience that Pius XI required of Catholic Action. This was spelled out by Cardinal Gasparri in a letter to Colombo of 2 October 1923:

In our opinion, the characteristics and advantages of the new Statutes are two-fold:

1) A much closer relationship between all the branches of Catholic Action, within a unified, centralised structure and under a single directing authority.
2) A greater and more effective subordination to the control of the ecclesiastical hierarchy, as a result of which Catholic Action is, much more so than in the past, an auxiliary and a supplement to the apostolic mission of the hierarchy.[38]

Such a system was the best guarantee that the Italian Catholic movement would never again stray from ecclesiastical control as it had done at the beginning of the century and in the years 1918–19. It also proved to be an important factor ensuring the very survival of Catholic Action as it faced Fascist attacks in the years to come.

The other means adopted by the Vatican in order to protect Catholic Action in the political uncertainty following the March on Rome was the adoption of a firmly non-political stance; again and again in this period

[35] I.e., Maria Rimoldi, President of the U.D.C.I. (1925–49), see Ubaldi, *Maria Rimoldi*, p. 66; and Armida Barelli, President of G.C.F.I.
[36] Padre Rosa was closely involved in the work of Catholic Action throughout the 1920s and 1930s, and played a particularly important role in the foundation of the I.C.A.S. which replaced the old Unione Economica e Sociale. He eventually became a firmly committed, conservative opponent of Fascism.
[37] Civardi, *Breve Compendio di Storia*, p. 186.   [38] As quoted in ibid.

it was stressed by the organs of the Vatican, by the bishops and by Catholic Action itself that it was above and beyond party politics. There was after all, nothing essentially new in this policy: similar declarations had also often been made during the reign of Pius XI's predecessor. What was new was the practical application of this policy: whereas Catholic Action carefully eschewed any contacts or associations with the P.P.I., it went out of its way to cultivate good relationships with those in power, that is with the Fascists after the March on Rome. Luigi Colombo was himself the staunchest upholder of this policy, indeed he initiated it in May 1923, when, in his role as President of Catholic Action in the large and very important diocese of Milan, he signed a 'pact of pacification' with the local Fascio. *L'Osservatore Romano* urged that this peace policy should be adopted everywhere, but unfortunately time proved that it was vulnerable to frequent and unilateral violations by the local squads. This did not deter Colombo from an even more spectacular act of submission to Fascism, his open letter of 1925 pledging the obedience and allegiance of Catholic Action to the recently established dictatorship.[39] Alas, this turned out to be no defence for Catholic associations against the wave of violence that followed the attempts on Mussolini's life in 1926.

The declining fortunes of the P.P.I. in the new pontificate were matched by the increasing sympathy being shown for Fascism in Catholic circles generally but especially in the Vatican. Since both of these tendencies undoubtedly date back to before the election of Pius XI, it would be unwise to make too much of the latter's Milanese experience of Fascism or of his brief meeting there with Mussolini.[40] The fact was that the P.P.I.'s intransigent parliamentary tactics during the long-drawn-out political crisis of the Summer and Autumn of 1922, which led to the collapse of the Facta Government in June and the still birth of a Giolittian coalition in October,[41] were alienating increasing numbers of conservative Catholics. In June 1922, the Milanese Catholic aristocrat and friend of Pius XI, Carlo Cornaggia-Medici, founded the short-lived Unione Costituzionale of like-minded Catholic conservatives outside of the P.P.I.; in July, the Roman aristocrat, Prince Francesco Boncompagni-Ludovisi, abandoned the *popolare* whip and joined the Nationalist group in the Chamber of Deputies, and in September the eight *popolare* Senators signed a letter to Sturzo protesting

[39] Margiotta-Broglio, *L'Italia e la Santa Sede*, p. 161 n. 87.
[40] For an account of Pius XI's early experience of Fascism when Archbishop of Milan, see Falconi, *The Popes in the Twentieth Century*, p. 180.
[41] As in January, so in October 1922 the most serious obstacle to another Giolittian ministry was the so-called 'veto Giolitti' of Sturzo. De Rosa, *Il Partito Popolare*, p. 181, demonstrates quite clearly that Sturzo's opposition to a Giolittian government in October 1922 was motivated not by his longstanding antipathy for the 'Grand Old Man' of Italian politics, but by his refusal to contemplate the inclusion of Fascists in the Cabinet, which was what Giolitti was proposing.

at the P.P.I.'s flirtation with the Reformist Socialists.[42] The direction in which all these elements were moving was that of P.P.I. participation in a government of 'National Order' presided over by Orlando, Salandra or Giolitti, and including the right-wing forces – the Fascists not excepted. On the other hand, Mussolini's policy towards the Church was winning favour, as was demonstrated by *L'Osservatore Romano* and *La Civiltà Cattolica*, which in a very short period of time moved from blanket condemnation of the rising Fascist movement to specific criticisms of its undesirable elements and their violent activities, coupled with a cautious recognition of its merits as a patriotic force fighting Communism.[43] Throughout 1921 and 1922, as well as endlessly reiterating the non-political character of Catholic Action, the Vatican had frequently issued instructions (for the most part ignored) that the clergy should abstain from party politics; since the only party which they were likely to support was the P.P.I., it was clear that the Vatican was in every way seeking to disassociate itself from that party.

In case anyone still entertained doubts on the subject, on 2 October 1922 Gasparri once again reminded the bishops that the P.P.I. had absolutely no connection with either the Church or Catholic Action, that the latter was a strictly non-political organisation and that the clergy were to refrain from any political activities with the P.P.I.[44] In some areas individual priests continued to defy the ban, the most notorious of course being Don Sturzo, but the Vatican's conscience was clear and it therefore felt ready to face the future whatever the outcome of the March on Rome.

THE RAPPROCHEMENT BETWEEN THE VATICAN AND FASCISM: FROM THE MARCH ON ROME TO THE MATTEOTTI CRISIS

When it came, the Vatican greeted the outcome of the March on Rome with relief and satisfaction.[45] Whether it could have anticipated it or not, Mussolini's appointment brought immediate benefits in the form of a series of measures to improve the position of the Church which he announced to Parliament early in November. Mussolini's religious 'package' was a purely opportunistic device to win further support in the Catholic world and, by stealing some of its policies, to isolate the P.P.I. and make it appear redundant in the eyes of many Catholics. The various measures, especially the introduction of religious instruction into the elementary schools, the

---

[42] See Molony, *The Emergence of Political Catholicism in Italy*, p. 158, and Reineri, *Il Movimento Cattolico in Italia*, pp. 39–40.

[43] For an account of this transformation see O'Brien, 'L'Osservatore Romano and Fascism', and Talluri, 'La Civiltà Cattolica', p. 300, where she says that after the March on Rome, 'With an abrupt change of tone...*La Civiltà Cattolica* also hastened to accept the fait accompli.' [44] For the text of the letter, see *Il Giornale d'Italia*, 20 October 1922.

[45] See the editorial in the Vatican newspaper of 1 November 1922.

appointment of military chaplains on the 'establishment', the improved salaries for the clergy and the return of the crucifix to public buildings in Italy, immediately created a very favourable impression in the Vatican.[46] It is important to grasp the full significance of Mussolini's gesture, and the impact which that gesture had upon Catholic opinion at the time. In taking these measures, Mussolini was doing something which none of his Liberal predecessors had dared to do, tied down as they were by the risorgimental, anti-clerical tradition of the Liberal State. Mussolini's originality and daring, therefore, blinded both the Vatican and conservative Catholic opinion generally to the sheer, cynical opportunism of the new Prime Minister's religious policy. The ecclesiastical measures announced in November 1922 were the logical development of that change in Mussolini's religious policy which dates from 1920/1. In this context, therefore, it is absurd to suggest, as at least one historian has done,[47] that there was a substantial continuity between the religious policy of Italian Governments, Liberal and Fascist, between the end of the First World War and 1924. On 20 January 1923, the first secret meeting between Gasparri and Mussolini took place in the house of the Catholic Senator Carlo Santucci.[48] It would seem that the only firm commitment that Mussolini entered into was a promise that his Government would save the tottering Banco di Roma (in which the Vatican had a large stake) from collapse in return for the replacement (as President of the bank) of Santucci by the philo-Fascist Catholic M.P. Prince Francesco Boncompagni-Ludovisi.[49] Thus Mussolini secured his first foothold in the Catholic world, and Gasparri for his part promised that the Vatican would do all in its power to induce the P.P.I. to adopt a more co-operative attitude towards the Fascist Government.

Initially at least, Gasparri's efforts were not very successful, but it is difficult to see how it could have been otherwise, given the size and complexity of a party like the P.P.I. The sympathy or support shown by the Vatican to the various Clerico-Fascist splinter groups inside and outside of the P.P.I., like the Unione Nazionale[50] or the Partito Nazionale Popolare,[51] which emerged as the crisis of the Party unfolded in the Spring and Summer of 1923, did not have the required effect. The activities of the philo-Fascist right-wing at the Turin Congress of the Party in March were also quite unsuccessful: instead of pushing the Party to the right, towards closer

---

[46] For the full list of the measures, see Jemolo, *Chiesa e Stato*, p. 256.

[47] See Margiotta-Broglio, *L'Italia e la Santa Sede*, p. 256.

[48] For an account of the meeting, See De Rosa, *I Conservatori Nazionali*, p. 63.

[49] See ibid.

[50] Like Cornaggia-Medici's earlier effort, the Unione Nazionale was an aristocratic clique which had virtually no impact on Italian politics other than the initial stir created by its manifestos of April and June 1923.

[51] Probably the biggest 'non-event' of Italian politics in 1923. Formed by the right-wing *popolari* L. Tovini and M. Postalozza, after the defeat of their pro-Fascist motion at the Turin Congress of the Party, it attracted few supporters and quickly faded away.

co-operation with Mussolini's Government and thus provoking the expulsion or secession of Miglioli's extreme 'socialistoide' left-wing, they ended up with a situation in which they were obliged to leave the Party, which under Sturzo's guidance voted only conditional support for the Fascist Government. For Mussolini and the Vatican this was the worst possible outcome imaginable, and the former's response to the situation was to declare war upon the Catholic party by expelling its ministers from his Cabinet.

The Vatican also had to take sides in the war; it was forced to make a decision of fundamental and lasting importance, whether to choose genuine neutrality in Italian politics (which could have only had beneficial effects for the P.P.I.), or to give active sustained support to Mussolini. That it chose the latter course was in large part due to blackmail by Mussolini, a threat to unleash a wave of violence against the Catholic clergy and institutions. But there was also a positive element in this choice, a shrewd calculation that Mussolini and Fascism seemed to offer to Italy, in the short term at least, protection from Communism, political stability and social peace, and to offer the Church an enormous improvement of the conditions in which it had existed under the Liberal Regime. And, of course, the Vatican's choice was crucial for Mussolini, because if its previous attempts to bring pressure to bear on the Party as a whole had failed, it did have the absolute, ultimate power over Don Luigi Sturzo, who thus became the Achilles' heel of the P.P.I.

On 10 July 1923 Sturzo was ordered to resign as Secretary-General of the P.P.I., which he duly did out of canonical obedience, and the Party was thus deprived of its most firmly anti-Fascist leader on the eve of the debates of the Acerbo Electoral Law, debates whose outcome was crucial not only to the P.P.I. but to the future of Italian democracy itself. Sturzo's exit undoubtedly contributed to the confusion and division which the P.P.I. displayed over the Acerbo Law, and, coupled with the trickery and treachery of the Party's right-wing, led by Cavazzoni, this ensured the safe passage of the bill, which guaranteed Mussolini a solid parliamentary majority in the future.[52]

L'Osservatore Romano greeted the passing of the Acerbo Law with the same relief and satisfaction it had exhibited after the March on Rome,[53] but what it almost certainly did not appreciate was that the divisions in the P.P.I. which had contributed to Mussolini's victory were going to pose serious problems for both the Vatican and the bishops, but especially the bishops,

---

[52] The Acerbo Law, with its central clause, giving two-thirds of the seats in the Chamber to the party or bloc of parties winning a quarter plus one of the votes, was meant to provide Mussolini with a solid, parliamentary majority. In fact, Mussolini's *Listone* won two-thirds of the votes in the 1924 general elections thanks to Fascist violence and intimidation and the divisions amongst the opposition parties.

[53] *L'Osservatore Romano*, 1 November 1923, editorial.

in their relations with the Catholic movement. The expulsion or secession of a sizeable number of right-wing M.P.s and Senators – the 'Clerico-Fascists' as Sturzo aptly named them – men like Cavazzoni, Martire, Mattei-Gentile, Crispolti and Grosoli, also involved a large part of the Catholic press (especially the papers in Grosoli's *Trust*) and large numbers of Catholic municipal and provincial councillors (as proved by the signatures on the pre-election Catholic 'Manifesto' of March 1924).[54] A split in the P.P.I. meant a split in the whole Catholic world, and particularly in Catholic Action, a split which was intensified by the campaign for the general elections of April 1924 in which sixteen Catholics stood in the Fascist *Listone*. For this reason alone, the Vatican was scrupulously careful to avoid being seen to be taking sides, even if all the evidence suggests that it was hoping for a Fascist victory.[55] This ambivalent attitude, which is faithfully reflected not only by the comments of *L'Osservatore Romano* but also by those of the integralist *L'Unità Cattolica* of Florence, and by Catholic journals like *L'Italia* of Milan which were firmly under the control of Catholic Action, continued right through the period of the Matteotti Crisis.[56] Whilst condemning the abduction and murder of Matteotti, *L'Osservatore Romano* and *La Civiltà Cattolica* refused initially to countenance the accusations of complicity against Mussolini, and even when they did implicitly accept the possibility of his guilt they argued for the defence of the status quo, for the maintenance of the lawfully, elected government on the principle of the lesser of two evils: for it is clear that the Vatican, like other sections of the Italian establishment, was convinced that if Fascism fell it would be followed by a Communist revolution. Like the King, they had little or no time for the Aventine Secession and its largely moral protests, and when the P.P.I. attempted to take more positive political action to remove Mussolini, that is when they proposed to join in an alternative coalition government with Turati's Reformist Socialists, their initiative was attacked by *La Civiltà Cattolica* as 'neither appropriate, opportune or permissible'.[57] And the condemnation was repeated in public by the Pope himself.[58]

In a very real sense the Vatican, like other conservative forces in Italian society, helped sustain Mussolini's government in its darkest hour and thus must accept some responsibility for the subsequent establishment of the dictatorship from the beginning of 1925 onwards.

[54] For the text of the manifesto, see *Il Popolo d'Italia*, 27 March 1924.
[55] See for example the editorial in *L'Unità Cattolica*, 31 March 1924.
[56] See *La Civiltà Cattolica*, 8 August 1924, 'La Parte dei Cattolici nella presenti lotte politiche'.
[57] Ibid.
[58] See the text of his address to an audience of F.U.C.I. members in *L'Osservatore Romano*, 10 September 1924.

THE CATHOLIC MOVEMENT AND THE PROCESS OF 'FASCISTISATION'

One of the inevitable consequences of the establishment of the dictator-ship was the disintegration and dissolution of the democratic opposition parties, including the P.P.I., which finally disappeared from the Italian political scene in November 1926.[59] This must have been welcome news to the men in the Vatican, for by then the Holy See was engaged in secret negotiations with the Italian Government to settle the 'Roman Question'. The demise of the P.P.I. meant that Pius XI and Gasparri had finally achieved their aim – the opportunity to conduct a relationship with the Italian State at the highest level without the embarrassing complications caused by the presence of a Catholic party in the Italian Parliament.

There was, admittedly, still a Catholic force active in Italian politics – the Clerico-Fascists. The largest grouping, comprising both M.P.s and Senators with a small grassroots following, was the C.N.I. which had been founded appropriately enough in August 1924 at the height of the Matteotti Crisis.[60] In addition there was the much smaller aristocratic clique, known as the Unione Nazionale, whose effective political membership was almost entirely confined to the Senate.[61] Though there were one or two moments of difficulty, these groups were too small and too obedient to papal directives to constitute a threat to the direct dialogue between the Church and the Regime. On the contrary, given their role as active supporters of the Regime and the resulting positions of influence held by some of the leading Clerico-Fascists – apart from the sixteen M.P.s there were almost as many Senators, one Minister, Nava, at National Economy and two Under-Secretaries, Boncompagni-Ludovisi at Finances and Mattei-Gentili, the President of C.N.I., at Justice – they were a positive asset to the Vatican.

The appointment to the Government of Paolo Mattei-Gentili, who was also editor of the Clerico-Fascist newspaper *Il Corriere d'Italia*, in June 1924 was, like the appointment of his fellow Clerico-Fascist Cesare Nava, the Liberals Casati and Sarocchi, and the ex-Nationalist Federzoni, primarily intended as a means of bolstering up Mussolini's very shaky political position at a time when the Matteotti Crisis was at its height. But a secondary purpose was to reinforce Mussolini's religious policy. Whilst the importance of Mattei-Gentili in a Ministry which also had responsibility for religious affairs at that time has not yet been properly investigated, his work

[59] For an account of the death throes of the P.P.I., see Camerini, *Il Partito Popolare*, chap. 3.
[60] For a history of the C.N.I. see Malgeri (ed.), *Storia del Movimento Cattolico in Italia*, Vol. IV, pp. 13–33, and J. F. Pollard, 'Italian Catholics and Fascism: The Clerico-Fascists, 1922–9', to be published in *Risorgimento*, 1985.
[61] After a bitter disappointment following Mussolini's rejection of Unione Nazionale candidates for his 'Big List' of candidates for the 1924 general elections, Cornaggia-Medici and his friends in the Senate kept themselves apart from the C.N.I. See A.C.S., A.A.G., letter from Cornaggia-Medici, 2 February 1924.

as chairman of the Ecclesiastical Legislation Reform Commission alone was to have a strong influence on the shape of the Concordat of 1929.

In addition, Clerico-Fascist figures also served on several governmental boards and committees[62] and others helped to provide useful, unofficial contacts between the Vatican and the Regime from time to time.[63] Last but not least of the services which the Clerico-Fascists rendered to the Church in this difficult period was their role in Catholic Action. During 1925 and 1926 many Clerico-Fascists were introduced into key positions in Catholic Action at a diocesan level, in an attempt to balance out the influence of the ex-members of the P.P.I. and thus provide some reassurance to the Fascist authorities of the political reliability and loyalty of the Catholic lay organisations.[64] Given the continued massive presence of former P.P.I. supporters inside Catholic Action it is surprising that the Regime did not show more anxiety about the issue, which rapidly became a bone of contention with the Church after the signing of the Lateran Pacts in 1929.

The very existence and activities of the C.N.I. gave an *appearance* of Catholic support for Fascism at a time when the Catholic masses were in fact largely indifferent or hostile. And this illusion was perpetuated by the Clerico-Fascist press, which became increasingly dominant in the Catholic world in the late 1920s due to the closure of anti-Fascist Catholic newspapers by the authorities. Despite the fact that the C.N.I., and the Clerico-Fascists generally, were eventually to fall out of favour in the Vatican, it would be true to say that between 1924 and 1929, the Clerico-Fascists made a significant contribution to the process which led to the *Conciliazione*.

The establishment of the dictatorship and the policy of 'fascistisation' was to have repercussions on the Catholic movement which went far beyond its effects upon the P.P.I., indeed in the mid-and late 1920s the Catholic organisations went through what the official historian of Catholic Action has described as 'the demolitions of Fascism'.[65] In the construction of their 'totalitarian' state the Fascists moved from the suppression of the opposition parties and press to the elimination of the free trade unions, including C.I.L. Like the Socialist confederation trade union C.G.L., C.I.L. had been reduced to a state of disintegration by mid-1925 under the impact of squadrist attacks and other forms of Fascist intimidation; the death blows came with the Palazzo Vidoni Pact of October 1925 which established

---

[62] I.e., Stefano Cavazzoni was to become President of the state-financed Istituto Centrale di Credito, and Francesco Mauro, as well as being the President of the Comitato Olimpico Nazionale, served on the national councils for the Economy and Education.

[63] For Carlo Santucci's role in 1925, see below p. 38.

[64] Gariglio, *Cattolici Democratici e Clerico-fascisti a Torino*, chap. 4, gives an insight into this phenomenon at Turin, and Fappani, *Giorgio Montini*, p. 118, offers another example of the application of this policy in Brescia.

[65] Civardi, *Breve Compendio di Storia*, chap. 14.

a bargaining monopoly between Confindustria, the industrial employers' organisation, and the Fascist trade unions, and with Rocco's labour legislation of 1926 which outlawed strikes and extended compulsory arbitration by the 'Labour Magistracy' into industry, thereby robbing the free trade unions of their *raison d'être*.[66] The position of C.I.L. was aggravated by the attitude of Catholic Action, which could not resist this opportunity to bring the errant, autonomous Catholic workers' organisation under its control.[67]

When it became clear that C.I.L. could not be saved, Catholic Action gave up the battle and henceforth restricted itself to criticisms of the *principle* of the single, state monopoly of trade union organisation.[68] Despite the very strong public protests of 'white' trade union leaders like Giovanni Gronchi and Achille Grandi,[69] Catholic Action now adopted a policy of *sauve qui peut* and taking advantage of those clauses of the Labour Law which permitted the existence of *de facto* organisations, set up *sezioni professionali* of Catholic workers in competition with the existing C.I.L. organisation, stressing that they had '... religious, moral, educational and social aims rather than trade union functions'.[70] In this way Catholic Action managed to retain a presence in the labour field after the dissolution of C.I.L. in the Winter of 1926/7. But resistance to this move was so strong amongst Fascist trade union leaders that the Regime only agreed to tolerate the *sezioni professionali* because the Vatican made it an essential pre-condition for the resumption of negotiations for the Lateran Pacts in the Summer of 1927.[71]

When it set up the *sezioni professionali*, Catholic Action placed them under the control of the Labour Commission of one of its dependent organisations – I.C.A.S., which had in its turn been established by the Giunta Centrale of Catholic Action in March 1925 to regroup those organisations that remained in the old Unione Economica e Sociale after the foundation of C.I.L.[72] In line with Piux XI's policy of keeping a tight control over all Catholic organisations, the direct dependence of I.C.A.S. upon the Giunta Centrale of Catholic Action was laid down in the Statutes of the new body, and in addition to the full-time Director – the Barnabite Father G. Balduzzi – who was naturally also a nominee of the Giunta Centrale, throughout the 1920s, and early 1930s at least, the Executive Committee of I.C.A.S. was almost entirely composed of members who either held important posts

[66] For an account of the demise of the free trade unions, see Lyttleton, *The Seizure of Power*, chap. 12.
[67] See Ferrari, *L'Azione Cattolica e il Regime*, pp. 12–13. Ferrari, formerly one of the leaders of the *popolare* left, was very bitter about the role which Catholic Action played in the downfall of the Catholic trade union confederation.
[68] Webster, *The Cross and the Fasces*, p. 104.
[69] Ibid.
[70] *Bollettino Ufficiale*, 1 May 1925, 'Atti della Giunta Centrale.'
[71] F. Pacelli, *Diario* ed. Maccarone, p. 60.
[72] The decision was announced in the *Bollettino Ufficiale*, 16 March 1925.

elsewhere in Catholic Action or were trusted servants, and often personal friends, of the Pope.[73]

Another significant aspect of the structure of I.C.A.S. was its inbuilt link with the Catholic University of Milan, which Pius XI intended to be the intellectual powerhouse of the whole Italian Catholic world and of Catholic Action in particular. And the President of the Research Commission of I.C.A.S. turned out to be none other than the Rector of the University, Agostino Gemelli, who along with some of his colleagues was to provide so much Catholic intellectual support for the corporatist, imperialist and racialist policies of the Regime in the mid- and late 1930s.[74]

As well as the Research and Labour Commissions, the Statutes provided for four others to deal with emigration, and with the Catholic peasant co-operatives and savings banks – the Casse di Risparmio – the mutual insurance societies and the Catholic recreational associations. For these branches of the Catholic movement the establishment of I.C.A.S. came not a moment too soon; the destruction of Catholic economic and social organisations continued through 1926, 1927 and 1928, partly as a result of fascistisation, and partly because of the economic climate. Whilst I.C.A.S. was not always able to save Catholic organisations from going under, it did much to help some others to survive.[75] The Catholic teachers' organisation, L'Associazione Magistrale di Nicolo Tommaseo went the same way despite the efforts of Fr. Tacchi-Venturi, who was by now established as one of the chief intermediaries between the Vatican and Mussolini.[76] The loss of the teachers' organisation did not, however, prove to be a serious one in the longer term, since the restoration of religious instruction in the secondary schools as a result of the Concordat of 1929 was to strengthen considerably Catholic influence in the schools. But the establishment of the Ente Nazionale della Co-operazione, a new body designed to fascistise co-operative enterprise in Italy, in December 1925 posed a serious threat to this traditional area of Catholic economic activity and but for the efforts of I.C.A.S., the network of Catholic co-operatives, which had already sustained heavy losses as a result of continuing squadrist violence, would have passed under complete state control.[77]

---

[73] I.e., Padre Rosa, Armida Barelli and Luigi Colombo.

[74] Gemelli was another friend of the Pope's from the period he went to Milan. For an account of the role played by this leading Catholic intellectual and his university in the 1920s and 1930s, see Webster *The Cross and the Fasces*, chap. 12. See also Ranfagni, *I Clerico-fascisti*. The 'Clerico-Fascisti' of the title were not, of course, the former *popolare* politicians who supported Fascism in the early and mid-1920s but Gemelli and his fellow academics, including Amintore Fanfani.

[75] This view of the role of I.C.A.S. is shared by the author of the only detailed study of the organisation that has emerged so far. See Brunori Di Siervo, 'L'Istituto Cattolico di Attività Sociali', p. 746, where she says: '...by founding I.C.A.S., it was hoped to save the "saveable", to prevent the fruits of fifty years of activity by Catholics in the social and economic fields from being lost to Fascism'.

[76] A.C.S., S.P.D., C.R. 88W/R, 'Tacchi-Venturi', letter to Mussolini of 21 October 1925.

[77] Brunori Di Siervo, 'L'Istuto Cattolico di Attività Sociali', p. 739.

Two other areas of Catholic activity which suffered severely both from Fascist policy and adverse economic circumstances at this time were banking and the press. The Italian banking system as a whole found itself in extreme financial difficulties in the mid- and late 1920s, but the Catholic banks were particularly badly hit.[78] Undermined by unfavourable economic conditions and defective management, the Catholic banks and the Casse Rurali were decimated between 1926 and 1929. Following the collapse of the Credito Nazionale, the lynchpin of the Catholic banking system, seventy-four banks and Casse Rurali – with 1,021 branches and a total loss of one milliard lire – either closed their doors completely or were bought out by more resilient institutions in these three years.[79] The presence of Clerico-Fascists on the boards of management of other Catholic banks probably saved them from the same fate, but government help was always paid for by greater Fascist control.[80]

Mussolini could hardly have been expected to shed many tears over the decline of Catholic financial interests and some Catholic historians have claimed that he deliberately discouraged the Banca d'Italia from mounting rescue operations in some cases.[81] On the other hand, the Government could not permit the complete collapse of the Catholic banking system owing to the grave damage it would have caused to the economic structure of the country as a whole. Furthermore, but for Mussolini, some of the larger Catholic banks would not have survived at all, and the foundation of the Istituto Centrale di Credito, which ultimately put the remaining Catholic banks on more secure foundations between 1929 and 1935, would have been impossible without his direct support. Indeed, it seems more than likely that the establishment of the Istituto was seen by the Vatican as an essential part of the 1929 *Conciliazione* 'package deal'. Once again, Clerico-Fascist influence with the Government, in this case that of Stefano Cavazzoni, a close friend of Luigi Colombo, was of decisive importance to the Catholic banking world.[82] Though Colombo had previously been on the boards of other Catholic banks (including that of the Banco Ambrosiano) it is clear that he was on the board of the Istituto not as a banking expert, but as a watchdog for the Vatican and Catholic Action.[83] The appointments of Cavazzoni and Colombo as President and Vice-President respectively of the Istituto guaranteed some autonomy for

---

[78] For an account of the troubles of the Catholic banks in this period, see Caroleo, *Le Banche Cattoliche*, chap. 4.

[79] De Stefani, *Baraonda Bancaria*, p. 496.

[80] Caroleo, *Le Banche Cattoliche*, pp. 146–7. From the *Annuario delle Banche Cattoliche*, 1925, it emerges that leading Clerico-Fascists sat on the boards of thirteen out of a total of seventeen major Catholic banks in the mid-1920s.

[81] See, for example, Civardi, *Breve Compendio di Storia*, p. 205.

[82] See Cavazzoni (ed.), *Stefano Cavazzoni*, p. 234. The book is a collection of essays on various aspects of Cavazzoni's life and work, put together with filial piety. The page cited is from an essay by Luigi Colombo.

[83] See Rossini, *Il Movimento Cattolico*, p. 42.

the remaining Catholic financial institutions, and provided a direct link with the 'general staff' of the Catholic movement – the Giunta Centrale of Catholic Action. In the end the vicissitudes of the Catholic banks provided more grist to Mussolini's mill; he took all the credit for the rescue operations and at the same time taunted Catholic Action with the accusation that: 'The Catholic banks have lost one milliard lire of money belonging to the poor.'[84]

The crisis of the Catholic banks could not have come at a worse moment for that branch of the Catholic movement which was so heavily dependent on them – the press. Whereas in 1923 the Catholic movement could boast of twenty-one daily newspapers, 90 per cent of which were to be found as one would expect in northern and central Italy, by 1929 that figure had been more than halved.[85] The central problem of the Catholic newspapers was, at it had always been, one of finance. The largest combine of Catholic papers, Count Grosoli's *Trust*, had lurched from one financial crisis to another ever since its birth at the beginning of the century.[86] Many of these papers only managed to keep going thanks to generous and regular subsidies from Catholic magnates and from the Catholic banks.[87] When the banks entered into crisis this source of funds began to dry up.[88] The financial problems of the Catholic newspapers were exacerbated by the political division which beset the Catholic movement from the Summer of 1923 onwards. After the defection from the P.P.I. of the Clerico-Fascists and their newspapers, a regular newspaper 'war' ensued between Clerico-Fascist organs like *L'Avvenire d'Italia* of Bologna, *Il Momento* of Turin and *Il Corriere d'Italia* of Rome on the one hand, and pro-P.P.I. newspapers like *Il Popolo di Roma*, *L'Eco di Bergamo* and *L'Ordine* of Como on the other. To make matters worse, two or three badly undercapitalised 'neutral' papers like *Il Corriere* of Turin and *Il Corriere Vicento* also entered into competition for the small Catholic readership, to the detriment of all concerned.[89]

Under these pressures *Il Momento* and *Il Corriere d'Italia* managed to maintain a precarious existence on government subsidies thanks to their Clerico-Fascist stance,[90] and *L'Avvenire d'Italia* and another Catholic paper *L'Italia* were only saved from complete financial collapse by ecclesiastical intervention.[91] But others were not so lucky, particularly the remaining members of the *Trust* which almost entirely vanished between 1926 and

[84] As quoted in ibid., p. 8.
[85] *Annuario della Stampa Italiana*, 1923 and 1929/30.
[86] Sgarbanti, *Ritratto Politico di Giovanni Grosoli*, p. 158.
[87] Caroleo, *Le Banche Cattoliche*, p. 105.   [88] Ibid.
[89] For the case of *Il Momento* of Turin, see Gariglio, *Cattolici Democratici e Clerico-fascisti a Torino*, chap. 4.
[90] Ibid., p. 169, and Castronovo and Tranfaglia, *La Stampa italiana dell'età Fascista*, p. 150.
[91] Majo, *La Stampa quotidiana cattolica Milanese*, p. 27; and for *L'Avvenire* see Onofrio, *I Giornali bolognesi del Ventennio Fascista*, pp. 69–70.

1929.[92] Another important factor in the survival of Catholic newspapers was the attitude of the Fascist authorities. As one historian of the Catholic press has pointed out, few Catholic newspapers were actually forced to close down by the Fascists, instead: '...they preferred to bring pressure to bear on the staff by introducing Catholic journalists sympathetic to Fascism, men who in the final analysis, were the heirs of the old Catholic Right'.[93] But when the method failed the Fascists were not slow to act: *Il Popolo*, the P.P.I. newspaper, disappeared with the Party in November 1926; *Il Corriere* of Turin was closed by prefectoral order at the same time as a result of high level Clerico-Fascist protests about its competition against *Il Momento*,[94] and *Il Cittadino* of both Brescia and Genoa were harried out of existence by the local *ras* because of their continued opposition to Fascism.[95] Others survived the temporary suspension of publication following the Zaniboni attempt on Mussolini's life in the Autumn of 1926 only by changing editorial staff and policy.[96] Thus by 1929, apart from those papers that were ostentatiously Clerico-Fascist anyway, the Catholic press was obsequious and obedient both to the ecclesiastical authorities and to the dictates of the Fascist press law. Only *L'Osservatore Romano*, the official organ of the Holy See, could afford the luxury, albeit rarely, of criticising the Regime.

On the eve of the *Conciliazone*, the Italian Catholic movement in nearly all its forms and activities was smaller than it had been when Mussolini came to power in 1922. In addition to the losses and trimmings already catalogued, the Catholic youth organisations were to be cut down to size by the Fascists in 1927/8 and all the affiliates of Catholic Action were to suffer a massive haemorrhage in membership in the late 1920s. In seven years the Catholic 'presence' in Italian society was considerably reduced in both size and effectiveness. But however much the Church might deplore the losses suffered, it could at the least congratulate itself on the fact that what remained – with the possible exception of the C.N.I. – had been brought back firmly and completely under its control.

THE 'FASCISTISATION' OF YOUTH AND THE OPENING OF THE
NEGOTIATIONS FOR A SOLUTION OF THE 'ROMAN QUESTION'

Though Pius XI may have more or less acquiesced in the 'demolitions' of other parts of the Catholic movement, when the Regime turned its policy of 'fascistisation' against the Catholic youth organisations, as it did from the beginning of 1926, the Pope became more alarmed. Indeed his fears

---

[92] Licata, *Il Giornalismo Cattolico Italiano*, p. 118.
[93] Gariglio, *Cattolici Democratici e Clerico-fascisti*, p. 182.
[94] Castronovo and Tranfaglia, *La Stampa italiana dell'età Fascista*, pp. 49–50.
[95] Ibid., p. 425.   [96] Ibid.

for the survival of Catholic youth groups in the face of legislation that was being pushed through Parliament to establish a new Fascist youth organisation – the Opera Nazionale Balilla (henceforth the Balilla) – largely explain his decision to take the initiative in seeking a definitive solution of the 'Roman Question' in the Spring of 1926.[97] Hitherto, he had shown very little optimism about the possibility of a settlement. Carlo Santucci records that when in 1925 he presented to the Pope his ideas for a settlement (which were substantially the same as those discussed in the Cerretti–Orlando conversations, except that instead of sovereignty he was proposing extra-territoriality for the Vatican) Pius XI's response was not very positive: 'The proposals greatly interested him, but he believed that they would be so difficult to implement, that he preferred to leave the solution of this grave problem to his successor.'[98]

Given the Vatican's attitude to what had been an initiative made with some support on the part of the Regime,[99] Mussolini's policy was naturally cautious, though not as fragmentary or incoherent as one contemporary observer has suggested.[100]

Since October 1923, when he had first attempted to persuade a reluctant Minister of Justice, Oviglio, to set the ball rolling in Cabinet, the main plank in Mussolini's policy towards the Church had been a proposal to carry out a comprehensive reform of Italy's ecclesiastical legislation. Early in 1925 an Ecclesiastical Legislation Reform Commission was set up under the chairmanship of Paolo Mattei-Gentili, with one other Clerico-Fascist, Senator Calisse, and more importantly three theological canons of the Roman Patriarchal Basilicas – Capitani, Talamo and Cisterna – as members.[101] The work of the Commission was both relevant and important and even if, as one historian has pointed out, the Commission's proposals were largely based on legal principles favouring the retention of State control over the property of the Church,[102] this would still not explain their eventual rejection by the Vatican, for the bulk of those same proposals were ultimately to be incorporated in the Concordat of 1929. It should also be borne in mind that the validity of the Commission's work was recognised by letters of support from no less than 10 cardinals and 125 Italian archbishops and bishops,[103] and was tacitly recognised by the Pope himself, for the Vatican would never have permitted the three canons to sit on the

---

[97] There is very little written on the Fascist youth organisations in the period before the setting up of the Balilla. For the background to the passing of the Balilla law of 1926 see Lyttelton, *The Seizure of Power,* pp. 408–10.

[98] As cited in Scoppola, *La Chiesa e il Fascismo,* p. 111.

[99] Ibid., where in the same document Santucci says that he was given moral support for his venture by Alfredo Rocco, the Minister of Justice.

[100] Gianinni, *Il Cammino della Conciliazione,* p. 41.

[101] Ibid., p. 129.   [102] Jemolo, *Chiesa e Stato,* p. 226.

[103] See Margiotta-Broglio, *L'Italia e la Santa Sede,* pp. 491–2.

Commission if it had not approved of what they were doing. Yet the Commission had barely completed its labours when, on 1 March 1926, in an open letter to his Cardinal Secretary of State, Pius XI repudiated the Government's initiative.[104]

The Pope justified his drastic and wholly unexpected decision on the grounds that the Holy See could never accept a revision of Italian ecclesiastical legislation law, even if that also included the Law of Guarantees, if it was imposed by the unilateral act of the Italian Parliament. This was palpably an excuse, for from the start the nature of the exercise had been clear to everyone concerned, including the Vatican. In the absence of evidence to the contrary, it is impossible to escape the conclusion that the law on the Balilla (which was at that time passing through its final stages in Parliament), with its implicit purpose of creating a Fascist monopoly of all Italian youth organisations, persuaded Pius XI that only through a negotiated settlement of *all* the outstanding issues between Church and State could he obtain the necessary legal guarantees for the remnants of the Catholic movement, and in particular, for the Catholic youth organisations, and this interpretation is borne out by the text of the letter which declared that the Holy See would only accept changes negotiated bilaterally.[105]

But why had the Pope become so optimistic about the chances of a negotiated settlement? Apart from the considerable progress made by the Commission, the answer to that question lies in the enormously strengthened position which Mussolini had achieved for himself both in the country at large and in the Fascist Party by the Spring of 1926. With the establishment of the dictatorship it was now clear that Mussolini and Fascism were here to stay. As a result, Mussolini was seen to possess a political authority, an ability to negotiate and enforce agreements, denied to both Orlando and Nitti, which explains why their talks with the Vatican had had no positive outcome.

Mussolini's strengthened position in the Party was of paramount importance to the Vatican because in practical terms it meant a significant diminution of anti-clerical influence inside the Regime as a whole. The first step in this direction had been achieved by the replacement of the philosopher Giovanni Gentile as Minister of Education by Pietro Fedele in June 1924. Gentile would never have agreed to the introduction of religious instruction into his newly reformed secondary school system nor to the ban against excommunicated priests holding teaching posts: on both these issues his Catholic successor was to prove more than

[104] For the text of the Pope's letter see *L'Osservatore Romano*, 27 February 1926.
[105] Ibid. See also Martini, *Studi sulla Questione Romana*, p. 110.

accommodating.[106] By 1926, Gentile's influence inside the Party was being bitterly contested, and his last public stand in 1928 against the imminent *Conciliazione* turned out to be a miserable failure.[107]

An even more crucial ministerial change was the replacement of the unco-operative Oviglio by the ex-Nationalist, Alfredo Rocco, as Minister of Justice in January 1925. Following Mattei-Gentili's earlier posting as Under-Secretary for Justice, Rocco's appointment meant that this ministry was now completely in the hands of pro-clerical elements. Already in his manifesto *Politica* of December 1918, Rocco had written that: '...Italy... cannot and must not neglect the favoured position that it holds by being Italian within the organised spiritual and traditional power of the Roman Catholic Church, that is to say, the institution that still enjoys the most universal prestige and the greatest potential of universal expansion'.[108] In a newspaper article published in April 1922, Rocco went further than this. He argued that the Liberal, secular traditions of the Risorgimento should be abandoned and that the Italian State must become more openly and more actively Catholic, promoting and defending the Catholic religion in return for the Church's loyal support of the social and political order in Italy.[109] In other words, he was advocating nothing less than a restoration of the nineteenth-century alliance of 'throne and altar'.

The immediate outcome of Rocco's appointment was an intensification of the campaign against freemasonry. The first shots in this campaign had been fired by Mussolini himself in February 1923 when he had declared membership of the masonic lodges to be incompatible with that of the Fascist Party. By the end of 1924, masonic premises in many areas of Italy were becoming the target of Fascist, squadrist violence as the Freemasons became identified as the new scapegoat.[110] In January 1925, Rocco introduced a bill into Parliament suppressing the masonic lodges, and making it a criminal offence for civil servants to belong to them or other secret organisations.[111] Whilst there was no explicit reference to the anti-Catholic activities of the Freemasons in the parliamentary speeches

---

[106] According to the most famous of all Italian apostate priests, Buonaiuti, *Pellegrino di Roma*, p. 245, though Pietro Fedele was his friend, he did not hesitate to forbid him to continue teaching at the University of Rome in order to please the Vatican. See also Jemolo, *Chiesa e Stato*, p. 225, where he says that Fedele '...was ready to concede anything to the Holy See'.

[107] See Mangoni, *L'Interventismo della Cultura*, p. 167, on the losing battle which Gentile fought with other Fascist intellectuals in the mid- and late 1920s. See also Gentile's article in *Il Corriere della Sera*, 20 October 1972. According to Biggini, *Storia inedita della Conciliazione*, p. 141, the *Foglio d'Ordini* replied to Gentile's article the next day, saying that it was possible to resolve the 'Roman Question', but that it would not be easy.

[108] As quoted in Lyttelton (ed.), *Italian Fascisms From Pareto to Gentile*, p. 267.

[109] See Sarti (ed.), *The Axe Within*, p. 37.

[110] For an interpretation and account of the Fascist campaign against freemasonry, see Lyttelton, *The Seizure of Power*, pp. 280–2.   [111] Binchy, *Church and State*, p. 143.

of either Rocco or Mussolini, the Vatican was understandably grateful for this attack on what it regarded as being the stronghold and headquarters of anti-clericalism in Italy. And, inevitably, the outlawing of the Freemasons had the effect of substantially reducing their influence in both the Fascist movement and Regime.

In these ways, Rocco's appointment opened the way to a further improvement in relations between the Church and Fascism, and eventually to the negotiations for the Lateran Pacts.

But ultimately the most significant change in the leadership of the Regime was the dismissal of Roberto Farinacci as Fascist Party Secretary in April 1926. Though this was a month *after* the Pope had taken his decision, Farinacci's departure was long expected in informed circles, not least in the Vatican.

As Farinacci's anti-clerical outburst of the following month demon-strates, the ex-masonic boss of Cremona was at this time the leading Fascist opponent of further concessions to the Church.[112] Farinacci's departure signalled Mussolini's final victory over the Party, and Farinacci's successor, Augusto Turati, was to give faithful and consistent support to the Duce's religious policy, and in his own way to work assiduously to promote good relations with the Church until he too was dismissed by Mussolini in October 1930. Looked at in these terms, then, the Pope's confidence in a positive response to his invitation to negotiate was more than justified in the Spring of 1926.

But Mussolini does not seem to have been quite as confident as the Pope, for two whole months were to elapse before he gave very cautious instructions to Rocco '...discreetly to sound out the Vatican on its view of the form which a satisfactory, legal settlement of relations between the Holy See and Italy might take'.[113] Perhaps the simplest explanation of his lack of enthusiasm at this point is to be found in his speech to the Chamber on the Lateran Pacts of 13 May 1929: 'Quite frankly, I was not thinking very seriously in terms of resolving the "Roman Question", in the Summer of 1926. The problem that was really worrying me at that time was the problem of the lira.'[114]

Certainly, at this stage of the game, it was the Vatican which was doing all the running, conveying through Tacchi-Venturi[115] and even through a rather more obscure intermediary, Mons. Haver, its eagerness to open

---

[112] *D.D.I.*, 7, Vol. VI, p. 227, letter of Tacchi-Venturi to A. Giannini in which the Jesuit priest protests against Farinacci's speeches against the Church and asks for a reassurance that Mussolini had nothing to do with them. In a marginal comment on the document, Mussolini refused to do so.

[113] Scoppola, *La Chiesa e il Fascismo*, pp. 117–18.

[114] *O.O.*, Vol. XXIV, p. 71.

[115] *D.D.I.*, 7, Vol. VI, p. 235, no. 322, Tacchi-Venturi to A. Giannini, 31 May 1926.

discussions as soon as possible.[116] It took several more months before the representatives of the two sides eventually met in August 1926.

THE NEGOTIATIONS FOR THE LATERAN PACTS, 1926–9

Both sides chose their representatives with skill. The Holy See selected Francesco Pacelli, brother of Mons. Eugenio Pacelli, who already held one of the Vatican's most important diplomatic posts – Nuncio to Germany – and was later to become Cardinal Secretary of State and then Pope. As a Consistorial lawyer, Francesco Pacelli was well-versed in the complexities of the 'Roman Question', and with his experience of handling the Vatican's interests in the Banco di Roma, he was eminently qualified to negotiate the financial aspects of the settlement. The Italian negotiatior, Domenico Barone, was equally well-placed to serve his country's interests. Also a lawyer, Barone had worked in the religious affairs department of the Ministry of Justice, and by 1926 he had risen to the highest rank in the Italian civil service, that of Consigliere di Stato.[117] From Mussolini's point of view, Barone's greatest recommendation was the fact that he was 'a faithful Fascist'.[118] Neither of the two men had diplomatic experience, but that hardly mattered given the fact that this was a 'family' affair and that both were obliged to refer back continually to their respective principals.

Pacelli and Barone made very rapid progress in the early stages of their negotiations: by November 1926 they had agreed on a provisional draft of the Treaty to liquidate the 'Roman Question' and had begun negotiations on a concordat.[119] On 30 December 1926, Mussolini gave Barone formal powers to negotiate on behalf of the Italian Government, having only then overcome the objections of the King, who was a notorious anti-clerical.[120] With the exceptions of the two periods when negotiations were suspended, from June 1927 to January 1928 and from April to May 1928, when the egregious Padre Tacchi-Venturi was employed to bring the two sides back to the negotiating table, Barone and Pacelli conducted the negotiations with great skill and secrecy until January 1929. At this point, Barone's untimely death obliged Mussolini to take over the final, critical stage of the negotiations himself.

The first major problem which Pacelli and Barone encountered in their

[116] According to Biggini, *Storia inedita della Conciliazione*, p. 77, in June 1926, the Vatican sent Mons. Haver to sound out both Barone and Federzoni: this is confirmed by F. Pacelli, *Diario*, ed. Maccarone, p. v.

[117] The Council of State, following the Napoleonic model which had been transmitted to United Italy by Piedmont, had the task of scrutinising draft legislation and treaties. It was composed of senior civil servants and judges.

[118] Binchy, *Church and State*, p. 172.

[119] F. Pacelli, *Diario*, ed. Maccarone, p. 263.

[120] Ibid., p. 35; Pacelli does point out, however, that the King's principal objections were to the Pope having 'sovereignty and subjects'.

negotiations for the Treaty was the question of the status of the Vatican City in international law. Initially, Barone was instructed to hold out against territorial sovereignty and to offer a more explicit form of that extra-territorial status which had been laid down by the Law of Guarantees.[121] He only gave way on this issue when Pacelli had made it clear that for the Holy See territorial sovereignty was the *sine qua non* of the whole settlement.[122] Even then it was not until late 1928 that Mussolini succeeded in persuading King Victor Emmanuel to accept the miniscule loss of territory that had already been made in his name.[123] The second major problem was thus the size of the restored 'papal state': while both sides had quickly agreed that it must obviously include the one-hundred-acre Vatican City, thus legitimising the *de facto* control which Pius IX and his successors had enjoyed there since 1878, the Pope also sought to annex the adjacent Janiculum Hill and the rather more distant Villa Pamfili. In the face of Mussolini's determined resistance to what would have been an unpopular, inconvenient and expensive cession of Italian territory, the Vatican abandoned its claims: indeed, as a goodwill gesture and a sop to Victor Emmanuel's lingering doubts, Piux XI opted for extra-territoriality rather than sovereignty over the Palace of the Holy Office which was contiguous with Vatican territory. In this way, the seventy-year-old dispute over the temporal power was finally resolved.

Pacelli and Barone encountered similar difficulties in their negotiations for the Financial Convention, whose purpose was to settle the question of compensation for the Holy See's loss of revenue from the former Papal States. The matter was complicated by the fact that the Holy See had steadfastly refused to accept the annual indemnity for which the Italians had made provision in the Law of Guarantees. After long-drawn-out negotiations on this issue, the Vatican eventually settled for 750 million lire in cash and 1 billion lire's worth of Italian Government Stock, plus an undertaking on the part of the Italians to pay for the cost of the engineering and technical works necessary to provide the Vatican City with the accoutrements of a modern state. Given the serious financial difficulties which faced the Holy See in the 1920s it is not surprising that Pius XI pushed Mussolini to the limit in the matter of financial compensation,[124] and this aspect of the Lateran Pacts was to arouse much criticism from Fascists and non-Fascists alike in the months immediately following the *Conciliazione*.

If the negotiations for the Treaty and the Financial Convention had been

---

[121] F. Pacelli, 'L'Opera di Pio XI per la Conciliazione con l'Italia', *Vita e Pensiero*, October 1929, p. 622. [122] Ibid.

[123] Biggini, *Storia inedita della Conciliazione*, p. 233.

[124] For an account of the negotiations for the Financial Convention see F. Pacelli, *Diario*, ed. Maccarone, p. 37.

far from easy, those for the Concordat proved to be fraught with difficulty. Whereas it had taken just over four months to reach agreement on the first two items in the Lateran 'package', it required well over two years from the presentation of Pacelli's 'punti formulati come base della trattative del Concordato' to arrive at a final draft. Though the Concordat dealt in the main with the kind of non-controversial matters common to most of the other concordats concluded by the Holy See with European governments in the 1920s there were a few items which were highly controversial, involving substantial concessions on Mussolini's part, and therefore gave rise to protracted negotiations. The Vatican's insistence on a clause excluding excommunicated priests from holding public office was fiercely resisted by the Italians,[125] and its proposals on marriage required such radical amendments to Italian matrimonial law that Mussolini resisted them until the last moment. But the most difficult problem, and one that nearly shipwrecked the negotiations on at least two occasions, was the question of the future of Catholic Action and in particular its youth organisations. This was hardly surprising in view of the fact that, as we have already seen, his desire to protect what remained of the Catholic movement from further 'fascistisation' had been a primary motive in Pius XI's decision to open negotiations in the first place.

The Pope's apprehensions for the survival of the Catholic organisations were wholly justified by the events of the Summer and the Autumn of 1926. The four attempts on Mussolini's life in this period prompted new waves of violence against the opponents of the Regime and against those organisations like Catholic Action which had declared themselves to be neutral in the political struggle. Catholic co-operatives and other economic organisations, Catholic printing presses and above all the Catholic youth groups found themselves amongst the principal targets.[126] Just as the assassination attempts offered an ideal pretext for the rapid construction of the apparatus of a police state,[127] so they gave the Fascist leaders the opportunity to press on with their campaign to achieve a Fascist monopoly in the youth field. The acts of violence against the Catholic organisations were accompanied by violent attacks in the Fascist press which denounced the Catholic Boy Scouts movement in particular as subversive and 'anti-Italian'.[128]

As usual, the most effective weapon in this campaign was legislation.

---

[125] See Margiotta-Broglio, *L'Italia e la Santa Sede*, pp. 176–7.
[126] F. Pacelli, *Diario*, ed. Maccarone, pp. 23–5, gives the text of the 'promemoria consegnata a Barone' containing a detailed list of the incidents of violence and acts of repression against Catholic organisations.
[127] See Seton-Watson, *Italy from Liberalism to Fascism*, p. 665, for a summary account of the legislative and police measures that followed the fourth attempt on Mussolini's life in October 1926.
[128] See for example *Il Tevere*, front page article of 18 September 1926.

The law on the Balilla of April 1926 had already taken a major step in this direction by re-organising and unifying the youth organisations and giving them that legal recognition which their rivals lacked – and of course their main rivals were the youth organisations of Catholic Action.[129] In an attempt to deprive these organisations of their *raison d'être* the 1926 law also provided for the appointment of chaplains to the Balilla and the inclusion of an element of religious instruction in the programme of activities to be followed by the Fascist youth organisations.[130] The same law gave the Ministry of Education wide powers to enact further measures governing the Balilla by decree. The full significance of this did not become apparent until January 1927, when the Ministry of Education conferred on the Prefects the power to dissolve all branches of the Catholic Boy Scouts in communes with less than 20,000 inhabitants.[131]

Pius XI's public defence of the Scouts and his threat to suspend the negotiations between Pacelli and Barone failed to save them. The Pope was forced to yield, and rather than accept such a dissolution at the hands of the authorities, he preferred to disband them himself.[132] Encouraged by this victory, the Regime delivered another serious blow to the Catholic youth groups by banning all organisations not affiliated to the Balilla from engaging in sporting or athletic activities.[133] The federation of Catholic Sports Club (F.A.S.C.) was thus forced to dissolve itself.[134] leaving Catholic Action with only the parochial cinemas, theatres and recreation centres of the G.C.I. Deprived of one of their most attractive activities, the Catholic youth organisations fought an increasingly losing battle to keep their members in face of the pressures and intimidation now being used to recruit new members to the Balilla. In a climate of general uncertainty over the future of the Catholic youth organisations their membership began to slump dramatically, and that of the Balilla rose accordingly.[135]

The enforced dissolution of the F.A.S.C. was also a blow to the Pope's confidence in the good faith of the men with whom he was negotiating, and from June 1927 until January 1928 the discussions between Pacelli and Barone were effectively suspended. They had barely resumed when the Vatican became aware of another, and this time, potentially mortal, threat to the Catholic youth organisations. In March 1928, to the usual accompaniment of fresh attacks in the Fascist press, the text of a decree law was published, banning '... all youth organisations, not belonging to

[129] For the text of the law on the Balilla see *Mediterranean Fascism*, ed. Delzell, pp. 139–43.
[130] These clauses were not actually published until January 1927. Martini, *Studi sulla Questione Romana*, p. 112, agrees with this interpretation of the aim of the Balilla religious instruction classes.
[131] F. Pacelli, *Dairio*, ed. Maccarone, p. 50.
[132] Ibid.　　　　　　　　　　[133] Binchy, *Church and State*, p. 414.
[134] Civardi, *Breve Compendio di Storia*, p. 207.
[135] Lyttelton, *The Seizure of Power*, p. 409 n. 70.

the Balilla, which are involved in moral and physical education'.[136] It seemed as if the fate of the Catholic youth organisations was finally sealed and that the Fascist youth leaders had at last achieved their goal of a monopoly in the youth field.

But this time Pius XI stood his ground and broke off the negotiations entirely.[137] In the end the Pope's famous intransigence paid off, for Tacchi-Venturi was able to contrive a solution whereby, in return for a resumption of the negotiations, Mussolini agreed to exempt the remaining Catholic youth organisations from the scope of the decree, accepting the principle that G.C.I., G.F.C.I. and the Catholic university student federations were an integral part of Catholic Action and therefore covered by a clause to be inserted in the Concordat recognising the legal status of Catholic Action – 'The Italian State recognises the affiliated organisations of Italian Catholic Action.'[138] Pius XI's intuition had been proved correct: only the prospect of a general settlement of the 'Roman Question' had persuaded the Regime to abandon its plans to eliminate Catholic Action from the youth field; but the price was a severe curtailment of its activities there.

By the beginning of February 1929 the remaining problems had been solved, and on the 11th of that month the agreements were finally signed in the Lateran Palace in Rome (hence their name, the Lateran Pacts). The *Conciliazione* between Italy and the Vatican had been achieved. Even allowing for the steady improvement in Church and State relations during the Liberal era and the considerable progress towards a settlement that had already been made in the negotiations between previous Prime Ministers and the Vatican, it has to be said that the *Conciliazione* was in large part the work of two bold, imaginative and ambitious men – Mussolini and Pius XI, but above all Mussolini. In all probability there would have been some kind of settlement of the 'Roman Question' had Mussolini and Fascism never come to power in Italy, but such a settlement would have been very different from the one reached in February 1929. A leading Italian Catholic historian has recently suggested that such a settlement would not have included a concordat.[139] It is inconceivable that as long as Pius XI was supervising negotiations from the Vatican side that some form of concordat would not have emerged as an essential part of the settlement. As we have already seen, by the end of the First World War, the temporal power was no longer the Vatican's main concern, even if it still demanded some more tangible sign of its independence – i.e., sovereignty over the Vatican City.

---

[136] As quoted in Civardi, *Breve Compendio di Storia*, p. 205.
[137] I.e., from April to May 1928: see F. Pacelli, *Diario*, ed. Maccarone, p. 25. According to Pacelli, the Pope believed that the regulation, 'would even permit the closing down of the seminaries'.
[138] See Appendix II, Article 43.
[139] Scoppola, 'The State and the Church in the Fascist Period in Italy 1922–1943' (paper given at Cambridgeshire College of Arts and Technology, 4 November 1979).

Far more important to Pius XI, as it would have been to any Italian Pope, was the recovery of at least some of the powers, privileges and property of the Church in Italy which had been taken away by the ecclesiastical legislation of the Moderate Liberals during the Risorgimento.

But a concordat concluded by the Holy See with a liberal, democratic Italian government would undoubtedly have been very different from the one concluded with Mussolini's Fascist dictatorship. In the first place, it would not have required the clause guaranteeing the juridical recognition of Catholic Action and its dependent organisations. Equally, no liberal, democratic government, not even one dominated by the P.P.I. – and a liberal, democratic regime could only have survived on that basis – would have accepted the enormous concessions which Mussolini was forced to make in the matter of the legal privileges of the clergy,[140] the ban on excommunicated priests, the reintroduction of religious instruction into the schools and, least of all, on the question of matrimonial law. For Pius XI these were the essential prerequisites of that Christian restoration of Italian society which was the main goal of his pontificate. Under a regime with totalitarian pretensions these gains were doubly necessary if the Catholic Church was to re-establish its strong presence in Italian society. Thus, in his quest for the historical glory and the immediate political prestige which a successful resolution of the 'Roman Question' would bring, Mussolini was forced to pay the price of the Concordat. Having finally achieved his goal, it remained to be seen whether Mussolini could persuade the Fascist Party and the Italian Parliament to accept his masterpiece. But as Mussolini is reputed to have said when asked by Gasparri what he would do if he encountered opposition in Parliament to his solution of the 'Roman Question': 'Then I will change Parliament.'[141] With the help of the Church, he proceeded to do precisely that in March 1929.

[140] See Appendix II, Articles 7 and 8.
[141] The conversation is reported in Charle-Roux, *Huit ans aux Vatican*, p. 47. Charle-Roux was French Ambassador to the Quirinale from 1919 to 1925 and Ambassador to the Holy See from 1933 to 1941.

CHAPTER 3

Reactions to the 'Conciliazione' and the ratification of the pacts

At the risk of stating the obvious, it needs to be said that the *Conciliazione* was an agreement reached at the highest levels of Church and State, the result of negotiations amongst a very few individuals at the highest level and conducted in the greatest of secrecy. On the Vatican side no more than half a dozen men were involved, led by Cardinal Gasparri – with the Pope himself frequently intervening.[1] The number of those involved in the negotiations, or at least kept informed of them on the Italian side, was probably much the same – Mussolini, Rocco, Mattei-Gentili, Barone – and in the background, the King.[2] For Mussolini, direct involvement in and responsibility for the negotiations ensured that it would be acclaimed as his achievement, and his alone. It was essential to prevent interference from the more anti-clerical elements of Fascism, like Balbo or Farinacci. It seems extremely unlikely that they would have allowed Mussolini to make the concessions which he actually did make on issues like marriage and Catholic Action; only by presenting them as a *fait accompli*, and by staking his authority on them could he hope to win acceptance for them from the Fascist Party.

Despite the increasing number of leaks of information in official circles as the negotiations neared their end in January and February 1929, the signing of the Lateran Pacts inevitably came as a complete surprise to the

---

[1] The others were Francesco Pacelli, who did most of the actual negotiating with Barone, Mons. Borgoncini-Duca, Secretary for Extraordinary Ecclesiastical Affairs and later first Nuncio in Italy, and Mons. Pizzardo, Borgoncini-Duca's deputy. According to Martini, *Studi Sulla Questione Romana*, p. 112, Padre Tacchi-Venturi was not informed about the negotiations until the beginning of 1928. It is interesting to note that Mons. G. B. Montini, who was working in the Vatican Secetariat of State as a junior *minutante* or clerk, did not hear of the negotiations till the beginning of 1929.

[2] The King was kept informed of the progress of the negotiations by regular reports from Mussolini who referred back to him on such sensitive issues as the sovereign status of the Vatican City. One or two officials of the Ministry of Public Works like Conte Cozza who, according to F. Pacelli, *Diario*, ed Maccarone, pp. 43 and 47, was consulted on questions relating to the boundaries of the future state of the Vatican City, also knew of the negotiations.

overwhelming majority of the Italian population. Whilst the majority of Catholics and Fascists probably approved in a general way of the agreements which their leaders had signed on their behalf, substantial numbers on both sides quickly began to raise doubts and criticisms of the agreements which belied the picture of universal joy and approbation presented by the Italian press: in two or three cases, indeed, neither Fascist press censorship nor ecclesiastical vigilance over the Catholic press managed to prevent some of this dissent appearing in print. These reactions point to a deep gulf between the leadership and the rank and file on both sides; they reveal the strength of continuing opposition to the policies of both Pope and Duce amongst their respective followers.

The Pope was perhaps in more need of a sharp reminder of the anti-Fascism widespread amongst Italian Catholics, both inside and outside Catholic Action, than Mussolini was of the undiminished ardour of Fascist anti-clericalism at all levels of the Party and its organisations – grassroots feeling that was to contribute enormously to the crisis of 1931. Catholic opinion was very quickly put to a public test in the so-called 'Plebiscite' of March 1929, when Italian Catholics were instructed by the ecclesiastical authorities and the leaders of Catholic Action to register their approval of the *Conciliazione* by voting for the single, Fascist list of candidates; unfortunately, given the nature of the 'Plebiscite' it is very difficult to measure the size of Catholic dissent.

The 'Plebiscite' offers even less indication of the extent of Fascist anti-clerical dissent, though it is interesting that no less a person than Arnoldo Mussolini attributed the 'no' votes in the Plebiscite '...to the few ill-advised anti-clericals who refuse to accept the Lateran Pacts'.[3] But even if there were no other evidence of Fascist opposition to the religious policy of the Regime, the way in which Mussolini steered the Pacts, and the implementation legislation through Parliament, and the tone of his accompanying speeches clearly demonstrate that he was well aware that it existed and that he took it very seriously. In his anxiety to reassure his followers and to gloss over the enormous concessions which he had been forced to make to the Church, Mussolini adopted an intransigent, statist stance and resorted to a brutal, bellicose rhetoric which deeply upset his Catholic admirers, infuriated Pius XI and nearly precipitated a rupture of Italo-Vatican relations on the eve of the ratification of the Pacts.

CATHOLIC REACTIONS TO THE *CONCILIAZIONE*

The official Catholic reaction to the Pacts was naturally one of unrestrained jubilation. *L'Osservatore Romano* led the Catholic press in celebrating the resolution of the 'Roman Question' with the famous words 'Italy has been

---

[3] Editorial in *Il Popolo d'Italia*, 26 March 1929.

given back to God and God to Italy.'[4] The Vatican organ then went on to render a generous, though by no means extravagant, tribute to Mussolini, Pius XI's 'Man whom providence has sent us', for his part in the achievement of a settlement. The other official Catholic journals, *La Civiltà Cattolica*, the *Bollettino Ufficiale* of Catholic Action and *Vita e Pensiero* of the Catholic University plus the diocesan press adopted much the same tone and like *L'Osservatore Romano* devoted many pages to a detailed analysis of the contents of the agreements and their implications.[5] The Clerico-Fascist papers like *Il Corriere d'Italia* and *Il Momento* needed no encouragement to indulge in sycophantic eulogies of the Duce, nor did they fail to point out that the *Conciliazione* was what they had been working for since 1923.[6]

This official journalistic euphoria was very much an expression of the feelings of triumph of the Pope, Cardinal Gasparri and the team of negotiators; it certainly was not an accurate reflection of all Catholic reactions; indeed, within the Vatican hierarchy and even amongst the members of the Sacred College itself there were several critics of the Lateran Treaties. According to Cesare Maria De Vecchi di Val Cismon, Fascist quadumvir and the first Italian Ambassador to the Vatican, Cardinals Merry del Val, Pompilji, Pignatelli di Belmonte, Lauri and Cerretti (the man who had conducted the negotiations with Orlando back in 1919), all senior members of the Roman Curia, believed that the Church had paid a very high price and had received too little in return,[7] and this impression of the balance of opinion inside the Vatican was confirmed by Mussolini in his speech to the Chamber during the debates on the ratification of the Pacts in May 1929.[8] And, despite the solemn re-opening of doors closed since 1870 and the holding of gala evenings in some Roman *palazzi* on the morrow of the signing of the Pacts, it is clear that the misgivings of these Princes of the Church were also shared by some members of the papal or 'black' aristocracy whose leading representative, Prince Ruspoli, Grand Master of the Sacred Hospice in the papal court, did not spare even the Pope himself from his criticisms.[9]

The *Conciliazione* could not have been greeted with unanimous approval by the Italian episcopate either. After seven years of Fascist religious policy which had without doubt raised the prestige and standing of the Church in Italian society enormously, increased its legal privileges and social

---

[4] *L'Osservatore Romano*, front page article of 12 February 1929.
[5] Ibid., 13–16 February. See also *La Civiltà Cattolica*, whose issue of 16 February 1929 was largely devoted to analysing the Pacts, and *Vita e Pensiero* which ran major articles on the *Conciliazione* by Filippo Meda, Francesco Pacelli and Agustino Gemelli in February, March, April, May, June and September 1929.
[6] See the article entitled 'Il Nostro Trionfo' in *Il Corriere d'Italia*, 12 February 1929.
[7] De Vecchi, *Memorie*, no. 15.   [8] *O.O.*, Vol. XXIV, p. 75.
[9] De Vecchi, *Memorie*, no. 15. He reports Ruspoli as saying: 'It is a pity that we are no longer in the Middle Ages when we could have administered a little poison to this Pope.'

influence and greatly improved its material conditions, twenty-one out of a total of two-hundred and fifty or so archbishops and bishops in Italy (not including the Slav and German bishops whose battles with Fascism will be described in Chapter 4) were still considered to be of doubtful loyalty to the Regime.[10] Such a figure might be regarded as insignificant were it not for the fact that two-thirds of this number were the ordinaries of large and important dioceses in northern and central Italy – Brescia, Bergamo, Como, Cremona, Fermo, Genoa, Novara, Padua, Parma, Piacenza, Rome (the Cardinal Vicar), Trento, Udine and Vicenza.[11]

Having witnessed the violence and destructiveness of Fascist anti-clericalism at work in their local areas in the same period, these prelates were understandably suspicious of the motives behind the Regime's assiduous wooing of the Church on a national level. Despite his instinctive patriotism and deference to the governmental authorities, Bishop Rodolfi of Vicenza was obliged to wage a private war against the local Fascio between 1924 and 1932 due to its violent treatment of clergy and laity alike,[12] and Archbishop Castelli of Fermo, whose instincts were equally conservative, was branded as being of an 'incorrigible mentality' because of his firm and dignified protests against Fascist excesses.[13]

On the other hand the vast majority of the bishops were favourably impressed by the achievements of the Regime in these years. The Bishops of Pavia and Vigevano, for instance, were deeply grateful for the fact that since the March on Rome the 'Reds' and their troublesome activities had been eliminated from their dioceses and that religious instruction had been introduced into the schools,[14] and the Bishop of Spoleto could be forgiven for failing to shed any tears over the fall of a Liberal Regime which in 1913 had done nothing to spare him the humiliation of being barred from his own cathedral by an anti-clerical demonstration; ten years later he was naturally more sympathetic to a Fascist Regime whose local representatives showed him the utmost respect and deference.[15]

In 1929, the vociferous anti-clericalism of the first Fasci could be

---

[10] The following bishops and archbishops were reported by the police as being in some way hostile to the Regime in this period: Brescia, Bergamo, Chieti, Colle di Val D'Elsa (Tuscany), Como, Cremona, Fermo, Genoa, Novara, Padua, Parma, Pavia, Piacenza, Piazza Armerina (Mario Sturzo – Luigi's brother), Reggio Calabria (coadjutor bishop), Rome (the cardinal vicar), San Severino (Campania), Senigallia, Trento, Udine and Vicenza.

[11] On the whole, southern dioceses were small, with an average population of between 100,000 and 150,000 souls and many were even smaller than this. The northern dioceses ranged from an average of 200,000 in Piedmont to 612,000 in Lombardy. Figures calculated from the *Almanacco Italiano*, 1933, pp. 372–8.

[12] See Zilio, *Un Condottiere d'anime*, pp. 211–34 and 269–331. Rodolfi's disputes with the local Federale are documented in A.C.S., D.G.P.S., G.I., bb. 93 and 94, 'Trimestrali'.

[13] A.C.S., D.G.P.S., G.I., b. 91, 'Fermo', 'Gioventù Cattolica' report from the Prefect of 21 June 1930.   [14] Guderzo, *Cattolici e Fascisti a Pavia*, pp. 53–4.

[15] R. Meloni, 'L'Episcopato Umbro Dallo State Liberale al Fascismo', in Monticone (ed.), *Cattolici e Fascisti in Umbria*, p. 149.

regarded as a part of history, and the more recent violence of the squads against various branches of the Catholic movement could be dismissed as an adolescent disorder: now the prospects for the Church in Italy looked very bright indeed, and not even the most anti-Fascist of bishops could fail to appreciate the further benefits which the Lateran Pacts brought to the Church, even if these were seen by some bishops as the Church's *rights* long denied.[16]

Nevertheless, whilst there were many effusive episcopal telegrams of congratulations to the Duce, there were also a lot of more guarded expressions of approval for the Lateran agreements which rather minimised the role of Mussolini in the negotiations.[17] This description of the reaction of Mons. Gazzani of Cremona to the events of February 1929 was typical of many of his episcopal colleagues:

From Cazzani there was neither a shout of unrestrained joy, nor a prejudiced reaction, but a calm and positive judgement; '...a happy event, and one from which much good will undoubtedly come for both the Church and Italy', was how he cautiously described it in his letter inviting the Prefect to a Te Deum in the Cathedral.[18]

For Cazzani, who had as his local *ras* the formidable Roberto Farinacci, as for other bishops who had lived through the fire and sword of Lombard and Emilian Fascism in the 1920s, there could be only one reaction to the *Conciliazione* and that was a cautious, circumspect policy of 'wait and see'.

In September 1929, in his address to the Grand Assembly of the Regime, Mussolini made this judgement of the behaviour of the Catholic clergy towards his Government: '...the Italian clergy are obedient to the laws of the State, and indeed are very often devoted to the Regime. Apart from a few border provinces, and three provinces in the North, in all the rest, and especially in the South, they desire only to co-operate with the authorities.'[19] He was undoubtedly correct about the southern clergy; they were more agnostic politically and conservative socially than their northern brethren, the result of their close contact with and in some areas economic dependence upon the local ruling class.[20] There was rather less of a tradition amongst the southern clergy of intransigent opposition to the Liberal State after unification than there had been in the North, very little experience of the Catholic social movement and even less interest in it;

---

[16] S. Tramontin, 'La Chiesa Veneta a la Conciliazione', in Pecorari (ed.), *Chiesa, Azione Cattolica e Fascismo*, p. 163.

[17] D. R. Nardelli, 'Il Clero nella Zona di Trasimeno', in Monticone (ed.), *Cattolici e Fascisti in Umbria*, pp. 211–12, cites the example of the telegrams sent by Mons. Angelucci, Bishop of Città di Castello.

[18] G. Gallina, 'Il Vescova di Cremona Cazzani', in Pecorari (ed.), *Chiesa, Azione Cattolica e Fascismo*, p. 511.   [19] *O.O.*, Vol. XXIV, p. 136.

[20] Borzomati, *I Giovani Cattolici*, p. 48, says that the resistance of Catholic youth groups to Fascism was weakened by the ties between the parochial clergy and the local notables.

politically active priests like Don Luigi Sturzo were very much exceptions which proved the rule.[21] All these factors rendered the southern clergy more inert yet more adaptable in the face of political events and more acquiescent in government policies whoever was in power.

Mussolini was also right about the Slav and German clergy of the new frontier provinces, whose dogged resistance to the Fascist policy of 'Italianisation' is discussed in Chapter 4. But, as far as the three provinces of northern Italy were concerned, he was understating the problem; at least nine strongly Catholic provinces, Bergamo, Brescia, Como, Padua, Trento, Treviso, Verona, Vicenza and Udine could have qualified for those three positions.[22] In these provinces were to be found a very large proportion of the 60,000 parochial clergy whom Salvemini estimated had belonged to the P.P.I. and who formed the backbone of the Party in many rural areas.[23] Many of them had not only witnessed at first hand squadrist attacks upon Catholic persons and assaults upon the premises of Catholic organisations, but had often themselves been the victims of such violence.

Admittedly, in five of these provinces – Bergamo, Trento, Verona, Vicenza and Udine – the prefects reported a significant improvement in the clergy's attitude towards the Regime in the early part of 1929 – attributing it to the *Conciliazione*; the Prefect of Trento, for example in his quarterly report for January–March 1929 informed the Ministry of the Interior that: 'The clergy used to be rather hostile to the Regime, but since the Lateran Pacts they have become more sympathetic.'[24] But this encouraging development did not last very long. As the Vatican and the Regime became involved in bitter arguments over the interpretation of the Pacts in May and June the situation deteriorated and by the end of the year the Prefects' reports had resumed their previous tenor, expressing concern over the activities of the clergy and Catholic organisations.[25] On the other hand it is quite clear that the majority of the Italian clergy welcomed and applauded the *Conciliazione*, and despite the public polemics of the Summer of 1929, looked towards the future with optimism.

It is obviously very difficult to gauge the feelings of the mass of the Catholic laity to the *Conciliazione*; after the dissolution of the P.P.I., the

[21] De Rosa, *Luigi Sturzo*, chap. 2, p. 25, provides an excellent insight into the absence in Sicily of an 'intransigent, papalist and *social* Catholicism', ascribing it to the absolute economic dependence of the clergy on the municipal authorities, and Bernabei, *Fascismo e Nazionalismo in Campania*, p. 242, explains how the Salernitan version of this economic dependence – the 'Chiese ricettizie' system effectively eliminated any social or political initiative amongst the local clergy.
[22] And also Milan: Rumi, 'Chiesa Ambrosiana e Fascismo', in *Dallo Stato di Milano alla Lombardia contemporansa*, p. 233, says '...according to the Ministry of the Interior, in June 1928, not long before the *Conciliazione*, only 8 out of 2,000 diocesan clergy supported Fascism'.
[23] See Molony, *The Emergence of Political Catholicism in Italy*, p. 71.
[24] A.C.S., D.G.P.S., G.I., bb. 93 and 94.
[25] Ibid., b. 94, 'Rovigo', 'Verona', 'Reggio', third and fourth quarters.

closure of the Party press and the passing of the rest of the Catholic press into the hands of either the Clerico-Fascists or the obedient agents of the bishops and Catholic Action, there was no one inside Italy to speak on their behalf. Catholic Action was committed to the official line and in public at least no murmurings of dissent were heard, except that is for a lone article by Guide Gonella in *Azione Fucina* which was confiscated by the police because it was judged hostile to the Regime.[26] The strong reservations about the Lateran Pacts which F.U.C.I. members expressed at their 1929 congress[27] were partly due to the influence of their spiritual director, Mons. G. B. Montini (later Pope Paul VI), who had voiced doubts about the value of a concordat even before the negotiations were completed – 'If the liberty of the Pope cannot be guaranteed by the strong faith of a free people, and especially by the Italian people, then no territory and no treaty will be able to do so.'[28] Similar feelings were rife in the other Catholic youth organisations in some dioceses, as this assessment of the situation in Padua indicates: 'There were fierce arguments inside Catholic Action',[29] and they must have been widespread in the adult sections too judging by the number of lectures, conferences and study weeks which were devoted to explaining the significance of the Pacts throughout 1929.[30]

The only spokesmen of Italian Catholics who were free from Fascist censorship and ecclesiastical censure were the members of the tiny band of *popolari* in exile outside Italy – Luigi Sturzo, Francesco Ferrari, Guido Donati and Guido Miglioli. In contrast to the other anti-Fascist politicians, the majority of the M.P.s and other leaders of the P.P.I. did not go into exile, but thanks to ecclesiastical help and protection stayed behind in Italy, usually retiring into a discreet and inconspicuous private life with very little further harassment from the police authorities.[31] Only a handful of the most notoriously anti-Fascist of the *popolare* leaders went abroad; Luigi Sturzo was obliged by the Vatican to leave Italy in 1924 ostensibly because it could not longer guarantee his safety from Fascist attacks: previous experience of Fascist violence also forced the left-wingers Ferrari and Miglioli to flee for their lives, and Giuseppe Donati, editor of the party newspaper and the instigator of the action in the High Court against De

---

[26] Marucci-Fanello, *Storia della F.U.C.I.*, p. 133.   [27] Ibid., p. 134.

[28] As quoted in Fappani and Molinari, *Giovanni Battista Montini Giovane*, p. 262.

[29] Agostini, 'Il Movimento Giovanile Cattolico Padovano, 1919–32', p. 261.

[30] Both the *Bollettino Ufficiale* of Catholic Action and the police reports on Catholic Action activities in the provinces testify to the numbers of meetings devoted to this theme culminating in the national Settimana Sociale held in August 1929 at which Francesco Pacelli spoke about 'L'Opera di Pio XI per la Conciliazione'.

[31] Few who stayed behind had much difficulty with the police; Angelo Mauri, editor of the strongly anti-Fascist Catholic newspaper *Il Cittadino* of Genoa, was the only *popolare* M.P. sent into internal exile. Others like Spataro, Prince Rufo Ruffo della Scaletta and Camillo Corsanego (the latter two were never actually elected to Parliament) were placed on the files of the Ministry of the Interior's index of political trouble-makers – the Casellario Politico Centrale – and subject to police surveillance for short periods of time.

Bono, also chose exile in order to escape Fascist revenge. The other major figure who attempted to take the path of exile, Alcide De Gasperi, Sturzo's successor as leader of the P.P.I. was caught, tried and imprisoned and then eventually released as a result of Vatican intercession.

It was difficult for the *popolari* to form a credible and effective party organisation in exile, as the parties of the Concentrazione Antifascista, i.e., the Socialists and Republicans, had done, for two reasons. In the first place only two other *popolari* followed their leaders into exile – Domenico Russo and Giuseppe Stragliati – neither of whom had ever been of great political weight in the party.[32] In addition, the *popolari* were not only widely scattered geographically – Sturzo in London, Ferrari in Brussels, Donati in Paris and Miglioli almost always on the move – but they did not always work in unison.[33] The *popolari* were also politically isolated, collaboration with the Concentrazione being made difficult by their ambiguous and embarassing relationship with the Vatican. Nevertheless, the exiled *popolari* kept in close touch with their colleagues in Italy by correspondence, and through that medium continued to exercise considerable influence over them.

The announcement of the *Conciliazione* was as much of a surprise to the exiles as it was to the majority of Italians; despite the hints about negotiations between Church and Regime that had been coming out of Italy since the beginning of the year, as late as 27 January 1929 Donati was writing to Sturzo in these terms: 'I do not believe a word of what the newspapers are saying – i.e. that an agreement is imminent.'[34] It also provoked very different reactions from such a small group of men.

The most critical judgement came from Guido Miglioli who, whilst not condemning the Pacts outright, made many criticisms of their contents, and in an interview which he gave to *Le Monde* he stated bluntly that for him: 'These two years have witnessed the gradual but inexorable submission of the Pope to the demands of the Regime.'[35] Ferrari also had strong reservations about the Pacts, particularly the Concordat which in his eyes represented a 'clericalisation of public and private institutions'.[36]

[32] For the role played by Russo and Stragliati during Sturzo's exile, see De Rosa, *Luigi Sturzo*, pp. 320–4.

[33] Ferrari and Sturzo worked fairly closely together but Donati was a loner, though initially at least he had had close ties with men like Salvemini, Sforza and Turati (Filippo). See F. Rizzo, 'Sturzo in esilio: Popolari e forze antifasciste dal 1924 al 1940', in Malgeri (ed.), *Luigi Sturzo nella Storia d'Italia*, pp. 531–56. Miglioli cut himself off entirely from the rest; for an account of his political odyssey in this period see Miglioli, *Con Roma e con Mosca*.

[34] *Luigi Sturzo: Scritti Inediti*, ed. Piva, Vol. II (1924–40), p. 217, no. 111, Donati to Sturzo, Paris, 27 January 1949.

[35] Interview with *Le Monde* as reproduced in the Italian immigrant newspaper *L'Italia del Popolo* of Buenos Aires, 'Fascismo e Vaticano', 9 May 1929.

[36] *Luigi Sturzo: Scritti Inediti*, ed. Piva, Vol. II p. 220, no. 114, Ferrari to Sturzo, Louvain, 13 February 1929.

The most balanced view of the Pacts, and the one which was probably shared by the majority of his ex-followers, came from Sturzo. He argued that '...as is so often the case, it is a mixture of good and bad'.[37] For Sturzo 'the good' lay in the fact that Italy had at last been freed from the burden of the 'Roman Question', and 'the bad' because this had been achieved by Fascism. Donati, however, frankly admitted that: 'the resolution of the "Roman Question" is largely Mussolini's work'.[38] This incautious remark brought down upon his head the wrath of the Concentrazione whose polemicists waged war against him in the various anti-Fascist publications for several weeks afterwards. The news of the *Conciliazione* came as a terrible blow to the other anti-Fascists in exile who had previously nurtured hopes that the Vatican would one day turn against the Regime.[39] By means of the Lateran Pacts Mussolini had succeeded in widening at least one division within the anti-Fascist movement in exile; henceforth Sturzo and his little band were ostracised by the supporters of the Concentrazione Parties.[40]

According to both Ferrari and Donati, the *Conciliazione* also had a divisive and disorientating effect upon the *popolari* in Italy; Donati cites the letter from a friend in Rome which said: 'The Clerico-Fascists are jubilant, the *popolari* disorientated.'[41] Their confusion could only have been increased by the appearance of articles by Filippo Meda in *L'Italia* and *Vita e Pensiero* which gave an entirely uncritical welcome to the Lateran Pacts.[42] In the absence of contrary voices, many *popolari* must have been won over by the arguments of a Catholic leader who, after a political career which had lasted nearly thirty years, still enjoyed enormous prestige and influence amongst Italian Catholics, and that, of course, was precisely why he was employed to explain the *Conciliazione* in the Catholic press and at Catholic Action meetings.

But there were other *popolari* who shared the opinion of another of their former leaders, Alcide De Gasperi; in a letter to his friend Don Simone Weber, De Gasperi warned of the dangers inherent in the new relationship between Church and State: '...The real danger lies in the policy of concordats, as a result of which the Church will be compromised, as happened in Spain with Rivera, or something even worse.'[43] Finally, it should not be assumed that all Italian Catholics felt so strongly either way

[37] Ibid., pp. 219–20, Sturzo to Nitti, London, 14 February 1929.
[38] See Delzell, *I Nemici di Mussolini*, p. 49.
[39] Zunino, *La Questione Cattolica*, pp. 243–4.
[40] Ibid., p. 269.
[41] *Giuseppe Donati: Scritti Politici*, ed. Rossini, pp. 358–9.
[42] *L'Italia*, 23 February 1929, 'La Riconciliazione', and *Vita e Pensiero*, June 1929, 'Pio XI e la Pace Coll'Italia'. See also the report on Meda's speaking activities for Catholic Action in A.C.S., D.G.P.S., G.I., b. 146, 'Azione Cattolica', sf. 2, report from Rome of 23 March 1929.
[43] De Gasperi, *Lettere sul Concordato*, ed. Romana De Gasperi, p. 64.

about the *Conciliazione*. Observers as diverse as Montini[44] and Togliatti[45] suggested that the *Conciliazione* was largely a journalistic event which left the Italian masses unmoved, and Miglioli agreed with them as far as his beloved peasants were concerned: '... Catholic proletarians have reacted to the Lateran Pacts with complete indifference'.[46]

CATHOLICS AND THE 'PLEBISCITE' OF MARCH 1929

During the course of 1928 the Fascist rump of the Italian Parliament had enacted a new electoral law to replace the Acerbo Law on which it had been elected in 1924.[47] The new electoral arrangements were a fitting crown to the Fascist, totalitarian dictatorship which had been under construction since 1925; by comparison the Acerbo Law was positively democratic. By the terms of the 1928 law, not only was the electorate significantly reduced by the introduction of new voting qualifications, but its freedom of choice was restricted to approving or rejecting a single list of candidates presented by the Fascist Party.[48] Mussolini had adopted the typically authoritarian device of a plebiscite to provide the necessary broad consensus for his Fascist State.

The 1928 law also laid down that the 'Plebiscite' had to take place not later than the end of April 1929. This explains Mussolini's anxiety to complete the negotiations for the Lateran Pacts as soon as possible in the New Year. In this way he was able to ensure that his greatest diplomatic triumph would have the fullest impact upon the electorate and he was also able to make use of the Vatican's pledge to mobilize the Catholic vote on his behalf. But why did the Vatican make this pledge? According to a letter which Tacchi-Venturi wrote to Mussolini shortly before the 'Plebiscite', the Vatican was motivated by a profound sense of gratitude to Mussolini and desired that: '... the coming elections should provide the clearest and most eloquent proof of the full support of Italian Catholics for the Government of the Hon. Mussolini'.[49] But this was not entirely an exercise in disinterested altruism; from the Vatican's point of view it was important that the Parliament which would have to ratify and implement the Pacts should be elected by the widest possible national consensus, albeit within a thoroughly undemocratic framework. And this was the justification given for instructing Catholics to vote 'yes'; thus the official appeal which Catholic Action issued to Italian Catholic voters on 12 March 1929 declared that a 'yes' vote 'Will signify a binding mandate to Parliament

---

[44] Fappani and Molinari, *Giovanni Battista Montini Giovane*, p. 261.
[45] 'Ercoli' (Palmiro Togliatti), 'La Situazione Italiana alla Vigilia del Plebiscito', in *Lo Stato Operaio*, February 1929, pp. 116 and 119.
[46] *Le Monde*, interview cited in n. 35.
[47] For the terms of the 1928 electoral law see De Felice, III, pp. 315–26.   [48] Ibid.
[49] A.C.S., S.P.D., C.R. 88W/R, 'Tacchi-Venturi', letter to Mussolini of 17 February 1929.

to ratify [the Pacts] and to approve the legislation necessary for the implementation of the Concordat.'[50] The Pope in his public speeches, *L'Osservatore Romano* and the Catholic Press, except for the Clerico-Fascist papers which also stressed the essentially economic and political merits of Fascism, stuck firmly and consistently to this line.

Despite the endless explanations and justifications offered by Catholic newspapers and organisations, the Vatican's voting policy perturbed the consciences of many Catholics, a serious problem being the composition of the Fascist list of parliamentary candidates. As Tacchi-Venturi pointed out to Mussolini, three-quarters of the original list of 1,000 names from whom the Grand Council eventually chose the 400 parliamentary candidates were unacceptable to the Catholic electorate, either because of their present moral conduct or because of their masonic/anti-clerical political past.[51] And to provide the Church with an alibi in case Catholic voters failed to heed ecclesiastical instructions, Tacchi-Venturi warned that confronted by such candidates '...the Catholic voter will feel compelled, in all conscience, to abstain from voting'.[52] Mussolini's response was not very helpful, as he only accepted five of the twenty-six alternative names which Tacchi-Venturi offered as a means of giving the list more credibility in Catholic eyes, but by now the Vatican was too heavily committed in public to be able to change its policy.[53]

The problem of how to vote, and how to advise the faithful about voting, continued to worry some of the clergy of northern Italy; Elia Dalla Costa, Bishop of Padua and later Cardinal Archbishop of Florence, in his perplexity approached his fellow prelate, Bishop Longhin of Treviso, asking for advice. Longhin's answer was to remind Dalla Costa that in the past Catholics had frequently been instructed to support Liberal candidates and he argued that it was therefore equally permissible to give their vote: '...to a government which is so well disposed towards our beliefs'.[54]

Another problem was constituted by the inevitable misgivings that many Catholics felt about the political implications of voting 'yes': did it mean that the Church was entering into a permanent political alliance with Fascism? Bishop Cazzani of Cremona insisted in his diocesan paper, *La Vita Cattolica*, that the Church was not about to ally itself with reactionary forces,[55] and on polling day itself *L'Avvenire d'Italia* thought it necessary to publish yet another clarification of the significance of Catholic support for the Fascist list, this time written by Padre Rosa who was at pains to

---

[50] *Bollettino Ufficiale*, 15 March 1929, 'I Cattolici e le Elezioni'.
[51] A.C.S., S.P.D., C.R. 88W/R, 'Tacchi-Venturi', letter to Mussolini of 17 February 1929.
[52] Ibid.   [53] Ibid.
[54] S. Tramontin, 'La Chiesa Veneta e la Conciliazione', in Pecorari (ed.), *Chiesa, Azione Cattolica e Fascismo*, p. 652, n. 69.
[55] C. Gallina, 'Il Vescovo di Cremona Cazzani', in Pecorari (ed.), *Chiesa, Azione Cattolica e Fascismo*, p. 511.

stress that 'It is worth repeating that our vote is a moral and religious rather than a political act.'[56]

Needless to say, all this tepidity in the Catholic camp did not go unnoticed; Mussolini denounced those who supported Fascism with 'mental reservations', and enlisted the campaigning support of members of the Centro Nazionale, and in some areas, the Unione Nazionale, as a useful reinforcement of the Church's voting instructions.[57] Indeed, it has been suggested that Mussolini's involvement of the Centro Nazionale in the election campaign and his inclusion of four out of its eight nominees in the final Fascist list was intended to embarrass the Vatican by pointing up the differences between the Centro Nazionale and Catholic Action, which was not allowed to nominate candidates to the list.[58]

Whilst there is absolutely no evidence that Catholic Action ever did ask for the right to nominate candidates,[59] and such a right would, of course, have conflicted with the longstanding policy of being above party politics, by 1929 the Centro Nazionale was very much out of favour with the Pope.[60] It therefore seems likely that the inclusion of the Centro Nazionale in the list caused as much irritation in the Vatican as it did in certain Milanese Catholic circles.[61]

After all the official and semi-official Catholic propaganda on behalf of Mussolini it would be very interesting to know exactly how Catholics voted in the 'Plebiscite' of March 1929. Ferrari offers this picture of a divided *popolare* response to the 'Plebiscite'; 'Some voted "yes", some voted "no", and some simply went into the country.'[62] The fear of physical violence or other equally effective sanctions must have intimidated many Catholics into voting for Fascism against their inclinations[63] – and these consider-

---

[56] *L'Avvenire d'Italia*, 24 March 1929, front page article, 'Oggi i Cattolici Reccheranno al Plebiscito il Contributo dalla loro Concorde e Consapevole Adesione.'

[57] Report on his speech in Milan, *Il Popolo d'Italia*, front page, March 1929. According to *Il Lavoro Fascista* of 13 March 1929, Stefano Cavazzoni and the Unione Nazionale campaigned on behalf of Fascism. Other leading Clerico-Fascists, like Martire and Mattei-Gentili, must also have worked in the campaign, since both the Centro Nazionale and the Unione Nazionale officially endorsed the Fascist list.

[58] De Felice, III, pp. 473–4.   [59] See front page article in *L'Italia* of 24 March 1929.

[60] In March 1928, the Centro Nazionale held its national conference in Rome, and though they were received in audience by Mussolini, they tactlessly failed to make a visit to the Pope. This omission, plus a few incautious remarks of Martire during the congress, provoked the wrath of Pius XI who publicly rebuked them. For an account of this episode see De Rosa, *Il Partito Popolare*, p. 302.

[61] See the article by Pio Bondioli of the Catholic University in *L'Italia*, 14 March 1949, 'I Miraggi e Le Mete', where he says of the Clerico-Fascist deputies and Senators '...they do not represent Catholics; they are merely Catholic personages involved in Fascist politics'.   [62] As quoted in F. Rizzi, 'Sturzo in esilio', p. 546.

[63] De Felice, III, p. 436, takes the view that these elections were conducted '...without any massive forms of coercion of the electorate: the only pressure used was an insistent propaganda campaign against abstentionism, and a careful check on those who did not vote'. What he fails to say is that different coloured cards were used for 'yes' and 'no' votes which then had to be deposited in a *transparent* 'urn'!

ations were, of course, just as valid for the rest of the Italian electorate. It should also be remembered that the electoral law of 1928 introduced a set of new voting qualifications which reduced the electorate from the figure of 12.5 million at which it had stood in 1924 to 9.7 million in 1929.[64] Of those excluded from the electoral registers, many were probably poor Catholic peasants who paid virtually no taxes and were not enrolled in any of the Fascist syndicates.[65] Unfortunately, the results of the 1929 'Plebiscite' give us only a very impressionistic idea of how Catholics voted.

A total of 8.63 million, 90 per cent of the registered electorate, actually went to the polls, of whom 135,761 voted 'no'.[66] More significant than these raw totals were the figures for 'no' votes and abstentions in the various regions. Whereas in the whole of the South the 'no' vote totalled 21,000, in the Catholic regions of Lombardy and the Veneto the figures were 37,000 and 20,800 respectively.[67] The figures for abstentions were even higher; the national average was about 10 per cent, but in the Catholic, Lombard province of Sondrio it rose to 17 per cent,[68] and in some parts of the Veneto it reached 30 per cent.[69] No doubt in some rural areas this was due to priests who positively dissuaded their parishioners from voting;[70] it certainly had little to do with the *popolari* in exile. Unlike the Communists who called upon their followers in Italy to vote 'no', or the parties of the Concentrazione Antifascista which recommended abstention, Sturzo and his friends remained silent, unable to contradict the Vatican's instructions to the Catholic electorate.[71]

The *Conciliazione* overcame the remaining doubts that many Catholics entertained about Fascism, and it also rendered the *popolari* in exile virtually impotent, but what it did not do was to eliminate the hardcore of Catholic anti-Fascists in Italy. In March 1930, the largest archdiocese in Italy, Milan, gave dramatic proof that Catholic anti-Fascism was far from being dead. In that month 200 Catholic laymen sent an anonymous letter to the archbishop, Cardinal Schuster, rebuking him for having publicly declared that 'From the very beginning, Catholic Italy and even the Pope himself, have blessed Fascism.'[72]

---

[64] *Ministero dell'Economia Nazionale, Compendio di Statistica Elettorale Politica,* 1921, 1924 and 1929, p. 213.

[65] For voting qualifications see De Felice, III, pp. 473–4.

[66] Ibid., p. 483.

[67] S. Tramontin, 'La Chiesa Veneta e la Conciliazione', in Pecorari (ed.), *Chiesa, Azione Cattolica e Fascismo,* p. 651 n. 65.

[68] See *L'Italia,* 26 March 1929, 'Le Cifre Complessive'.

[69] See above, n. 67.   [70] Ibid.

[71] For the policy of the *Concentrazione* see De Felice, III, p. 472, for that of the Communist Party see the article cited in n. 45.

[72] As quoted in Pellicani, *Il Papa di Tutti,* p. 37 n. 3.

Distributed to the higher clergy and bishops of Italy,[73] the letter denied that the Pope had ever blessed Fascism and went on to remind the archbishop of the devastating damage to Catholic institutions and the appalling violence to Catholic clergy and laity inflicted by the Fascists in the diocese of Milan. And the letter concluded by affirming the fundamental incompatibility of Fascism and Catholicism: '...there is an unbridgeable gulf between the principles of Fascism and the law of the Gospel'.[74]

As the Ambassador to the Holy See admitted in a report to Grandi, the Foreign Minister, the letter was symptomatic of strong and widespread feelings among the clergy and in Catholic Action.[75] And here was the danger, for the Concordat with its juridical recognition of Catholic Action seemed to offer to Catholic anti-Fascists greater scope and greater security for their activities and their influence, thus ensuring that sooner or later Catholic Action would come into conflict with the Regime.

FASCIST REACTIONS TO THE *CONCILIAZIONE*

The official Fascist reaction to the announcement of the *Conciliazione* was as unrestrainedly enthusiastic as that of the Catholic press, but, unlike the latter, it was carefully organised and orchestrated, the lead being taken by *Il Popolo d'Italia*, whose editor, Arnaldo Mussolini, was a staunch supporter of his brother's religious policy.[76] In its treatment of the Pacts, the Italian press naturally laid great stress upon the achievement of Mussolini, the victory of the Regime and the benefits that the *Conciliazione* would bring Italy. *Il Popolo d'Italia* hailed the Lateran Pacts as 'A great moral and political victory of the Regime', attributing it to the diplomatic skill of Mussolini,[77] and repeated the expressions of admiration for the Duce which had appeared in the foreign press.

The Fascist press displayed an intense interest in all the details of the implementation of the Pacts and a genuine pride in the fact that the 'Roman Question' had been settled by the Fascist Regime and, of course, some newspapers argued that the problem could not have been solved by any other government.[78] Fascist reactions were also strongly conditioned by those of the foreign press: the opposition of the Italian anti-Fascist press was inevitably dismissed out of hand and the Fascists were half-elated, half-insulted by the criticisms of the French press – especially those of the

---

[73] The text of the letter is to be found in A.C.S., F.C., Serie IV, 'Vescovi', b. 100, 'Milano', Telespresso no. 1006 from De Vecchi, Ambassador to Holy See, to Grandi, Minister of Foreign Affairs, 4 May 1930.
[74] Ibid.
[75] Ibid., De Vecchi also drew attention to the fact that though the letter had been widely distributed among the higher clergy, not one of them had reported it to the authorities!
[76] Binchy, *Church and State*, p. 123.
[77] *Il Popolo d'Italia*, 12 February 1929, 'Ora del Luce'.   [78] Ibid.

anti-clerical and masonic papers like *L'Oeuvre* and *L'Ere Nouvelle*, which interpreted the *Conciliazione* as either a defeat for the Church or a defeat for Fascism.[79] In this situation, the Fascist papers were on common ground with *L'Osservatore Romano* and the rest of the Italian Catholic press. This convergence between Fascism and Catholicism reached its high point in an editorial of Arnaldo Mussolini in *Il Popolo d'Italia* on the morrow of the signing of the Pacts '...we Fascists, as Italian Catholics who were born and educated according to Christian principles, baptised in our churches, which are full of national memories, are transported with joy by the resolution of the "Roman Question".'[80]

Arnaldo, unlike his brother Benito, was a fervent, practising Catholic, and as one contemporary observer has pointed out, 'The fact of Arnaldo's Catholicism was to be of immense importance in the history of Fascist relations with the Church.'[81] In the matter of Church and State relations, Arnaldo Mussolini was certainly one of the 'doves' of Fascism, frequently intervening to dampen down polemics between the Catholic and Fascist press, and pressing his brother to adopt a more conciliatory line towards the Church. But his sentiments by no means represented the feelings of all Fascists, as the coming months were to show.

Despite the official jubilation, many Fascists were not so impressed by the *Conciliazione*, but like their Catholic counterparts, these Fascist critics of the Lateran Pacts were given little or no opportunity to express their misgivings publicly in a regime of press censorship, though they did so frequently and vigorously in private. There was bound to be some criticism of the Pacts from the Fascist side given the strong anti-clerical element amongst the Fascists of the 'First Hour', such as revolutionary syndicalists of the calibre of Michele Bianchi, or the Futurists like Marinetti – not to mention the virulent and violent anti-clericalism of agrarian Fascism in Lombardy and Emilia as represented by such figures as Roberto Farinacci of Cremona and Italo Balbo of Ferrara.[82]

There are reports of violent scenes at the Grand Council Meetings held to approve the Pacts on 25 and 26 February 1929,[83] and we have other evidence of the critical attitude of *gerarchi* like Bottai and De Bono. In a telephone conversation with De Bono, Bottai expressed what was probably a widespread feeling in Fascist leadership circles, '...he has made far too

[79] See Missiroli, *Date a Cesare*, p. 32.
[80] *Il Popolo d'Italia*, 12 February 1929, 'Ora del Luce'.
[81] Binchy, *Church and State*, pp. 126–7.
[82] As might have been expected, Gabriele D'Annunzio also disapproved of the Lateran Pacts. In a letter to Mussolini of May 1931, he wrote: 'I always disapproved of the Conciliation because I know how irreducible the mercantile, intrusive spirit of the Vatican is.' As quoted in Hamilton, *The Appeal of Fascism*, p. 63, where the author says that this letter was censored when his correspondence with Mussolini was published.
[83] Binchy, *Church and State*, pp. 118–19.

many concessions to the Church', and in reply, De Bono lamented the fact that '...while he [Mussolini] has given away a fortune to the Vatican, government ministries are having to tighten their belts'.[84] In another of De Bono's indiscreet telephone conversations, Italo Balbo gave vent to the frustration of many members of the Grand Council when he complained that Mussolini, by signing the Pacts before consulting the Grand Council, '...diminished the prerogatives of the supreme organ of the Regime'.[85]

For obvious reasons, very little criticism of the Lateran Pacts was allowed to appear in the Italian Press. Usually, the most that was permitted was some expression of anxiety about the way in which the Concordat would be implemented, hardly justifying the claims of one writer that there was, '...a kind of revolt of the Fascist Intelligentsia'.[86] The historian, Volpe, for instance, limited himself to warning of the danger that the Church's new power might put in jeopardy, '...the benefits of the spirit of modernism'.[87] His most serious concern was for the educational system, and in particular for the effects of the introduction of religious education into the secondary schools, which he felt would not be very compatible with other subjects.[88] The same question preoccupied the Fascist Senator and educationalist, Luigi Credaro, whose heretical claim that 'As far as modern philosophy is concerned, Thomism, that is the philosophy of the Church, is entirely obsolete'[89] brought down upon his head the wrath of *L'Osservatore Romano*.[90] Ugo Ojetti even asked whether the *Conciliazione* might not lead to an attack upon the freedom of expression of artists and intellectuals, for which impertinence he was firmly rebuked by Padre Rosa of *La Civiltà Cattolica*.[91]

These comments on the part of Fascist intellectuals, even if they were not actually organised by Mussolini, were certainly grist to his mill, serving the purpose of warning off future clerical pretensions. It also gave the press an opportunity to reassure Fascists that in the process of implementing the Pacts Mussolini's wisdom would conquer all, indeed, Giovanni Gentile, the 'doyen of Fascist intellectuals', was prevailed upon to answer all fears and anxieties on this score by an article in *L'Educazione Fascista* which declared that '...the Concordat...is a programme whose precise meaning will be determined by the way it is implemented by the Duce of Fascism'.[92] In view of the fact that Gentile had publicly maintained his opposition to the idea

---

[84] Guspini, *L'Orecchio del Regime*, p. 55.
[85] As quoted in ibid., p. 97.
[86] Pellicani, *Il Papa di Tutti*, p. 17.
[87] G. Volpe, 'Il Concordato e la Scuola', *Gerarchia*, March 1929. [88] Ibid.
[89] L. Credaro, 'L'Insegnamento della filosofia in Italia dopo il Concordato con la Santa Sede', *Rivista Pedagogica*, February 1929.
[90] *L'Osservatore Romano*, 28 March 1929, 'Un Referendum'.
[91] U. Ojetti, 'Lettera al Padre Enrico Rosa S. I.', *Pegaso*, March 1929; and the reply of Enrico Rosa, 'Intorno alla Conciliazione', *La Civiltà Cattolica*, 6 April 1929.
[92] G. Gentile, 'La Conciliazione', *Educazione Fascista*, February 1929.

of a settlement with the Church until as late as October 1928, this must be regarded as a particularly cynical manoeuvre on Mussolini's part.[93] In 1931 Gentile was allowed to express his real feelings about the Concordat: 'We were never very enthusiastic about the Concordat; we always regarded it as merely the unavoidable prerequisite for the *Conciliazione*.'[94]

It is significant that the only major section of the Fascist press which departed from the official line on the *Conciliazione* was the small-circulation youth magazines like *Il Saggiatore, Il Cantiere* and *L'Universale,* which exhibited less than the required enthusiasm for Mussolini's masterpiece. Another such magazine, *La Camicia Rossa,* was suspended from publication for eighteen months after the appearance in its pages of a violently anti-clerical article,[95] and yet another, *A e Z* was confiscated by the police for publishing a bitterly satirical poem by Emilio Settimelli entitled, 'Mussolini Inter Grato Re';[96] Settimelli, an ex-Futurist and editor of the national daily *L'Impero* also suffered the temporary loss of his party card.[97] In his speech to the Chamber of 13 May, Mussolini dismissed Fascist opposition to his religious policy as the work of a few remaining masonic groups,[98] but the criticisms of the youth press, only one of whose editors, Ezio Garibaldi of *La Camicia Rossa,* could fairly be described as a Freemason, gives the lie to his claim. Opposition to the *Conciliazione* was widespread in the Fascist movement, and the rabidly anti-clerical youth magazines were but the tip of the iceberg – and an ominous portent of the grassroots, Fascist intolerance of Catholic youth activities which was to contribute substantially to the crisis of 1931.

THE IMPLEMENTATION AND RATIFICATION OF THE PACTS

Like all international treaties, the Lateran Pacts required the approval of the legislative authorities of the respective parties before they could be formally ratified. In the case of the Holy See nothing could have been simpler and more straightforward because the sole source of all power, legislative, executive and judicial, was the Pope himself; but as far as Fascist Italy was concerned, it was still necessary to seek parliamentary sanction for the Treaties, with full-dress debates in both the Chamber and the Senate. Mussolini allowed himself just under four months in which to conduct the plebiscitary elections, obtain parliamentary approval for the

[93] See chap. 2, p. 56.
[94] *Educazione Fascista,* May 1931, p. 579.   [95] Pellicani, *Il Papa di Tutti,* p. 9.
[96] E. Settimelli, 'Mussolini Inter Grato Re', *A e Z,* 12 February 1929.
[97] Lyttelton, *The Seizure of Power,* p. 365, says: 'Emilio Settimelli and Mario Carli, the editors of the extremist *L'Impero* were old futurists and their paper continued to defend the identity of the true spirit of Fascism with futurism.'
[98] *O.O.,* Vol. XXIV, pp. 75–6.

Treaties and to draw up the most important items of the necessary implementation legislation, the latter task being entrusted to a Joint Implementation Commission of Italian and Vatican representatives, as laid down by Article 45 of the Concordat.[99]

Given Mussolini's overwhelming political dominance in Italy, and the fact that the members of the newly elected Chamber had been handpicked by the Grand Council and Mussolini himself, there was never any real danger that the Pacts would be rejected by the Italian Parliament, but Mussolini was acutely aware of the extent of Fascist opposition to his religious policy and he accordingly took steps to deal with it. Once the 'Plebiscite' was over, and the Catholic vote had been safely delivered into his hands, Mussolini, in his speeches to the Chamber and the Senate, was free to adopt a tough, aggressive, even mildly anti-clerical attitude towards the Church, in order to reassure his followers that he had not sold out to the Vatican.

Furthermore, in the speech at the opening of the new Parliament on 21 April, the King announced that: 'The implementation of the Concordat will require enactment of a series of legislative measures; one for the regulation of marriage, one to deal with ecclesiastical corporations and one to regulate the activities of the *culti amessi*.'[100] Whilst the first two bills were a necessary consequence of the Concordat, the bill on the *culti amessi* (literally, 'the permitted cults') – the Protestant denominations – was emphatically not: nothing in the Concordat necessitated the introduction of such a measure, as Rocco was forced to admit to the Vatican representatives on the Implementation Commission when they challenged him on this point.[101] The Vatican objected strongly to the *culti amessi* bill, which was exactly what Mussolini wanted because the bill was intended to divert attention from the concessions he had made in the Concordat, and to offer positive proof to the Fascist anti-clericals and the Liberal supporters that the risorgimental, secular character of the Italian State had not been abandoned – or at least not entirely. It was also meant to allay the fear of Mussolini's admirers in Protestant countries that the *Conciliazione* would be followed by the persecution or harassment of Italy's Protestant

---

[99] For the text of Article 45 see Appendix II. The Commission, which had as its chairman Alfredo Rocco, Minister of Justice, and as its vice-chairman Mons. Raffaele Rossi, Secretary of the Sacred Congregation of the Consistory, began its labours on 11 April 1929 and held its twenty-fifth and last session on 25 November of the same year. Amongst other members of the Commission were R. Jacuzio, Director-General of the Fondo per il Culto, the Ministry of Justice's office for religious affairs, and Francesco Pacelli, the chief Vatican negotiator of the Lateran Pacts. For the minutes of the Commission meetings see *Dossier Conciliazione* ed. Cavaterra, pp. 9–257.

[100] As quoted in *L'Osservatore Romano*, 21 April 1929, report on the opening of Parliament.

[101] *Dossier Conciliazione*, ed. Cavaterra, p. 85.

minority, fears which were expressed in the newspapers of Britain and America in February 1929.[102]

When the debates on the Pacts took place in the Chamber in May 1929[103] the voice of Fascist anti-clericalism was barely heard; indeed a number of speakers, like Paolo Orano, fell over backwards to disassociate themselves from the critics of the *Conciliazione*.[104] Those Fascist *gerarchi* who had so strongly dissented in private clearly lacked the courage to criticise Mussolini's policy in public; and Roberto Farinacci, that most anti-clerical of Fascist *ras*, even delivered a panegyric to Mussolini's masterpiece.[105] The rest of the speakers toed the line, except for Ezio Garibaldi, whose speech according to *L'Osservatore Romano* was heard by an almost deserted Chamber.[106] The grandson of the Risorgimento hero expressed anxiety about the future: 'Will you permit me to express my earnest hope that the Catholics do not go too far. Unfortunately, there are already signs that they are doing just that.'[107]

Apart from De Vecchi's profuse praise of Mussolini, the debates in the Senate were rather less marked by exaggeration and effusiveness than those of the Lower House. On the whole, the Upper House exhibited more honesty and independence of mind on the questions raised by the *Conciliazione*. An example of this was the request by Professor Vitalli of the University of Florence for an assurance that university teachers would continue to enjoy complete freedom to enjoy teaching what they believed, to which Mussolini replied clearly in the affirmative.[108]

Another aspect of the debates in the Senate was the major contribution made by the Clerico-Fascist members. Five out of fifteen took part in the committee stage of the legislation and another four, Crispolti, Santucci, Soderini and Cornaggia-Medici, spoke in the debate on the floor of the house, symbolising their belief that this was the last act in the reconciliation between Italian Catholics and the Italian State.[109] Not to be outdone by their Catholic colleages, the representatives of the Liberal supporters of Fascism, Boselli, Scialoja, Bevione and Vittorio, also took a prominent part in the discussions; whilst praising the Lateran Pacts, they were at pains to defend the Law of Guarantees from the criticisms of the Clerico-Fascists, arguing that it had been the essential starting point on the long road towards the *Conciliazione*.[110]

---

[102] See for example *The Observer*, 17 February 1929, which reported that efforts were already being made to curtail the activities of the Y.M.C.A. in Italy, and that eventually all Protestant activity would be banned.
[103] For an account of the debates see Jemolo, *Chiesa e Stato*, pp. 233–50.
[104] *Atti*, 1929, Vol. I, Camera, Discussioni, p. 34.
[105] Ibid., p. 36.
[106] *L'Osservatore Romano*, 14 May 1929, 'Notizie Italiane – Camera dei Deputati'.
[107] *Atti*, 1929, Vol. I, Camera, Discussioni, p. 214.
[108] Ibid., Senato, Discussioni, pp. 197–8.
[109] Ibid., pp. 162–84.   [110] Ibid., p. 202.

Only one Senator, the philosopher and historian Benedetto Croce, had the courage to make any serious criticisms of the Pacts. Speaking on behalf of many others of the same mind, both inside and outside of Parliament, Croce declared that it was not so much the idea of the reconciliation which he objected to as the manner in which it had been brought about.[111] In particular he regretted that the eighty-year-old secular policy of Liberal Italy had been abandoned. Croce was especially critical of the Concordat and the many concessions to the Church which it contained, and he warned of the danger of an anti-clerical backlash, signs of which he already detected amongst the supporters of the Government.

Mussolini was acutely stung by Croce's speech, particularly by the reference to the dissidents inside the Fascist Party and Government, and despite his attempts to dismiss Croce's comments as irrelevant and unimportant, he devoted a disproportionately large part of his own speech in the Senate to refuting them, and he ended up by describing Croce, rather absurdly, as 'a deserter from history'.[112] Croce's speech had elicited no rapturous applause from his fellow Senators, but it did represent the feelings of many Liberals throughout Italy. One group of Genoese Liberals who publicly applauded his stand were arrested by the police.[113]

When Parliament got down to discussing the details of the Pacts and implementation legislation, undoubtedly the most difficult aspect of the Concordat to defend was the clauses relating to marriage. As Mussolini admitted in a letter to the King, during the negotiations for the Concordat, he had been obliged to make an enormous surrender of State jurisdiction over Italian marriage law:

> I cannot conceal the fact that the greatest obstacle to overcome has been the clauses relating to marriage. Here the State has conceded a great deal, indeed, it now has virtually no say in this most important aspect of the life of the family. On the other hand, the Holy See has insisted that this is an essential condition for the successful outcome of the negotiations.[114]

The Government's embarrassment over these concessions came out very clearly in the speeches of Mussolini himself and in those of Asquini, one of the sponsors of the implementation legislation. Mussolini was reduced to demonstrably invalid comparisons with other concordats,[115] and Asquini rather gave the game away when he concluded his report on the committee stage of the Marriage Bill by saying, 'There has been no apocalypse of the State, nor has there been any abdication by the State of its jurisdiction over marriage.'[116]

Working out the arrangements for the application of the concordatory

---

[111] Ibid., p. 192. [112] Ibid., p. 207.
[113] Jemolo, *Chiesa e Stato*, p. 185.
[114] As quoted in Santarelli, *Storia del Movimento e del Regime Fascista*, Vol. I, p. 568.
[115] *O.O.*, Vol. XXVI, p. 392. [116] *Atti*, 1929, Vol. I, Camera, Discussioni, pp. 11–14.

matrimonial system proved to be a very difficult and contentious issue for the Implementation Commission. After the legal and technical problems involved in the transfer back to the Church of the ecclesiastical property appropriated by the Governments of Piedmont and United Italy, and those relating to the setting up of the State of the Vatican City, revision of the Italian marriage laws made the largest demand on the Commission's time. The major points of difficulty were:

1. The form in which the civil effects of matrimony were to be announced by the celebrant of the religious (Catholic) ceremony.
2. The transfer of exclusive jurisdiction over the annulment of marriages from Italian courts to those of the Church.
3. The question of whether or not Catholics should be obliged in law to go through a religious ceremony.

Since the 1865 Marriage Act, the religious ceremony had not been recognised as sufficient in the eyes of the State which had insisted on the necessity of a civil ceremony as well, and, moreover, had demanded that this precede the ceremony in Church.[117] According to Article 34 of the Concordat, the religious ceremony would henceforth suffice as long as declaration of the civil effects of the marriage thus celebrated was read out by a priest, who would for this purpose function as an official of the State, and as long as the registration of the marriage with the civil authorities was completed within a specified period of time. Such a system was not substantially different from that in force in other countries both Catholic and non-Catholic (e.g., Britain), but the Vatican representatives on the Implementation Commission demanded that the declaration of the civil effects be read in the Sacristy after the end of the religious ceremony, thus rather diminishing the dignity and role of the State in the affair.[118] In order to spare their Government further humiliation, the Italian representatives resisted the Vatican's demand and succeeded in establishing that the reading of the civil effects should take place towards the end of the ceremony and in full view of the congregation.[119]

The Government could not, however, avoid the humiliation of having to transfer jurisdiction over cases of annulment from its own courts to those of the Church, decisions in these cases then being automatically ratified by the Italian regional Courts of Appeal.[120] Only cases of legal separation were reserved to the exclusive competence of the Italian Courts. Despite this enormous surrender of legal jurisdiction, which implicitly denied the Italian State the right to legislate for divorce,[121] Asquini persisted in

[117] For a clear and concise account of Italian marriage law between 1865 and 1929 see Binchy, Church and State, chap. 14, especially pp. 390–3, See also Coletti, Il Divorzio in Italia.   [118] Dossier Conciliazione, ed. Cavaterra, pp. 91–3.
[119] Ibid.   [120] Jacuzio, Commento della Nuova legislazione, p. 344.
[121] The indissolubility of marriage was reaffirmed in the Codice Rocco; see the text in Manuale Hoepli, p. 37.

declaring that 'The system established by the Concordat remains one which is still essentially governed by the laws of the State.'[122] A rather more realistic assessment of the situation was given to the Senate by D'Amelio, the President of the Corte di Cassazione, Italy's Supreme Court:

Ecclesiastical jurisdiction in these cases [annulment etc.] is very wide...the Holy See has agreed, however, that cases of separation shall be decided by the civil courts...this is a real concession on the part of the Holy See. In this respect our marriage law is quite different from that of all other countries.[123]

The Italian representatives on the Implementation Commission had to fight off yet another potential embarrassment for their Government, the demand by the Holy See to make the religious ceremony a legal requirement for all Catholics.[124] The question was easily the most contentious that the Commission had to deal with, as is demonstrated by the heat generated during its discussion;[125] and it became clear from his letter to Cardinal Gasparri of 15 May that the Pope only accepted with a very bad grace the Italian Government's adamant refusal to impose such an obligation by law.[126] Naturally, much was made of this 'victory' during the debates in Parliament and Rocco made a particular point of referring to it in his speech to the Chamber '...every citizen is free to choose the form of marriage which suits him'.[127]

During the divisions on the various items of the legislative package for the implementation of the Pacts, members of both Chambers of the Italian Parliament registered their feeling on the matrimonial question. Whereas in the Chamber only two votes were cast against approving the Pacts themselves, the number rose to four in the vote on the marriage laws.[128] In the Senate six voted against the Pacts – Albertini, Croce, Bergamini, Ruffini, Paterno and Sinibaldi – thirteen against the law on the restitution of ecclesiastical property, but seventeen against the marriage law.[129] That the opposition to the marriage law was not still greater can partly be explained by the strong attachment of Liberal/masonic Italy to the institution of Christian marriage, which is attested by the failure of no fewer than nine attempts to pass a divorce bill through the Italian Parliament between 1865 and 1929.[130] Nevertheless, Mussolini had made concessions on the marriage question which no Liberal statesman would have dreamt of making, with the result that there were now three types of marriage in Italy.

[122] *Atti*, 1929, Vol. I, Camera, Discussioni, p. 114.
[123] Ibid., Senato, Discussioni, p. 195.
[124] *Dossier Conciliazione*, ed. Cavaterra, p. 32.
[125] Ibid. The argument became so intense that the meeting was suspended, and the Holy See only formally accepted the Italian refusal on 17 October 1929.
[126] For the text of the letter see *L'Osservatore Romano*, 6 June 1929.
[127] *Atti*, 1929, Vol. I, Camera, Discussioni, p. 112.
[128] Ibid., p. 167.
[129] Ibid., Senato, Discussioni, pp. 210–11.
[130] Coletti, *Il Divorzio in Italia*, pp. 91–8.

1. Religious (Catholic) marriage with civil effects.
2. Religious (non-Catholic) marriage with civil effects.
3. Civil marriage.

And to add to this confusion, there was the extraordinary anomaly whereby anyone who had previously contracted a civil marriage was eligible in Canon Law to enter into a Catholic religious marriage with another partner.[131] As the great Catholic constitutional and ecclesiastical lawyer Arturo Carlo Jemolo has observed: 'In this way there was foisted upon the country the most chaotic and anomalous marriage law that could possibly be imagined...which left its regulation entirely in the hands of the Church.'[132] And this, of course, remained the situation in Italy until the passing of the Divorce Law in 1970.

In the debates in the Chamber and the Senate, Mussolini had both the first and last word. His speech to the Senate was relatively short, being largely devoted to attempting to rebut Croce's criticisms of his religious policy, but that in the Chamber was a ponderous, three-and-a-half-hour set piece, studded with potted histories of early Christianity, the Risorgimento, and the 'Roman Question' together with the previous attempts to solve it.[133] Mussolini's attempts to show off his knowledge of other recent concordats between the Holy See and European powers were rather less successful than his displays of historical erudition: his comparison of the marriage clauses of the Italian and Bavarian concordats merely revealed a profound misunderstanding of the latter.[134]

Whilst his remarks on the Treaty were proud, confident and convincing, those on the Financial Convention and the Concordat were increasingly defensive. In his attempt to prove that Italy could afford the 1,750 million lire which he had contracted to pay the Holy See, he soon lost himself in elaborate and rather meaningless calculations.[135] Above all, Mussolini was anxious to minimise the concessions which he had made to the Vatican in the Concordat. Speaking of Article 5 which forbade apostate or defrocked priests from holding public office and teaching posts, in particular he stressed that contrary to the wishes of the Pope this measure would not be made retrospective.[136] What he did not tell his audience was that during the course of the negotiations for the Concordat pressure had been brought to bear on Ernesto Buonaiuti, probably the most famous excommunicated priest in Italy, to give up his chair at the University of Rome.[137]

The Duce used the same tactic when he dealt with the introduction of religious instruction into the secondary schools, a development which

---

[131] *Dossier Conciliazione*, ed. Cavaterra, pp. 81–2.
[132] Jemolo, *Chiesa e Stato*, p. 240.
[133] The text of the speech is in *Atti*, 1929, Vol. I, Camera, Discussioni, pp. 129–54.
[134] Ibid., p. 152.   [135] Ibid.
[136] Ibid.   [137] See Buonaiuti, *Pellegrino di Roma*, p. 75.

seriously impaired the integrity of Gentile's secondary school reform of 1924 and in consequence had given rise to much anxiety among Fascist educationalists. To divert attention from this, he made much of the fact that religious instruction was not going to be extended to the universities, 'You will note that I categorically rejected the demand that religious instruction be introduced into the universities.'[138]

When he came to that part of the Concordat which undoubtedly gave rise to the greatest apprehension among the *gerarchi*, Article 43 dealing with Catholic Action and its youth organisations, Mussolini adopted a predictably aggressive and threatening tone. As usual, he was at pains to stress that Article 43 was no different from articles dealing with Catholic Action in other concordats, citing as examples those of Latvia and Lithuania.[139] But implicit in his remarks was the view that Catholic Action was irrelevant and superfluous in post-*Conciliazione*, Fascist Italy.

Mussolini went on to indicate in the clearest terms his awareness of the fact that Catholic Action intended to take advantage of the Concordat and expand its membership and extend its activities, and he warned that the Regime would be extremely vigilant against the threat of 'aggression' from that quarter.[140] And with the customary graphic reminder of how Fascism defended itself against its enemies, the Duce made the first of what were to become frequent warnings against any attempt to use Catholic Action as a camouflage for the re-organisation of the P.P.I.: 'We will not permit the resurrection of those parties or organisations which we have destroyed.'[141] With these statements Mussolini was announcing the beginning of a new policy of police surveillance over Catholic Action which was rapidly to become evident to its leaders and members over the next few months.

Throughout his speech, Mussolini had exalted the secular glories of Italy as against those of the Church. He was preaching a version of *Romanità* rather different from that of his brother Arnaldo and the School of Fascist Mysticism which Arnaldo was to establish in Milan in 1930.[142] Whereas Arnaldo saw the Catholic Church as the essential element of historical continuity between the values of ancient Rome – order, discipline and hierarchy – and their modern reincarnation in Italian Fascism, in Benito's scheme of things there was little place for the Church. Thus, in his justification of that article of the Concordat which imposed on the Italian Government an obligation to defend the 'sacred character' of Rome, he stressed that this character was not solely the result of its Christian past but was also, and more importantly, the consequence of the presence in

[138] *Atti*, 1929, Vol. I, Camera, Discussioni, p. 152. [139] *O.O.*, Vol. XXIV, p. 88.
[140] Ibid. [141] Ibid.
[142] For the School of Fascist Mysticism see D. Marchesini, 'Romanità e Scuola di Mistica Fascista', *Quaderni di Storia*, Vol. IV (1976), pp. 55–73.

Rome of three secular shrines – the Tomb of the Unknown Warrior, the Altar of the Fatherland (the ghastly 'Wedding-cake' construction in Piazza Venezia) and the Altar to the Fallen of the Fascist Revolution, all on the Capitol – which was thus both literally and metaphorically a *contraltare* to the Vatican.[143] Rome was only in fourth part sacred because of the Catholic Church, because it was the 'cradle of Catholicism', and here Mussolini added those remarks which demonstrated his instinctively secular outlook, and which must therefore have delighted the anti-clericals:

We should be proud of the fact that Italy is the only European nation which contains the headquarters of a world religion. This religion was born in Palestine but became Catholic in Rome. If it had stayed in Palestine, then in all probability it would have shared the fate of the many sects, like the Essenes or the Therapeutae, which vanished without trace.[144]

Once again, Mussolini had put the Church in its place, just as he had done at the beginning of his speech, when he had defined the very circumscribed limits in which he intended it should operate in post-*Conciliazione* Italy. In response to a re-evocation by Arrigo Solmi of Cavour's 'Free Church in a Free State' formula, Mussolini declared:

Inside the State the Church is not only not sovereign it is not even free. It is not sovereign because that would be a contradiction of the concept of the State, and it is not free because it is subject to the institutions and the laws of the State, and, indeed, to the terms of the Concordat.[145]

With this speech Mussolini brutally shattered the post-*Conciliazione* honeymoon between Church and State, for within the space of three months he had overthrown the premises on which the Vatican believed that it had been negotiating for three years. Whilst the speech had great success in Parliament and the Press, and went a long way towards reassuring the more doubtful of Mussolini's colleagues and supporters, it had a devastating effect in the Vatican. *L'Osservatore Romano*, which up to this point had obviously been devoting a great deal of space to reporting the parliamentary debates on the Pacts, limited its coverage of Mussolini's long-awaited speech to these few terse lines, 'We will not comment on a speech of an essentially political and, frequently, polemical nature, a speech with which for the most part, we cannot agree.'[146]

Pius XI was profoundly shocked, angered and alarmed by the speech, feelings which were shared by Catholics throughout Italy.[147] The Pope took the opportunity of an audience which he had granted to the students of the Collegio Mondragone[148] the morning after the speech to give vent to

[143] *Atti*, 1929, Vol. I, Camera, Discussioni, p. 152.   [144] Ibid.
[145] Ibid., p. 131.
[146] *L'Osservatore Romano*, 17 May 1929, 'Notizie Italiane – Camera dei Deputati'.
[147] *The Times*, 14 May 1929, 'Lateran Treaty-Ratification by the Chamber'.
[148] The text was published in *L'Osservatore Romano*, 15 May 1929.

his feelings on Mussolini's comments about education, but his full reply to the speech was more meditated; it came in a letter to Cardinal Gasparri dated 30 May, but only published in the Vatican newspaper on 6 June.[149] The choice of this date, the eve of ratification ceremony, was obviously no casual one: on the one hand it was unlikely that Mussolini would be prepared to risk losing face by calling off the ratification at this stage, and on the other hand, in any future disputes over the interpretation of the Pacts, Pius XI would always be able to claim that he had made his position clear before the Pacts were ratified. Certainly, interpretation of the Pacts was what the Pope's letter was all about.

Pius wasted little time on the embarrassing question of Mussolini's gratuitous remarks about the origins of Catholicism, simply condemning them as '...heretical and worse than heretical'.[150] Nor did he mince words when it came to defending the Church's rights: in response to Mussolini's remarks about the sovereignty and liberty of the Church he categorically reasserted the absolute superiority of the Church over the State and in particular its precedence in the question of the education of youth: '...the full and effective right to the education of the child belongs to the Church and not to the State'.[151]

But he was primarily concerned with correcting Mussolini's erroneous interpretations of the Concordat and the implementation legislation. Line by line he analysed Mussolini's commentary on the salient points of the legislative package, and his bitter disappointment showed through when he took the Italian Head of Government to task for his 'errors of judgement' in interpreting these documents: for example, speaking of Mussolini's statement that '...the State has the right of veto over all ecclesiastical appointments'.[152] Pius XI replied quite correctly that '...the Concordat never once uses such an expression'.[153] He was thus drawing attention to the subtle but important difference between a right of absolute veto over ecclesiastical appointments and the right of the Italian Government to be consulted in advance about such appointments, which was the system adopted by the Concordat of 1929.[154] And with the same firmness, he attacked Mussolini's statements about the non-retrospective nature of the ban on excommunicated priests, the new status of the *culti amessi* and the Italian refusal to make religious marriage obligatory for Catholics.

Whilst the Pope concluded his letter on a more conciliatory note, expressing the hope that relations between Church and State would soon

[149] Ibid., 6 June 1929, front page.   [150] Ibid.
[151] Ibid.   [152] *Atti*, 1929, Vol. I, Camera, Discussioni, p. 152.
[153] *L'Osservatore Romano*, 6 June 1929.
[154] See Appendix II. In fact the Italian Government never did veto an episcopal appointment in the period 1929–32, though it did raise initial objections to at least five nominations: (1) Bressanone – see A.C.S., F.C., Serie IV, 'Vescovi', b. 68, 'Bressanone'; (2) Florence – ibid., b. 85, 'Firenze'; (3) Milan – ibid., b. 100, 'Milano'; (4) Reggio Calabria – ibid., b. 117, 'Reggio Calabria'; (5) San Severino – ibid., b. 120, 'San Severino'.

begin to improve, he made it clear that if they did not then the whole of the Lateran package would be at risk; that if the Concordat could not be made to work then the Treaty would be in danger as well: 'They stand or fall together: if one goes, then so does the other, and with it goes the Vatican City and its State.'[155] The State of the Vatican City did not fall; the constitution of that State was proclaimed on 7 June while Cardinal Gasparri and Mussolini were solemnly ratifying the Pacts in the Apostolic Palace. But Church and State were far from being reconciled; on the contrary, in Mussolini's speech and the Pope's letter the battle lines of future conflict had been traced out. Throughout 1929 and 1930, Italy and the Vatican skirmished again and again over such issues as Catholic Action, the Catholic youth organisations and the Catholic press, or the propaganda and proselytising activities of the *culti amessi*, until in the Spring of 1931 they reached a state of open war. But already in the Summer of 1929, against the background of polemics between *L'Osservatore Romano* and the Fascist press, confiscations of Catholic newspapers and the first police investigations into Catholic Action, a serious deterioration in relations between the Church and the Regime seemed imminent, and as the Pope revealed in another letter to Cardinal Gasparri, he was preparing himself for the test.[156]

[155] *L'Osservatore Romano*, 6 June 1929.
[156] The letter is quoted in another of Gasparri to the Pope of 17 September 1929, see Martini, *Studi sulla Questione Romana*, p. 100.

CHAPTER 4

The diplomatic dimension: Italian Foreign Policy and the Vatican, 1929–31

The *Conciliazione* of 1929 brought Mussolini and Fascist Italy great diplomatic prestige. Mussolini's personal achievement in solving the sixty-year-old 'Roman Question' was everywhere recognised by the foreign press; *The Times*, for instance, hailed him as 'the greatest Italian statesman',[1] and the Hungarian Minister of Religious Affairs was reported as saying that Mussolini was '...the leading statesman of the post-war period'.[2] As a result of this great personal triumph, the Duce's already high standing as a moderate, conservative statesman was enhanced. In the eyes of foreign observers, he added the re-establishment of religious peace to his long catalogue of domestic triumphs – the restoration of law and order, the attainment of political stability and the revitalisation of the economy. The *Conciliazione* was seen to have strengthened Italy diplomatically, especially in relation to France, the former 'Elder Daughter of the Church', and the French themselves felt this very deeply as their press comments on the *Conciliazione* demonstrate. Many Italians must have shared the exultation of the Clerico-Fascist Martire, who declared that with the decline of Spain and the demise of Habsburg Austria, Italy was now the leading Catholic power. In his triumphant celebration of the *Conciliazione*, Martire wrote that 'It seems clear to us that Italy must now take on the historically necessary task of saving European civilisation.'[3]

Naturally, Mussolini wished to exploit his new position of strength and he desired to use the 'special relationship' between Italy and the Vatican to further the aims of Italian foreign policy. The Italian Foreign Office, which was now becoming more markedly expansionistic and adventurous as a result of the recent influx of Fascist cadres, sought the aid of the Vatican in certain colonial schemes and other projects aimed at extending Italian territory or influence, in return for the protection or extension of Catholic interests. Another important area in which Italy attempted to

---

[1] *The Times*, 12 February 1929, 'The End of the Roman Question'.
[2] As quoted in *Il Popolo d'Italia*, 14 February 1929, front page article.
[3] Martire, *La Conciliazione*, p. 219.

exploit its Vatican connections was its troubled relations with Yugoslavia and the concomitant problem of the Slav (and German) minorities inside the new north-eastern border provinces. But the *Conciliazione* was also recognised internationally as a great achievement for the Pope, and the Holy See emerged with its diplomatic standing and prestige greatly strengthened. The Vatican certainly did not desire a special relationship which ran counter to the Holy See's traditional policy of diplomatic independence and neutrality, and it managed to defend both, skilfully eluding Mussolini's efforts to involve it in his schemes.

THE DIPLOMATIC ESTABLISHMENTS OF THE VATICAN AND ITALY

Before embarking on an analysis of the diplomatic dimension of the relationship between the Church and the Regime in this period, it would be useful to cast a glance at the diplomatic establishment on both sides in order to understand the shape of the policy-making structures and to identify the chief policy makers. On the morrow of the *Conciliazione*, the Vatican 'Foreign Office' – the Secretariat of State – was still headed by Cardinal Gasparri, the leading advocate, after the Pope himself, of the policy of co-operation with Fascism, and Gasparri's influence was all the more powerful now that this policy had been crowned with success in the Lateran Pacts. His lieutenant, Mons. Borgoncini-Duca was appointed first Nuncio to Italy on 8 June 1929 and thus by custom became the doyen of the diplomatic corps accredited to the Quirinale. Despite the somewhat poisoned atmosphere at the time, Italian reaction to his appointment was uniformly favourable. His opposite number, De Vecchi, described him as '...one of the leading architects of the *Conciliazione*'.[4]

However, De Vecchi also claimed that Borgoncini-Duca was the leader of the pro-*popolare* faction in the Vatican and that his intrigues on its behalf were the cause of many unnecessary misunderstandings between the Vatican and the Regime, especially in the critical months of 1931.[5] Fascist police reports tend to confirm De Vecchi's claim, which he repeated several times in his memoirs, and there are no available sources on the Catholic side to challenge this view.

The other important figure in the Secretariat of State was Mons. Pizzardo, who was made Secretary for Extraordinary Ecclesiastical Affairs in July 1929 in succession to Borgoncini-Duca. Pizzardo was also the ecclesiastical head of Italian Catholic Action. This dualism had its counterparts in other areas of Catholic Action: for example, Augusto Ciriaci, President of F.I.U.C. and later President of Catholic Action in the whole of Italy, was manager of the Vatican printing press; Mons. Fernando Roveda was Rector of the German Seminary in the Vatican and Secretary-

⁴ De Vecchi, *Memorie*, no. 10.   ⁵ Ibid.

General of Catholic Action; Mons. Domenico Tardini was Under-Secretary for Extraordinary Ecclesiastical Affairs in the Secretariat of State and National Chaplain for the Catholic women's organisations; and Mons. G. B. Montini was a *minutante* in the Secretariat of State and National Chaplain of F.U.C.I. It irked Mussolini and his colleagues who believed that the holding of high office in an Italian organisation was incompatible with the service of a 'foreign state'.

De Vecchi had little to say about Pizzardo, but by 1931 the police had compiled a very fat dossier on his activities inside of Catholic Action.[6] In 1931, Pizzardo became the major scapegoat during the crisis over Catholic Action, being subjected to a vicious newspaper campaign which relied almost entirely upon information from the police files.[7] In the circumstances, Pizzardo's alleged anti-Fascism was a gross distortion of the facts, as is borne out by other sources.[8]

The inauguration of formal diplomatic relations between Italy and the Vatican by no means rendered redundant those unofficial channels of communication which had flourished since the establishment of the Regime: Monsignori Pucci and Caccia-Dominioni continued to play a role in the background,[9] as did Padre Tacchi-Venturi, whose good offices were resorted to when diplomatic channels failed, the most notable example being his mediation during the crisis of 1931.[10] Exactly a year after the signing of the Lateran Pacts, in February 1929, Cardinal Gasparri was replaced by Eugenio Pacelli: whilst this was to have some repercussions on the conduct of the Vatican's relations with Italy,[11] one thing remained emphatically unchanged – the Pope continued to be the major policy maker, frequently intervening to stiffen the Vatican side in his public pronouncements, and even on occasion writing pungent editorials for *L'Osservatore Romano*.[12]

On the Italian side the dominating figure was Mussolini who held the portfolio of Foreign Affairs until September 1929, when, in a general Cabinet reshuffle, Dino Grandi, hitherto Under-Secretary at Palazzo Chigi, took his place. Even then, Mussolini continued to have the last word in the formulation of foreign policy and, as De Vecchi's memoirs show, he retained a close control over the day-to-day conduct of relations with the Vatican.[13] Mussolini was also head of the Ministry of the Interior, which

---

[6] A.C.S., S.C.P., b. 44, f. 2, 'Mons. Pizzardo'.

[7] See below Chapter 6, p. 146.

[8] *The Times*, in its report of 25 March 1929, 'The First Fascist Elections', said that Pizzardo gave the Facist salute on leaving the polling booth.

[9] See below Chapter 5.   [11] See below Chapter 6.

[10] See below Chapter 6.

[12] This was particularly true during the crisis of 1931, see P.R.O., F.O. 137, C. 3795/2810/22, Sir R. Graham to Henderson, 12 June 1931.

[13] De Vecchi may well have exaggerated the frequency of his audiences with Mussolini in order to bolster his own importance, but he rarely mentions meetings with Grandi after the latter's appointment as Foreign Minister. See De Vecchi, *Memorie*, no. 10.

through the police forces exercised a continuous surveillance over the activities of the clergy and Catholic Action. Though the Under-Secretary of the Interior, first Michele Bianchi and then Leandro Arpinati, was responsible for the activities and budget of the Ministry before Parliament, the Police Chief Bocchini was directly responsible to Mussolini and to him alone.[14] It was Bocchini's spies inside the Vatican who kept Mussolini provided with up-to-date and usually very accurate reports on the balance of power and opinion in the highest circles of the Roman Curia and even supplied precisely detailed résumés of the meetings of the Giunta Centrale of Catholic Action.

From July 1931, probably as a result of the crisis with the Vatican, the Fondo per il Culto, the office responsible for scrutinising the nominations of bishops and parochial clergy and for the administration of ecclesiastical property and the payment of State subsidies to the Church, was transferred from the jurisdiction of the Ministry of Justice to that of the Interior:[15] there was thus concentrated in Mussolini's hands ultimate control of all aspects of religious policy. In any case, the moderating voice of the Ministry of Justice had been somewhat muffled by the removal of Under-Secretary Mattei-Gentili in the Cabinet reshuffle of September 1929: clearly, with the conclusion of the Lateran Pacts, the presence of a Clerico-Fascist in the Government was no longer regarded as either useful or necessary.[16]

Undoubtedly the most important personality on the Italian side, after Mussolini, was Cesare Maria De Vecchi di Val Cismon, quadumvir or general of the March on Rome, Senator, Minister of State and former Governor of Somalia, who was appointed as Italy's first Ambassador to the Holy See and presented his credentials in the Vatican on 23 June 1929.[17] De Vecchi's entry into the Diplomatic Service did not pass without comment; in some Fascist circles the appointment of this slightly comic, 'swashbuckling' figure was regarded as nothing less than an outrage.[18] But the Vatican was quite happy with him, if only because he was one of the few Fascist *gerarchi* who was also a practising Catholic and was highly regarded in ecclesiastical circles in Turin:[19] indeed there is evidence to suggest that De Vecchi came to be genuinely liked and respected in Vatican

[14] For an account of the internal power structure of the Ministry of the Interior see Iraci, *Arpinati Oppositore di Mussolini*, p. 121. Iraci was Secretary-General of the Ministry when Arpinati was Under-Secretary of State.

[15] The change was confirmed by a Royal Decree Law published in the *Gazzetta Ufficiale* of 20 July 1932.

[16] The only Clerico-Fascists, apart from M.P.s and Senators, to remain in high public office after the *Conciliazione* were Boncompargni-Ludovisi, Governor (Mayor) of Rome, and G. B. Imberti who was Podesta (Mayor) of his home town, Cuneo.

[17] The figure of De Vecchi has been largely neglected among the ranks of the Gerarchi; the only biographical works available are the sycophantic book by Orano, *De Vecchi di Val Cismon*, and the rather less enthusiastic study by Montanelli, *Padre della Patria*.

[18] A.C.S., M.P.P., P.154, Cat. M.29, 'Ambasciata Italiana presso la Santa Sede', report of 11 June 1929.   [19] Ibid., report of 20 October 1930.

circles, not least by the Pope himself.[20] They seemed to have been willing to tolerate his diplomatic gaffes, though they drew the line at his appearing in party uniform on festive occasions, and there was real regret in the Vatican when he left diplomacy to become Minister of Education in January 1935.[21]

The more astute observers close to the Government perceived the wisdom of Mussolini's choice: a career diplomat would have been too low in status for such an important and prestigious post: De Vecchi was an established and influential *gerarca*, who combined sincere Catholic convictions with a tough, combative Fascist spirit.[22] The appointment continued to serve Mussolini's interests long after he had handed over Foreign Affairs to Grandi, for De Vecchi, who was certainly equal in party ranking to Grandi, also considered himself to be so in diplomatic terms and in consequence tended to report directly to Mussolini thus preserving the latter's overall direction of religious affairs.

ITALO-VATICAN RELATIONS ON THE MORROW OF THE *CONCILIAZIONE*

The 1929 settlement brought about peace and reconciliation and the establishment of diplomatic relations between two very different kinds of international entity – the Kingdom of Italy and the Holy See. The latter was, to say the least, an anomaly in the international order,[23] for although it had lost its territorial, 'temporal' power at the hands of the creators of United Italy, in its sixty-year-old conflict with that State it had retained the attributes of sovereignty in the eyes of the other European powers thanks to the enormous spiritual and moral authority derived from the Pope's headship of the universal Catholic Church: that was, after all, the *raison d'être* of the Papacy. As a leading international lawyer has conclusively demonstrated, '...between 1870 and 1929, the Holy See possessed, as it possessed before, legal personality and sovereignty in the international sphere.'[24]

---

[20] See Castelli, *Il Vaticano nei tentacoli del Fascismo*, p. 13.
[21] So much so that he was made a member of the Papal Order of the Golden Spur, which counted foreign kings and princes amongst its members, but no other diplomats accredited to the Vatican. See the *Annuario Pontificio*, 1948, p. 874.
[22] This view is shared by Montanelli, *Padre della Patria*, pp. 248–9.
[23] Though not the only one: the Sovereign Military Order of St John of Jerusalem, Rhodes and Malta, having led a peripatetic existence since its expulsion from Malta by Napoleon, by 1929 was firmly installed in two extra-territorial palaces in the centre of Rome and continued to conduct diplomatic relations with a number of Catholic states. The analogy between the S.M.O.M. and the Vatican is very close indeed as both had lost their territorial sovereignty, but succeeded in maintaining recognition of their sovereign attributes by other powers. See C. d'Olivier Farran, 'The Sovereign Order of Malta in International Law', *International Law Quarterly*, April 1954.
[24] Falco, *The Legal Position of the Holy See before and after the Lateran Agreements*, p. 17.

One of the essential features of the 1929 settlement, however, was precisely that it 'reclothed' the Holy See with territorial sovereignty over the miniscule State of the Vatican City. In more than one sense this did not represent any significant change in the relationship between Italy and the Holy See. The Italian Ambassador who presented his credentials in the Vatican in June 1929 was accredited to the Holy See, that is to the central governing body of the Catholic Church, as were all the rest of the Vatican diplomatic corps, and not to the State of the Vatican City. It was by virtue of this fact, and not because the Pope was Sovereign of the State of the Vatican City, that foreign governments had, and still have, relations with the Vatican. The area of the Vatican City had been 'out of bounds' to officials of the Italian State ever since the occupation of Rome by Italian troops in September 1870,[25] even though the Italian Parliament had implicitly asserted its sovereignty over the Vatican by the Law of Guarantees of the following year. In any case, the overwhelming not to say over-powering presence of the Holy See in the Italian capital had long been established by the countless shrines, churches and monuments, by the dozens of offices of the Roman Curia and Congregations, by the embassies and legations accredited to the Pope, and by the thousands of colourfully dressed seminarians from all parts of the globe. Victor Emmanuel's fears that the Pope would soon be processing freely through the streets of his capital were proved groundless: Pius XI very tactfully limited his public appearances to the balconies of St Peter's and the Vatican Palace, and on his visits to the new papal summer palace at Castel Gandolfo he took the most discreet route across the Eternal City.[26]

The emergence of the new independent and neutral State of the Vatican City, whose boundaries had been agreed and demarcated by the represen-tatives of both sides and which had been provided with most of the facilities of a modern state by the time the Lateran Pacts were ratified in June 1929, had very little immediate impact. Not until Mussolini constructed the Via della Conciliazione, in 'Fascist' style, from the Tiber to St Peter's was there any really visible sign of the new order of things.

But in another sense the creation of the new State did change the relationship between Italy and the Vatican; it had a powerful impact upon the Italian mind which Mussolini found altogether unhealthy. In the weeks and months following the *Conciliazione*, the Italian Fascist press developed an almost obsessive interest in the goings-on inside Peter's City, from the public building works in progress to the 'in' gossip about Vatican personalities – the greatest offender being *Il Popolo d'Italia* which devoted

---

[25] This was in pursuance of Article 7 of the law which forbade Italian officials to enter the palaces or offices of the Pope or those of Ecumenical Councils or Conclaves. See Appendix I.

[26] *Dossier Conciliazione*, ed. Cavaterra p. xviii.

several column inches to Vatican news in most editions.[27] Ironically, the chief instigator of this coverage was the editor of *Il Popolo d'Italia*, the devout Catholic Arnaldo Mussolini, which must have greatly displeased his brother, Benito.

Mussolini's exasperation at this irritating phenomenon expressed itself in a telegram to the Prefects ordering them to instruct newspaper editors to desist from this 'exaggerated' coverage – to no avail.[28] Behind the keen interest of the Italian press in Vatican affairs lay a strong sense of pride – in the Papacy as an historically Italian institution and in the Vatican State, which was after all an exclusively Italian creation. This feeling of pride was obviously shared by Italian Catholics, whose traditionally fervent devotion to the Holy See, it seemed, need no longer conflict in the remotest way with their loyalties to King and Country. But Mussolini did not see it in this light, he remained intensely jealous of the strong attachment of Italian Catholics to what he would describe as a 'foreign state'. He found the practice of Italian Catholic associations, including Catholic Action, of using the papal banner in ceremonies and processions extremely irritating, and he rebuked the Prefects for permitting the use of this 'foreign flag'.[29] Another undesirable by-product of the creation of the new Sovereign State was the fact that it inevitably acquired citizens. In the months following the ratification of the Pacts, Mussolini repeatedly asked through De Vecchi for a list of persons on whom Vatican citizenship had been conferred.[30] His anxiety to know who had acquired the much coveted status was determined by fears that Vatican citizenship would be used to shield undesirable *popolare* elements from Fascist justice. As it turned out, Vatican citizenship was not used in this way, but the territorial sovereignty of the Vatican did encourage a number of prominent *popolari* to gather there. The police seem to have been very slow to detect their presence, the first report to Mussolini is dated mid-1930,[31] but thereafter the police maintained the closest surveillance over these 'exiles' in Peter's City.[32]

In this way, the new status of the Vatican encouraged fears and fantasies about the activities and influence of the *popolari* there and in Catholic Action generally. In the eyes of Mussolini and his ministers, the Vatican had become a 'foreign country' whose enormous social and political influence in Italy could only be regarded with suspicion.

[27] See also *Il Lavoro Fascista* and *Il Popolo di Roma* for the period February–July 1929.
[28] A.C.S., S.P.D., C.R. 6/97/R, 'Questione Romana', sf. II, telegram to the Prefects, no. 7127, of 24 February 1929.
[29] See B. *Mussolini: Corrispondenza Inedita*, ed. Susmel, p. 112, which reproduces the text of Mussolini's telegram to the Prefect of Treviso of 11 December 1929.
[30] De Vecchi, *Memorie*, nos. 14 and 15.
[31] A.C.S., M.P.P., Pacco 100, K.7, report of 28 August 1930.
[32] Ibid., report of 15 June 1931.

THE VATICAN AND THE LEAGUE OF NATIONS

In the weeks following the *Conciliazione* Mussolini had another reason for regretting his role as midwife in the birth of the State of the Vatican City, for the 'baby' seemed to be rapidly turning into a monster beyond his control. News reached the Italian Foreign Office that the Vatican was considering the possibility of registering the Lateran Pacts at the League of Nations in Geneva, and even of applying for membership of the international organisation.[33] The registration of international treaties had become a practice of the League as a result of President Wilson's desire to eliminate 'secret treaties', to which he ascribed much of the blame for the outbreak of the First World War.[34] In the case of the Lateran Pacts, registration at the League would have given them that international recognition which the Holy See had always insisted on as an essential element in any satisfactory settlement of the 'Roman Question': in a letter to Francesco Pacelli, the chief Vatican negotiator, of 24 October 1926, Gasparri had underlined the importance for the Holy See that '...the new territorial and political order be recognised by the powers', and that the responsibility for securing this recognition should rest with Italy.[35] It should be noted that Gasparri spoke of international recognition, that is the explicit acceptance by other countries of the sovereignty of the Vatican City State, not international guarantees which would have involved formal treaty agreements by other powers to defend that sovereignty.

The idea of international guarantees had been popular in Vatican circles in the reigns of Leo XIII and Pius X as a means of 'internationalising' the Law of Guarantees, which was after all merely a unilateral act of the Italian Parliament.[36] The Italians rejected 'internationalisation' as an affront to their national independence and integrity, and the idea also fell out of favour in the Vatican; as Pius XI explained in an address given to the parish priests of Rome at the very moment that the Pacts were being signed in the Lateran Palace, the Vatican no longer desired international guarantees, if only because they had proved absolutely worthless in defending the temporal power during the previous century.[37]

International recognition was a different matter, but how Mussolini intended to satisfy the Holy See's demand for this is simply not known; he certainly gave no hint in his parliamentary speeches of how he proposed to obtain it, and there is absolutely no evidence that Italian diplomats made approaches to foreign governments in this sense. Paradoxically, the easiest

[33] D.D.I., 7, Vol. VII, pp. 279–80, no. 250.
[34] For the text of Article 18 covering registration see Walters, *A History of the League of Nations*, Vol. I, p. 54.
[35] O.O., Vol. XXIV, p. 75.
[36] Jemolo, *Chiesa e Stato*, p. 79.
[37] *Discorsi*, Vol. II, p. 10, 'Ai parroci e quaresimalisti di Roma', 11 February 1929.

and most convenient method of obtaining international recognition for the Pacts was to register them at the League, which strictly speaking Italy was obliged to do anyway as a signatory to the League Covenant.[38] But this was the last thing that Mussolini intended to do; he was determined that the Pacts should remain a purely bilateral affair between Italy and the Holy See and he was most anxious that the latter should not increase its independence and room for manoeuvre in the relationship with Italy, which is exactly what he feared would happen if the State of the Vatican City joined the League.

Against a background of intense speculation at Geneva a campaign was mounted in the Italian press aimed at discouraging the Vatican from having anything to do with the League of Nations. *Il Popolo d'Italia* argued that registration of the Pacts at Geneva was tantamount to seeking guarantees which would be an affront and a humiliation for Italy,[39] and in another article the President of the Council of State, Santi Romano, claimed that registration of the Pacts at the League was not necessary to give them international recognition, a view which was to be borne out by events.[40] *La Stampa* enlisted the services of Padre Rosa, who reiterated the Pope's statement that international guarantees were not necessary and stated quite specifically that the Holy See would not accept membership of the League of Nations, '...because it could not agree to one of the conditions of membership, that is to take part in wars against members who violated the Covenant, members which might be Christian States'.[41]

This eminently sensible clarification of the issue by one of the most authoritative spokesmen for the Vatican failed to convince Mussolini; on learning that Sir Eric Drummond, the Secretary-General of the League, intended to visit the Pope in the near future, Mussolini through Grandi instructed the Italian Under-Secretary-General of the League, Paulucci, to use all possible means to prevent or postpone Drummond's visit lest it should encourage the Pope to register the Pacts. The Duce's anxiety may be judged from the vehemence of the language used by Grandi in his note to Paulucci:

...The Italian Government does not (I repeat, does not) wish that the Lateran Pacts should be registered at the League of Nations. It has got nothing to do with the League. Any initiative taken by the Secretary-General of the League in this matter will only arouse the displeasure of Italy. It is important that you make Drummond understand that even the merest hint of such a thing would be inopportune. *The Treaty between Italy and the Holy See has got nothing to do with the League of Nations* [Grandi's italics]...this is a very delicate and important matter.[42]

[38] Walters, *A History of the League of Nations*, Vol. I, p. 54.
[39] *Il Popolo d'Italia*, 13 February 1939, 'L'Accordo col Vaticano e le garanzie internazionali'.
[40] Ibid., 14 February 1929, 'I Patti Lateranensi e le garanzie internazionali'.
[41] *La Stampa*, 12 February 1929, 'Intervista col Padre Enrico Rosa'.
[42] *D.D.I.*, 7, Vol. VII, p. 281, no. 258.

Paulucci was unable to prevent Drummond from visiting the Vatican or from presenting the Pope with a technical brief on the process of registering treaties at the League, but he did succeed in making Drummond understand that any unilateral initiative by the Vatican in this matter would greatly displease Italy.[43] The other object of Paulucci's anxious attentions was Mons. Ritter, the Papal Nuncio to Switzerland, who also had the task of monitoring any developments at Geneva that might be of interest to the Vatican. During one of his many visits to Geneva which had given rise to speculation about the Vatican's intentions, Mons. Ritter was cornered by Paulucci who endeavoured to persuade him that the only benefit which registering the Lateran Pacts at the League would bring to the Vatican would be a little extra publicity, nothing more.[44] Meanwhile, in Rome, Grandi and De Vecchi lobbied their Vatican opposite numbers to the same effect, with a little help from Mussolini who in his speech to the Chamber of 13 May declared that the terms of the Treaty ruled out Vatican involvement with the League.[45]

The fact that the Pope in his reply to that speech did not repudiate this interpretation suggests that by then the Vatican had already rejected the idea of an approach to the League; nevertheless it was not until February 1930 that De Vecchi was able to inform Grandi that the Vatican had definitely abandoned the plan.[46] The principal factor in this decision was undoubtedly the strong Italian opposition to registration, but there was also another important consideration; apart from the likelihood of strong opposition on the part of anti-clerical and Protestant powers in Geneva, there was no precedent in international law for the recognition or guaranteeing of a concordat. As we have already seen, it was axiomatic to Pius XI's policy, as laid down in his letter to Cardinal Gasparri of June 1929, that the Treaty and Concordat stood together; to have had only the Treaty (and Financial Convention) registered at Geneva would have left the Concordat dangerously isolated, vulnerable to unilateral amendment or even repeal by the Italians, as the Law of Guarantees had been. The Pope and his Secretary of State preferred to rely upon the force of Italian and world public opinion to defend the Lateran Pacts from attack, a confidence that was only partly justified by the events of 1931 and not at all by the crisis over the Racial Laws in 1938.[47] As for Vatican membership of the League, it is unlikely that this was ever seriously considered in the Secretariat of State for all the good reasons advanced by Mussolini and the Fascist press: both the Holy See's traditional policy of non-involvement in

[43] Ibid.
[44] Ibid., Vol. VIII, p. 251, no. 258.
[45] *O.O.*, Vol. XXIV, p. 78, 'Finally... the Vatican City declares itself neutral in all international disputes... and that it will not take part in international conferences, whatever their purpose,... or in the meetings of the League of Nations.'
[46] *D.D.I.*, 7, Vol. VIII, p. 352, no. 387.   [47] See below, Chapter 7, pp. 189 and 193.

international disputes and the specific terms of the Treaty in this regard did indeed make it impossible for the Vatican to subscribe to the League Covenant. Another consideration must have been the attitude of the existing members of the League: according to Paulucci, neither the British nor the French, the dominating powers at Geneva, would have welcomed the prospect of Vatican membership, fearing the strong influence it might have on Catholic powers to their detriment,[48] a judgement confirmed by other sources.[49]

The most significant aspect of this episode was Mussolini's almost paranoid reaction to the possibility of Vatican involvement with Geneva: registration of the Pacts there would have carried with it the danger of the Vatican appealing to the League in any disputes over interpretation of the Treaties. Furthermore, Vatican involvement with the League would have strengthened the influence of the world body, which is why its Secretary-General was so enthusiastic about registering the Pacts.[50] Fascist Italy, as a power with moderately 'revisionist' intentions towards the Treaty of Versailles, was already adopting a rather equivocal attitude towards the League of Nations in the late 1920s, was resentful of the joint British–French hegemony at Geneva, and had no interest in strengthening their meddlesome organisation. But Mussolini's primary anxiety was that the Vatican should not escape his embrace, the restricting 'special relationship' with Italy, by means of which he intended to use the Vatican for the purposes of Italian foreign policy.

MUSSOLINI'S ATTEMPTS TO EXPLOIT THE NEW VATICAN
CONNECTION: THE NEAR EAST AND AFRICA

In the years following the *Conciliazione*, Mussolini and the Italian Foreign Office endeavoured to make use of their new relationship with the Vatican to further Italian ambitions in the Middle East and the Mediterranean. Fascism had always been the standard-bearer of the 'Mutilated Victory' lobby, with its bitter resentment of the refusal by Britain and France to honour the admittedly rather vague promises of Italian colonial gains contained in the Treaty of London. International recognition of Italian sovereignty over the Dodecanese Islands, acquired in the Libyan War of 1911–12, and the cessions by Britain to Italy of Jarabub and Jubaland were hardly adequate compensation for the Franco-British carve-up of the Turkish Empire or the fact they had taken the lion's share of the German colonies without offering Italy anything. And despite Mussolini's hopes, Kemal Ataturk's new, secular Turkish Republic did not disintegrate, thus preventing the realisation of the Italian dream of a colony in Asia Minor.

[48] *D.D.I.*, 7, Vol. VII, pp. 279–80, no. 250.
[49] Ibid., Vol. VIII, p. 215, no. 203.   [50] Ibid.

In this situation, the Italians sought to undermine French and British influence in the Balkans, Turkey, Palestine and Malta, frequently attempting to exploit religious questions in which the Vatican had an interest, to this end.

The policy of trying to use the Vatican in support of Italian foreign policy was not new. Both Vittorio Emmanule Orlando and Francesco Nitti had tried to take advantage of their improving relations with the Vatican to extend Italian influence in Palestine, the most notable example of this being the attempt to obtain control of the Cenacle, the site of the Last Supper in Jerusalem, for Italian priests.[51] The failure of this attempt, and the lukewarmness which the Vatican displayed towards it, did not prevent the Fascist Regime from seeking to repeat the experiment. Some years before the signing of the Lateran Pacts, Mussolini was already seeking to profit diplomatically from the rapprochement with the Church.[52] In December 1925, Giannini wrote to Fr. Tacchi-Venturi asking that the French Vicar Apostolic (bishop) of Salonika be replaced by an Italian on account of the fact that many of the Catholic community in that Greek city were Italians: '...even though the Parish Priest of Salonika is French as is the Apostolic Nuncio at Athens'.[53] Though he received no satisfaction in this matter. Giannini tried again in 1927; this time he sought to increase Italian influence at the expense of the French in Bulgaria where he demanded that Italian diplomats be accorded the same liturgical honours in Catholic churches as were enjoyed by the French.[54]

These liturgical honours had originated in the 'protectorate' over the Catholics within the territories of the Ottoman Empire granted by the Sultan to the French in 1790. France continued to enjoy the political prestige and influence and some commercial advantage deriving from this traditional role in the Levant, reinforced now by the conferment on her of the League of Nations' mandates for the Lebanon and Syria, and in December 1926, as a result of the negotiations between the French Foreign Minister, Briand, and the Papal Nuncio to France, Maglione, the Holy See had renewed the protectorate.[55] Though Italy protested about this to the Vatican, it was to no avail,[56] and thus in the matter of Bulgaria its efforts were doomed to failure. It was precisely this kind of French influence which Palazzo Chigi sought to undermine: thus it was anxious for a successful outcome to the negotiations undertaken by the Holy See in 1928 and again in 1929 to re-establish full diplomatic relations with Turkey, because in the words of Orsini Barone, Italian Ambassador at Ankara, '...it seems to me that this would put an end to the privileged position which the French

---

[51] Minerbi, 'The Italian Activity to Recover the "Cenacolo"', pp. 181–209.
[52] Carocci, *La Politica Estera dell'Italia Fascista*, pp. 202–5.
[53] *D.D.I.*, 7, Vol. IV, p. 154, no. 209.
[54] Ibid., p. 313, no. 405.
[55] Carocci, *La Politica Estera dell'Italia Fascista*, p. 204.   [56] Ibid.

claim for themselves, but which they are unable to maintain, that it would also, therefore, coincide with our interests'.[57] Orsini Barone's efforts to help the negotiations along did not bear fruit. In fact, Italian efforts were counter-productive. The Turks were justifiedly suspicious of Italian motives, and the opposition of the Moslem clergy to a link with the 'Infidel' shipwrecked the negotiations.[58] The Vatican continued to be represented in Turkey for many years to come by an Apostolic Delegate, that is by an envoy without official diplomatic status.

As the French were the first to admit, the *Conciliazione* of 1929 strengthened Italy's diplomatic position vis-à-vis France; liberated from the burden of the 'Roman Question' and the resulting stigma of anti-clericalism, Italy was now the leading Catholic power, a fact also recognised by foreign commentators.[59] Bitterness at this diplomatic defeat for France was compounded with anti-clerical and anti-Fascist feelings in the reactions of those newspapers of a masonic or democratic tinge: *L'Ere Nouvelle* wrote, 'L'Alliance des deux Romes est conclusé contre la France de '89, contre la France de la Liberté.'[60]

Not all foreign papers agreed but all did stress the *diplomatic* consequences of the *Conciliazione*, that in both the Middle East and Africa Italy stood to gain enormously increased prestige and influence at the expense of France, as a result of the new relationship with the Vatican.[61] The Fascist press luxuriated in the warm glow of all this foreign interest in Italy, throughout February 1929 Italian newspapers abounded in equally optimistic predictions of the future Italian diplomatic success. *Il Lavoro Fascista*, for example, claimed that the *Conciliazione* had greatly increased Italy's prestige in the Balkan countries.[62]

But this diplomatic success simply did not materialise, Fascist Italy made no concrete gains in this direction, indeed when in 1930 the Italian Foreign Office once more passed its claims to the much-coveted liturgical honours, it received a polite refusal from the Vatican.[63] The Vatican refused to take sides between Italy and France, preferring to give them equal consideration in its policy calculations. Mussolini had to rest content with a less tangible benefit, the knowledge that Italy now enjoyed greater prestige and respect in all her dealings with France.

An important ingredient in the success of French imperialism in Africa

[57] *D.D.I.*, 7, Vol. VII, p. 108, no. 119, note of 20 February 1928.
[58] Kent, *The Pope and the Duce*, p. 90.
[59] See, for example, *The Observer*, 17 February 1929.
[60] As quoted in Missiroli, *Date a Cesare*, p. 32.
[61] Ibid., p. 35, where he cites comments to this effect in *Neues Wiener Tagblatt*, the *Berliner Tagblatt*, the *Frankfurter Zeitung* and *The Observer*.
[62] *Il Lavoro Fascista*, 28 February 1929.
[63] *D.D.I.*, 7, Vol. VII, p. 239, no. 314. In this report the Italian Consul at Aleppo explained to Mussolini that the Apostolic Delegate in Syria had refused to permit the holding of a Te Deum to celebrate the *Conciliazione* for fear of offending the French colonial authorities.

and elsewhere had always been the scale of French missionary activity and the role France had assumed as 'protector' of Catholic missions – factors which remained largely unaffected by the anti-clerical policies pursued within metropolitan France. By comparison with France, Italian missionary activity was small beer, but immediately after the *Conciliazione* there was much speculation in the foreign[64] and Italian press that Italy would now be in a position to challenge France and with the tacit support of the Vatican be able to exploit its influence in the missionary field on a scale hitherto unknown.[65] In the three years following the signing of the Lateran Pacts, the Regime showed a strong interest in the Italian missionary organisations in the deluded hope that it could use them to counter French influence and spread Italianità.[66] There was even talk of a special, secret agreement concluded during the course of the negotiations for the Pacts, whereby the Vatican was supposed to have promised a significant proportion of the funds it was to receive under the terms of the Financial Convention to the enlargement of Italian missionary activity,[67] an allegation quickly and indignantly denied by *L'Osservatore Romano*[68] and by the Clerico-Fascist Francesco Mauro, who in a long article on the subject for *L'Italia* stressed that it was not and never had been the policy of the Catholic Church to permit its missions to be used for narrow, nationalistic ends.[69]

This would explain why the only recorded instance of an approach by the Italian Government to the Vatican for the purpose of using Catholic missions to assist its colonial administration was a signal failure. In November 1929, the Italian Ministry for the Colonies urged an approach to the Vatican with a view to intensifying Catholic propaganda and proselytism in Eritrea, in order to combat the influence of the Ethiopian-dominated Coptic Church in that colony. In a note to Grandi, De Vecchi reported that he had not made any specific request in this regard because of Gasparri's manifest lack of interest in the matter on previous occasions.[70] De Vecchi argued that such a move was unlikely to succeed because of the strenuous opposition of Mons. (later Cardinal) Marchetti-Selvaggiani, the head of the Vatican's missionary department Propaganda Fide, whom he quoted as saying that the Church '...must prevent religion from being exploited by various colonial powers'.[71]

[64] See *The Observer*, 12 February 1929, article by E. Oldmeadow.
[65] Missiroli, *Date a Cessare*, pp. 43–4.
[66] See the very detailed report on the Italian missionary conference held in Turin in August 1930 in A.C.S., D.G.P.S., G.I., b. 146, 'Azione Cattolica', sf. III, 'Conference e Convegni', 3 September 1930. As well as providing a brief profile of Italian missionary activity, the author underlines the Vatican's policy of keeping Catholic missions, including those of Italy, out of international politics.   [67] Missiroli, *Date a Cessare*, p. 44.
[68] *L'Osservatore Romano*, 20 February 1929, 'Dubbi Impertinenti'.
[69] *L'Italia*, 23 March 1929, 'Le Missioni Cattoliche'.
[70] D.D.I., 7, Vol. VIII, p. 6, no. 57.
[71] Ibid., Vol. IX (proofs), pp. 5, 6 and 7, no. 5.

Gasparri's coolness on this matter was probably also influenced by the fact that the colonial authorities in Eritrea were opposing the Vatican's appointment of a native as head of the Catholic Coptic Church there on the grounds that this would undermine the natives' sense of inferiority towards their white masters.[72] This forward-thinking, so typical of Vatican policy towards colonial peoples in the inter-war period,[73] was not appreciated by the now racially conscious Italians.

When De Vecchi raised the matter again, in April 1930, the Vatican was as unenthusiastic as before, indeed in view of the fact that the Pope had made a public pronouncement on the missions in between times, it is surprising that he bothered.[74] Pius XI shared Marchetti-Salvaggiani's views on the question and in his address to an audience of missionaries in December 1929, he stated the Church's policy unequivocally: 'The missions must have absolutely nothing to do with nationalism. They must be solely concerned with Catholicism, with the apostolate...nationalism has always been a calamity for the missions, indeed, it would be no exaggeration to say that it is a curse.'[75] The refusal of the Vatican to be drawn into the Italian Government's colonial schemes almost certainly cost it the decision of the Ministry of the Colonies not to extend the provisions of the Concordat to Italy's overseas territories.[76] After sitting for two years, the Commission appointed by that Ministry to study the question gave a generally negative report, and the Concordat was eventually only applied to the Dodecanese Islands, and then only because the newly appointed Archbishop of Rhodes was an enthusiastic supporter of the Italian, Fascist cause.[77] The attitude of the Vatican also contrasts sharply with the later enthusiasm of the Italian clergy for the Ethiopian War, which many of them dubbed a 'Christian Crusade'.

Throughout the 1920s and the 1930s, the Fascists continued the Italian Foreign Office's longstanding policy of strengthening Italian influence in Palestine by a variety of means including that of financing Italian religious works in general, and the Latin Patriarchate (Archbishopric) of Jerusalem in particular[78] on the one hand, and flirting with Zionism on the other.[79]

---

[72] Ibid., Vol. VIII, p. 205, no. 190, telegram from the Minister for the Colonies, De Bono, to Grandi, in which he says: 'The conferment of such an important office upon an Eritrean would have the effect of undermining the Eritreans' necessary sense of inferiority towards Europeans.'

[73] Neill, *A History of Christian Missions*, pp. 522–3.

[74] *D.D.I.*, 7, Vol. IX (proofs), pp. 5, 6 and 7, no. 5.

[75] *Discorsi*, Vol. II, pp. 214–5, 'Ai Religiosi Missionari', 7 December 1929.

[76] On 6 December 1930, De Bono formed a working party within his Ministry to consider whether the Concordat should be extended to the colonies: see *D.D.I.*, 7, Vol. VIII, p. 6, no. 57, Note 1.

[77] See A.C.S., F.C., Serie IV, 'Vescovi', b. 138, 'Rodi', letter of 12 July 1938 from the Minister of the Interior to the Ministry of Foreign Affairs.

[78] Rhodes, *The Vatican in the Age of the Dictators*, p. 67.

[79] De Felice, *Storia degli ebrei*, p. 130.

Mussolini's ultimate aim was very ambitious: to bring about the transfer of the League of Nations' mandate over Palestine from Britain to Italy.[80] In this he had the support of many Italian Catholics, and not only those in Clerico-Fascist circles: Fr. Barduzzi, by no means a Clerico-Fascist, made a strong attack on British policy in Palestine and explicitly demanded that the mandate be handed over to Italy or to a condominium of Italy and Spain under the aegis of the Holy See.[81] But the Vatican was in fact much more moderate and circumspect in its view than either Fr. Barduzzi or the numerous and very vocal Italian Catholic associations 'interested in the Holy Places'.[82]

The Vatican's interest in Palestine was restricted to the troubled question of access to the Holy Places for Latin Christians. When, as a result of an outburst of fisticuffs between Catholics and Orthodox in the Church of the Nativity, Bethlehem in January 1928, the British administration banned five Italian monks from the Church, the Italian press was quick to champion the cause of its co-nationals against British 'injustice'.[83] This policy was continued over the much wider question of the composition of the international commission to adjudicate disputes over the Holy Places; Italy supported Vatican objections to the proposed appointment of an American, Protestant chairman to the commission.[84] When the British invited the Latin countries to work out an alternative solution, the project was doomed by Italo-French rivalry. Very probably this was what the British were both hoping and expecting, since it prevented either power from gaining a foothold in the Palestinian mandate. In the circumstances the Vatican could hardly have been very impressed with the effectiveness of Italian diplomatic help.

The troubled affairs of Malta, on which Mussolini had designs as an 'Italian' island, also offered, so it seemed, an opportunity for Italy to exploit its Vatican connections. In the 1920s, Fascist Italy nurtured vague aspirations towards the 'return' of Malta, and another historically Italian island, Corsica, to the *patria*, aspirations which in the 1930s broadened into the policy that, 'The Mediterranean is an Italian lake.' At this stage, with no chance of wresting the strategically vital island fortress from British control, Italian policy was limited to preserving its interests and influence there. In 1927, after his Constitutional Party had won a majority in the general election and he had been appointed the Prime Minister of Malta, Lord Strickland, a half-Maltese, half-British aristocrat abolished the use of Italian as an official language. Whilst the vast majority of the population only spoke Maltese, and the colonial authorities were not unnaturally

[80] Rhodes, *The Vatican in the Age of the Dictators*, p. 67.
[81] De Felice, *Storia degli ebrei*, p. 129.   [82] Ibid., p. 130.
[83] Rhodes, *The Vatican in the Age of the Dictators*, p. 65.
[84] D.D.I., 7, Vol. VIII, p. 212, no. 163.

promoting the use of English, the Italian language (a relic of Malta's medieval connections with Sicily) was still spoken by the business and professional classes and was vigorously defended by the pro-Italian Nationalist Party.

As was usually the case when Italian interests were threatened, the Italian Nationalist newspaper, *La Tribuna*, leapt into the fray: with the approval of Mussolini, the editor launched a bitter attack on Strickland and his anti-Italian policy, and Palazzo Chigi backed this up with protest notes to the British Government.[85] There seemed for a time to be a convergence of interests between the Vatican and Italy over Malta, for Strickland also managed to offend the Church. Since his election he had allowed himself to become involved in a bitter dispute with the ecclesiastical authorities on the island and since one of the points at issue was the question of the deportation of an Italian friar, the Italians waded in on the Vatican side.[86] But this Italo-Vatican convergence did not last long; as the dispute hardened, the Bishops of Malta threatened to excommunicate anyone who voted for Lord Strickland in future elections.[87]

The significance of this development, and the resulting fall of Lord Strickland's Government, was not lost on the Italians; it provided a sobering reminder that the Church, which had played such an important part in the overwhelming victory of Fascism in the 1929 'Plebiscite', could also be a powerfully dangerous enemy in an election.[88] By the summer of 1931, under the influence of the crisis in its own relations with the Vatican, the Italian Government had changed sides in the Maltese dispute, and Grandi was enthusiastically recommending the British Government to take a tough line with the Vatican.[89] Regardless of this peculiarly ironical twist to the Maltese affair, it is difficult to see how Mussolini imagined that Italy was going to profit from it. Whilst Anglo-Vatican relations did go through a difficult period as a result of the dispute over Malta, it is inconceivable that the Vatican would have allowed itself to become identified with Italian interests there; the Holy See could not afford to jeopardise its long-term relations with the British Empire in whose dominions, protectorates and colonial territories there were very substantial numbers of Catholics.

THE MINORITIES PROBLEM AND YUGOSLAVIA

The other major geographical area in which Palazzo Chigi hoped that Italian foreign policy would be able to benefit from the Vatican connection was the Adriatic: here, despite Italian complaints about a 'Mutilated Victory', the Versailles Peace Settlement had fulfilled the most important

[85] E. M. Robertson, *Mussolini as Empire-Builder*, pp. 18–19. [86] Ibid.
[87] Ibid. [88] Ibid.
[89] P.R.O., F.O. 371 C.3914, Graham to Henderson, 8 June 1931.

of Italy's war aims and nearly all her irredentist aspirations as laid down in the Treaty of London of May 1915. The defensible frontiers which Italy had so long desired were now provided by a new boundary running along the Brenner, down the watersheds of the Carinthian and Julian Alps, and into the Adriatic, thus bringing within the Kingdom of Italy all those parts of the former Habsburg Empire – Trento and the South Tyrol, Venezia Tridentina, Gorizia, Trieste, Istria and various islands and cities of Dalmatia (Venezia Giulia) – in which large numbers of Italians lived. But as was so often the case with the Versailles Peace Settlement, Italian national self-determination was achieved at the expense of the national rights of others; two large minority groups – 250,000 Germans in Venezia Tridentina and 500,000 Slavs (mostly Slovenes) in Venezia Giulia – ended up inside Italy's new borders.[90] Outside stood the newly created 'Kingdom of the Serbs, Croats and Slovenes' – Yugoslavia – which repeatedly denounced Italy's aggressively nationalist repression of the Slav minority, and also served to bar the way to further Italian expansion in the Adriatic area. It was the hope and expectation of the Regime that the Vatican would be able to help in its twin aims of 'Italianising' the Slavs and the Germans in the border areas, and of undermining its troublesome Adriatic neighbour.

The German and Slav minorities got their first taste of the Fascist policy of forcible 'Italianisation' with the violent occupation by the Fascist squads of Trento in 1921 and Trieste in 1922. The 'Italianisation' policy imposed by the Regime from 1923 onwards was a clear breach of the spirit of the League of Nations Covenant, but Italy was able to pursue the policy without interference because as a 'Great Power' she was exempt from the provisions of the Minorities Treaty of 1919 and from the scrutiny of the League's Minorities Commission.[91] Between 1923 and 1927, a series of Royal Decree Laws sought to extirpate the minority cultures through the abolition of the teaching of the German and Slav languages in the schools, the dismissal of teachers who opposed this measure, the closure of German and Slav newspapers and the Italianisation of geographical and family names.[92] Whilst the opposition of the German minority to this policy was fairly passive and ineffectual, Slav resistance was obstinate, tenacious and frequently violent – after the Communists, the Slav terrorists were the largest single group to be dealt with by the Tribunale Speciale in its seventeen-year existence.[93]

In the forefront of both German and Slav resistance to the 'Italianisation' policy were the clergy. According to one of the leading authorities on the minorities question:

[90] The figures for the German and Slav minorities are those given in Wiskemann, *Europe of the Dictators*, p. 267.   [91] Ibid., p. 48.
[92] Rusinow, *Italy's Austrian Heritage*, p. 194.   [93] Dal Pont, *Aula IV*, p. 17.

The favourite target of Fascist abuse before 1922, the priest, remained the heart of Slav resistance to Fascism until the War, his traditional leadership and patriotic role reinforced by the Regime's suppression of every other form of normal, secular political life and the intimidation or physical removal from the area of alternative cadres, of the Slav intelligentsia and middle class.[94]

This was also a true, but to a lesser extent, of the German clergy of the South Tyrol who, like their Slav brethren, by the continued use of the minority language in preaching, religious instruction classes, in those services requiring the use of the vernacular – like Baptism (and in the case of the Slav clergy, the use of the Old Slavonic liturgy), and in parochial notices and bulletins helped to preserve the separate cultural identity of their parishioners. Some of the Slav clergy in particular also preserved links with the 'motherland' across the border, with minority political organisations, and there were allegations, admittedly never substantiated, that some priests even had contacts with terrorist groups.[95]

The 'Italianisation' policy, and the clergy's opposition to it, presented the ecclesiastical authorities with a serious problem. The Vatican was willing to meet reasonable demands, like the adjustment of diocesan boundaries to fit the new national ones as it had done in 1925 when it set up the Diocese of Fiume and separated the non-Italian parts of the Diocese of Bressanone (Brixen) to form the new Diocese of Innsbruck, and as it was to do in 1932 when it set up the Diocese of Zara as laid down by Article 16 of the Concordat. It even accepted rather less reasonable government measures like the expulsion of non-Italian religious communities from the border areas,[96] but it was not prepared to condone attempts virtually to suppress the use of the Slav and German languages in the life of the Church in those areas. On several occasions before 1929, the Vatican protested to Mussolini through Tacchi-Venturi about the Ministry of Education's policy of progressively eliminating the teaching of religion in the pupils' mother tongue, and also about attempts by the police to prevent such instruction in the priest's own home.[97]

The Vatican was not helped in its stand by the attitude of some of the local bishops; whereas those of the ethnic minorities like Sedej of Gorizia could be expected to defend their clergy come what may, Italians like Endrici of Trento or Pederzolli of Pola and Parenzo (Istria) fell over backwards to please the authorities.[98] When *La Tribuna* sounded off against the Slav and German clergy and suggested that they be replaced by

[94] Rusinow, *Italy's Austrian Heritage*, p. 202.
[95] Binchy, *Church and State*, p. 565 n. 2.
[96] Reut-Nicolussi, *The Tyrol under the Axe of Fascism*, p. 232, gives an account of the expulsion of German nuns from the Tyrol.
[97] See the letter of Tacchi-Venturi to Mussolini of 1 December 1929, in Margiotta-Broglio, *L'Italia e la Santa Sede*, pp. 472–4, and the letter of Tacchi-Venturi to Mussolini in A.C.S., S.P.D., C.R. 88W/R 'Tacchi-Venturi', sf. 1924–37, 11 February 1927.
[98] Binchy, *Church and State*, pp. 561–4.

Italians,[99] *L'Osservatore Romano* was quick to reply, re-asserting the time-hallowed custom of the Western Church of ministering to the faithful in their mother tongue and defending the rights of the minority clergy.[100]

But it cannot be said that the Church was very successful in defending the rights of the Slav and German minorities in the long term; indeed the Pope himself admitted as much publicly. In 1928, *Der Reichspost* of Vienna published the report of an audience Pius XI had granted to the Austrian Cardinal Pfiffl during which he said, 'Tell your flock that the Pope has done what he could (for the Germans in the South Tyrol) but that he is not free.'[101] During the course of the negotiations for the Lateran Pacts, Borgoncini-Duca made an equally candid admission of the Vatican's helplessness in the matter when he demanded of Barone the insertion into the Concordat of clauses providing that religious instruction classes in the State Schools should be in the pupils' mother tongue, arguing that this was necessary in order to prove to the world that the Holy See had done all it could to protect the interests of Italy's Slav and German minorities.[102] Borgoncini-Duca was no more successful than Tacchi-Venturi had been; Barone flatly rejected the proposed clause, and another which would have made it possible to 'import' priests from Austria and Yugoslavia in order to make up for a lack of German and Slav-speaking priests in the border areas.[103]

All that the Vatican was left with was a vague commitment to '...religious services in the language of the faithful according to the rules of the Church'.[104] As a result, religious instruction in the primary and secondary schools continued to be given in Italian, and those parents who wanted their children instructed in their mother tongue were obliged to send them to additional classes conducted by the priest outside of school hours. In addition, Article 22 of the Concordat insisted that anyone who held an ecclesiastical benefice (i.e., parish priests and bishops) in Italy had to be an Italian citizen and had to speak Italian, thus barring the path of promotion to those Slav and German priests who did not.[105] It would be fair to say that this was the one and only area of the Concordat in which the Church had had to make substantial concessions and where, conversely, Mussolini had achieved a real victory.

Mussolini's victory and the Church's defeat was seized on by the foreign press, though they undoubtedly exaggerated the extent of that defeat. *Le Popolaire* of Paris, for example, claimed that the Vatican had been forced to concede a veto power to the Italian Government over episcopal

[99] *La Tribuna*, 21 August 1927.
[100] *L'Osservatore Romano*, 22 August 1927.
[101] As quoted in Binchy, *Church and State*, p. 545.
[102] Biggini, *Storia Inedita della Conciliazione*, p. 191.   [103] Ibid.
[104] See Article 22 of the Concordat in Appendix II.   [105] Ibid.

nominations in the border areas, when in fact such a power had long been exercised prior to 1929 by Italian and Habsburg Governments alike.[106] The French paper could be forgiven for this slip, since the same mistake was also made by a leading contemporary authority on the question.[107] Another exaggeration was the claim that 'Signor Mussolini has succeeded in forcing the German priests of those dioceses to support their new fatherland in their sermons. What will Catholic Austria think of this?'[108] As we shall see, Catholic Austria never ceased to express its concern for the situation in the South Tyrol, much to Mussolini's annoyance, but neither the German nor the Slav clergy for that matter could be induced to support the Fascist list in the Plebiscite of 1929 from the pulpit, even if some felt obliged to vote for it at the polls. The minority clergy expressed no joy for the *Conciliazione*, and their leaders, Muntschleichner and Sedej, managed to avoid all references to it in their communications to the clergy.

Many minority clergy felt that the *Conciliazione* was yet another blow to their cause, but, contrary to their expectations, the Vatican did not abandon them in their battles with the authorities – and it goes without saying that by far the largest number of priests in trouble with the authorities in this period came from the border areas. In November and December 1930, Borgoncini-Duca protested to the Italian Government about the arbitrary treatment of six priests from the Diocese of Gorizia, who, having fallen foul of the authorities, were placed under house arrest and eventually sent into internal exile whithout reference to their bishop, contrary to the provisions of Article 19 of the Concordat.[109] When the matter was raised in Parliament, in an atmosphere already highly charged by the murder of an Italian teacher by Slav terrorists, Arpinati warned that if the ecclesiastical authorities did not bring the anti-Italian clergy to heel, the Government would take drastic measures.[110] Arpinati's statement elicited a strong protest from *L'Osservatore Romano*, but Borgoncini-Duca failed to obtain satisfaction in the matter.

The Gorizia affair was only the tip of the iceberg, the Prefects' reports for 1929–32 clearly indicate their continuing preoccupation in this period with the activities of the minority clergy, the Slavs in particular: in report after report, the Prefect of Gorizia complained that 'The clergy are actively hostile to the Italian State',[111] and the reports of the Prefect of Pola and Trieste tell much the same story.[112] The Prefect of Bolzano wrote in the

---

[106] Missiroli, *Date a Cesare*, p. 32.   [107] Binchy, *Church and State*, p. 560.

[108] As quoted in Missiroli, *Date a Cesare*, p. 32.

[109] D.D.I., 7, Vol. IX (proofs), p. 703, no. 476.

[110] *Atti*, 1930, Vol. III, Camera, S.H. 23, 26 November 1930.

[111] See his reports for September 1930 and June and December 1929 in A.C.S., D.G.P.S., G.I., b. 93, 'Trimestrali'.

[112] A.C.S., S.P.D., P.N.F., S.P.P., b. 15, 'Pola', report of 9 February 1931, and A.C.S., F.C., Serie IV, 'Vescovi', b. 137, 'Trieste e Capodistria'.

same vein about the activities of the German-speaking clergy, informing his superiors that despite a slight but short-lived improvement brought about by the news of the *Conciliazione*, the parochial clergy of his province continued to maintain '... an attitude of reserve and hostility towards the Italian State'.[113] The more realistic of the Prefects of these provinces realised that there could be no easy, short-term solution to the problem – as the Prefect of Trieste admitted in his report of 26 October 1931, 'The Slav clergy cannot be transferred *en masse*, and in any case, they would be very difficult to replace'.[114] The Vatican would never have countenanced such a step, as the reactions of *L'Osservatore Romano* to previous suggestions of this kind demonstrate.

On the other hand, the removal of those bishops belonging to the ethnic minorities and their replacement by prelates of unimpeachably patriotic sentiments could reasonably be expected to yield results, and this was the policy pursued by the Fascist authorities. Here the Vatican was in a weaker position given the Government's 'veto' power over episcopal nominations, nevertheless it did not give in easily to Fascist demands. In 1928, on the eve of the *Conciliazione*, the Italian Government rejected the Vatican's German-speaking nominee for the vacant Bishopric of Bressanone and urged instead the appointment of an Italian, Mons. Beltrami.[115] The Vatican fought a long rear-guard action and it eventually managed to persuade the Italians to accept their original candidate, Mons. Geisler, in late 1930,[116] this success being largely due to the rapprochement between Austria and Italy arrived at in February 1930, a development which was greatly welcomed in the Vatican.[117] On the other hand, the Vatican was clearly defeated in the battle over the Prince-Archbishopric of Gorizia where the episcopal throne was occupied by the most intransigent and immovable of the Slav bishops, Mons. Francesco Sedej. In January 1926, Rocco, as Minister responsible for Affari di Culto, had written to Sedej complaining of the support which he had given to those of his clergy in trouble with the police for 'propaganda anti-nazionale', and had threatened him with '... measures which the Government would be obliged by law to take against him'.[118] This warning did not frighten Sedej who continued to defend his clergy. To add insult to injury, he refused to attend the handing-over ceremony of his reconstructed cathedral, badly damaged in the fighting between the Italians and the Austrians during the First World War.[119]

---

[113] A.C.S., D.G.P.S., G.I., b. 94, 'Trimestrali', 'Bolzano', report for the second quarter of 1929.
[114] A.C.S., S.P.D., P.N.F., S.P.P., b. 27, 'Trieste', report of 26 October 1931.
[115] The long tortuous battle over this appointment is fully documented in A.C.S., F.C., Serie IV, 'Vescovi', b. 127, 'Bressanone'.
[116] Ibid.   [117] Kent, *The Pope and the Duce*, p. 107.
[118] A.C.S., F.C., Serie IV, 'Vescovi', b. 88, 'Gorizia', letter of Rocco to Sedej of 3 January 1926.
[119] Ibid., letter of the Federale of Gorizia to the Prefect, 31 October 1926.

By late 1930, as a result of the incidents already recounted, complaints from the Prefect and Federale of Gorizia had reached such a pitch that the Ministry of Foreign Affairs instructed De Vecchi to press strongly at the Vatican for the removal of Sedej, unless there was a dramatic change in his attitude.[120] The Vatican at first resisted this demand, but when Sedej made a solemn, public reaffirmation of his policy, and that of the Vatican, that school-children should receive religious instruction in their native language, the pressure from the Government became so great that the Vatican eventually yielded and in October 1931 Borgoncini-Duca informed De Vecchi that Sedej's retirement had been arranged.[121] Finding a suitable replacement was not so easy, as the three-year tenure of Mons. Sirotti as Apostolic Administrator bears out: only in 1934 did the Vatican find a permanent replacement for Sedej who was acceptable to the Italian Government – Mons. Margotti, whose zeal in the cause of 'Italianisation' was soon to be rewarded by the conferment of a Royal decoration.[122]

Sirotti's tenure as Apostolic Administrator also demonstrates that even when the Regime did succeed in obtaining the appointment of an Italian bishop, this did not always guarantee the implementation of a pro-Italian policy by the local ecclesiastical authorities, and even less an improvement in the behaviour of the clergy.[123] Not all Italian bishops abandoned their clergy to the tender mercies of the Fascists; Mons. Luigi Fogar, who was hailed as 'Fascist bishop' on his appointment to Trieste in 1923, stood by his clergy and ended up being vilified by the local press and hounded from his see in 1934.[124] But with his replacement Fascist policy had achieved success, all of the bishoprics in the border areas were now in the hands of reliable and compliant tools of the 'Italianisation' policy. While the Slav clergy in particular continued to defy the authorities, their resistance became less and less effective; only Italy's defeat in the Second World War saved the minority cultures from extinction.[125] If there was precious little the Vatican could do to help the German and Slav minorities before 1929, after the signing of the Concordat it was completely impotent, indeed one is forced to the conclusion that as a result of the *Conciliazione* the Vatican

---

[120] Ibid., see the letters from De Vecchi to Rocco of 28 August 1930 and 30 September 1930 regarding the pressure he put on the Vatican to remove Sedej.

[121] Ibid.

[122] According to Binchy, *Church and State*, p. 556: 'In October of 1936 Mgr. Margotti received the Order of SS. Maurice and Lazarus from the King of Italy: the official press remarked at the time that few recipients of the high honour had earned it so well.' Sedej, on the other hand, was even refused a state pension on his retirement!

[123] Ibid., p. 566.

[124] Ibid., pp. 566–7.

[125] Most of Italy's First World War gains in Gorizia, Istria and Dalmatia were transferred to Yugoslavia by the terms of the Peace Treaty of 1947 – thus removing the Slav minority from within Italy's borders, and after 1945 the 'Italianisation' policy was abandoned in the South Tyrol and the German minority was given guarantees respecting its language and culture.

became a wholly unwilling but nevertheless extremely useful partner in the Fascist Regime's first venture in applied racialism.

Inevitably, the Regime's 'Italianisation' policy provoked a barrage of criticism from neighbouring countries, Austria, Bavaria and Yugoslavia. After the *Conciliazione* Mussolini clearly expected that the Vatican would silence any Catholic newspapers in these countries which indulged in such criticism. He was mistaken. When the frequent criticisms of Fascist policy towards the German minority by the Bavarian newspaper *Germania* stung Mussolini into protesting at the Vatican, he got a sympathetic reception but ultimately no satisfaction of his demands. As the Italian Consul-General in Munich explained to Grandi in February 1930, these protests were to no avail because the Papal Nuncio to Bavaria, Mons. Vassallo de Torregrossa, was '...a dyed-in-the-wool supporter of Sturzo', who had not hesitated to criticise publicly the way in which Italy had implemented the Concordat, and the way that the Regime had treated the Catholic youth organisations.[126] The Consul-General went on to say that there was little hope that he could persuade the Nuncio to exercise a restraining influence on the Bavarian Catholic press because Mons. Torregrossa had consistently shown sympathy for the Germans of the South Tyrol.[127] Despite the vulnerability of the Nuncio's position, the Vatican appears to have been unable or unwilling to force him or *Germania* into line, and the latter continued to thunder against Italy's policy in the South Tyrol until it was closed down by the Nazis in 1934.

Another foreign newspaper which incurred Mussolini's wrath was the Catholic Slovene daily *Slovenec* of Lublyana against whose violently anti-Italian attitudes he protested to Borgoncini-Duca in September 1930.[128] In his reply the Nuncio to Italy limited himself to informing Mussolini that he had asked the Nuncio in Belgrade, Mons. Pellegrinetti, to look into the matter and to see what could be done.[129] This could hardly have brought much comfort to Mussolini since he was well aware that Mons. Pellegrinetti had not previously shown willingness to help further Italian interests in Yugoslavia.[130] And so, as usual, nothing was done.

Overall Vatican policy towards Yugoslavia in the 1920s and 1930s was a great disappointment to the Italians, and one made all the more bitter by the fact that in neighbouring Albania, which was already an informal Italian protectorate, the Italians had helped the Vatican in its negotiations for a Concordat.[131] As well as being a member of the French-dominated 'Little Entente', Yugoslavia was the chief foreign critic of the 'Italianisation' policy and the major obstacle to further Italian expansion in the Adriatic.

[126] *D.D.I.*, 7, Vol. VIII, p. 392, no. 378.   [127] Ibid.
[128] Ibid., Vol. IX (proofs), p. 335, no. 246.   [129] Ibid., p. 340, no. 245.
[130] See the report on Mons. Pellegrinetti in ibid., Vol. VIII, p. 260, no. 251.
[131] P.R.O., F.O. 371, C. 1344/1344/90, report of the British Minister to the Vatican, September 1929.

It was thus an essential element of Italian foreign policy at this time that Yugoslavia be kept weak, or better still encouraged to split into its original component parts – Serbia, Croatia, Slovenia and Montenegro – so that she would present less of a threat in the Adriatic and offer less resistance to Italy's treatment of the Croat and Slovene minoritories. In pursuit of this policy, Mussolini harboured the Croatian separatist leader, Anton Pavelitch, and provided for the training of members of his Croatian Fascist/terrorist organisation 'Ustachi', a useful card in the struggle against the Serbian-dominated Government of Belgrade.

Given the attachment of the bulk of the Serbs to the Orthodox Church, the Italians counted on the diffidence of the Vatican towards the Belgrade Government and expected it to be sympathetic towards the separatist tendencies of the Croats and Slovenes, the majority of whom were Catholics. On the contrary, as the Italian Minister in Belgrade revealed to Grandi, '...the Vatican is using its enormous moral and religious influence to bolster up a state, the Kingdom of Yugoslavia, which is engaged in an underhand campaign against us and our interests'.[132] As Galli also pointed out, the result of the Vatican's policy had been that instead of supporting the Croatian Nationalists '...the Croatian higher clergy have come out openly in the favour of the Belgrade Government, and against Croatian nationalism', and Galli further claimed that the explanation for the Vatican's benevolent attitude towards the Belgrade Government '...is to be found in its hopes for an eventual union between the Serbian Orthodox Church and Rome'.[133]

Reunion with the Eastern Churches had certainly been one of Pius XI's most fervent ambitions ever since his Polish experience[134] and may well have been a secondary consideration in the Vatican's assessment of the situation in Yugoslavia, but in the end its policy there was determined by more immediate and realistic considerations, the need to maintain good relations with those in power and the possibility of concluding a concordat with them. As we have seen, the reign of Pius XI might almost be called the 'Age of Concordats', since Vatican diplomats became almost obsessed with them, believing that the concordat was the only way of guaranteeing the rights of the Church, particularly in the new states. Yugoslavia was no exception: here the Vatican was anxious to obtain juridical guarantees for what was in fact a Catholic numerical majority.[135]

When in 1930 the attitude of the Croatian clergy appeared to have changed drastically, as the result of a dispute between Archbishop Bauer of Zagreb and the Yugoslavian Minister of Religious Affairs, the Italian

---

[132] *D.D.I.*, 7, Vol. VIII, p. 260, no. 251.   [133] Ibid.
[134] See Falconi, *The Popes in the Twentieth Century*, p. 177.
[135] See Rhodes, *The Vatican in the Age of the Dictators*, pp. 157–60, for an account of the political battle over the Concordat.

Foreign Ministry was interested to know how this would affect the attitude of the Holy See, and De Vecchi was accordingly instructed to take soundings on the matter in the Vatican.[136] He reported back that the Secretariat of State was being extremely careful, not to say cagey, in the matter and that though it was publicly supporting the stand taken by Mons. Bauer, in private it was encouraging the fresh approaches being made by the Yugoslavs for a concordat.[137] Matters came to a head at the end of January 1931 when Bauer was reconciled with the Belgrade Government. As proof of his re-established loyalty, Bauer published a pastoral message to his fellow bishops and to the whole Croat and Slovene clergy calling for prayers and masses to be offered on behalf of their 'persecuted brethren' in Italy.[138] The Italians were predictably furious,[139] though the reaction of the Fascist press was strangely muted – *La Tribuna*, the nationalist watch-dog, did not comment until 10 March, and the rest of the Italian press was virtually silent.[140] The explanation for this untypical display of Fascist 'phlegm' in the face of the Yugoslav provocation is to be found in the tone and content of the *La Tribuna* article which suggests that Mussolini was expecting a repudiation of Bauer by the Vatican. But it did not come, and *L'Osservatore Romano* was obliged to maintain an embarrassed silence throughout the affair. The Vatican's attitude deeply angered Mussolini,[141] and contributed in no small way to the rapid deterioration in Italo-Vatican relations during the Spring of 1931.[142]

Though hopes of a concordat came to nothing thanks to the opposition of the Orthodox Church, the Vatican's policy towards Yugoslavia remained substantially unchanged, and not in the least helpful to Italian interests; so much so that in July 1931, Bauer once more snatched the headlines in Italy with a call on behalf of the Croatian and Slovene hierarchies for prayers in aid of the persecuted brethren in Italy.[143]

Mussolini's failed attempt to use the Vatican as an 'instrumentum regni',

[136] *D.D.I.*, 7, Vol. VIII, p. 442, no. 380.
[137] Ibid., p. 463, no. 396.
[138] Binchy, *Church and State*, p. 564.
[139] P.R.O., F.O. 371, C. 1550/1550/22, annual report of the Ambassador to the Holy See, 19 February 1932.
[140] *Il Popolo d'Italia* and *Il Corriere della Sera*, for example, restricted their coverage of the affair to reproducing the *La Tribuna* article.
[141] Tamaro, *Venti anni di Storia*, Vol. II, p. 441.
[142] Kent, *The Pope and the Duce*, p. 118, sees the Bauer incident as being virtually the catalyst of the 1931 crisis: 'In pledging his loyalty to Yugoslavia, and thereby choosing sides in the Italo-Yugoslav dispute, Archbishop Bauer brought down the wrath of the Italian Fascists on the Italian Church...The pastoral of the Archbishop of Zagreb seems to have been the incident which sparked off the Fascist attack on the Church in 1931, as the press attacks dated from the day after the pastoral was issued.' In fact the press attacks did not really start until the middle of March, and, as Tamaro, *Venti anni di Storia*, Vol. II, p. 442, points out, whilst the Yugoslav problem was important, '...the conflict with the Vatican would appear to have been the result of a combination of many different factors'.
[143] See *La Gioventù Fascista*, 14 July 1931.

as an auxiliary in the service of Italian foreign policy, was the result of a profound misunderstanding of the Vatican and of the motives and mentality of those who ruled it. Such a mistake on the part of an instinctive and lifelong anti-clerical is entirely understandable. But he was encouraged in his mistaken belief by two men who should have known better, his Catholic brother Arnaldo and the Clerico-Fascist Martire, whose re-evocation of the Giobertian idea of the civilising, Catholicising mission of Italy undoubtedly fostered the illusion that the Church would be happy to play a subordinate role in a new Italian, Fascist 'Roman' Empire, if only out of gratitude for the *Conciliazione*. Mussolini made the same mistake as some of his left-wing foreign critics, like the French newspaper *L'Oeuvre* which declared that 'there was an Italian pope, but now Mussolini has made the Pope an Italian'.[144] This was based on the cynical assumption that because the vast majority of the men in the Vatican, from the Pope downwards, were Italians,[145] as a result of the *Conciliazione*, they would betray their sacred duty to the universal, international mission of the Catholic Church, and use the diplomatic resources of the Vatican to further Mussolini's schemes for the greater glory of the *patria* – just as Paulucci, Under-Secretary-General of the League of Nations, happily subordinated his loyalty to that international organisation to the service of his own country. Men such as Ratti, Gasparri and Pizzardo were indeed Italians, and like Pius IX they were patriotic ones at that, but they were also Catholic priests who had dedicated themselves to serving the interests of the Catholic Church throughout the world. Faced with the dilemma of serving the Church or Italy, again like Pius IX they had no hesitation in choosing the former. This precluded them from favouring Italian interests over those of say France, Britain or Yugoslavia. Even in the case of the Slavs and Germans *inside* Italy they cannot be said to have allowed their national feelings to influence their policy: if that policy was in the end a failure it was for quite other reasons.

Like other contemporary authors writing about the *Conciliazione*, Palmiro Togliatti predicted Mussolini's attempts to exploit the Vatican connection for diplomatic purposes, he also forecast their inevitable failure:

[The Fascists]...are hoping to obtain certain advantages in the international sphere, advantages which will be useful to them in their efforts to realise the imperialistic ambitions of the Italian bourgeoisie. But these advantages will not be very great nor of long duration, because the Church will go to any lengths to preserve its universal character.[146]

Togliatti had understood what Mussolini seemed incapable of understand-

---

[144] As quoted in Missiroli, *Date a Cesare*, p. 32.
[145] In 1928, out of a total of ninety leading officials in the *Curia Romana* only *six* were not Italians and out of twenty-two Papal Nuncios only *one* was a non-Italian. Figures calculated from the *Almanacco Italiano*, 1928, pp. 233–9.
[146] *Stato Operaio*, February 1929, 'La fine della Questione Romana'.

ing, that the Vatican would take the utmost care and go to any lengths to preserve its universal character, to prevent its reputation for neutrality and impartiality in international affairs being compromised by Italian diplomatic manoeuvres. By 1931 he seems to have learnt his lesson. But the lesson was a painful one, leaving Mussolini with a deep sense of disappointment and disillusionment which contributed in no small way to the bitterness of the 1931 crisis.

CHAPTER 5

The Catholic offensive: Catholic Action and the Regime, 1929–31

Throughout the negotiations for the Lateran Pacts and during the three-year period that followed, relations between the Church and the Regime were ultimately determined by one central problem – Catholic Action and its youth organisations. As we have already seen, the Pope's decision to seek a general settlement of outstanding disputes between the Holy See and Italy was strongly motivated by the imperative need to safeguard the future of the Catholic organisations during the period of 'fascistisation', and this thorny question nearly shipwrecked the negotiations for the Lateran Pacts on more than one occasion. The Pope finally obtained the juridical guarantee of Catholic Action's future in Article 43 of the Concordat,[1] and armed with this 'licence' he embarked on a campaign to expand the activities and influence of Catholic Action in Italian society. Mussolini, however, having made this paper concession in order to obtain the rest of the Lateran 'package', was equally determined that Article 43 should not be exploited in this way, that the Catholics should not use it to provide immunity for their aggressive, expansionist activities. In consequence, the history of Church and State relations in Italy in this period is in large part a history of the struggle between the Pope and the Duce over Catholic Action.

THE CHRISTIAN RESTORATION OF SOCIETY

For Pius XI, the *Conciliazione* of 1929 marked both an end and a beginning. The end lay in the Treaty, which had reconciled the Holy See and Italy and thus resolved the 'Roman Question', and the beginning was to be found in the Concordat, which set down a new pattern of relations between the Church and the Italian State, and, in a broader sense, the relations between the Church and Italian society. For the Concordat had brought about the restoration of vital ecclesiastical powers and privileges

---

[1] For an analysis of the juridical implications of Article 43 see Beccaria, 'L'Azione Cattolica e la norma concordataria'.

which Pius XI hoped would provide the basis for a '...Christian restoration of society', as La Civiltà Cattolica described it:[2] the Christian reconquest of an Italian society which had for so long been steeped in the anti-Catholic, anti-clerical values of Liberalism, and had more recently been polluted by the pagan elements of Fascism. In the process of restoring the dominance of Catholic values in every aspect of Italian life, the Church's chief instrument was to be Catholic Action, now legally recognised by the Concordat.

The Christian restoration involved not only the usual aspects of public morality such as the anti-blasphemy campaign and the crusades against immoral films, plays and books, but also the battle against Protestant propaganda and proselytism, and the revival or reinforcement of Catholic influence in the educational, youth and labour fields – areas in which the Catholic movement had had a strong presence until the 'demolitions of Fascism'. It was through the influence exercised by Catholic cadres in these fields in particular that the Pope and Catholic Action hoped to Catholicise and clericalise the Fascist Regime.[3]

Whether, as one historian has suggested, Catholic Action intended to use these cadres '...to create its own ruling class which could eventually become the successors of Fascism at a social and political level'[4] is rather more debatable. There is certainly no evidence to suggest that Pius XI had a medium-or even long-term vision that included the collapse of Fascism, least of all in 1929 when the 'Plebiscite' had confirmed and reinforced the solidity of Mussolini's Regime: the most that he could hope for was a 'partnership' between Fascists and Catholics, the two most vital and dynamic forces in the 'new' Italy. But Fascism sought no partners, and given the strong influence of the popolari inside Catholic Action, Mussolini and his followers were bound to regard the emerging cadres of that organisation with great suspicion, seeing in them a threat to the authority and survival of the Regime.

After the violence and 'demolitions' of the previous six or seven years, Article 43 now seemed to give Catholic Action the chance to develop freely without fear of further Fascist harassment. Certainly, both the leaders and the rank and file of Catholic Action believed this, and they were strongly encouraged to believe it by the Pope; in a speech he made to the Uomini Cattolici just before the signing of the Pacts he urged them to '...double your membership: strengthen the Christian army, quantitively and quali-tively', and in its report on the speech the Bollettino Ufficiale stressed that this appeal was addressed to all branches and all members of Catholic Action.[5] The response to the appeal as far as the recruitment of new

[2] La Civiltà Cattolica, 6 April 1929, 'Preparazione Elettorale'.
[3] Scoppola, La Chiesa e il Fascismo, p. 255.
[4] De Felice IV, p. 248.   [5] Bollettino Ufficiale, 1 January 1929, p. 2.

members was concerned was for some time rather slow and patchy, except, that is, for the youth organisations of Catholic Action whose phenomenal growth in this period is discussed elsewhere. Dissatisfied with the results of the first appeal, Catholic Action issued another in mid-May 1929, but without any more success.[6] By the end of the year, the Giunta Centrale was plainly becoming impatient, and as a desperate measure Mons. Pizzardo proposed that they take over such essentially religious organisations as the Confraternities, Sodalities, the Legion of Mary and other pious lay associations in order to fill out the ranks of Catholic Action.[7] The proposal was never implemented, presumably because Article 29 of the Concordat forbade any change in the status or purpose of these bodies.[8]

The failure of the Catholic organisations to grow as fast as the Pope and their leaders desired, and especially the slow growth of the key adult organisation, the Uomini Cattolici, which had only just over 100,000 members in the whole of Italy,[9] began to provoke a serious crisis of confidence amongst the leaders of Catholic Action during the Summer of 1930. Extreme dissatisfaction with the recruiting figures was voiced at the summit meeting of the Catholic organisations, the Convegno dei Consigli Superiori dell'Azione Cattolica, and many speakers expressed particular unease about the fact that in many parishes in the poor dioceses of the South support for Catholic Action was either minimal or non-existent.[10] Following the meeting, Raimondo Manzini, the editor of *L'Avvenire*, brought the debate out into the open by publishing a distinctly depressing article on the subject in his newspaper.[11] Both the Vatican newspaper and the journal of Catholic Action rushed to reply in order to calm Catholic anxieties.[12] But the debate continued, and one police informer alleged that so serious was the crisis inside the Catholic movement that the Giunta Centrale cancelled the annual, national conference, the Settimana Sociale, in order to avoid further damaging controversy.[13]

There were many different reasons for the slow response to the Catholic

[6] Ibid., 15 May 1929, 'Atti della Giunta Centrale dell'A.C.I.'.
[7] A.C.S., D.G.P.S., G.I., b. 146, 'Azione Cattolica', sf. 2, anon. report on a meeting of the Giunta Centrale of 1 January 1930, p. 9.
[8] Ibid., the informant makes the point that Article 29 of the Concordat '...has very clearly laid down the rule that the aims and objectives of the confraternities may not be changed in any way'.
[9] *Annali dell'Italia Cattolica*, 1931, p. 85.
[10] A.C.S., D.G.P.S., G.I., b. 146, 'Azione Cattolica', sf. 2, anon. report (almost certainly by the author of the report of 1 January 1930) 2 October 1930.
[11] See his editorial in *L'Avvenire*, 3 August, 1930.
[12] See, for example, *L'Osservatore Romano*, 6 August 1930.
[13] A.C.S., D.G.P.S., G.I., b. 146, 'Azione Cattolica', sf. 2, anon. report of 2 October 1930. The *Annali dell'Italia Cattolica* 1931, p. 387, gives as the reason for cancelling the 1930 Settimana Sociale the need to commit all resources and efforts to the National Eucharistic Congress which was to be held in September at Loreto. This does not sound very convincing, and the tone of the 1931 *Annali* is less than jubilatory.

Action recruiting campaign. As far as the South was concerned, it has already been seen that the Catholic movement here was always very weak due to the general social, economic and political backwardness of the Mezzogiorno, and throughout Italy many bishops remained intensely suspicious of lay initiatives and jealous of the power of the lay leaders of Catholic Action. They, therefore, did little to encourage the development of the movement in their dioceses, despite repeated appeals from the Vatican.[14] The failure to arouse greater enthusiasm for Catholic Action amongst adult Catholics can also be explained by an insidious combination of factors; on the one hand many Catholics were inclined to feel that since the *Conciliazione* had 'given back God to Italy and Italy back to God', Catholic Action no longer served a useful function, a view that was naturally supported by Fascist propaganda.[15] On the other hand, many were discouraged from joining Catholic organisations by the intense police surveillance of Catholic Action during the second half of 1929 and the early months of 1930.[16] Towards the end of 1930, however, it became evident that the membership of Catholic Action was now beginning to grow steadily.[17] This picture was confirmed in 1931: in January of that year the *Bollettino Ufficiale* announced that in Pavia, not a particularly 'Catholic' area, the membership of Catholic Action had risen from 9,000 to 11,000,[18] and in March it reported a similar success in Padua where it was claimed that membership of the Catholic organisations had jumped from 45,355 to 55,773 in the same period.[19] At the end of 1930, the membership figures for the whole of Catholic Action touched the one million mark for the first time in several years.[20] Only the crisis of 1931 halted this expansion, and then but temporarily.

CATHOLIC ACTION ON THE MARCH

Secure in the knowledge that its activities were formally sanctioned by the Concordat, Catholic Action embarked upon its mission to re-Christianise Italian society. The result was a massive increase in its activities on all fronts in the months following the signing of the Pacts. This dangerous

[14] A.C.S., D.G.P.S., G.I., b. 146, 'Azione Cattolica', sf. 2, anon. report of 1 January 1930. This is also borne out by the reports on the activities of the diocesan *giunte* in the *Bollettino Ufficiale* for the period, where the South is disproportionately less represented than northern or central Italy.

[15] See, for example, Mussolini's speech of 13 May 1929 in which he rejects the need for Catholic Action; in *O.O.*, Vol. XXIV, p. 89.

[16] See below, pp. 124–7, and also the protest letter of Gasparri to De Vecchi in *D.D.I.*, 7, Vol. VIII, p. 296, no. 284.

[17] *Annali dell'Italia Cattolica*, 1931, pp. 285–7.

[18] *Bollettino Ufficiale*, 15 January 1931, p. 75.

[19] Ibid., 1 March 1931.

[20] Calculated from the membership figures for the branches of Catholic Action to be found in *Annali dell'Italia Cattolica*, 1931.

development in the Catholic world did not go unnoticed by the authorities; from about the middle of 1929 the Prefects of the Catholic provinces in particular began to report intensified activity on the part of the Catholic organisations, which continued for the rest of the year.[21] Nor does there appear to have been any slackening off in activity in 1930, as this extract from the report of the Prefect of Udine for the second half of that year demonstrates: 'The diocesan boards of Catholic Action are still carrying out an intensive programme of activities.'[22] Needless to say, all this activity brought Catholic Action into contact, and very often conflict, with the State authorities and the organisations of Fascism at every level, giving rise to serious apprehension on their part.

Apart from the spiritual formation of its members and their education in Catholic Social Teaching, Catholic Action's most persistent activity was its crusade 'for public morality' aimed at eliminating immoral films, plays, cabarets and books, as well as public dances and female athletics. This campaign had been running for a number of years prior to 1929 under the aegis of a special secretariat of Catholic Action presided over by Camillo Corsanego, the former president of the male Catholic youth organisation.[23] The public morality campaign was carried on by means of exhortations in the pages of *L'Osservatore Romano*, the *Bollettino Ufficiale* and the diocesan publications of Catholic Action, through public meetings and through the individual efforts of the parochial branches of the Catholic organisations.[24] Catholic Action was also responsible at a diocesan and parochial level for the campaign against blasphemy: no less a person than Mussolini was the national president of The National Anti-Blasphemy Committee, which must have caused not a little embarrassment in the Vatican and much hilarity in Fascist circles since Mussolini was notoriously prone to blasphemy himself![25] In addition to the campaigning at a local level, representations on these issues were made at the highest levels by the Clerico-Fascist parliamentarians,[26] by Padre Tacchi-Venturi[27] and even

---

[21] Scoppola, *La Chiesa e il Fascismo*, pp. 241–51, which reproduces all the Prefects' quarterly reports.

[22] A.C.S., D.G.P.S., G.I., b. 94, 'Udine', report for third quarter. See also 'Pistoia' in the same *busta*.

[23] *Bollettino Ufficiale*, 19 July 1924, 'Atti della Giunta Centrale dell'A.C.I.'.

[24] Catholic complaints over abuses and demands for government action were often coupled with praise of measures already taken. See the *Bolletino Ufficiale*'s lavish praise for the introduction of regulations for female teachers' dress in the issue of 1 April 1929; also reports of complaints against 'Lo Sport femminile' and against books placed on the Index, yet still for sale, at the Fascist publishing house Littorio in A.C.S., D.G.P.S., G.I., b. 146, 'Azione Cattolica', sf. 2, of 11 October 1929 and March 1930.

[25] The 1 January 1929 issue of the *Bollettino Ufficiale* urged members of Catholic Action to co-operate faithfully with the National Campaign against Blasphemy.

[26] *Il Popolo d'Italia*, 25 March 1929, 'Vita Parlamentare', which reports the exchanges between Cavazzoni and other Clerico-Fascist Senators and Arpinati over the Government's tutelage of public morals.

[27] A.C.S., S.P.D., C.R. 88W/R, 'Tacchi-Venturi', letter to Mussolini of 3 February 1929.

by the Pope, who on more than one occasion complained publicly about the spread of pornography, immoral stage shows, the failure to observe the Sabbath and other moral evils, especially in 'his' own city of Rome.[28]

Another important activity of Catholic Action in this period was the campaign it waged against the Protestant denominations, a campaign which generated much friction between the Church and the Regime. Indeed, in a telegram sent to the Italian embassies abroad on 29 May 1931, at the height of the crisis of that year, Mussolini claimed that the Church's presumptuous and exaggerated complaints against the activities of the Protestant Churches was the main cause of the conflict.[29] In the telegram he accused the Church of seeking '...the suppression of Protestant propaganda and of freedom of worship'.[30] Whilst it was nonsense to suggest that this was the main issue at stake in 1931, Mussolini's description of the Church's aim was not far wrong. After the *Conciliazione*, the Vatican expected the active support of the Regime in the restriction, if not the total suppression, of Protestant propaganda and proselytism, and through the organisations of Catholic Action it brought pressure to bear at both a central and provincial government level to this end.

It has been seen how Mussolini sought to calm fears that the secular character of the State was being abandoned by introducing the law on the *culti amessi*, and roughly a year later, a similar law was introduced to regulate the affairs of Italy's 40,000-strong community of Jews who had also expressed apprehensions about the implications of the Lateran Pacts.[31] The law on the *culti amessi* was especially necessary in order to reassure the religious minorities that the *Conciliazione* would not affect their freedom and their rights.[32] A great deal of anxiety was generated by the fact that Article 1 of the Treaty re-affirmed the first part of Article 1 of the 'Statuto', which proclaimed that Catholicism was the sole religion of the State, but did not mention the second part, which stated that other religions were tolerated by the law.[33] Rocco went out of his way to stress that religious freedom would be maintained in Italy,[34] and in his address to the 'summit

---

[28] *Discorsi*, Vol. II, p. 237, 'Al Collegio Cardinalizio', 24 December 1929; ibid., p. 371, 'Ai Consigli Superiori dell'A.C.I.', 28 June 1930; ibid, p. 379, 'Allocuzione Concistoriale, Indicatam Ante', 30 June 1930; and ibid., p. 487, 'Ai Quaresimalisti e Parroci di Roma', 16 February 1931.

[29] *D.D.I.*, 7, Vol. X (proofs), T.S.S.O.R., 29 May 1931.

[30] Ibid.

[31] For details of the law, and reactions to it among the Jewish community, see De Felice, *Storia degli ebrei*, pp. 118–20.

[32] For the reactions of the Protestants to the *Conciliazione* see Piacentini, *I Culti Amessi*, p. 33; for those of the Jewish community see De Felice, *Storia degli ebrei*, pp. 110–13.

[33] Piacentini, *I Culti Amessi*, p. 32. For the text of Article 1 of the Statuto see *Manuale dei Senatori del Regno*, pp. 1–10.

[34] According to Piacentini, *I Culti Amessi*, p. 33, Rocco called the Moderator of Waldensian Church to a special meeting at the beginning of March 1929, to assure him that the position of the Protestant Churches would not be adversely affected by the *Conciliazione*.

meeting' of the national and local leaders of the movement and the officials of the Regime, in September 1929, Mussolini assured his audience that 'We have recognised the pre-eminent role which the Catholic Church plays in the religious life of the Italian people...but it goes without saying, that this does not mean that the other denominations which hitherto have been tolerated must from now be persecuted, suppressed or even harassed.'[35] The easy passage of the *culti amessi* bill, which alone of the implementation legislation was approved without a single contrary vote, seemed a good augury for the future.

The presence of the Clerico-Fascists in Parliament, however, ensured that there was a strong expression of Catholic views on the subject; Egilberto Martire, for example, made it clear that he did not approve of the purpose of the bill[36] and the participation of two other Clerico-Fascists, Aristide Carapelle and Ernesto Vassallo, at the committee stage of the bill meant that the report back to the Chamber contained strong criticisms of the proselytising methods of the Protestants, together with an ominous warning that the Government would take action against any 'excesses'.[37] But anti-Protestantism was no monopoly of the Clerico-Fascists; the editor of *Fides*, the leading journal in the crusade against the Protestants, was Igino Giordani, the former *popolare* activist and author of the famous anti-Fascist and anti-Clerico-Fascist pamphlet, *La Rivolta Cattolica*.[38] Protestant propaganda and proselytism was a concern of the whole Catholic movement, and as such a high priority on Catholic Action's list of evils to be eradicated from Italian society.

From the moment that the bill on the *culti ammesi* was announced, the Church made its displeasure clear; the Pope especially attacked the change in the status of the Protestant churches from *culti tollerati* (tolerated cults) which, whilst it involved some State intervention and regulation of their affairs, also meant official, legal recognition.[39] But in the Church's eyes the most dangerous part of the new law was Article 5: 'There is complete freedom of discussion as far as religious matters are concerned.'[40] This word-for-word reproduction of Article 2 of the Law of Guarantees cut the ground from under the feet of those Catholics who had imagined that with the signing of the Pacts, and the consequent abrogation of the Law of Guarantees, the propaganda and proselytising activities of the Protestants could be controlled by the somewhat ambiguous clauses of the 'Statuto',

[35] For the text of Mussolini's speech, see *O.O.*, Vol. XXI, p. 14.
[36] *Atti*, 1929, Vol. I, Camera, Discussioni, p. 119.
[37] Ibid., p. 98.
[38] But according to Riccardi, *Roma 'Città Sacra'?*, p. 85: 'The journal *Fides* directed by Igino Giordani, though involved in polemics with the Protestants, never descended to the level of other, more scandalous publications.'
[39] See Pius XI's letter to Cardinal Gasparri, in *L'Osservatore Romano*, 6 June 1929.
[40] For the text of the law see *Gazzetta Ufficiale*, Vol. I, 1929, pp. 197–200.

and in particular by Article 28, which stated that, 'Bibles, missals and prayer books may not be printed without the prior approval of the bishop.'[41] Despite this defeat, the Church continued to pursue its crusade against the Protestants.

In the three years following the *Conciliazione*, the Catholic observers became convinced that the proselytising activities of the Protestants were on the increase, and that they were also bearing greater fruit,[42] a view which is borne out by Protestant sources.[43] Naturally, the Catholics ascribed this increase to the permissive atmosphere created by the law on the *culti amessi*, and De Vecchi agreed with them. In a report to Grandi of early 1931, De Vecchi warned that 'As a result of reports from a number of bishops, the Holy See has expressed serious apprehension about the revival of the Protestant movement which has become stronger in Italy, thanks to the provisions of the law on the "permitted cults".'[44]

In the face of this mounting threat, the Church took counter measures: already, in January 1929, the Giunta Centrale of Catholic Action had issued fresh directives to the diocesan *giunte* on the need to intensify resistance to Protestant propaganda, and throughout the period regular meetings were held at this level to brief militants on their role in the battle.[45] As well as holding lectures and seminars aimed at exposing the fallacy of Protestant teaching, Catholic Action organisations took the lead in making complaints to the police against the activities of the Protestant Churches.

The response of the authorities to this kind of Catholic pressure varied throughout the country; in many cases the Prefect or police chief firmly ignored Catholic complaints against Protestant activities,[46] some Prefects warned Catholic priests who preached violently against the Protestants and they forbade Catholic counter-propaganda and demonstrations – these measures later being endorsed by the Ministry of the Interior.[47] On the other

[41] *Manuale dei Senatori del Regno*, p. 1, text of the *Statuto*.

[42] Giordani, *I Protestanti alla conquista d'Italia*, pp. 9–10.

[43] A.C.S., D.G.P.S., G.I., b. 105, 'Firenze', 'Propaganda Evangelica' (henceforth 'P.E.'), report of police spy of 4 June 1931 on the national synod of the Wesleyan Methodist Church.

[44] *D.D.I.*, 7, Vol. IX (proofs), p. 45, no. 113. It is indicative of the Vatican's growing concern about the Protestant threat in Rome that in August 1930 it appointed Mons. Marchetti-Sevaggiani as head of the Opera per la Preservazione della Fede...per Roma, the Vatican organisation responsible for combating Protestantism and building new churches in the capital; see Giordani, *I Protestani alla conquista d'Italia*, p. 12.

[45] *Bolletino Ufficiale*, 15 January 1929, 'Atti della Giunta Centrale', p. 61.

[46] A.C.S., D.G.P.S., G.I., b. 123, 'Potenza', 'P.E.', report of 31 March 1930.

[47] Ibid., b. 108, 'Genova', 'P.E.', report of the Prefect to Michaele Bianchi, Under-Secretary of State, dated 25 May 1929: 'A local Catholic club has asked permission to distribute flysheets protesting against Protestant propaganda. I have refused to give permission and I am informing you of my decision in case this proves to be more than an isolated incident and you therefore wish to issue general instructions.' Bianchi approved his decision, and Bianchi's successor, Arpinati, was equally firm in his refusal to countenance such Catholic reactions.

hand, the police frequently accepted and pursued Catholic complaints,[48] the explanation being found at the level of common ignorance and prejudice – most Italians shared the anti-Protestant feelings and suspicions disseminated by the Catholic Church.

At another level, the police were very suspicious of Protestant activity because of the foreign origins and connections of most of their Church organisations. The Anglican, German Lutheran and Presbyterian Churches, serving as they did mainly foreign residents, were treated with diplomatic respect, but the Baptists, the Methodists, the Seventh-Day Adventists and the Y.M.C.A. were the subject of frequent investigations.[49] The Catholics naturally exploited the authorities' anxiety about the foreign links of these Churches in their campaign of harassment against the Protestants.[50]

Another factor influencing police attitudes towards the Protestants was the masonic and anti-Fascist past of some of the Protestant clergy. The close links between the Craft and Protestantism in Italy were first investigated by the police in 1927; though they found little evidence of continuing masonic activity within the Churches, they did identify a significant number of Protestant pastors as masons,[51] and even several anti-Fascists and other political suspects.[52] All this was grist to the Catholic mill, giving some credence to their view of the Protestants as politically unreliable and anti-nazionale.

Despite this convergence of interest between Catholics and Fascists, there was no uniformly hostile government policy towards the Protestants. Indeed, the Church was far from satisfied with government policy towards the Protestants, as the Pope explained during his meeting with Mussolini in 1932.[53] As for the Protestants, whilst conditions were difficult for them during the Fascist period, they could have been worse off – as is proved by the systematic harassment of the religious minorities under the Christian Democratic Regime in the 1940s and 1950s.[54]

---

[48] Ibid., b. 95, 'Agrigento', 'P.E.', report of 28 August 1931; b. 113, 'Massina', 'P.E.', report of 1 July 1928; and b. 120, 'Palermo', 'P.E.', report of 17 February 1929.

[49] Ibid., b. 155, 'P.E.', sf. 2, contains several reports which demonstrate the intense interest of the Political Police in the 'Mother' Churches of these organisations. See also b. 105, 'Firenze', 'P.E.', report of 2 March 1929 which describes the Salvation Army as 'a masonic organisation of British origins'.

[50] Ibid., b. 132, 'Roma', 'P.E.', report of 9 July 1926.

[51] Ibid., b. 155, 'P.E.', sf. 2, contains a report from the Ufficio Provinciale di Investigazion Politica listing twelve Protestant pastors as masons of grade 33 (the highest grade).

[52] Ibid., b. 96, 'Avellino', 'P.E.', report of 21 August 1931; b. 102, 'Chieti', 'P.E.', report of 14 June 1927, 'Como', 'P.E.', report of 8 September 1927 and 'Cossenza', 'P.E.', report of 29 January 1932; b. 120, 'Parma', 'P.E.', report of 15 August 1928; b. 121, 'Perugia', 'P.E.', report of 27 January 1928; b. 147, 'Chiesa Avventista', report of 12 March 1929. See also A.C.S., C.P.C., under the following names: C. Ferreri, E. Maschellano, V. Melodia, C. Pristunzani and E. Sbaffi.

[53] Corsetti, 'Dalla preconciliazione ai Patti del Laterano', p. 222, 'Colloquio col Papa, ore 11 del giorno 11th Febb. 1932, in Vaticano'.

[54] Bucci, *Chiesa e Stato*.

As if Catholic Action did not have enough to do with its existing responsiblities, in March 1929 the Pope gave it the new task of assisting in the implementation of the Concordat.[55] The Giunta Centrale took up this additional responsibility with enthusiasm; throughout 1929 and to a lesser extent 1930, numerous lectures at diocesan level and national conferences and study weeks were devoted to the theme of the *Conciliazione*, and in particular to the role which Catholic Action was expected to play in implementation of the Pacts.[56] But when Catholic Action offered the Government its co-operation, 'For the full and integral application of the Concordat', the Fascist press replied that the Government needed no help from anyone to apply one of the fundamental laws of the State.[57] In fact, it is difficult to see what help Catholic Action could have given the Government in the implementation of the Concordat, apart from the provision of training facilities for those teachers who were to give the religious instruction lessons which now became obligatory in secondary schools.[58]

Unable to give any other really practical help, Catholic Action took upon itself the task of *monitoring* the implementation of the Pacts instead. Like *L'Osservatore Romano*, the official organ of Catholic Action carried regular progress reports on the process of implementing the Pacts, reports which frequently contained advice on, and even criticism of, the measures adopted by the Government.[59] Catholic Action was particularly interested in the implementation of Article 11 of the Concordat, dealing with the observance of Sundays and Holy-days of Obligation, since it had been conducting a crusade for *il riposo festivo*, that is for the observance of Sunday as a day of rest, for many years.[60] Thus while *L'Osservatore Romano* greeted with satisfaction the establishment of the feast of St Joseph the Worker (19 March) as a national holiday, as laid down by Article 11, Catholic Action did not let up in its campaign to enforce observance of the Sabbath.[61] Local committees of Catholic Action were very active in this period, denouncing both traders and employers who violated Sunday working laws, and the Government authorities who condoned those violations.

[55] *Discorsi*, Vol. II, p. 43, 'Agli Uomini Cattolici di Roma', 19 March 1929.
[56] See reports on such meetings in A.C.S., D.G.P.S., G.I., b. 91, 'G.I.A.C.', sf. 3, 'Settimana Sociale di Stresa', 29 August 1929, and ibid., b. 146, 'Azione Cattolica', sf. 3, 'Parma', 16 June 1930, and 'Velletri', 6–9 August 1930.
[57] *Italy Today*, September 1931, F. L. Ferrari, 'The Vatican and the Fascist State'.
[58] See the report on the course established at the Catholic University of Milan for this purpose in A.C.S., D.G.P.S., G.I., b. 146, 'Azione Cattolica', sf. 2, 6 February 1930.
[59] See *L'Osservatore Romano* and the *Bollettino Ufficiale* for the period February–June 1929.
[60] The *Bollettino Ufficiale* had a special column devoted to the *riposo festivo* campaign, see, for example, the issue of 1 January 1929. See also *L'Osservatore Romano*, 15 March 1929, 'Disposizioni del Prefetto di Lucca per il riposo festivo'.
[61] *L'Osservatore Romano*, 2 March 1929, 'Festa religiosa e di San Giuseppe'.

Catholic Action also supported the Vatican in its effort to bring about the abolition as a national holiday of the 20th of September, the commemoration of the fall of Papal Rome to Italian troops in 1870. In his diplomatic note of September 1929, Borgoncini-Duca argued that the abolition of the feast, and the transfer of the national holiday to the 11th of February, was a natural and logical consequence of the resolution of the 'Roman Question', even if Italy had made no actual commitment to such a course of action in any of the Lateran Treaties.[62] The Papal Nuncio also stressed the strong personal feelings of the Pope, who was offended and distressed by the continued celebration of the feast.[63] The youth sections of Catholic Action were particularly agitated by the question, and the G.C.I. federation of the diocese of Como, a notoriously *popolare* stronghold, actually sent a telegram to the Pope expressing its sympathy and condolence for the continued celebration of the hateful event.[64] Mussolini's reaction to this 'impertinence' was swift and crushing; he ordered the Prefect of Como to dissolve the youth federation, and when its journal, *L'Idea Giovanile*, protested, it too was closed down.[65] The Como incident, and the flurry of diplomatic exchanges which followed it, contributed to the steadily deteriorating relations between the Church and the Regime in the Autumn of 1929.

With or without the help of Catholic Action, the Vatican eventually managed to persuade Mussolini to remove the 20th of September from the calendar of Italian national holidays. Whereas in September 1929 Mussolini had written to Borgoncini-Duca that 'I have no intention of changing the law',[66] a year later he had changed his mind and did exactly what he was asked by the Vatican, that is he abolished the feast of the 20th of September and transferred the national holiday to 11th of February as a commemoration of the *Conciliazione*.[67] He even used the Vatican's own arguments as an explanation for the change, describing the 20th of September as a 'masonic feast'![68] This was hardly a very convincing justification for the loss of an important part of Italy's risorgimental heritage, for the 20th of September had latterly been much more of a national, patriotic celebration of the establishment of Rome as the Capital of Italy rather than a Liberal anti-clerical commemoration of triumph over the Papacy, and Mussolini's decision must therefore have disturbed and distressed many of his followers.

After two years of incessant Catholic complaints over the state of public morality and related matters, and Protestant propaganda and proselytism,

---

[62] *D.D.I.*, 7, Vol. VIII, p. 10, no. 7.   [63] Ibid.
[64] For an account of the Como affair see A.C.S., D.G.P.S., G.I., b. 102, 'Como', 'Fed. Giov. Catt. 1929–30'.   [65] Ibid.
[66] *D.D.I.*, 7, Vol. VIII, p. 6, no. 3.
[67] *Il Lavoro Fascista*, 20 September 1930, 'L'Abolizione della festa del 20th Settembre'.
[68] Ibid.

the Government's patience finally snapped. On 16 February, 1931, in his customary Lenten address to the clergy of Rome, Pius XI once more returned to these themes; the address became a veritable catalogue of complaints about all the evils of Italian society plus a more specific allegation that the Government had failed in its concordatory obligation to preserve the 'sacred character' of Rome.[69]

In the past such complaints had either been dealt with at a diplomatic level, or simply ignored. On this occasion, however, the response was sharp and extremely public. A fortnight after the Pope's speech, in a parliamentary debate on the budget of the Ministry of the Interior, its Under-Secretary, Arpinati, defended his Ministry's record as far as maintenance of public morality was concerned: he rejected the bulk of the Pope's complaints observing that 'Of course, we can never be zealous enough for those who demand perfection.'[70] Arpinati's other sharp comments on the attempts by Clerico-Fascist M.P.s to tell the Government how to run the new film censorship boards and how to interpret the laws on Sunday working[71] should have given ample warning to the Vatican of the changing mood inside the Fascist Government. But the Vatican ignored the warning and chose instead to mount a dignified but wholly ineffective diplomatic protest about the tone of Arpinati's remarks.[72]

CATHOLIC ACTIVITIES IN THE ECONOMIC AND SOCIAL FIELDS

Another cause of considerable friction between the Fascist organisations and Catholic Action in this period were the latter's activities in the economic and social fields, and especially the activities of I.C.A.S. in the area of labour relations. During the early months of 1929, the spokesmen of the Fascist trade unions appeared to have no worries about competition from Catholic Action; on the contrary there were convinced that the *Conciliazione* had finally put the chrism of Catholic approval on the trade union monopoly of the Corporative State. *Il Lavoro Fascista*, the organ of the Fascist trade unions, flattered itself that 'Pius XI would never have recognised the King of Italy if the essential policies of the Regime had been effectively hostile or even neutral towards the Catholic point of view...in fact, Fascist corporativism fits in perfectly with the Catholic concept of social justice.'[73]

During the course of the election campaign for the 'Plebiscite' of March 1929, Clerico-Fascist speakers took the same view: the Hon. Pezzoli, for

[69] *Discorsi*, Vol. II, p. 487, 'Ai Quaresimalisti e Parroci di Roma', 11 February 1929.
[70] *Atti*, 1929–31, Vol. IV, Camera, Discussioni, pp. 4034–5.
[71] Ibid.
[72] See De Vecchi, *Memorie*, 16.
[73] *Il Lavoro Fascista*, 20 February 1929, leading article by Paolo Orano. Most of the other articles cited from this mouthpiece of the Fascist trades unions are by the editor, De Marsanich.

instance, sought to persuade his Catholic audience that the 'Fascist Revolution' had made the Social Teaching of the Church into a living, institutional reality in Italy.[74] But Catholic Action speakers were generally more reserved in their praise of Fascist Corporatism, and one or two individuals were even critical of it: a police report on March 1931 on Federico Alessandrini and Igino Righetti, two of the leaders of F.U.C.I., claimed that they were '... bitterly criticising the Fascist trade union system and praising the former Catholic trade unions'.[75] In fact the official Catholic Action line lay somewhere in between the two extremes and is typified by this statement of its President, Luigi Colombo, at the Settimana Sociale in 1928: 'After fifty years of study, commitment and work, the essence of the great corporative idea has finally been embodied in the laws of the State. As a result, Catholics now have the duty to ensure that its practical application is in keeping with the social principles of the Church.'[76]

Reading between the lines of this extract and the rest of his speech, it is clear that Catholic Action considered the corporative system to be not only incomplete but also imperfect, and that it believed that the process of perfection and completion could only be carried out with Catholic assistance. To this end, in April 1929, the Giunta Centrale of Catholic Action drew up a plan of campaign to be implemented by I.C.A.S. in the labour field, '... with the aim of establishing close collaboration between the institutions of the Corporate State and Catholic Action for the provision of moral and religious support for the workers'.[77]

This uninvited and unwelcome venture into the labour field, so typical of the new-found confidence of Catholic Action, was bound to cause friction with the Fascist unions, but to make matters worse, I.C.A.S. went beyond its brief by issuing advice, information and instructions on a wide variety of social and labour problems. In June 1929, for example, through the medium of the *Bollettino Ufficiale*, I.C.A.S. focussed attention on the problems of the rice fields of North-West Italy, urging an intensification of efforts aimed at '... the elimination of the many moral and health dangers which we have complained about in the past'.[78] Amongst the other problems which received the attention of I.C.A.S. were those of the share-croppers, the spiritual needs of migrants and the operation of the new labour contracts.[79] The instructions which I.C.A.S. gave to its branches on the latter were very precise and specific: they were to monitor the application of the new contracts in order to ensure '... that the spiritual

[74] Ibid., 24 March 1929, 'Il Sindacalismo Fascista e la scuola cristiana, Conference dell'On. Pezzoli alla Sala Borromini'.
[75] A.C.S., D.G.P.S., G.I., b. 155, 'F.U.C.I.', report of 20 April 1931.
[76] Ibid., b. 146, 'Azione Cattolica', sf. 3, report by the Prefect of Milan, 14 September 1928.
[77] *Bollettino Ufficiale*, 15 April 1929, editorial, 'La Nostra Collaborazione'.
[78] Ibid., 1 June 1929, 'L'Assistenza in Risaia', p. 410.
[79] Ibid., 1 February 1931, 'La Adunanza della Giunta Centrale dell'A.C.I.'.

and health needs of the working girls were safe-guarded, and that the Sabbath day was observed'.[80]

The job of monitoring the application of the contracts was entrusted to the *sezioni professionali* whose members were urged to get themselves elected onto trade union committees with appropriate responsibilities wherever possible.[81] And in order to provide a steady stream of properly trained cadres to do this work, in September 1929, I.C.A.S. and the Catholic University of Milan jointly set up a new '...introductory course on the Institutions of the Corporate State';[82] as a basis for this course and a working manual for Catholic militants in the field, the Director of I.C.A.S., Padre Balduzzi, produced a commentary on Fascist labour legislation.[83]

The Fascist response to this rapid development of Catholic activity inside the Corporate State was predictably swift and sharp: on 19 September 1929, *Il Lavoro Fascista*, the official newspaper of the Fascist trade unions, came out with the banner headline: 'Surveillance which we cannot accept.'[84] The headline was a parody of the Pope's recent complaint that Catholic Action was under surveillance, indeed it was clearly intended as an answer to it, for *Il Lavoro Fascista* alleged that a vast campaign of propaganda was being mounted by Catholic Action inside the Fascist trade unions.[85] And of course, that claim was substantially correct. Over the next three weeks, *Il Lavoro Fascista* waged war against Catholic Action and its pretensions in the labour field.

One of the particular targets of its wrath was Padre Balduzzi's little pamphlet: whilst Balduzzi presented a generally positive analysis of the Charter of Labour 1927, he did make one or two serious criticisms of that cornerstone of Fascist labour policy; in particular he condemned the fact that, contrary to the Catholic Social Teaching, the Charter gave a monopoly to the Fascist trade unions, and expressed the hope that it would once more be permissible to organise 'free associations' in the labour field.[86] *Il Lavoro Fascista* rejected this 'heresy' and claimed that Balduzzi's little book was inspired by anti-Fascist sentiments.[87] Furthermore, it accused the leaders of Catholic Action of seeking nothing less than the revival of the system of free trade unions as it had existed under the Liberal Regime, and of using the *sezioni professionali* as a Trojan Horse inside the Fascist unions with the ultimate aim of making them into a rival trade union organisation.[88] De Marsanich, the editor of *Il Lavoro Fascista* probably hit the nail on the head when he wrote: 'Let us not deceive ourselves. Catholic Action does not believe in the vitality of the Corporative system and it is indeed looking to the future.'[89]

[80] Ibid., 1 May 1929, column devoted to I.C.A.S.
[81] Ibid.
[82] *Vita e Pensiero*, September 1929, p. 575.
[83] Balduzzi, *Brevi Note*.
[84] Il Lavoro Fascista, 19 September 1929, 'un controllo che non si può accettare'.
[85] Ibid.
[86] Balduzzi, *Brevi Note*, p. 21.
[87] *Il Lavoro Fascista*, 28 September 1929, 'L'Azione Cattolica e la Carta del lavoro'.
[88] Ibid.
[89] Ibid.

There were indeed men inside Catholic Action who believed that the Regime could not last for ever, and who were therefore preparing, albeit in a general way, for the post-Fascist future; these press polemics put them temporarily on their guard, and in consequence, I.C.A.S. kept a lower profile for the rest of 1929 and throughout 1930. The broadsides of *Il Lavoro Fascista* ended as abruptly as they had begun – as the anti-Catholic polemics of the Fascist press were apt to do – but the question of the *sezioni professionali*, together with the wider question of Catholic Action's attitude to Fascist social and corporative policy, lingered on under the surface, only to re-emerge with explosive force when I.C.A.S. once again came into the public eye, during the celebrations for the fortieth anniversary of Leo XIII's social encyclical *Rerum Novarum* in March 1931.

A LOSING BATTLE – CATHOLIC ACTION AND THE CATHOLIC PRESS

Ever since the mid-1920s, when political divisions in the Catholic camp and problems of a financial nature had led to the closure of a number of Catholic newspapers, Catholic Action had become more and more directly involved in the running of the Catholic press (see Chapter 2, pp. 36–7). Such was its concern with the declining fortunes of the Catholic press, that in 1926 the Giunta Centrale of Catholic Action set up a Secretariat for the Diffusion of the Catholic Press which sought to increase the quality and quantity of Catholic newspapers and promote their circulation amongst the Catholic masses.

At the beginning of 1929, the state of the Catholic press was far from healthy and the situation was to deteriorate further during the course of the year. In the whole of Italy there were ten Catholic dailies, thirty-eight weekly, fortnightly or monthly publications, mostly controlled by the diocesan curia, and thirteen assorted, specialist national journals like the *Bollettino Ufficiale* of Catholic Action itself, the *Rivista del Clero* and *Vita e Pensiero* (both edited by Padre Gemelli of the Catholic University of Milan) and the fortnightly Jesuit journal *La Civiltà Cattolica*.[90] There was also, of course *L'Osservatore Romano* which was directly controlled by the Secretariat of State and which, after 1929, was printed inside the Vatican City. Raimondo Manzini (the editor of *L'Avvenire* and later of *L'Osservatore Romano*) estimated that in 1929 the Catholic press had a readership of 100,000 out of a total circulation of two million, 200,000 for the Italian press;[91] not a very impressive figure, even if one also takes into account the wide circulation of parish news sheets which were often the only reading of the faithful in rural areas.

By the end of 1929, five out of the ten Catholic dailies had ceased to

[90] *Annuario della Stampa Italiana*, 1929, p. 216.
[91] A.C.S., D.G.P.S., G.I., b. 92, 'F.I.U.C.', report on the congress of F.I.U.C., 17 September 1929.

exist. *L'Unità Cattolica* of Florence disappeared with the death of its editor, Ernesto Calligari. *Il Corriere della Sardegna* went under due to the declining fortunes of the De Teulada family who owned it, and the three remaining Clerico-Fascist papers, *Il Momento* of Turin, *Il Corriere della Tre Venezia* and *Il Corriere d'Italia* finally expired after the removal of the Clerico-Fascist Mattei-Gentili from his post at the Ministry of Justice and the consequent withdrawal of Government financial aid. These papers had only managed to survive the never-ending financial difficulties of the Grosolian *Trust* to which they belonged thanks to the subsidies which they earned as journalistic supporters of the Regime.[92] With the signing of the Lateran Pacts, and, even more importantly, the successful outcome of the 'Plebiscite', there was no further need of the Clerico-Fascists or their newspapers. The bitterness of those who were abandoned in this way was voiced by *Il Corriere d'Italia*. In its farewell edition, the Roman paper informed its readers that it had suddenly had its financial support cut off, despite the fact that 'Since the March on Rome, the *Corriere* has supported the Regime with tenacious loyalty.'[93]

The crisis of the Catholic press went further, involving two other dailies, *L'Italia* of Milan and *L'Avvenire* of Bologna. Faced by this situation, the Vatican attempted to save the saveable, which also coincided with Pius XI's longstanding policy of bringing all Catholic lay initiatives and activities under the control of Catholic Action. Whereas the Vatican was happy to let the badly undersubscribed, and somewhat eccentric newspaper *L'Unità Cattolica* follow its owner to the grave,[94] and showed no interest in saving the troublesome and independent Clerico-Fascist organs like *Il Corriere delle Tre Venezia*, *Il Corriere d'Italia* or *Il Momento*,[95] it did support the Milan and Bologna curias in their continuing efforts to prop up *L'Avvenire* and *L'Italia*, which were now placed under the control of the respective *giunta diocesane* of Catholic Action.[96] The replacement of *Il Cittadino* of Genoa, another Clerico-Fascist paper which had ceased publication in 1928, by *Il Nuovo Cittadino* was also carried out under the aegis of the local archbishop and diocesan Catholic Action.[97]

---

[92] Castronovo and Tranfaglia, *La Stamp italiana*, p. 72.
[93] *Il Corriere d'Italia*, 22 September 1929, front page article.
[94] Ballerini, *Il Movimento Cattolico a Firenze*, p. 415.
[95] According to Tramontin, 'Patriarca e cattolici veneziani di fronte al P.P.I.', in *Cattolici, Popolari e Fascisti nel Veneto*, p. 59, the local *curia* refused to have anything to do with the *Corriere* from the moment that it was established in 1926, because of its political alignment with the C.N.I. In his report on the meeting of the Giunta Centrale of Catholic Action of 21 December 1929, the police spy stated that Catholic Action was not anxious to see the re-publication of *Il Corriere d'Italia*, because of its '...irritatingly pro-Fascist tone'.
[96] For the complicated vicissitudes of *L'Avvenire* see Onofrio, *I Giornali bolognesi*, pp. 69–70. For the *L'Italia* rescue operation, see Majo, *La Stampa quotidiana cattolica Milanese*, pp. 27–30.
[97] *Bollettino Ufficiale*, 1 January 1929, p. 25, 'Il Segretariato Diocesano per la Stampa'.

Henceforth the three newspapers followed a new editorial line very similar to that of *L'Osservatore Romano*, though since they were vulnerable to Fascist press censorship, unlike the Vatican paper, they were less outspoken. The other major element in Catholic Action's press policy, the campaign to increase the readership of Catholic newspapers, bore little fruit in this period: despite the authoritative pronouncements of *L'Osservatore Romano* and the *Bollettino Ufficiale* there was no significant increase in circulation, and in consequence *L'Avvenire* continued to need substantial subsidies.[98] Catholic Action's further efforts to found new Catholic newspapers in the South and Sicily also came to nothing.[99]

To add to its other difficulties, during the course of 1929 the Catholic press came under the increasingly repressive surveillance of the Regime, which in 1923 and again in 1928 had equipped the Prefects with more than adequate instruments of press censorship.[100] In his speech to the Chamber of 13 May 1929 Mussolini had proudly declared: '...I have confiscated more Catholic newspapers in the last three months than in the preceding seven years!', and he went on to assure his listeners that, 'Make no mistake about it, Mussolini is kept informed of every parish magazine which is published in Italy.'[101] The Catholic press failed to heed this warning and continued to believe that the *Conciliazione* had opened up a new era of freedom. As a result, the confiscations of various Catholic publications continued throughout the Spring and Summer of 1929: *La Civiltà Cattolica* suffered because of an article by Padre Rosa which criticised Mussolini's religious policy and compared him with Napoleon,[102] the *Rivista del Clero* was suspended for an article discussing the controversial question of education,[103] and a half-dozen broadsheets of Catholic youth organisations were confiscated or suspended for the same reason.[104] In addition, the Government blocked an attempt by the *giunta diocesana* of Turin to inaugurate a replacement for *Il Momento*.[105]

When, in his Allocution of Christmas 1929, the Pope complained that 'The publications of Catholic Action are treated badly, shamefully badly',[106] he received an aggrieved and angry reply from the Italian Government. De Vecchi strongly denied that the Catholic press was being treated badly and he justified the measures taken on the ground that they were necessary in order to put an end to the dangerous activities of a residue of anti-Fascist journalists on the Catholic papers.[107] This kind of

[98] A.C.S., D.G.P.S., G.I., b. 146, 'Azione Cattolica', sf. 2, anon. report of 1 January 1930.
[99] Ibid.
[100] For the text of the 1923 law on the press see *Mediterranean Fascism*, p. 53.
[101] *O.O.*, Vol. XXIV, p. 89.
[102] *D.D.I.*, 7, Vol. VIII, p. 296, no. 284, Gasparri to De Vecchi, 29 December 1929.
[103] Ibid.   [104] Ibid.   [105] Ibid.
[106] *Discorsi*, Vol. II. p. 237, 'Al Collegio Cardinalizio', 24 December 1929.
[107] *D.D.I.*, 7, Vol. VIII, p. 295, no. 280, De Vecchi to Gasparri (no date but presumably between 26 and 28 December 1929).

counter allegation was scarcely credible as an explanation of the majority of confiscations and suspensions, and both sides knew it, but by now it was rapidly becoming the stock response to Vatican complaints.

There were very few police measures against Catholic newspapers in 1930 or 1931, largely because by the end of 1929 the Catholic press had learnt the hard way to be more cautious and circumspect than it had been during the heady months following the *Conciliazione*. The Catholic journalistic voice was to be further weakened during the Fascist period by the closure of yet more Catholic newspapers, leaving *L'Osservatore Romano* virtually alone to face the Fascist press. It therefore seems impossible to escape the conclusion that in its campaign to maintain and even strengthen the Catholic presence in Italian society, Catholic Action had lost the battle as far as the Catholic press was concerned.

CATHOLIC YOUTH AND FASCIST YOUTH, 1929–31

Of all the branches of Catholic Action, the youth organisations gave most concern to the Fascist authorities precisely because it was among the young people that Catholic Action was to have its greatest recruiting success in this period. The figures shown in the table speak for themselves.

Catholic youth organisations

| | G.C.I. (male) | | |
	Probationary members	Full members	Totals
1928	84,647	121,763	206,410
1929	91,291	131,465	222,756
1930	101,346	145,028	246,374
1931	116,264	151,065	267,329[108]

| | G.C.I. (female) | | |
	Leaders and full members	Probationary members	Beginners	Totals
1928	196,832	93,858	103,561	394,251
1930	211,359	97,305	137,630	446,294[109]

[108] Statistics are given in *Annuario LXXVI della Gioventù Cattolica Dell'A.C.I.*, p. XV. Angelo Jervolino, President of G.C.I. between 1928 and 1934, claims in 'Lo Scioglimento dei Circoli' (copy of typescript given to the author by Jervolino in 1975), p. 20: 'We had 370,000 members at that time.' However, the figure quoted in the returns to the police circular on the 1931 dissolution of G.C.I. in A.C.S., D.G.P.S., G.I., bb. 95–124; in A.C.S., S.C.P., Pacco 13; and in A.C.S., S.P.D., C.R. 31252/R. 'Riunioni del Direttoro del P.N.F.', sff. I–II, confirm the earlier statistics.

[109] *Annali dell'Italia Cattolica*, 1931, p. 91.

At the beginning of the Fascist period G.C.I. had had nearly half a million members, but by 1928, Fascist violence and harassment, and especially the dissolution of the Scouts and the sporting organisations, had taken their toll.[110] From 1928 onwards, once their future had been guaranteed by Mussolini, the remaining Catholic youth organisations began to recover, their membership growing steadily until the crisis of 1931. This recovery constituted a serious threat to the Regime's recently acquired hegemony over Italian youth, and it is not surprising, therefore, that the Catholic youth organisations loomed large in the disputes over Catholic Action in 1929, 1930, not to mention 1931.

Fascist observers of the period frequently and loudly complained about the resurgence of the Catholic youth organisations; indeed the chief anxiety of most Prefects, when reporting on the state of Catholic Action in the provinces under their control, was the particularly flourishing condition of its youth wings.[111] The Prefect of Bergamo, for example, in a report to the Ministry of the Interior of July 1929 expressed concern over the rapid growth of G.C.I. in his province – by 2,000 in one year.[112] It was particularly galling to Fascist youth leaders that in some areas the Catholic youth organisations were better equipped to attract new members than was the Balilla, due to the fact that the Church possessed numerous cinemas, theatres and sporting facilities. Thus the Prefect of Ancona complained that G.C.I. in his province was drawing away members of the Fascist youth organisations as a result of facilities provided for it by the *giunta diocesana* of Catholic Action.[113] Naturally enough, when the Catholic youth groups were dissolved by the Regime in the Summer of 1931, local Fascist youth leaders demanded that these facilities be handed over to them.

For the Fascist authorities, one of the most worrying aspects of the growth of the Catholic youth organisations was their activities inside the educational system. At the end of 1928 the authorities were particularly alarmed by G.C.I.'s campaign to attract greater support in the secondary schools: under the dynamic leadership of Francesco Alessandrini, G.C.I. set up a network of special secretariats at a diocesan and parochial level to recruit members in the *licei* or grammar schools. The Direzione Generale of the Police took this new development sufficiently seriously to launch an investigation in December 1928, though the replies to its questionnaire

---

[110] E. Tannenbaum, *Fascism in Italy*, p. 222, where he also says, 'G.C.I., which had been 500,000 strong on the eve of the March on Rome, had declined in numbers to 160,000 by early November 1926 by its own President's admission', citing an interview given by that President to *La Civiltà Cattolica* on 20 November 1926.

[111] For examples of this anxiety see A.C.S., S.P.D., P.N.F., S.P.P., b. 19, 'Treviso', report of 24 October 1930, and also A.C.S., D.G.P.S., G.I., b. 94, report for the first quarter of 1930 for Messina, Reggio Emilia, Udine and Vincenza.

[112] Report of the Prefect of the Province of 6 July 1929 in A.C.S., D.G.P.S., G.I., b. 94.

[113] Ibid., b. 91, 'Ancona', 'Giov. Catt.', report of the Prefect of 25 March 1930: see also ibid., b. 120, Novara, 'A.C.I. 1929–40', report of the Prefect of 8 December 1929.

suggest that the campaign had hardly got off the ground in the majority of provinces.[114]

The ultimate purpose of Alessandrini's efforts was to prepare more members of G.C.I. for entry into F.U.C.I., the Catholic university students' association of which he was a leading member. The membership of F.U.C.I. was small in comparison with that of its Fascist counterpart, the G.U.F.; like other Catholic youth organisations, it had suffered badly during the period of 'the demolitions of Fascism'. As well as being harassed by officials and subjected to squadrist violence in the early and mid-1920s, F.U.C.I. also suffered a crisis in its relations with the Vatican. In 1925, the leaders of the organisation unwisely accepted the advice of the Prefect of Bologna, Bocchini, to place its annual congress under the patronage of the King. The Pope was deeply offended by this 'ghibelline' initiative, and as a result ordered the leaders to resign.[115] In the consequent reshuffle, F.U.C.I. lost the remaining vestiges of democratic organisation, the last wing of Catholic Action to do so. But the new president, Igino Righetti, and the new national chaplain, G. B. Montini, worked miracles to restore the intellectual and spiritual vitality of the organisation, with the result that F.U.C.I. in the late 1920s and early 1930s constituted an obstinate residue of Catholic, intellectual anti-Fascism. Under the leadership of Righetti, and Montini, F.U.C.I. offered to university students an intellectually stimulating atmosphere free from the usual Fascist conformism, and F.U.C.I.'s journals – *Studium* and *Azione Fucina* – reflected the same spirit of freedom; indeed they alone of Catholic publications somehow contrived to avoid offering up the obligatory grain of incense to the Fascist Regime.

F.U.C.I. was still further compromised in the eyes of the Fascist authorities by its continuing, close links with the former leaders of the P.P.I. Many of the leading figures in that Party, Cingolani, Dore, Ferrari, De Gasperi, Migliori, Spataro, etc., were either products of F.U.C.I. training or had taken a benevolent interest in it,[116] and some, like Spataro for example, continued to be associated with it; thus the principles and programme of the Catholic party continued to exert a strong influence on Catholic university students.[117] In consequence of this, F.U.C.I. was inevitably the

---

[114] On 14 December 1928, the D.G.P.S. issued circular no. 442/37820, claiming that '...the leaders of the Catholic youth organisations have decided to intensify their activities in the schools, with the aim of recruiting to their ranks as many pupils as possible, and especially the pupils of the middle schools'. The circular went on to request information on G.C.I. activity in this sphere, and to ask whether teachers were also involved. Out of seventy-six replies, only eleven reported any significant activity directed towards *scuola media* pupils, and only one (Cuneo) reported the involvement of State School teachers, not surprisingly, in view of the pressure brought to bear on them to recruit for the Balilla. For the text of the circular and the replies, see A.C.S., D.G.P.S., G.I., b. 91, 'Circolari'. There were no further inquiries into this matter between 1929 and 1932.

[115] For an account of this episode see Marcucci-Fanello, *Storia della F.U.C.I.*, pp. 113–14.

[116] Ibid., p. 105.

[117] Ibid. A leading member of F.U.C.I. in the 1930s explained the situation in these terms: 'We were regarded with suspicion [by the Fascists], and not without reason because the

object of particular police attention, its conferences and study weeks were always kept under close surveillance, and in some cases banned altogether.[118] Not surprisingly, when Catholic Action began organising nuclei of ex-F.U.C.I. members and other Catholic graduates into a Segretariato di Cultura, the police took the view that it was nothing less than a conspiracy to bring the professions under Catholic control.[119]

Relations between the Catholic and Fascist youth organisations in the period 1929–31 were marked by intense rivalry and friction, which occasionally degenerated into violence on the Fascist side.[120] Amongst both the organisers and members of the Fascist youth formations there was a growing intolerance of their Catholic counterparts which chiefly took the form of declarations of incompatibility between membership of the two organisations, young Fascists who were simultaneously enrolled in the youth groups of Catholic Action being frequently pressurised into abandoning the latter.[121] This practice, and the difficulties placed in the way of young Fascists wanting to attend Mass on Sundays, had become so widespread by early 1930 as to provoke a diplomatic protest on the part of the Vatican, and was one of the major topics of discussion during the visit of P.N.F. leader Turati to the Pope in February of that year.[122] One of the few positive results of the visit was Turati's subsequent policy directive forbidding such practices.[123]

It should be said, however, that such discrimination was not confined to the Fascist side alone: many priests and lay Catholic youth organisers also attempted to discourage their charges from belonging to the Balilla.[124] Adherence to Fascist organisations was already very low amongst members of Catholic Action organisations, and nowhere lower than amongst those who belonged to its youth groups. F.U.C.I. officially disapproved of those

ideas of Sturzo were still a powerful influence among us...we proudly maintained ideals that were not those of Fascism, the universalist ideals of the Church as opposed to the nationalistic ideals of Fascism. The authorities did not look upon us with favour, indeed they barely tolerated us; no Prefect, no mayor nor university rector wanted to have anything to do with us, for fear of offending their superiors.' G. Olivero, 'L'Azione Cattolica e il Fascismo', in *Trent'Anni di Storia Italiana*, p. 178.

[118] Marcucci-Fanello, *Storia della F.U.C.I.*, p. 69.
[119] A.C.S., D.G.P.S., G.I., b. 146, 'Azione Cattolica', report of the Political Police of 14 March 1931. See also Chapter 6, pp. 140–1.
[120] On 8 June 1931, the British Ambassador in Rome wrote to the Foreign Secretary, Henderson, explaining that there had long been trouble between Catholic and Fascist youth groups, citing the incidents which had taken place between members of F.U.C.I. and G.U.F. at the Universities of Turin and Bari. P.R.O., F.O. 371, C. 3908/2810/22, 1931. This is confirmed by other sources.
[121] *D.D.I.*, 7, Vol. VIII, p. 269, no. 284, Gasparri to De Vecchi, late December 1929, lists various incidents of this kind.
[122] Ibid., and the report of Turati to Mussolini on his audience with the Pope as reproduced in De Begnac, *Palazzo Venezia*, p. 700n. XXVIII.
[123] See *Foglio d'Ordini*, no. 69, 'L'Anniversario della Conciliazione'.
[124] A.C.S., D.G.P.S. G.I., b. 120, 'Novara', 'A.C.I.', Prefect's report of 4 December 1929, and ibid., b. 123, 'Ragusa Ass. Giov. Catt.', Prefect's report of 1 June 1931.

of its members who belonged to the G.U.F., and at its September 1929 congress an attempt was made to exclude G.U.F. members altogether, the move being defeated by Righetti and Montini, who managed to win a majority for the official Catholic Action line which decreed that Fascists should only be excluded from national office in Catholic Action organisations.[125] These attempts to exclude Fascists were another sign of the feelings of pride and confidence that permeated the Catholic youth organisations after the *Conciliazione*, feelings which helped to offset the pressures from the Fascist authorities and thus encouraged young people to join Catholic Action youth groups in ever growing numbers. In this period, as indeed during the later years of the Regime, the Catholic youth organisations helped set their members apart from the common, Fascist herd, operating as a kind of quarantine, albeit not entirely effective, against the infectious, undesirable influences of Fascism.

THE FASCIST RESPONSE – CATHOLIC ACTION UNDER SURVEILLANCE

Mussolini's warning, contained in his speech to the Chamber of 13 May 1929, that he would always keep a vigilant eye upon the activities of the Catholic organisations, very quickly proved to be no empty threat. Within a few days of the ratification of the Pacts, in his role as Minister of the Interior, Mussolini issued instructions to the Prefects on how they should interpret and implement Article 43 of the Concordat concerning Catholic Action. Since the circular very effectively sums up the policy adopted by Mussolini and the Regime towards Catholic Action, we shall quote it in full:

> This clause lay down both a guarantee and a limitation. The guarantee lies in the formally recognised right of the organisations affiliated to Catholic Action to live and develop freely inside the national community; the limitation consists of the need to observe an essential, binding pre-condition, that is that their activities should be exclusively outside the sphere of petty politics. Your excellencies will understand that Article 43 of the Concordat must be enforced with great vigilance.[126]

This vigilance soon manifested itself: it came in the form of an investigation by the Carabinieri into the activities of the clergy and of Catholic Action in July 1929.[127]

    This was certainly not the first time that Catholic organisations had been under investigation by the authorities, nor was it to be the last – by the end of 1931 a total of ten separate inquiries had been carried out by the police into the activities of one or more branches of Catholic Action. The earliest police files on Catholic Action date back to 1927 when the Ministry

[125] Marcucci-Fanello, *Storia della F.U.C.I.*, p. 140.
[126] A.C.S., S.P.D., C.R. 6/97R, 'Questione Romana', 16 June 1929.
[127] *D.D.I.*, 7, Vol. VIII, p. 269, no. 284, Gasparri to De Vecchi, late December 1929.

of the Interior first issued instructions to the Prefects to collect data on the numerical strength of the Catholic organisations in their provinces. It also became normal practice in 1927 for the Prefects to seek prior authorisation from Rome for the holding of large Catholic Action gatherings.[128] Then in December 1928, as has been seen, the Ministry of the Interior ordered an investigation into G.C.I.'s campaign to recruit more members in the secondary schools. But the Carabinieri investigations of July 1929 were on an entirely different scale; the circular which was sent out being in effect an extremely comprehensive questionnaire asking for information on, amongst other things, the political activities of the clergy, their work in the Catholic organisations – especially the youth groups – the membership figures for all the Catholic organisations and their activities in the educational sphere.[129]

The most important fact which these and other inquiries inevitably revealed was the continued massive presence of *popolari* amongst both the rank and file and the leadership cadres of Catholic Action.[130] It could hardly have been otherwise; the P.P.I. had been formed in 1919 largely of members of the existing Catholic Action movement, especially in the South,[131] and many continued to work for both organisations until the demise of the Party in 1927. Thereafter they remained inside Catholic Action, without ever abandoning their allegiance to the concept of a democratic, reforming Catholic party, ideals which naturally coloured their approach to activities involving Catholic Social Teaching and relations between the Church and the Regime. The *popolari* in Catholic Action, as one Fascist remarked, '...persist in quite open hostility towards Fascism, despite several explicit or implicit requests from the ecclesiastical authorities that they co-operate, or at least co-exist, with the Regime'.[132] The ecclesiastical authorities were not the only ones to give such advice; Francesco Pacelli, writing in *Vita e Pensiero* in October 1929, warned that '...it is quite clear that anyone who tries to use the organisations of Catholic Action for political purposes is certainly not conforming to the wishes of the Pope'.[133]

These warnings had little effect. The *Conciliazione*, and in particular the juridical recognition of Catholic Action afforded by Article 43 of the Concordat, gave the *popolari* inside the Catholic organisations a false sense

[128] A.C.S., D.G.P.S., G.I., 'Anno 1927', 'Consistenza delle Forze Cattoliche nel Regno al 15 agosto 1927', and ibid., b. 146, 'Azione Cattolica', sf. III.

[129] *D.D.I.*, 7, Vol. VIII, p. 269, no. 284, Gasparri to De Vecchi, late December 1929.

[130] See De Vecchi, *Memorie*, nos. 13, 14 and 15. In these instalments of his memoirs, De Vecchi, without ever specifying which of the branches of the police forces was supplying the information, repeatedly cites police reports for the Summer of 1929, listing *popolari* active at the highest levels of Catholic Action.

[131] Borzomati, *I Giovani Cattolici*, p. 44.

[132] A.C.S., D.G.P.S., G.I., b. 146, 'Azione Cattolica', sf. 2, anon. report of 1 January 1930.

[133] *Vita e Pensiero*, 'L'Opera di Pio XI per la Conciliazione con l'Italia', p. 626.

of security, and the declining presence of the Clerico-Fascists made it more difficult to contain or even to hide their growing influence there and in the Vatican itself. In September 1929, Luigi Colombo resigned as national President of Catholic Action, later justifying his decision on the grounds that he was no longer '...willing to take responsibility for those groups which sought to drag Catholic Action into a political struggle against the Regime'.[134] Colombo may well have had other reasons for resigning, including a desire to devote more time to his legal practice back in Milan, but the reasons which he stated were undoubtedly the most important ones. The exit of this philo-Fascist friend of Pius XI did not, as some Fascist newspapers tried to suggest, result in a fundamental change of policy on the part of Catholic Action, but it did mean that the strongest hand restraining the influence of the *popolari* had been removed.[135] It also had the effect of strengthening still further the joint dominance of Mons. Pizzardo and Count Dalla Torre over Catholic Action: the new national President Augusto Ciriaci had no special relationship with the Pope and earned his living as an employee of the Vatican, running its printing presses.[136]

According to De Vecchi, Mussolini was genuinely angry at the reports which he was now receiving about the activities of the *popolari* inside Catholic Action, and the Italian Ambassador was sent by the Duce to protest to the Pope about these activities.[137] The Pope in his turn was outraged by the fact that the investigations were taking place at all, and his answer to the Italian accusations was to charge the Regime with 'bad faith', with having violated the Concordat.[138] The gist of the Vatican's case, as presented by *L'Osservatore Romano*, was that though Article 218 of the *Legge di Pubblica Sicurezza* did give the police the power to investigate the activities of certain organisations, Catholic Action was not one of them, since Article 217 of the same law expressly defined these organisations as 'political organisations', and, of course, Catholic Action was 'purely religious'.[139]

The Fascist press was not convinced by these arguments and dredged up numerous, plausible quotations from Catholic Action publications to prove that 'Catholic Action does not debar its members from taking part in public life.'[140] Mussolini was determined that the Regime should not be deprived of the means of exercising control over Catholic Action merely because of the wording of a law and on 28 August the Council of Ministers

---

[134] As quoted in Cavazzoni (ed.), *Stefano Cavazzoni*, pp. 232–3.
[135] *Il Lavoro Fascista*, 15 October 1929, 'Il Nuovo Presidente dell'A.C.I.'.
[136] See the anon. report of 20 May 1931, in A.C.S., D.G.P.S., G.I., b. 146, 'Azione Cattolica', sf. II, where the informant illustrates the dominance of Pizzardo and Dalla Torre over Ciriaci.
[137] De Vecchi, *Memorie*, no. 13.   [138] Ibid.
[139] *L'Osservatore Romano*, 22 August 1929.   [140] *Il Popolo D'Italia*, 23 August 1929.

resolved the problem by repealing Article 217 of the Law on Public Security. As the Fascist press now gleefully pointed out,[141] the Vatican had very definitely lost this round of the battle. Its belief that Article 43 of the Concordat gave Catholic Action complete exemption from Italian law had been proved illusory, and it was obliged to advise the officials of Catholic Action that in the event of any future police investigations they were to declare emphatically that Catholic Action was *not* a political organisation, but to furnish the information requested.[142]

The Regime did not reduce the pressure on Catholic Action, even after this clear-cut victory: speaking to the Congress of the Fascist Party on 14 September 1929, Mussolini reminded his audience that he was carefully monitoring the way in which the Pacts were implemented, and in a thinly veiled reference to Catholic Action he declared: '...the Regime has 9,000 watchmen in every corner of Italy, watchmen who are trained to report any violations [of the Concordat] to a very vigilant Government in Rome'.[143] Despite the generally optimistic tenor of his remarks on the state of relations with the Church, including praise of the majority of the clergy, his reference to the Carabinieri (who were probably still collecting information on Catholic Action in the more remote provinces of Italy at that moment) struck home in the Vatican. The Pope himself took up the challenge on the following day. During an audience granted to members of G.C.I., the Pope warned: 'The Pope knows, the young people all know, and it has been admitted by the authorities themselves that the Catholic Youth organisations are under the surveillance of thousands of watchmen'.[144] For good measure he repeated his remarks to a group of chaplains of G.C.I. the next day. Within a few days, *Il Lavoro Fascista* began its campaign against I.C.A.S., and over the next three and a half months there developed what can only be described as a 'creeping' crisis in the relations between the Church and the Fascist Regime.

THE 'CREEPING' CRISIS OF 1929-30

The 'creeping' crisis of 1929–30 bears so much resemblance in its major elements to the more serious conflict of 1931 that it could almost have been a dress rehearsal for it. As in 1931, so in 1929 the central dispute over Catholic Action, over the activities of its youth and labour wings and over the presence of the *popolari*, was conducted both at a diplomatic level and in the press. In reply to the Regime's allegations about the political activities of Catholic Action, in late October 1929 the Vatican delivered

---

[141] *L'Impero*, 26 August 1929, 'L'A.C.I. e la legge di P.S.'.
[142] *Bollettino Ufficiale*, 15 October 1929, 'Atti Ufficiali-Circa le inchieste sulle associazioni cattoliche'.
[143] *O.O.*, Vol. XXIV, p. 135.
[144] *Discorsi*, Vol. II, pp. 164–5, 'Alla Gioventù Cattolica Italiana', 15 September 1929.

a stiff diplomatic protest about police harassment of Catholic organisations and the Catholic press.[145]

Thus began a long exchange of notes and counternotes which went on fruitlessly until 1930. Diplomatic relations were further soured by a series of incidents, such as the arguments over the continued celebration of the 20th of September (see above, p. 113), the publication in November 1929 of M. Missiroli's book *Date a Cesare* – a pungent defence of Mussolini's religious policy – and the unseemly squabble over the granting of a papal dispensation for the mixed marriage of Princess Giovanna of Savoy to King Boris of Bulgaria.[146] Meanwhile, the Fascist newspapers continued to press their charges against Catholic Action: *Il Popolo di Roma*, for example, informed its readers that 'There can be no doubt about it, Catholic youth is a political organisation',[147] and, naturally, *L'Osservatore Romano* rushed to the defence of the Pope's 'favourites' followed by the rest of the Catholic press. Given the number of the Fascist newspapers, and the size of their circulation, not to mention the tight censorship imposed upon their Catholic rivals, the polemics were bound to be an unequal contest.

When Pius XI realised that the Church was fighting a losing battle on both the diplomatic and journalistic fronts, he resorted once more to the weapon which Mussolini feared the most because it got most attention in the foreign press – the public speech. In his Allocution to the College of Cardinals on Christmas Eve 1929, the Pope delivered a stinging attack on the policy of the Regime: 'Catholic Action . . . is not being treated in the way that an explicit article of the Concordat expressly demands, to say that Catholic Action is violating the article by involving itself in politics is quite plainly contrary to the truth, it is nothing less than a slander.'[148] And the Pope went on to make those remarks about the treatment of the Catholic press which have been mentioned earlier, and to attack the proposed erection on the Janiculum Hill of a statue to Anita Garibaldi.[149] This was not a particularly happy note on which to end the first year of the *Conciliazione*, but for the Pope this first year had not been a happy one, on the contrary, it had turned increasingly sour with bitterness and frustration at the disappointing fruits of the great event. Whilst the official organs of the Regime kept silent in order not to give the Pope's remarks a wider circulation than they had already received, Mussolini gave free rein to the more anti-clerical newspapers whose excesses he could conveniently disavow. Thus Settimelli published a satirical commentary on the Pope's

---

[145] *D.D.I.*, 7, Vol. VIII, p. 149, no. 132, De Vecchi to Grandi, 2 November 1929. This contains both the text of the Vatican Note and the text of De Vecchi's reply.
[146] De Vecchi, *Memorie*, no. 14.
[147] *Il Popolo di Roma*, 21 September 1929, leading article on the front page.
[148] *Discorsi*, Vol. II, p. 237, 'Al Collegio Cardinalizio', 24 December 1929.
[149] Ibid.

speech entitled 'Anita sul Gianicolo',[150] and on the diplomatic front De Vecchi sent yet another outraged note of protest to the Vatican.[151]

These disputes cannot be properly understood except in the context of the further steps which the Regime had been taking in 1929 and 1930 to complete the 'fascistisation' of education and youth. In February 1929, primary and secondary school teachers were ordered to swear an oath of loyalty to the Regime, a move that has been interpreted by various authors as an attempt to counteract the increased Catholic influence in education which was expected to follow the introduction of religious instruction in the secondary schools as laid down by the Concordat.[152] A few months later, in September 1929, Mussolini took the opportunity of a general Cabinet reshuffle to replace Pestro Fedele by Balbino Giuliano as Minister of Public Instruction.[153] In addition, the name of that government department was changed to 'Ministry of National Education', a change which signified Fascism's intention to exercise responsibility and control over the whole education and *upbringing* of the Italian child.[154] And to underline this intention, the Balilla organisation was placed under the nominal jurisdiction of the new ministry, the head of the Balilla, Renato Ricci, being nominated Under-Secretary of State for Youth and Physical Education.[155]

Early in 1930, the Fascist Grand Council further decreed that the rectors of universities and the heads of schools should henceforth be chosen from party members of not less than five years standing, and a few weeks later, Giuliano announced that from the beginning of the 1930/1 academic year only state-approved and published textbooks would be used in Italy's schools.[156] In these various, concrete ways Mussolini's Regime renewed its claim to the total monopoly of education and youth. This was a challenge that Pius XI was not slow to take up.

As in 1931, so in 1929, the last act of the crisis opened with the publication at the beginning of January 1930 of a solemn papal encyclical, *Rappresentanti in Terra* (or, in its English version, 'On the Christian Education of Youth').[157] According to De Vecchi, the encyclical burst like a bomb attack upon the policies of the Regime.[158] Why he should have regarded the encyclical as a bomb is hard to imagine; neither its timing nor its content could have come as much of a surprise to Mussolini, for, as De Vecchi himself admits, it had been ready since October of the previous

[150] *L'Impero*, 29 December 1929, 'Anita sul Gianicolo'.
[151] *D.D.I.*, 7, Vol. VIII, p. 291, no. 280, 26 December 1929.
[152] E.g., Tannenbaum, *Fascism in Italy*, p. 184; and Guerri. *Giuseppe Bottai: un fascista critico*, p. 157.
[153] E. Tannenbaum, *Fascism in Italy*, p. 184.   [154] Ibid.
[155] Ibid.   [156] Guerri, *Giuseppe Bottai*, pp. 156–7.
[157] For the text of the encyclical see *The Papal Encyclicals*, ed. Freemantle, p. 226.
[158] De Vecchi, *Memorie*, no. 14.

year.[159] Pius XI had held it in reserve in the hope that the crisis could be resolved by less drastic means, but the Fascist response to his Christmas Allocution convinced him that only the most solemn, public and dogmatic defence of the rights of the Family and the Church against the totalitarian monopoly of the education of the young would suffice to prevent a renewed Fascist assault upon the youth organisations of Catholic Action.

De Vecchi tried very hard to pour oil on troubled waters by claiming that the Vatican was alarmed and upset about the way in which the foreign press was interpreting the encyclical as an attack on the Regime and he attempted to persuade Mussolini that since the majority of educational practices condemned in the encyclical, like co-education and sex education, were not practised in Italy, the document was really directed at other countries.[160] This was quite patently not true; that the encyclical was directed at Fascist Italy is proved by the fact that along with *Non Abbiamo Bisogno*, the encyclical issued during the 1931 crisis, *Rappresentanti in Terra* was the only encyclical in the whole of Pius XI's seventeen-year reign written in Italian and addressed to the Italian bishops.

The core of the encyclical was a reiteration of the prior rights of the Family and the Church over those of the State in the education of youth, rejecting the State's monopoly of education in the wider, Italian sense of the word, i.e., control of all youth organisations and activities.[161] More specifically, the encyclical criticised various aspects of the activities of the Fascist youth organisations, particularly the policy of giving military training to the very young. Here Pius XI condemned the exaggerated nationalism which led to the military training of both young boys and girls, '...contrary to the very instincts of human nature'.[162] In addition, the Pope attacked the Fascist youth organisations for monopolising children's time on Sundays, when they should have been devoting themselves to religious duties and to family life at home.[163] This was clearly a reference to the obstacles which many Balilla officials continued to place in the paths of those children who wished to attend Mass on Sundays. All of this was, of course, cloaked in general and anonymous terms yet their target – the Fascist Regime – was crystal clear as the foreign press so rightly pointed out.

The Italian press, on the other hand, was virtually silent about the encyclical, the only real comment being made by Mussolini himself in *Foglio d'Ordini*.[164] But even this was little more than a ritual reaffirmation of the Fascist State's totalitarian claim to a monopoly of the education of youth. If, as we shall see, Mussolini did little or nothing at this point to bring about

[159] Ibid.
[160] A.C.S., P.C.M., '1930', S.3 10278, 'Enciclica del Santo Padre sulla Cristiana Educazione della Gioventù' (containing De Vecchi's letter to Mussolini).
[161] *The Papal Encyclicals*, ed. Freemantle, p. 226.
[162] Ibid.   [163] Ibid.
[164] *Foglio d'Ordini*, no. 64, 20 January 1930, B. Mussolini, 'Punti Fermi sui Giovani'.

a resolution of the dispute, neither did he risk inflaming it further by more press polemics. By the end of January, therefore, a stalemate had been reached in the dispute between the Church and the Regime, with each side waiting for the other to take the initiative.

But at this time there were still powerful forces at work inside the Regime seeking to ease the tensions. Apart from the indefatigable De Vecchi, there was Mussolini's brother Arnaldo who was undoubtedly responsible for the comparatively moderate line which most of the Fascist press took towards the Pope's encyclical. Most important of all was the Party Secretary, Augusto Turati, for it was he who took the initiative which ended the crisis by seeking an audience with the Pope, despite the opposition of Mussolini.[165]

Whilst we can discount the report of one of the Regime's informers inside the Vatican – no less a person than Mons. Caccia-Dominioni, the papal Maestro di Camera – that the meeting was an unqualified success, Turati's visit to the Pope broke the deadlock between the Vatican and the Regime and dissipated the atmosphere of tension which still prevailed on the eve of the first anniversary of the *Conciliazione*.[166] It is clear from Turati's own report to Mussolini that Pope and party leader could only agree to differ on such fundamental issues as the *raison d'être* of Catholic Action in a Catholic, Fascist State, and the exact division of responsibilities between the Church and the State in the sphere of education, yet agreement was reached on the vexed question of compatibility of membership between the organisations of the Party and those of Catholic Action, Turati agreeing to issue a declaration to the effect that members of Catholic Action could belong to the party organisations and vice-versa.[167]

The Pope and Turati warmed to each other, and the feelings of optimism generated by the meeting were borne out by events in the short term: the first anniversary of the *Conciliazione* was celebrated with great cordiality and festivity on both sides, and when Turati issued his promised party directive, *L'Osservatore Romano* replied in terms which could only be interpreted as a public acceptance and recognition on the part of the Vatican of the totalitarian nature of the Regime.[168] This was in its turn warmly welcomed by the Fascist press, and to seal the reconciliation

---

[165] Attilio Tamaro, who was a very well-informed observer of the Fascist scene, says that Turati did not inform Mussolini of his request for a papal audience until after the Pope had agreed to see him, which may well account for Mussolini's displeasure. He goes on to say that, 'Mussolini did not interfere but merely insisted on being kept informed. However, his estrangement from Turati began to make itself felt more and more': Tamaro, *Venti anni di Storia*, Vol. II, p. 428. De Vecchi, *Memorie*, no. 14, also says that Mussolini tried to prevent the meeting.

[166] De Begnac, *Palazzo Venezia*, p. 700 n. XXVIII. This contains the texts of the reports of both Caccia-Dominioni and Turati.   [167] Ibid.

[168] Bendiscioli, 'I Patti lateranesi', p. 173, says that the *L'Osservatore Romano* article '...could be interpreted as an acceptance by the Church of the totalitarian character of the Fascist State'.

between the Vatican and the Regime, Arnaldo Mussolini pronounced a solemn anathema against 'Fascist' journalists and authors like Mario Missiroli who disturbed the serenity of relations between the Church and the Regime by their writings.[169] The 'doves' were clearly still in control of the Regime's religious policy and apart from a few minor hiccups, the rest of 1930 passed without any incident.

Mussolini's instructions to the Prefects of June 1929 demonstrate that he did not believe that he had entirely resolved the problem of Catholic Action by subscribing to Article 43 of the Concordat. He was clearly expecting trouble because, as he knew only too well, Catholic Action in 1928 was already showing signs of recovery after the 'demolition' of the previous two years. Despite the 'stasis' of Catholic Action, the Catholic organisations were growing and their activities expanding, even if some leading members of those organisations had their doubts about this. It is ironical, therefore, that Raimondo Manzini should have found it necessary to urge members of Catholic Action 'to explore, to invade, and to get the upper hand', for it was exactly these existing tendencies of Catholic Action which created so much alarm in Fascist circles. If relations between the Church and the Regime arrived at a crisis point early in 1931 it was precisely because of the continuing aggressive and expansionist tendencies of Catholic Action, which reached new heights during the celebrations of the fortieth anniversary of *Rerum Novarum* in the Spring of that year.

[169] '...writers who before and after the March on Rome had nothing to do with Fascism, and in fact in some cases, had masonic connections': as quoted in Pellicani, *Il Papa di Tutti*, p. 38. Arnaldo was referring to Missiroli, *Date a Cessare*, and Anon., *Stato Fascista, Chiesa e Scuola*, both of which were apologies for Mussolini's religious policy, and as such were part of Mussolini's tactic of getting others to help in the task of reassuring Fascist followers that he had not sold out to the Church, i.e., *Date a Cesare* contained hitherto unpublished documents relating to the *Conciliazione* which only Mussolini possessed. Arnaldo's strictures about the dubious Fascist faith of these authors is certainly borne out in the case of Missiroli. Lyttleton, *The Seizure of Power*, p. 299, says of him: 'Even Mario Missiroli, one of the leading critics of Fascism up 'till 1924, found a protector in Arpinati. He was the author of the most persuasive eulogy of Mussolini's social and religious policies, although it seems that Mussolini never entirely forgave him for his remarks during the Matteotti Crisis.'

CHAPTER 6

The crisis of 1931

The public harmony between the Vatican and the Regime, which had been re-established by Turati's visit to the Pope in February 1930, lasted for little over a year; in mid-March 1931 the tensions which had been accumulating below the surface broke out in a succession of public disputes, culminating in Mussolini's dissolution of the youth organisations of Catholic Action on 30 May, and the resulting suspension for all practical purposes of diplomatic relations between the Vatican and Italy. The Vatican's intransigent response to the dissolution, and in particular Pius XI's hard-hitting encyclical *Non Abbiamo Bisogno*, prolonged the crisis for a further two months until its resolution by the *Accordi per l'Azione Cattolica* of 2 September 1931. Why did things reach so serious a pass? Why did the press polemics not exhaust themselves, as they had done several times in 1929 and 1930, and why were relations not patched up earlier at a personal or diplomatic level?

The answer lies in the fact that the background to the crisis of 1931 was different in several fundamentally important respects from that prevailing in 1929 and 1930. By the Spring of 1931, the last vestiges of the honeymoon atmosphere of 1929 had evaporated; two years of living under the Concordatory 'system' had hardened attitudes on both sides and made them resistant to the shock of public disputes. This hardening of attitudes was reinforced by the changes in leadership which had taken place on both sides during 1929 and 1930, for in addition to Colombo's retirement from the presidency of Catholic Action in September 1929, Cardinal Gasparri was replaced as Vatican Secretary of State by Cardinal Pacelli in February 1930, and in October of that year Turati was replaced by Giovanni Giurati as Fascist Party Secretary. The new leaders were either too weak, like Pacelli and Ciriaci, to neutralise the entrenched 'hawks', like Pizzardo and Borgoncini-Duca, or they were more 'hawkish' than their predecessors, like Giurati and his lieutenant Scorza.

The appointment of Giurati and Scorza also signified the launching of a new phase of the Fascist Regime's drive towards a totalitarian monopoly of youth organisations, leading inevitably to a conflict with the youth organisations of Catholic Action. And the hardline attitude of the leaders was reinforced by strong grassroots feelings in both camps, especially among the younger members. The Spring of 1931 also witnessed a new, unprecedently public, manifestation of Catholic activism, centred around the celebrations for the fortieth anniversary of the Leonine encyclical *Rerum Novarum*. It was this development more than any other which actually provoked the dispute between the Church and the Regime in 1931. But by far the most important change was that which had taken place in the overall economic and political climate in Italy. It was the effects of the 'Great Depression', and in particular the encouragement which it gave to Catholic anti-Fascism, which forced Mussolini to take drastic measures against Catholic Action and thus brought relations between the Church and the Regime to crisis point at the end of May 1931.

THE LEADERSHIP CHANGES AND THEIR REPERCUSSIONS

The first of the leadership changes that were to have such a crucial bearing on relations between the Church and the Regime in 1931 actually took place a year earlier when on 11 February 1930, it was officially announced by the Vatican that Cardinal Gasparri had retired and that Mons. Eugenio Pacelli (Nuncio to Germany and brother of the chief Vatican spokesman in the negotiations for the Lateran Pacts) had been appointed Secretary of State in his place. There is some evidence to suggest that Gasparri's retirement was motivated by the kind of policy disagreements which were to induce Mussolini to dismiss Turati a few months later,[1] but though Gasparri went reluctantly he did at least have confidence in his successor.[2] The Italian Foreign Ministry also had confidence in Pacelli,[3] but De Vecchi, on the other hand, was rather less sanguine about this change at the top of the Vatican hierarchy for he perceived that it would have the effect of strengthening the influence of Pizzardo, and also of Borgoncini-Duca, whom he regarded as the leading exponent of the *popolare* faction in the Secretariat of State.

The events of 1931 were to prove De Vecchi correct. Pacelli's absence in Germany during the formative period of relations between the Vatican and the Regime, that is from 1926 to 1930, put him in a weak position vis-à-vis his two subordinates. As a result, Pizzardo was left in virtually

---

[1] See De Felice, III, pp. 201–8.
[2] According to Falconi, *The Popes in the Twentieth Century*, p. 154: '...Gasparri was summarily dismissed by his former protégé'. This interpretation is supported by Gannon, *The Cardinal Spellman Story*, p. 167, where he quotes from a letter of the then Mons. Spellman: 'Now Cardinal Gasparri is more reconciled and contented. And he and all my friends here are happy that it is Mons. Pacelli who steps into the greatest position in the Church after the Pope...'.   [3] *D.D.I.*, 7, Vol. VIII, p. 45, no. 237.

complete control of Catholic Action, whose annual review for 1931 waxed lyrical, not about Pacelli's appointment as Secretary of State and his elevation to the Sacred College, but about Pizzardo's consecration as archbishop.[4] Similarly, Pacelli's weakness left Borgoncini-Duca free to conduct the Vatican's day-to-day relations with Italy in an intransigent fashion, with damaging effects during the course of the 1931 crisis. It was in large measure due to the encouragement of Pizzardo and Borgoncini-Duca, and contrary to Pacelli's own inclinations, that Pius XI pursued a policy of 'brinkmanship' towards the Regime in the Spring and Summer of 1931. As the British Ambassador to the Quirinale explained to the Foreign Office: 'Gasparri's resignation was a great misfortune, the Pope is too impulsive, too undiplomatic...Pacelli has been unable to moderate his actions and his utterances.'[5]

By the Autumn of 1930, the disagreements between Mussolini and his Party Secretary Turati on major policy issues had widened considerably,[6] and, as had become clear when Turati decided to make his visit to the Pope earlier in the year, the Duce and his lieutenant no longer saw eye to eye on the question of relations with the Church. Whereas in March 1929 Mussolini had been unable to afford the luxury of dismissing Turati for fear of weakening his own position vis-à-vis the Fascist anti-clericals, by October 1930 he had nothing to lose by dropping a Party Secretary whose attitude to the Church was decidedly less intransigent than his own. Turati continued to believe passionately in the need for good relations with the Church,[7] and his departure meant the loss of a major moderating influence in the highest counsels of the Regime.

Giovanni Giurati, whom Mussolini appointed to replace Turati as Party Secretary on 8 October 1930, was by no means an anti-clerical of the Farinaccian stamp, but he could be relied upon to take a tougher line with Catholic Action and its youth activities, as indeed he did during the crisis of 1931. Another 'hawk' who moved to the top of the party hierarchy as a result of the October 1930 reshuffle was Carlo Scorza, who was given responsibility for those youth organisations directly controlled by the Party – the G.U.F.s and the University Militia.[8] Like Giurati, Scorza did much to exacerbate the crisis of 1931. Indeed, as more than one contemporary observer has noted, Giurati and Scorza were the driving forces behind the campaign against Catholic Action.[9]

[4] *Annali dell'Italia Cattolica*, 1931, pp. 67–72.
[5] P.R.O., F.O. 371, C. 3795/2810/22, Graham to Henderson, 3 June 1931.
[6] De Felice, IV, p. 201.
[7] See his letter to Mussolini in A.C.S., S.P.D., C.R. 92/WR, 'Turati', sf. I, 27 August 1931.
[8] Scorza had already served in the Party Direttorio of Turati.
[9] See, for example, De Begnac, *Palazzo Venezia*, p. 440, where he says that '...Scorza spearheaded this campaign', and also Iraci, *Arpinati Oppositore di Mussolini*, pp. 141–2, where he claims that Arpinati attempted to plead moderation against the 'hawkishness' of Giurati and Scorza.

The most significant aspect of Scorza's appointment was not so much his 'hawkishness' as the fact that he was taking over the party youth organisations at one of the turning-points in their history. Throughout 1929 and in early 1930, there had been much debate and discussion in the Fascist press about the role of youth in the life of the Party and the Regime.[10] In the same *Foglio d'Ordini* article which he had used to reply to the Pope's encyclical *Rappresentanti in Terra*, Mussolini had concluded the debate by stressing the vital importance of youth to the survival of the Regime:

The Regime intends to train spiritually the whole of Italian youth, from which, by a process of rigorous selection, will emerge the Italian ruling class of the future. For this purpose, it has created organisations like the Balilla, the Avanguardisti, and the Fascist University Groups alongside the civil militia of Fascism. The totalitarian nature of the Fascist educational system thus meets the supreme necessity of the Fascist Revolution, that is to last, to continue into the future.[11]

When the new Party Secretary and Direttorio were installed in October 1930, Mussolini entrusted them with the special task of strengthening and expanding the Fascist youth organisations, an area of party activity which had been somewhat neglected by Turati.[12] Thus the 'Changing of the Guard' of October 1930 marked the beginning of a new phase in the development of the Fascist youth organisations, and one which was almost as important as that initiated in 1926 with the foundation of the Balilla, and, like that of 1926, the phase inaugurated in 1930 led inevitably to a clash between the Fascist youth organisations and those of the Church.

As well as introducing a more aggressive policy of recruitment for the Balilla,[13] Giurati and Scorza responded to Mussolini's call by making more resources available to the Fascist youth organisations, and by launching two major initiatives in the youth field. In December 1930, the *Foglio d'Ordini* announced the formation of a new Fascist youth group, the Fasci Giovanili di Combattimento (henceforth Fasci Giovanili), designed to bridge the gap between the Avanguardisti, the oldest age range in the Balilla, and the adult Party, and thereby provide more recruits for the latter at the annual *leva*.[14] The absence of a party youth section for the eighteen and twenty-one age group had in the past resulted in the loss of many potential recruits to the Party proper; it also exposed this age group to the alternative attractions of the Catholic youth organisations which were particularly active among the eighteen- to twenty-one-year-olds.[15]

In his efforts to build up the new youth formations as quickly as possible,

[10] For an account of this debate, see De Felice, IV, pp. 228–37.
[11] *Foglio d'Ordini*, no. 64, 20 January 1931, 'Punti Fermi sui Giovani'.
[12] *O.O.*, Vol. XXIV, pp. 282.
[13] See the article by Palmiro Togliatti in *Stato Operaio*, no. 2, 1931, p. 510.
[14] Ibid.
[15] Tannenbaum, *Fascism in Italy*, p. 137.

Scorza trod on the toes of Renato Ricci, head of the Balilla, who complained to Mussolini that Scorza was 'poaching' schoolboys between fourteen and eighteen years old from his own organisation.[16] There may have been an element of personal and local rivalry in this quarrel, for Scorza and Ricci were the *ras* of the neighbouring provinces of Lucca and Massa Carrara respectively, but the substance of Ricci's complaint was justified, and by fair means or foul Scorza succeeded in building up the Fasci Giovanili to a membership figure of 479,000 within the space of six months.[17] Giurati and Scorza also took measures in 1931 to improve the preparation of Italian youth for their destiny; pre-military training was made obligatory for all males between eighteen and twenty-one, military training (including street-fighting) was introduced into the universities, and it was decided that in future mobilisation would include all males over fourteen years of age.[18] In addition, Giurati provided funds for a new youth magazine, *Il Gioventù Fascista*, which appeared for the first time in March 1931, under the editorship of Scorza. *Il Gioventù Fascista* was to play an important role in the Fascist press campaigns against Catholic Action during the crisis of 1931.

Scorza's efforts to increase the membership and extend the influence of the two existing party youth organisations, the G.U.F.s and the University Militia proved less successful than those for the Fasci Giovanili. In a report to the Direttorio in May 1931, Scorza expressed his dissatisfaction with the success of efforts to bring about '...the 'fascistisation' of university students',[19] and he was forced to admit that out of a total university population of 47,950 (which remained more or less stable in this period) membership of the G.U.F.s stood at 30,803, a drop of about 25 per cent since the Summer of 1930.[20] His disappointment at this setback undoubtedly contributed to the bitterness of his campaign against F.U.C.I. in May 1931,[21] though F.U.C.I., with at the most 3,000 members, could hardly have accounted for more than a fraction of the losses from the G.U.F.s. But by the Spring of 1931, the growing friction between the Fascist and Catholic youth organisations was by no means restricted to the universities. As Togliatti predicted at this time, the creation of the Fasci Giovanili was bound to intensify the pressure on all Catholic youth organisations and would, sooner or later, lead to a clash between the Church and the Regime on this issue.[22]

---

[16] A.C.S., S.P.D., C.R. 31 242/R, 'Adunanze del Direttorio del P.N.F.', 6 June 1931.
[17] *Il Lavoro Fascista*, 5 June 1931.
[18] Togliatti, in *Stato Operaio*, no. 2, 1931, p. 510.
[19] As quoted in Aquarone, *L'organizzazione dello stato totalitario*, p. 516.
[20] A.C.S., S.P.D., C.R. 242/R, 'Adunanze del Direttorio del P.N.F.', 23 May 1931.
[21] For an account of Scorza's persecution of F.U.C.I. in 1931, see M. C. Giuntella 'I Fatti del 1931', in Scoppola and Traniello (eds.) *I Cattolici tra Fascismo e Democrazia*, p. 209.
[22] Togliatti, in *Stato Operaio*, no. 2, 1931, p. 510.

THE ORIGINS OF THE 1931 CRISIS: FASCIST REACTIONS TO THE
RERUM NOVARUM CELEBRATIONS.

If 1930 had been a disappointing year for Catholic Action from a number
of points of view, 1931 promised to be different. Catholic Action was
committed to an ever-expanding programme of activities for that year,
centred around the celebrations for the fortieth anniversary of Leo XIII's
great social encyclical *Rerum Novarum*. Naturally, I.C.A.S. was to be
primarily responsible for organising the celebrations which would culmi-
nate in a massive international Catholic rally before the Pope in Rome on
15, 16 and 17 May. At the same time, the Giunta Centrale was also
planning a Marian congress and general assemblies of the various wings
of Catholic Action, all to be held in the Italian capital.

There was considerable apprehension in Fascist circles about this
extremely public manifestation of the strength of Catholic Action, and
police reports for the early months of 1931 indicate growing feelings of
irritation and unease at the amount of attention that was going to be
focussed on Catholic Action as a result of the celebrations. One such report,
on a meeting of the Giunta Centrale of Catholic Action held in late March
1931, declared that the forthcoming publication of Pius XI's commemora-
tive encyclical *Quadragesimo Anno* was nothing less than a provocation for
it would be dealing exclusively with economic and social questions.[23]
Mussolini's own concern about the contents of the forthcoming encyclical
may be gauged from the fact that at the beginning of April he explicitly
instructed De Vecchi to demand of the Pope 'To praise Italy during the
celebrations of *Rerum Novarum*.'[24]

Fascist press comments on the celebrations tried to play down the
importance and influence of *Rerum Novarum*, arguing that in any case its
ideals and objectives had all been realised by Fascism: thus *Il Lavoro Fascista*
published a cartoon of an old lady in Victorian clothes surrounded by others
dressed in the latest fashion with the caption: 'She is really rather old
fashioned...', and went to to say that 'the best commemoration of this
document [*Rerum Novarum*] has already been made by Fascism, which has
gone well beyond the proposals that were regarded as audacious forty years
ago'.[25] *Critica Fascista*, the organ of Giuseppe Bottai, was even more hostile
to the celebrations, arguing that the Church had no business getting
involved in economic and social questions anyway: a naive view, but one
that was very common in Fascist circles.[26]

When Pius XI's long awaited contribution to Catholic Social Thought

[23] A.C.S., D.G.P.S., G.I., b. 146, 'Azione Cattolica', sf. 2, report from the Rome Police of
25 March 1931.
[24] As quoted in Martini, *Studi sulla Questione Romana*, p. 137.
[25] *Il Lavoro Fascista*, 28 March 1931, 'Dalla Rerum Novarum al Fascismo'.
[26] *Critica Fascista*, 1 June 1931, 'Vecchie Cose Nuove'.

eventually appeared, Bottai's journal greeted it as a damp squib but it also did not fail to remark on the encyclical's grudging acknowledgement of the corporative institutions of Fascist Italy: '...that which was possible had been put into effect in the Corporative State, yet it would appear from the encyclical that the Pope is not aware of the fact'.[27] Other authoritative representatives of the Italian Catholic world did not seem to have noticed either, for Cardinal Minoretti of Genoa managed to write a lengthy article on *Quadragesimo Anno* for the journal of the Catholic University of Milan without once mentioning Fascist Italy.[28]

But by far the most serious defect of Pius XI's encyclical in the eyes of the Fascists was its explicit criticisms of the single, State trade union system which they had established in Italy:

We must also point out that the State itself has taken over the functions of the free organisations, instead of limiting itself to adequate and necessary assistance. The new system is also excessively bureaucratic and political: despite the general advantages already referred to, it is more likely to serve particular political interests rather than lead to a better social order.[29]

The force of this criticism of the Fascist Corporate State was, admittedly, blunted by the fact that the encyclical was addressed to Catholics throughout the world, but despite this universality, there was yet another pointed reference to the Italian situation when Pius XI affirmed the right and duty of Catholics to contribute to the process of establishing social peace and justice. Whilst the Pope stressed that Catholic Action did not itself intend to carry out political or trade union activities,[30] he reaffirmed the right of individual Catholics, trained in Catholic social principles by Catholic Action, to do so within the framework of the *sezioni professionali*: 'It has been officially stated that the legally constituted trade unions do not exclude the existence of *de facto* professional associations.'[31] This was obviously intended as an authoritative reply to the renewed attack on the *sezioni* which *Il Lavoro Fascista* launched in the middle of March, and which can be regarded as the beginning of the crisis of 1931.[32]

THE ATTACK ON THE *SEZIONI PROFESSIONALI*

The development of the *sezioni* had gone on apace since the first attack upon them by *Il Lavoro Fascista* in September 1929, and in addition to the efforts of I.C.A.S., other Catholic organisations were now rapidly extending

[27] Ibid.
[28] *Vita e Pensiero*, May 1931, 'Leggendo l'Enciclica Quadragesimo Anno'.
[29] The text of the encyclical is to be found in *Bollettino Diocesano di Padova*, Vol. XVI, no. 6, 15 June 1931, pp. 309–48.
[30] Ibid., p. 333. [31] Ibid., p. 332.
[32] The campaign began on 19 March with an article in *Il Lavoro Fascista* entitled 'Professionisti Cattolici or Cattolici Professionisti?'.

their presence amongst various groups of workers and professional people. The Opera dei Ritiri Operai (henceforth O.R.O.), which had been founded in 1904 by the Jesuit, Padre Masella, to provide spiritual retreats for working people, was particularly active in the late 1920s and early 1930s. The O.R.O. first came to the attention of the police in 1928 but they were persuaded to take their inquiries no further by the protests of Padre Tacchi-Venturi and the reports of the Prefects that the O.R.O. had strictly religious objectives.[33] Police interest was re-awakened in 1929 after the *Il Lavoro Fascista* campaign against the *sezioni* and by the beginning of 1931 they had pieced together an alarming picture of the geographical spread of the O.R.O. in Italy: 'It has branches in all the major cities of Italy, especially in those places which have tram or railway workshops, and it has also infiltrated all the branches of the State administration.'[34]

Another Jesuit-run operation which aroused the suspicions of the police was the Opera Di Assistenza Religiosa per i militari, which included amongst its patrons the Commander of the Carabinieri, General Vaccaro, and the wife of Marshal Pietro Badoglio.[35] Though infinitely less developed than the O.R.O., the authorities took a dim view of the fact that there was another Catholic organisation at work among the Armed Forces in addition to the Military Chaplains of the Vicario Castrense (the Military Chaplaincy) which was already looked upon with disfavour in Fascist circles.[36]

In March 1931, the Giunta Centrale of Catholic Action decided to extend the *sezioni* movement into the professions on an organised basis, using nuclei of ex-members of F.U.C.I. for this purpose; the new organisation received official recognition in the Catholic movement in 1932 under the title of Movimento Laureato.[37] Dubbed as 'an organisation of intellectuals' by the police, their inquiries quickly revealed that the movement already existed in practice in various Italian dioceses, and that in their efforts to establish its presence among Catholic secondary school teachers, and amongst doctors and engineers, the leaders of Catholic Action were using the files of government departments![38] *Il Lavoro Fascista*, supplied as usual with very accurate information by the Ministry of the Interior, warned its readers on 26 March that many of the leaders of the infant movement were 'Men whom the Fascist Revolution seemed to have swept from the Italian political scene forever.'[39] What the police had discovered was the involve-

---

[33] See the voluminous file on the Opera in A.C.S., D.G.P.S., G.I., b. 154, 'Opera dei Ritiri Operai'.
[34] Ibid., report of 30 October, 1928 from the Rome Police containing a copy of Tacchi-Venturi's letter.
[35] A.C.S., M.P.P., Pacco 107, K. 14, reports from Rome of 23 July 1930, and 30 September 1931.   [36] De Vecchi, *Memorie*, no. 14.
[37] A.C.S., D.G.P.S., G.I., b. 146, 'Azione Cattolica', sf. II, report of Rome Police, 25 March 1931.
[38] Ibid., sf. III, report of Rome Police, 14 April 1931.
[39] Il Lavoro Fascista, 26 March, 1931.

ment in the movement of such important *popolari* as Camillo Corsanego, Edoardo Clerici, Giorgio Colombo, G. B. Migliori and one of the sons of Filipo Meda.[40] Even more sinister than this was the discovery, through some judicious phone-tapping, of the involvement of Padre Enrico Rosa in the movement.[41] Rosa was already under suspicion for his contacts with the anti-Fascist Alleanza Nazionale and this discovery, therefore, placed the whole Jesuit order under suspicion, with the result that the Jesuits became the object of a sustained Fascist press campaign in late May and early June 1931.

The campaign against the *sezioni* came to a head at the end of March with a report in *Il Lavoro Fascista* about the 'trade union' activities of the youth wings of Catholic Action, whose own *sezioni* were growing in number as a result of intensified efforts connected with the *Rerum Novarum* celebrations.[42] This was the last straw as far as *Il Lavoro Fascista* was concerned, for the mouthpiece of Fascist trade unionism seems to have been genuinely surprised to discover that the Catholic youth formations were also organising their members into occupational groups, and it was particularly exercised by a circular of Traglia, the Rome diocesan president of Catholic Youth, which urged individual groups to give their members 'technical training'.[43] *Il Lavoro Fascista* took this to mean training in trade union rules and practices, which would constitute an invasion of Fascism's monopoly in the labour field,[44] an interpretation which appeared to be borne out by the subsequent repudiation of the Traglia memorandum by the Giunta Centrale of Catholic Action: 'As far as the professional associations are concerned, it should be noted that the circular sent out on the 19th of March by the Catholic Youth Federation of Rome was not in conformity with instructions issued by the national officers of Catholic Action.'[45]

This was a very embarrassing admission to have to make, but it did not satisfy *Il Lavoro Fascista* or deflect it from its campaign against Catholic Action. On the last day of March, the trade union mouthpiece published an article which amounted to a declaration of war against Catholic Action, spelling out with the greatest clarity its main fears:

1. That the *Rerum Novarum* celebrations were being used as a cover for the expansion of Catholic Action on an unprecedented scale.
2. That the *sezioni* were being used in a campaign of infiltration, propaganda and proselytism aimed at securing Catholic Action a powerful influence in the labour field.

---

[40] A.C.S., D.G.P.S., G.I., b. 146, 'Azione Cattolica', sf. II, report of Rome Police, 25 March 1931.   [41] Ibid.
[42] *Il Lavoro Fascista*, 31 March 1931, 'Alle Carte Scoperte Antifascismo Cattolico'.
[43] Ibid.   [44] Ibid.
[45] *L'Osservatore Romano*, 15 April 1931, 'Chiaramenti'.

3. That a particular object of these activities was the conversion of workers from a Fascist to a Catholic allegiance.
4. That the whole campaign was inspired and directed by *popolare* elements.

This article concluded with a sharp reminder about the cleansing power of Fascist violence and a highly coloured assessment of the situation: 'Catholic Action is openly taking up a position of anti-Fascism and illegality vis-à-vis the Regime.'[46]

THE CRISIS DEEPENS – THE FASCIST ATTACK ON CATHOLIC YOUTH

The article of 31 March in *Il Lavoro Fascista* marks a significant turning-point in the 1931 dispute, and not only because of the gravity of the allegations which is contained. Other sections of the Fascist press took their cue to join in the battle against Catholic Action, and their principal target became increasingly the Catholic youth organisations. The hand of Mussolini is clearly discernible in this press campaign, for throughout the crisis of 1931 Fascist newspapers were regularly supplied with information about the activities of Catholic Action by the Political Police section of the Direzione Generale della Pubblica Sicurezza, that department of the Ministry of the Interior over which the Duce had complete and direct control. Many of the articles in *Il Lavoro Fascista*, *Il Gioventù Fascista* and other Italian newspapers contained long, word-for-word extracts from police reports compiled only the day before publication.[47] Virtually the only Fascist newspaper which did not imitate the frenzied, hysterical style of *Il Lavoro Fascista* was *Il Popolo d'Italia* edited by Arnaldo Mussolini: unlike his brother, Arnaldo maintained a moderate, conciliatory line towards the Church throughout the 1931 dispute. Whilst the moderation of his brother's newspaper was to prove useful in July and August, when Mussolini was bent on compromise with the Vatican, he did not welcome it in April and May when he believed that only a tough line towards the Vatican would induce it to change direction and at the same time placate the party intransigents who were breathing down his neck.[48]

But Mussolini's hardline policy had a disappointing response from the Catholic side: the Catholic press risked confiscations and suspensions by

---

[46] *Il Lavoro Fascista*, 31 March 1931, 'Alle Carte Scoperte Antifascismo Cattolico'.
[47] Compare the police reports of 25 March 1931, in A.C.S., D.G.P.S., G.I., b. 146, 'Azione Cattolica', sf. 2, with the *Il Lavoro Fascista* article of March 1931, 'Manovre Cattoliche', and a police report of 7 July 1931 in the same *sottofasciolo* with *Il Lavoro Fascista* (front page, headline) of 10 July 1931.
[48] According to De Vecchi, *Memorie*, no. 16, Mussolini was not happy with Arnaldo's handling of the subject in *Il Popolo d'Italia*: this is borne out by the transcript of an intercepted telephone call between the two brothers (1931, but no precise date) in Guspini, *L'Orecchio del Regime*, p. 97.

the Prefects and the police in its efforts to defend Catholic Action and its activities.[49] *L'Osservatore Romano*, which had no reason to fear Fascist press censorship, carried on the battle against *Il Lavoro Fascista* and its sister papers, correcting their factual errors and rejecting their allegations against Catholic Action with a ponderous, operatic dignity which earned it the title of 'The Dancing Elephant' from its opponents.[50]

The Vatican itself was even less intimidated by the broadsides of the Fascist press. On 8 April, Mussolini sent De Vecchi to see the Papal Nuncio, confident that the press barrage had softened up the Vatican and that it would therefore be willing to apply the brakes to Catholic Action. De Vecchi gave Borgoncini-Duca a list of demands, the most important being that the Pope should refrain from public protests, that the Vatican should use its authority to moderate the Catholic press, that Catholic Action '...should not become, as it is already showing signs of becoming, a political party, but that it should operate solely within the terms laid down by the Concordat, and that it should refrain from any trade union activities', and that 'The *popolare* ring-leaders should be ordered out of Rome.'[51] The Vatican refused even to discuss the demands, and far from ceasing to speak on these matters in public, on 19 April, Pius XI solemnly reaffirmed in a public audience that Catholic Action was necessary, legitimate and irreplaceable, and defended its right to interest itself in questions of social morality and justice.[52]

Mussolini's diplomatic initiative having failed to persuade the Vatican to change direction, the new, hardline party bosses entered more directly into the fray. On 5 April, Scorza instructed the provincial Fascist leaders to carry out their own investigations into the activities of the Catholic youth groups and report back to him,[53] and that order was to be repeated by Giurati towards the end of May,[54] and in addition, he used the pages of the journal *La Gioventù Fascista* to attack Catholic Action and in particular its youth organisation. Here he took advantage of the rather belated comments of *L'Osservatore Romano* on an article published a month before about a certain Mons. Galosi, who had been sent into internal exile for having sexually assaulted one of his charges.[55] Naturally, *La Gioventù Fascista* had made much of the incident, arguing that it demonstrated that the Catholic youth organisations were not fit to have responsibility for the future

[49] For example, 29 May 1931, *L'Avvenire d'Italia* was confiscated by the Prefect of Bologna for an article deploring Fascist violence, see A.C.S., D.G.P.S., G.I., b. 98, 'Bologna', 'Ass. Giov. Catt. Scioglimento', report of 1 June 1931.
[50] *Il Lavoro Fascista*, 7 April 1931, 'L'Elefante che balla'.
[51] As quoted in Martini, *Studi sulla Questione Romana*, p. 137.
[52] For the text of Pius XI's speech, see *La Polemica per l'Azione Cattolica*, p. 49.
[53] For the text of Scorza's circular, see Tramontin, 'La crisis del 1931 nella documentazione veneta', p. 516.
[54] Ibid.
[55] *La Gioventù Fascista*, 9 March 1931, 'Notizie dalle Provincie'.

generations of soldiers and industrial heroes.[56] *L'Osservatore Romano* in its turn had taken Scorza and his newspaper to task for their lack of charity and their unremitting '...hatred for enemies of the Revolution and the Fatherland'.[57] The inevitable press polemics followed between the Vatican newspaper on the one hand, and *La Gioventù Fascista* and the rest of the Fascist press on the other, in which *L'Osservatore Romano* battled to uphold the biblical precept 'Love thine enemies' and the Fascists argued that such a principle undermined the formation of a tough, healthy, fighting force to defend the Fatherland.[58] This particular round of the press battle is remarkable for the fact that it was one of the few moments during the 1931 dispute when some of the fundamental, philosophical differences between Fascism and Catholicism were revealed, differences that were later to have an echo in the Pope's encyclical *Non Abbiamo Bisogno*.

But it was a very brief moment, because towards the end of the month the debate had descended from the philosophical plane, and on the Fascist side had degenerated into a general attack on the aims and objectives of Catholic Action. In a front page article of 24 April entitled, 'Note Chiarissime', *La Gioventù Fascista* repeated the accusation that 'An attempt is being made to constitute a real political party, organising, or attempting to organise, a part of Italian youth behind the washed up remains of the old Sturzian programme.'[59]

On 19 April, in a speech to an important gathering of party leaders in Milan, Giurati spoke out against Catholic Action, the first time that a P.N.F. Secretary had publicly intervened in relations between the Church and the Regime since the resignation of Farinacci in 1926. Giurati made all of the by now well-rehearsed allegations against Catholic Action, but he took the crisis one step further by introducing a new note of menace. Commenting on Pius XI's recourse to Article 43 of the Concordat, Giurati declared: 'And to those who seek to justify their futile and perhaps dangerous actions by recourse to an article of the Concordat, we will simply say that the Concordat was stipulated with a totalitarian Fascist Regime and with the Fascist Corporative State.'[60]

For a moment it seemed as if Giurati's tough policy had paid off, for the Pope's reply to the Party Secretary, which came in the form of an open letter, was remarkably conciliatory: firm, but conciliatory.[61] The Fascist press reaction was equally firm, and equally conciliatory. Taking its cue from Arnaldo Mussolini, who in *Il Popolo d'Italia* suggested a solution of

---

[56] Ibid.
[57] *L'Osservatore Romano*, 13 April 1931, 'Carità'.
[58] Ibid.
[59] *La Gioventù Fascista*, 24 April 1931, 'Note Chiarissime'. Most of the articles cited in the Fascist youth journal were written by Scorza himself.
[60] *La Polemica per l'Azione Cattolica*, p. 61.
[61] The text was published in *L'Osservatore Romano* on 26 April 1931.

the dispute through a clearer demarcation of the respective sphere of influence of Church and State, the Fascist press suddenly began to urge conciliation.[62] By way of reply, *L'Osservatore Romano*, in a front page editorial of 6 May, requested that everyone should refrain from further comment so that '...the supreme authorities may negotiate in whatever manner they think fit'.[63] But the negotiations did not materialise, the journalistic truce lasted only a few days; by the middle of May the Fascist press had resumed the offensive. At the end of the month Mussolini dissolved the Catholic youth groups and Italo-Vatican relations reached an all-time low.

The immediate cause of the breakdown at this point was the *Rerum Novarum* celebrations. Undeterred by the tensions of the previous two months, Catholic Action went ahead with the celebrations which surpassed even the worst Fascist expectations in their success. Ten thousand foreign delegates of Catholic social organisations joined their Italian colleagues to render homage to the Pope, and to commemorate Leo XIII's great social encyclical.[64] These celebrations constituted the high-water-mark of post-*Conciliazione* Catholic 'triumphalism', and, like Pius XI's own encyclical, *Quadragesimo Anno*, which was published on 15 May, they were endured in painful silence by the Fascist press. Once the foreign delegates had left Rome, however, the rancour and the resentment of the Fascist newspapers burst forth. The object of their anger was the series of 'summit meetings' of the various branches of Catholic Action which were held in the days following the celebrations. At these meetings, Pizzardo and Ciriaci were hard put to restrain the open expression of feelings of hostility against Fascism which had been accumulating amongst the rank and file of the movement over the years: frustration at police harassment and surveillance, anger at the persecution of members of the Catholic youth groups by their Fascist opposite numbers and bitterness over the months of Fascist press attacks.[65] That these diocesan delegates faithfully represented the feelings of their members is amply confirmed by recent local studies of Catholic Action.[66]

For *Il Lavoro Fascista*, which had as usual been supplied with detailed

[62] *Il Popolo d'Italia*, 29 April 1931, 'Sopranaturale e Naturale', and *Il Lavoro Fascista*, 30 April 1931, 'Una questione di Limiti'.
[63] *L'Osservatore Romano*, 6 May 1931, front page editorial.
[64] P.R.O., F.O. 371, C. 3541, British Minister to the Holy See to the Foreign Secretary, 18 May 1931.
[65] A.C.S., D.G.P.S. G.I., b. 146, 'Azione Cattolica', 'Roma', Rome Police report of 20 May 1931.
[66] See for example L. Balestrieri, 'I Fatti del 1931 a Genova – Fascismo e Giovane laicato cattolico', in Pecorari (ed.), *Chiesa, Azione Cattolica e Fascismo*, p. 40; M. Begozzi, 'Fonti per la storia della Gioventù Cattolica Novarese', in ibid., p. 170; and M. C. Giuntella, 'Circoli Cattolici e organizzazioni giovanili fasciste in Umbria', in Monticone (ed.), *Cattolici e Fascisti in Umbria*, p. 36.

information by police spies,[67] the meetings confirmed all its worst suspicions. The organ of Fascist syndicalism splashed the story across the front page of its edition of 27 May and quoted delegates as saying, amongst other things, that 'Catholic Action must prepare itself to take power', and that 'It is necessary to make our activity appear to be of a purely religious character, so that if they attempt to attack us, we can then denounce them before world public opinion.'[68] *L'Osservatore Romano*, as well as defending Mons. Pizzardo, the particular object of Fascist ire, rejected these allegations as fabrications, pointing out that many bishops and clergy had been present at the meeting.[69]

But for the next four days the Fascist press raged against Catholic Action and a rash of anti-Catholic incidents took place in several Italian cities, especially Rome: members of Catholic youth organisations were beaten up, F.U.C.I. taking the brunt of this,[70] Catholic premises were attacked, including the palace of Bishop Rodolfi at Vicenza,[71] and in Rome the printing presses of *La Civiltà Cattolica* were damaged by young blackshirts.[72] Whilst there was undoubtedly a certain amount of organisation and orchestration on the part of P.N.F. officials,[73] they should nevertheless be taken as an expression of the strength of Fascist feelings against Catholic Action, which was generally seen to have gone too far. After an acrimonious diplomatic exchange over responsibility for the incidents,[74] which were frighteningly reminiscent of the waves of Fascist violence against Catholic

[67] Compare the front page article in *Il Lavoro Fascista* of 27 May 1931 with the police report of 20 May 1931, in A.C.S., D.G.P.S., G.I., b. 146, 'Azione Cattolica'.

[68] Front page article in *Il Lavoro Fascista*, 27 May 1931.

[69] *L'Osservatore Romano*, 31 May 1931.

[70] Marcucci-Fanello, *Storia della F.U.C.I.*, p. 143; this is borne out by P.R.O., F.O. 371, C. 374/28/0/22, British Minister to the Holy See to the Foreign Secretary, 2 June 1931, reporting attacks on F.U.C.I. members in Parma, Bari and Modena.

[71] The number of attacks on Catholic Action members and premises in May 1931 is too great to list separately; the 'Associazioni Giovanili Cattoliche-Scioglimento' files to be found in A.C.S., D.G.P.S., G.I., bb. 98, 103, 107, 109, 120, 121 and 123 indicate that anti-Catholic violence was fairly general. See also *L'Osservatore Romano*, 31 May 1931 for a full catalogue of the incidents.

[72] Ibid., b. 131, 'G.C.I.', 'Incidenti fra Cattolici e Fascisti', report from the Rome Police of 30 May 1931.

[73] It cannot be a pure coincidence that in so many of the incidents described in the police files, officials of the Party or the Militia were to be found conveniently at hand to put an end to the disturbance!

[74] This diplomatic 'quadrille' began with Borgoncini-Duca's note of 29 May, demanding an apology for the anti-Catholic incidents that had taken place in Rome over the previous three days, and an assurance that they would not happen again. The Nuncio's intemperate wording of the note, which set a twenty-four-hour deadline for satisfaction, conveniently placed the Vatican in the wrong just at the moment when Mussolini was issuing his orders for the dissolution of the Catholic youth organisations. Grandi was thus able to reject the note as 'unreceivable'. The Vatican retaliated by refusing De Vecchi's request for an audience with the Pope, whereupon the Nuncio was also deprived of access to Mussolini. Then followed the exchange of notes which continued fruitlessly throughout June. All but the Vatican's note of 29 May are to be found in *D.D.I.*, 7, Vol. X, pp. 42–73.

organisations in 1926 and 1927, Mussolini dealt Catholic Action a 'short, sharp shock': on 30 May he instructed the Prefects to dissolve the Catholic youth organisations.[75]

THE DISSOLUTION OF THE CATHOLIC YOUTH ORGANISATIONS

With Mussolini's order to the Prefects to dissolve the Catholic youth organisations, the crisis of 1931 reached the first of two climaxes (the second being the publication of Pius XI's encyclical *Non Abbiamo Bisogno* on 29 June 1931). What prompted this drastic measure on Mussolini's part? Part of the explanation is to be found in the enormous pressure which was exerted on Mussolini at this time by the 'hawks' in the Fascist hierarchy, Giovanni Giurati and Carlo Scorza, who in their turn represented the feelings of many officials of the Party and its youth organisations at a local level. The events of May 1931 presented Giurati and Scorza with a golden opportunity to get rid of the Catholic youth organisations once and for all and thus achieve that totalitarian control of Italian youth which had always been the ultimate objective of Fascist policy. It seems likely that under the influence of Giurati and Scorza, Mussolini decided to dissolve the Catholic youth organisations in the hope that he would be able to persuade the Vatican to accept this loss in return for the survival of the adult sections of Catholic Action (which were obviously less dangerous to the long-term future of the Regime), just as, in 1927, he had traded the dissolutiom of the Catholic Boy Scouts and sports organisations in return for the survival of the remaining Catholic youth organisations. To have dissolved the whole of Catholic Action would have been too serious a breach of the Concordat, leaving no room for negotiations with the Holy See and running the serious risk of the denunciation by the latter of the Lateran 'package' as a whole.

The decision to dissolve the Catholic youth organisations, the most unpopular of all the sections of Catholic Action, was also a response to the grassroots, Fascist feelings against them; feelings that had been brought to boiling point by the campaign waged against Catholic Action in the Fascist press between March and May 1931. Mussolini himself believed that this violence was a genuine, spontaneous expression of strong and widespread Fascist hostility to the Church and Catholic Action, as this Note, intended for purely internal distribution, clearly demonstrates: '...the incidents are highly indicative of a state of mind which is both deep-seated and widespread, a strong feeling against any organisation or interference of the clergy in the social and political life of the Nation'.[76] Mussolini's claims are borne out by other evidence of Fascist hostility towards the

---

[75] The text of Mussolini's telegram to the Prefects is in A.C.S., D.G.P.S., G.I., b. 146, 'Azione Cattolica', sf. I (no date).
[76] *D.D.I.*, 7, Vol. X (proofs), 'Appunto per il Capo di Gabinetto', 30 May 1931.

Church, which was accused of black ingratitude to the Regime. This feeling is eloquently expressed by a leaflet widely distributed in Fascist circles in the Summer of 1931 which graphically contrasted the persecution of the Church in Lithuania, Russia, Mexico and Spain with its secure, comfortable and privileged existence in Fascist Italy.[77]

Mussolini was not a leader who allowed himself to lag behind the opinion of his followers. In this sense his decision to dissolve the Catholic youth organisations was an assertion of his authority, a demonstration of the power of his leadership.

Mussolini was, however, motivated by another consideration, and one that was even more crucial to his survival as leader of Fascism; indeed it was crucial to the survival of Fascism itself. The dispute between the Church and the Fascist Regime in 1931 took place against the background of a deteriorating economic and political situation, for by the Spring of 1931 the effects of the Great Depression were beginning to weigh heavily upon Italy, giving rise to a resurgence of social protest and political dissidence, and in particular the flowering of Catholic anti-Fascism. Whereas during the earlier disputes of 1929 and 1930, Italians had been barely aware of the implications of the Great Crash, by the Spring of 1931 the economic and political effects of the Great Depression were making themselves felt in Italy, even if the gravity of those effects was hidden from many Italians, and from most foreign observers, by heavy press censorship, the regimentation of the workers by the Fascist trades unions and the tight grip of the Fascist police-state.

According to all the major statistical indicators, the condition of the Italian economy deteriorated rapidly during 1930; both the index of production[78] and the value of exports[79] dropped by 18 per cent in that year, and even more dramatically, unemployment doubled in the same period.[80] Almost as devastating in its effects as the rise in unemployment was the decline in living standards in Italy, which was in large part due to government-enforced reductions in money-wages – in the year ending December 1930, average earnings fell by 4 per cent.[81] The fall in living standards was most marked in the countryside;[82] it is no wonder, therefore, that in June 1931, after the publication of the Church's ban on Corpus Christi processions, Mussolini accused the Vatican of attempting to '...stir up the masses, especially those in the countryside, against the Regime'.[83] Disturbances of that kind were, after all, the most normal of occurrences in Italy in times of widespread economic and social distress. The rural masses did not rise up on this occasion, but police statistics testify to the

[77] A copy of the leaflet is to be found in A.C.S., D.G.P.S., G.I., b. 113, 'Milan', letter from the Prefect of 29 October 1931.

[78] De Felice, IV, p. 58 n. 2.   [79] Ibid., p. 61.
[80] Ibid., p. 63 n. 1.   [81] Ibid., p. 58 n. 2.
[82] Ibid.   [83] As quoted in ibid., p. 252 n. 2.

serious repercussions of the Great Depression on the law and order situation in Italy during 1931 – spontaneous but short-lived strikes, demonstrations, bread strikes and the daubing of anti-Fascist graffiti reached a high point in 1931, more than double the figure recorded in any of the previous four years.[84]

These spontaneous protests by the working population of Italy against the effects of the Great Depression were accompanied by an upsurge in organised activity on the part of the anti-Fascist forces, for, naturally, the opponents of Fascism, both at home and abroad, were eager to exploit the economic misfortune of the Regime. Apart from the Slav terrorists who were extremely active in this period,[85] both the Italian Communist Party and the Giustizia e Libertà movement waged an intensive propaganda war against Fascism and in consequence suffered heavily at the hands of the police.[86]

Italy's worsening economic situation also excited the Catholic opponents of the Regime, and as a result the year 1931 witnessed the greatest flurry of Catholic anti-Fascist activity since the end of the Matteotti Crisis seven years before. According to the Political Police, the mounting effects of the Depression in Italy encouraged hopes among the *popolari* that the collapse of the Regime could not be far off, and led to a revival of their clandestine political activities including a renewal of contacts with the Vatican[87]. A resurgence of 'the spirit of popolarism' was reported among Catholics in the Veneto (including members of the former Centro Nazionale), inspired in great part by rumours that the State was facing a serious financial crisis.[88] In August 1930, police interest was centred on Milan, that hotbed of Catholic anti-Fascism and the home of the Jacini group of *popolare* politicians,[89] and in September the Political Police were drawing attention to the links being forged between *popolari* in the provinces and their leaders in Rome.[90]

The tiny band of *popolari* in exile also began to wake up to the possibilities of the new political situation that was developing at home. In October 1930, a police spy in Paris sent information on their activities: he reported that at a meeting of the Executive Committee of the International of Christian Democratic Parties, Francesco Ferrari had claimed that '...the head of the Fascist Government has been making overtures to the Vatican with the purpose of inserting into the Government some eminent person-

---

[84] Ibid., p. 78.
[85] Dal Pont, *Aula IV*, p. 17.
[86] For Giellista activity in Italy in the period 1930–1, see Delzell, *I Nemici di Mussolini*, pp. 69–70, and for that of the Communists, ibid., p. 121. For both see also Tamaro, *Venti anni di Storia*, Vol. II, p. 454.
[87] A.C.S., M.P.P., Pacco 100, K. 7, report from Rome, 8 March 1930.
[88] Ibid., report from Rome of 18 July 1930.
[89] Ibid., report from Milan of 23 September 1930.   [90] Ibid.

alities from the Partito Popolare'.[91] The 'eminente popolare' in question was believed to be Filippo Meda, and according to the spy the Committee then resolved that '...if any leader of the dissolved Partito Popolare allows himself to be persuaded into supporting the Fascist Government, he is to be immediately excluded from affiliated organisations'.[92]

The Meda story sounds highly improbable,[93] but it illustrates perfectly the state of mind of *popolare* politicians in Italy and in exile at this time, as do reports of the same period that Sturzo and Ferrari were seeking to rebuild their links with the anti-Fascist Concentrazione,[94] and that they were in unusually frequent contact with Nitti and Sforza.[95]

In February 1931, Ferrari, on behalf of the Segretariato del Partito Popolare Italiano in Brussels (which consisted of himself and exactly one other – Luigi Sturzo!), began circularising his party's sympathisers in Italy, including parish priests and members of Catholic Action. The circular, which fell into the hands of the Political Police, whilst discouraging hopes of an early and complete collapse of the Regime, affirmed that '...we must stress the gravity of the present economic and political crisis and the fact that the Fascist leaders are unable to cope with it'.[96] It is impossible to gauge the effects of the letter on its recipients, but the police took it very seriously, as they did the anti-Fascist propaganda being sent to parish priests by the Giustizia e Libertà movement at this time.[97]

Added to the conspiracy theories multiplying in police and Fascist circles generally in the Spring of 1931 was knowledge about the activities of two clandestine anti-Fascist organisations with strong Catholic connections – the Alleanza Nazionale of Lauro De Bosis, and the Movimento Guelfo d'Azione of Piero Malvestiti and his friends.[98] De Bosis has been chiefly remembered for his airborne leaflet raids over major Italian cities, which eventually led to his death in October 1931, but the distribution of Alleanza propaganda was more successful, if less spectacular, on the ground, especially in the 'Catholic provinces of the Veneto, Lombardy, Le Marche, and in and around Rome'.[99] As one author has pointed out, De Bosis,

[91] Ibid., report from Nice of 23 December 1930.
[92] Ibid.
[93] Nevertheless, *Mussolini* took it very seriously because it helped to give credence to stories in other foreign newspapers which pointed up the weakness of the Regime: see De Felice, IV, p. 128 n. 3.
[94] A.C.S., C.P.C., b. 4980, 'Luigi Sturzo', report from the Paris Embassy of 23 September 1930.   [95] Ibid.
[96] Ibid., a report from the Prefect of Turin containing a typed copy of Ferrar's circular.
[97] Garosci, *Storia dei fuorusciti*, p. 202.
[98] For the Alleanza Nazionale, see M. Vinciguerra, 'L'Alleanza Nazionale e Lauro de Bosis', in *Trent'anni di Storia Italiana* and De Bosis *Storia della mia morte*; for the Movimento Guelfo d'Azione, see G. Malavasi, 'Il Processo dei Guelfi', in *Fascismo e Antifascismo*, and G. Brezzi, 'Il Gruppo Guelfo tra Gerarchie ecclesiastica e regime Fascista', in Scoppola and Traniello, *I Cattolici tra Fascismo e Democrazia*, pp. 235–99.
[99] See the reports in A.C.S., M.P.P., Pacco 100, K. 14.

'Despite his "crocean" agnostic attitude to Catholicism as a religion...
accepted the reality of Catholicism as a social and political force.'[100] Thus
the propaganda leaflets were from the start designed to arouse the
sympathy and the support of conservative Catholics.

The second manifesto of the Alleanza dealt at length with the Catholic
role in the fight against Fascism and in particular made the following very
significant assertions: 'We would have to be blind not to recognise the fact
that the Monarchy with the Army, and the Vatican with Catholic Action,
are the two greatest forces in Italy outside of Fascism. No one can doubt
that both the King and the Pope are anti-Fascists at heart.'[101] Whilst De
Bosis was almost certainly wrong in thinking that the Pope and the King
were really anti-Fascists, his assessment of the importance of Catholic
Action was undoubtedly correct, as was this further statement of the likely
role of Catholic Action in the event of the collapse of the Regime: 'The
Pope equals Catholic Action. The latter is the largest organisation outside
of Fascism and is latently anti-Fascist. When the crisis comes it will be a
valuable rallying-point against Fascism, but also against any subversive
agitation unleashed by the crisis. It is necessary to operate in agreement
with Catholic Action and not against it.'[102]

Even though, as the best police analyst of information on the Catholic
world pointed out, De Bosis had over-estimated the organisational effectiveness of Catholic Action,[103] the police were seriously concerned about
his activities, if only because of the wide penetration of his propaganda
in Catholic circles: not only was Padre Rosa, one of the most powerful of
the 'eminence grises' in the Vatican, found to be in contact with the
Alleanza,[104] but, as the Special Tribunal trial revealed in December 1931,
the death of De Bosis had not been in vain, for he had succeeded in
recruiting several active supporters from the ranks of Catholic organisations
for his short-lived movement.[105]

Ultimately, the intuitions of De Bosis about Catholic Action were proved
correct; by 1943 Catholic Action had become the largest and most
influential mass movement in Italy, and its head, Luigi Gedda, was to place
the resources of this formidable organisation at the disposal of Marshal
Badoglio and his post-Fascist Government for precisely the purposes
envisaged by De Bosis.[106]

At the same time that the activities of the Alleanza Nazionale movement

[100] Garosci, *Il Secondo Risorgimento*, pp. 168–9.
[101] See the original of number 2 in A.C.S., M.P.P., Pacco 100, K. 14.
[102] Ibid.
[103] Ibid., report of Rome Police, 1 December 1930.
[104] Ibid.; see also Bendiscioli, *Antifascismo e Resistenza*, p. 170, where he mentions '...relations
established in Rome between Liberal opposition circles and the new Catholic opposition
of Padre Rosa'.
[105] A.C.S., M.P.P., Pacco 100, K. 14, report from Rome of 25 December 1931.
[106] Scoppola, *La proposta politica di De Gasperi*, p. 46.

were in full swing, the police became aware of the existence of an anti-Fascist movement of an even more explicitly Catholic kind: the Movimento Guelfo d'Azione, whose manifesto, entitled *Cristo Re e il Popolo*, was being distributed in Catholic circles in mid-May 1931, as the dispute between the Church and the Regime was reaching its climax.[107] The manifesto was written by Catholic Action militants, for, as was to become clear at the trial before the Special Tribunal in 1933, Malvestiti and his friends were active, influential members of Milanese Catholic Action.[108] Addressed to 'The Christian Democrats gathered around the Chair of St Peter on the fortieth anniversary of *Rerum Novarum*', in other words to the activists in Catholic Action, the 'Guelf' manifesto had a pronounced anti-capitalistic/Catholic integralist flavour, and though it showed no sympathy towards the former P.P.I., it professed a deep hatred of Fascism and a supreme confidence in the early demise of the Regime.[109] The Ministry of the Interior was not to know until much later that the Movimento Guelfo was an extremely small, isolated group with no organisational links with either the Alleanza Nazionale or the nuclei of *popolare* members inside or outside of Catholic Action. It took this new threat at its face value, and fearing that 'Guelf' propaganda might reach the thousands of foreign Catholics gathered in Rome for the *Rerum Novarum* celebrations, on 24 May, it issued instructions to provincial police chiefs to report immediately the appearance of further manifestos of what turned out to be the only clandestine, Catholic anti-Fascist group to be tried and convicted during the years of Fascism.[110]

The police inevitably connected these overt manifestations of Catholic opposition to the Regime with the activities of the *popolari* inside Catholic Action and the Vatican, regarding them as nothing less than an organised conspiracy against the Regime. As had been revealed by the police investigations of 1929 and 1930, and indeed as was only to be expected, large numbers of *popolari* continued to hold important positions in Catholic Action, especially in the diocesan boards.[111] In the South, the *popolare* presence was less marked, and, in contrast to the North, many members and officers of Catholic Action held a Fascist Party card testifying to the time-honoured southern habit of political re-insurance,[112] but in the North, whole diocesan boards of Catholic Action, priests included, were found to

---

[107] The police reports on the first appearances of the Guelf manifestos are to be found in A.C.S., D.G.P.S., G.I., b. 65, 'Movimento Guelfo'.
[108] For an account of the trial, see C. Brezzi, 'Il Gruppo Guelfo tra Gerarchie ecclesiastica e regime Fascista', in Scoppola and Traniello (eds.), *I Cattolici tra Fascismo e Democrazia*, pp. 260–72.
[109] An original of the first Guelf manifesto is to be found in A.C.S., D.G.P.S., G.I., b. 65, 'Movimento Guelfo'.   [110] Ibid., circular to Prefects of 24 May 1931.
[111] See the replies to circular no. 4163, 10 January 1930, in A.C.S., D.G.P.S., G.I., bb. 1–93.
[112] For example, see the replies to circular no. 33148, 28 November 1931, regarding the reconstitution of the Catholic Action *giunte*, in A.C.S., D.G.P.S., G.I., b. 123, 'Potenza', 17 June 1932, and 'Ragusa', 7 September 1931.

be composed entirely of *popolari*.[113] In addition, it was common knowledge that several prominent politicians of the former Catholic party, men like Mario Cingolani, Edoardo Clerici, Giorgio Colombo, Filippo Meda and Gian Battista Migliori, were still very active on the Catholic Action speaking circuit.

To make matters worse, by the Autumn of 1930, the Political Police had compiled an impressive list of notorious *popolari* living or working within the Vatican. The majority, like Padre Guilio Bevilacqua, who '...appears to have had various brushes with the Honourable Turati' (i.e., Turati the former P.N.F. Secretary), were purely and simply refugees, but others like Comm. Beccaria and Mons. G. B. Montini held important positions in the various branches of the Vatican administration.[114] A particularly large group were employed by the Vatican newspapers including Mons. Piantelli, '...who was forced to flee from Lodi on account of his anti-Fascism',[115] Dott. Margotti, '...ex-editor of *Il Popolo*' (the newspaper of the P.P.I.),[116] and Cesidio Lolli, '...another journalist from the P.P.I. who is now the Pope's typist',[117] not to mention Igino Giordani, who divided his journalistic talents between *L'Osservatore Romano* and *Fides*, the organ of the campaign against Italian Protestantism. And, of course, there was Alcide De Gasperi, who, although actually resident outside the boundaries of the Vatican, worked inside its library.[118] When, in May 1931, reports reached Mussolini of meetings inside the Vatican between Cingolani, Paolo Cappa (former *popolare* M.P. for Genoa) and G. Dore, it must have seemed as if a large part of the leadership of the former P.P.I. was systematically regrouping in preparation for the expected fall of the Regime, and that it was receiving some moral support from the Vatican.[119]

From Mussolini's point of view, these manoeuvrings seemed all the more sinister given the widely growing belief in the fatal weakness of the Regime in establishment circles in Italy, among former Liberal politicians like Bonomi and Orlando,[120] in the Army and at Court,[121] and even in the

---

[113] For example, Parma where a police report of 30 October 1931 said that twelve out of thirteen members of the diocesan board were *popolari* – in A.C.S., D.G.P.S., G.I., b. 112, 'Parma', f. I, and ibid., b. 98, 'Bergamo', f. I, where *all* the members of the *giunta* were *popolari*.

[114] A.C.S., M.P.P., Pacco 100, K. 7, report from Milan of 23 September 1930.

[115] Ibid.   [116] Ibid.   [117] Ibid.   [118] Ibid.

[119] Ibid., report from Rome of 15 June 1931.

[120] Ibid., Pacco 140, K. 14, report from Naples, 21 November 1930, saying that Bonomi and Salandra had escaped punishment for their involvement in an unspecified anti-Fascist movement (presumably the Political Police believed it was linked with the Alleanza Nazionale): '...thanks to the protection of the Royal Family'. (Both were members of the Order of the SS.Annunziata, and therefore 'cousins' of the King.) A report from the British Ambassador to the Foreign Secretary of 17 November 1930 in P.R.O., F.O. 371, C. 8407/55/22, says that Bonomi signed a petition to the King, along with one hundred other notables, asking for more liberty.

[121] A.C.S., M.P.P., Pacco 100, K. 7, report of 10 October 1930, concerning growing opposition to the Regime in army and court circles, especially in Piedmont. According to the report there was also a lot of dissension amongst ex-Nationalists centred around

highest ranks of the Vatican hierarchy itself. As early as February 1931, the authoritative *Berliner Tagblatt* had suggested that the Vatican was about to abandon the Italian Fascist Regime because of its growing weakness, a suggestion of which Mussolini took very careful note.[122] On 22 March 1931, De Vecchi heard from Pacelli's own lips of the increasing doubts being entertained in the Vatican about Fascism's ability to survive the crisis: '...he has asked me several times whether the Government had confidence in itself and whether it felt itself to be strong'.[123] And a letter from the Pope himself declared that 'Fascism has already lost a lot of ground and it loses more every day. Listen carefully to this advice which is given in a friendly spirit.'[124] Whilst De Vecchi gives no indication of the precise nature of that advice, it undoubtedly was given in a friendly spirit; though the Vatican was dissatisfied with the Government's religious policy for much of this period, the Pope for his part did not desire the downfall of the Regime.

Nevertheless, the leaders of the Regime had strong reasons for believing that a conspiracy was forming against them in Catholic and conservative circles. In these circumstances, Mussolini could not back down: he had to take up the challenge offered by Catholic Action's 'provocative' activities. To have allowed the press campaigns against Catholic Action quietly to be dropped after having mobilised Fascist opinion against the Catholic organisations would have been a most dangerous admission of weakness. It would have been interpreted by both the allies and opponents of Fascism as a serious political defeat for the Regime, one from which it might never have recovered.

THE CATHOLIC RESPONSE TO THE DISSOLUTION

As the prefectoral reports testify,[125] Mussolini's instructions to dissolve the Catholic youth groups were carried out with virtually no resistance or unpleasant incidents, even if one over-zealous Prefect interpreted the orders to include the adult sections of Catholic Action as well.[126] It is equally true that few even remotely compromising documents were found when the police searched Catholic Action premises, though Jervolino, President of Catholic Youth at this time, has admitted that he was afraid lest some correspondence concerning his movement's early relations with

Federzoni, and even De Vecchi was considered to be lukewarm in his support for Mussolini.

[122] Kent, *The Pope and the Duce*, p. 119.
[123] *D.D.I.*, 7, Vol. X (proofs), 'Ambasciatore presso la Santa Sede' (to Grandi), 9 June 1931.
[124] Ibid.
[125] See the prefectoral reports on the dissolution in their provinces in A.C.S., D.G.P.S., G.I., b. 131, 'G.I.A.C.', f. I, 'Ass. Giov. Scioglimento'.
[126] Ibid., b. 121, 'Pescara', sf. I, Prefect's report, 12 March 1931.

the P.P.I. would fall into the hands of the police.[127] Nevertheless, the depth of the opposition to the Government's measure amongst Catholics was progressively revealed throughout June and July: there were pro-Catholic demonstrations in a number of areas, posters and pamphlets attacking the dissolution appeared in the streets,[128] and many bishops condemned the dissolution in their pastoral letters or protested in person to the local or central government authorities.[129] The prefectoral reports for the second two quarters of 1931 speak of an upsurge of feeling against the Regime amongst the clergy of the 'white' provinces in particular,[130] and the Pope was inundated with messages of sympathy and support from both the laity and clergy alike.[131]

Mussolini also received telegrams of support and loyalty, though rather fewer, with some even from Catholic clergy and a few lay members of Catholic Action.[132] The majority of the latter came from the South, whose greater indifference to the fate of Catholic Action and ignorance of the issues at stake in the dispute were reflected in the fact that the southern clergy largely ignored the ban on the holding of Corpus Christi processions imposed by the Vatican Secretariat of State, a ban which was intended as a form of protest against the dissolution. The failure to observe the ban in so many places throughout the peninsula was greeted with considerable satisfaction in Fascist circles.

The ban on the Corpus Christi processions was one of the Vatican's first reactions to the dissolution, along with a formal note of protest by the Papal Nuncio, and, more significantly, an order placing Catholic Action under

---

[127] Jervolino, 'Lo Scioglimento dei Circoli', pp. 20–1.

[128] De Felice, IV, p. 259, says: 'Given the gravity of the measures taken, Catholic reactions were quite mild.' Given the fact that the dissolution was a deliberate act of intimidation by a police state which also controlled the press, there were hardly likely to have been mass, Catholic, protest demonstrations in every Italian city! But the Pubblica Sicurezza files offer ample evidence of acts of protest in places throughout northern and central Italy.

[129] Here again, the files on the dissolution in A.C.S., D.G.P.S., G.I., bb. 95–125, show that the majority of bishops in northern and central Italy protested to the local authorities in one form or another. The Bishops of Piedmont and the Veneto also protested *en bloc*, and the Bishops of Vicenza and Trento went to Rome to protest to Mussolini in person: see Zilio, *Un Condottiere d'anime*, p. 309. To make this point, the Bishop of Pesaro preached in his cathedral on the horrors of the Diocletian Persecution!

[130] For example, A.C.S., S.P.D., P.N.F., S.P.P., bb. 6 and 7 'Milano', 2 August 1931; see also 'Pola' and 'Novara', same date.

[131] P.R.O., F.O. 371, C. 3914. British Minister to the Holy See to the Foreign Secretary, 8 June 1931, where he says that telegrams of condolence had also been pouring in from all over the world, especially the U.S.A. This is confirmed by the list of such messages in the pages of *L'Osservatore Romano*, 4–21 June 1931.

[132] Ibid., for the telegram from the Bishop of Caltanissetta reaffirming his loyalty to the Duce. See also A.C.S., D.G.P.S., G.I., b. 119, 'Avellino', telegram of support for Mussolini from the Sodalizio Cattolico, 19 June 1931, and *ibid.*, b. 124, 'Reggio Calabria', 'Ass. Catt.', report from the Prefect that the local branch of the Catholic men's organisation had dissolved itself in protest at the policies of the national Catholic Action leaders.

the direct control of the bishops.[133] In this way the Vatican hoped to protect what remained of the Catholic organisations from further government measures. The move was also interpreted by both Grandi and Mussolini as offering the basis for a possible settlement of the dispute; thus in his Note of 1 June, Mussolini wrote: '...the Pope's decision to place Catholic Action under the direct control of the bishops could provide the basis for discussions whose object would be to secure a supplementary agreement regarding the interpretation of Article 43'.[134] Mussolini believed that the transfer of control over Catholic Action to the bishops would reduce the influence of Pizzardo and Dalla Torre and would diminish the effectiveness of Catholic Action as a *national* organisation, and, by virtue of the oath which the bishops had taken to the King, it would make it easier to remove the *popolari* and the anti-Fascist influence which they exercised inside the movement.

But if Mussolini believed that the shock of dissolution had rendered the Vatican willing to negotiate, he was wrong; it had had quite the reverse effect; it left Pius XI feeling bitterly aggrieved and outraged as his public speeches throughout June demonstrate.[135] In consequence, the position of the 'hawks' like Mons. Borgoncini-Duca was considerably strengthened, and that of the more pacific Cardinal Pacelli correspondingly weakened. In fact, throughout June 1931 Vatican policy towards the Regime was firmly in the hands of the Pope and his Nuncio, with the result that relations with Italy were reduced to a futile exchange of diplomatic notes, each side stating its grievances only to have the other rebut them.[136] De Vecchi attempted to break the impasse by talking only to Pacelli, but his interview only confirmed how weak the position of the Cardinal Secretary really was: though Pacelli was fearful of the consequences of further conflict, and therefore more than anxious to bring the dispute to an end as soon as possible, he could do nothing against the intransigence of Borgoncini-Duca and Pius XI.[137]

Nevertheless, the Vatican 'doves' did make some attempt to re-open channels of communication with the Regime. Cardinal Sbarretti sent the Father-General of the Salesians, Padre Tommassetti, to take soundings from his old friend Luigi Federzoni, a mission doomed to failure since the former Nationalist leader by now possessed no influence over the Duce.[138] The Cardinal Secretary of State chose both his emissary and target more

---

[133] For the text of the circular see *L'Osservatore Romano*, 30 June 1931, 'Direttive del Segretario di Stato per L'Azione Cattolica'.

[134] *D.D.I.*, 7, Vol. X (proofs), 'Appunto per il Capo del Gabinetto', 1 June 1931.

[135] See Jervolino, 'Lo Scioglimento dei Circoli', p. 23, for the Pope's reactions to the news of dissolution. Pius XI commenced his public protests on the morrow of the dissolution; *Discorsi*, Vol. II, p. 114, 'Per la Proclamazione delle Virtu eroiche di Glicero Landriani – La Difesa di Azione Cattolica Perseguitata', 31 May 1931.

[136] See above, p. 146, n. 2.

[137] *D.D.I.*, 7, Vol. X (proofs), 'Ambasciatore presso la Santa Sede' (to Grandi), 1931.

[138] Ibid., Federzoni, 13 May 1931, for Federzoni's account of his interview.

carefully; on 10 June he sent his brother to see Giurati. But despite the fact that Francesco Pacelli enjoyed considerable prestige in Fascist circles by virtue of his role as chief Vatican spokesman during the negotiation for the Lateran Pacts, he made little impression on the hardline Party Secretary.[139]

The only enterprise that was likely to succeed in these difficult circumstances was an approach to Mussolini by an authoritative representative of the Pope himself – in other words Padre Tacchi-Venturi – but given the intransigence of Pius XI this was out of the question. As De Vecchi explained to Grandi, the Pope had no more intention of backing down than had Mussolini.[140] De Vecchi knew the Pope, Mussolini did not. How could he? Despite all of De Vecchi's urgings since the *Conciliazione*, the Duce had refused to meet Pius XI on the grounds that this would be interpreted as a sign of weakness on his part.[141] So these two men who had only met briefly, and accidentally, ten years before,[142] but who lived within two miles of each other in the same city, maintained their obstinate, intransigent positions, and as a result the crisis of 1931 moved inexorably towards its final climacteric, the publication of the encyclical *Non Abbiamo Bisogno*.

NON ABBIAMO BISOGNO AND THE RESOLUTION OF THE CRISIS

Dated 29 June 1931, *Non Abbiamo Bisogno* was not in fact published in Italy until 7 July, in order that the encyclical could be distributed to the world by the enterprising Mons. Francis Spellman, later Archbishop of New York.[143] The Fascist press denounced this precaution as 'disloyalty' on the part of the Vatican, but Pius XI judged rightly that since the Regime was bound to censor the publication of the encyclical in Italy, his strongest weapon in the battle with Mussolini was an appeal to Catholic opinion throughout the world.[144] Such a step was also necessitated by the fact that Mussolini had sent a very one-sided account of the dispute to foreign governments,[145] and that Radio Nazionale had broadcast a similarly biased account of events in its international services.[146]

---

[139] A.C.S., S.P.D., C.R., 44 242/R, Giurati, contains a typed copy of Giurati's account of his talk with Pacelli, dated 10 June 1931. De Vecchi, *Memorie*, no. 17, says that an unspecified person in the Vatican also sent Count Pocci, a well-known Clerico-Fascist in the Papal Court, to sound him out on the possibility of negotiations.

[140] See *D.D.I.*, 7, Vol. X (proofs), 'Ambasciatore presso la Santa Sede' (to Grandi), 9 June 1931.

[141] De Vecchi, *Memorie*, nos. 14 and 15.   [142] De Begnac, *Palazzo Venezia*, p. 441.

[143] For an account of Spellman's mission to Switzerland, and the bitter Fascist reactions see Gannon, *The Cardinal Spellman Story*, pp. 74–9.

[144] As a further precaution against Fascist censorship, *L'Osservatore Romano* was put on sale at the news-stands five hours earlier than usual!

[145] See the text of the telegram sent to Italian missions abroad citing Vatican demands for the suppression of Protestant propaganda, and the anti-Fascist activities of Catholic Action, in *D.D.I.*, 7, Vol. X (proofs), T.S.S.O.R., 29 May, 1931.

[146] Ibid., no. 1806, 'Nunziature Apostolica d'Italia' (to Grandi), 6 June 1931 – contains Borgoncini-Duca's protest about the Radio Nazionale broadcasts.

The Pope, therefore, devoted a large part of his encyclical to discrediting these statements, and the accusations made against Catholic Action by the Fascist press, describing them as downright lies.[147] In particular, Pius XI rejected the claim that Catholic Action was dominated by members of the P.P.I.: '...in all there are only four cases where ex-leaders of the Partito Popolare have become leaders of Catholic Action'.[148]

It has to be said that whatever criterion is used to define local leaders of the P.P.I., including restricting it to that of the local branch secretary of the dissolved Party, the Pope's statement was manifestly incorrect, as *Il Lavoro Fascista* proceeded to demonstrate in the ten days following the publication of the encyclical, listing on its front pages the names of all those members and officials of Catholic Action who had previously held office in the P.P.I.[149] The Pope's statement, therefore, only confirms De Vecchi's claim that Pius XI was genuinely unaware of the extent of the *popolare* presence inside Catholic Action.[150]

The Pope was on safer ground when he denounced the orchestration by Fascist Party officials of the 'spontaneous' demonstrations and acts of violence against Catholic Action and when he pointed out that the innocence of the Catholic youth organisations had been established beyond question by the failure of the police to find any incriminating documents on their premises.[151] These were statements that no one could challenge.

The Pope then turned to the doctrinal and educational errors of the Regime, condemning it for '...out and out pagan worship of the State' and for educating Italian youth '...in hatred, in violence and even irreverence towards the Pope himself'.[152] For the Regime the most unpalatable part of the encyclical was that in which Pius XI cast serious doubts upon the propriety of the Fascist oath imposed on members of the Party and its organisations, and on various categories of public servants, implying that the oath was not in the main taken out of conviction or commitment to the Fascist faith, but, as the popular Roman joke had it, 'for familiar necessity'.[153] In these circumstances, the Pope recommended Catholics who had to take the oath to make the mental reservation: '...saving the laws of God and the Church – or saving the duties of a good Christian'.[154] But like Mussolini himself, who allowed his brother Arnaldo to continue to publish conciliatory articles in *Il Popolo d'Italia* whilst the rest of the Fascist press was inveighing against Catholic Action, in order to allow some possibility of a rapprochement with the Vatican, so Pius XI

---

[147] For the text of the encyclical in English, see *The Papal Encyclicals*, ed. Freemantle, pp. 243–9, and in Italian, *L'Osservatore Romano*, 7 July 1931, whole of the first two pages.
[148] Ibid.
[149] See the front page articles in *Il Lavoro Fascista*, 8–16 July 1931.
[150] De Vecchi, *Memorie*, nos. 14 and 15.
[151] *L'Osservatore Romano*, 7 July 1931.
[152] Ibid.   [153] Ibid.   [154] Ibid.

in his encyclical was careful not to rule out hopes of an agreement; thus he made a point of saying: '...we do not wish to condemn the Party and the Regime as such, but we do mean to point out those of their policies which are contrary to Catholic theory and practice'.[155]

All in all, *Non Abbiamo Bisogno* was a masterpiece combining a clear warning to the Regime of the dangerous consequence of a continuation of the dispute with an implicit invitation for negotiations to bring it to an end.

Fascist reactions to the encyclical were violent, almost uncontrolled: once again Mussolini let the Fascist anti-clericals off the leash, as he had threatened to do.[156] The result was a rash of anti-clerical pamphlets containing direct personal attacks on Papa Ratti, and a series of newspaper articles which were barely less disrespectful towards the Pope and the Church.[157] *Il Lavoro Fascista* produced yet more stories of Catholic conspiracies against the Regime, including a highly imaginative but extremely implausible account of Jesuit 'conclaves' against Fascism.[158] And the Party Direttorio, at its meeting on 14 July, adopted a tough but dignified stand against the encyclical, denying its accusations about the Balilla and its claims of masonic influences at work in the Fascist camp with the counter-assertion that there had been a '...scandalous, unheard of collusion between the Vatican and the masonic lodges, which are joined together in common hostility towards the Fascist State'.[159] The Party Direttorio felt most keenly, of course, the Pope's strictures about the Fascist oath, which it defended with the same passion as the Fascist press,[160] and by way of reply it took the very serious step of declaring that henceforth membership of Catholic Action organisations was incompatible with that of the Party.[161] As a result, hundreds of Catholics felt compelled to resign from Catholic Action during the following weeks.[162]

This dramatic decision of the Party turned out to be the swansong of Giurati and Scorza, because already more pacific spirits were at work in both camps to bring about a reconciliation between the Church and the Regime. In the Vatican both Cardinals Gasparri and Sbarretti made approaches to Pius XI with a view to opening negotiations with representatives of the Italian Government,[163] and Gasparri also made use of the

---

[155] Ibid. [156] Tamaro, *Venti anni Storia*, Vol. II, p. 450.
[157] Amongst others, Settimelli, *Preti Adagio*, and *Svanticanamento* – the latter was particularly vicious in its attacks on the Pope – and Ricci, *Duello col Papa*, Rome, 1931. Mussolini permitted the publication of a sharp criticism of the Concordat by V, Morello, as a warning to the Vatican of the increasing disillusionment with the *Conciliazione* in the Fascist camp.
[158] *Il Lavoro Fascista*, 16 July 1931, 'Riunioni sospette alla Casa Generalizia dei Gesuiti'. Once again, most of its information came from the police.
[159] A.C.S., S.P.D., C.R., 3/242/R.P.N.F., 'Riunioni del Direttorio', meeting of 14 July 1931.
[160] Ibid., see the paragraph of the statement headed 'Giuramento'.
[161] Ibid. [162] Martini, *Studi sulla Questione Romana*, p. 153.
[163] Ibid.

enormous credit which he still enjoyed at Palazzo Venezia to counsel moderation, ably seconded by Arnaldo Mussolini, who travelled to Rome in order to persuade his brother to take the initiative in seeking a solution to the dispute.[164]

These pressures reinforced Mussolini's growing conviction that the dispute was damaging Italy's reputation abroad, especially in Catholic countries. This had already become clear immediately after the dissolution in June 1931 when messages of sympathy had flooded into the Vatican from Catholic bishops, clergy and lay organisations all over the world.[165] The publication of *Non Abbiamo Bisogno* had had the intended effect of consolidating this sympathy for the Pope, and his claim to be defending religious liberty even evoked a sympathetic response in Protestant and masonic circles.[166]

Eventually, in mid-July, an article appeared in *Gerarchia*, the authoritative organ of Fascist thought edited by Mussolini himself, urging the need to seek a reconciliation with the Church.[167] Written by Crispolto Crispolti, the journalist nephew of the eponymous Clerico-Fascist Senator, the article contained a cool, detached and very perceptive analysis of the causes of the dispute, as well as drawing attention to the effects which it was having on public opinion abroad. In addition, Crispolti put his finger on one of the main reasons for the Pope's intransigence: '...the Holy See is chiefly concerned to prove to the whole world, both Catholic and non-Catholic, that it is in every respect, completely free and independent of Italy'.[168] Crispolti concluded his article with what was clearly intended both as an olive branch to the Vatican and notice to Italian public opinion that a reconciliation was not far off: '...the policy of states towards the Church, if it is aimed at harmonious relations, cannot be anything other than a policy of compromise'.[169]

The olive branch was seized upon quickly and eagerly in the Vatican where Pius XI was coming under strong pressure to resolve the dispute with the Regime, as a result of a meeting of Curia Cardinals held on 23 July.[170] Another consideration which weighed heavily with the Pope at this time was the fear that if the crisis dragged on for very much longer, then the Regime might unilaterally denounce the Concordat, a course of action

[164] Ibid.
[165] See above, p. 155, n. 131.
[166] See Diggins, *Mussolini and Fascism*, p. 199, where he cites the cases of several leading Protestant pastors and journals who gave their support to Pius XI in his stand against Fascism. In France, democratic and masonic politicians and newspapers applauded Pius XI for his resistance to Mussolini; the Socialist, Torres, for example, defined *Non Abbiamo Bisogno* as 'L'Encyclique des droits de l'homme' in *Oeuvre*, 26 July 1931.
[167] C. Crispolti, 'Da Roma al Vaticano. Psichologia di un Contrasto', *Gerarchia*, July 1931, pp. 558–68.
[168] Ibid.   [169] Ibid.
[170] Martini, *Studi sulla Questione Romana*, pp. 158–9.

that was hinted at in several Fascist newspapers.[171] On the Italian side, the decks had been cleared as early as 11 July, when Grandi sent De Vecchi off on holiday in order to avoid having to negotiate with Borgoncini-Duca,[172] whom Gasparri aptly described as a 'war-monger'.[173] By the end of July, Padre Tacchi-Venturi had been commissioned by the Pope to sound out Mussolini on the prospects of a settlement, and in a Rome lulled into unconsciousness by the August heat, the subtle Jesuit carried out his 'shuttle' diplomacy between the Vatican and Palazzo Venezia.

The two main obstacles to an agreement were inevitably the Catholic youth groups and the *sezioni professionali*: under pressure from Giurati and Scorza, Mussolini resisted at length the Vatican demand to hand back the premises and property of the dissolved organisations, hoping that a further deterioration of the situation in the new Spanish Republic (where widespread anti-clerical violence was causing serious alarm in the Vatican) would make the Vatican more amenable to his terms.[174] In the event, Mussolini's ploy failed, as did his attempt to force the Vatican to dissolve the *sezioni professionali*, on which issue Giurati had made a last desperate stand.[175] Despite these difficulties, the negotiations went ahead fairly quickly:[176] on 11 August, normal relations were resumed between the Vatican and Italy, and on 2 September, Tacchi-Venturi and Mussolini reached an agreement; the crisis of 1931 was over.

RECONCILIATION – THE SIGNIFICANCE OF THE SEPTEMBER ACCORDS

L'Accordo per l'Azione Cattolica, as the agreement was officially called, dealt with three central issues:

1. The organisational structure and the leadership of Catholic Action.
2. The aims and objectives of the *sezioni professionali*.
3. The youth groups of Catholic Action.

Clause 1 of the agreement opened with the statement that Catholic Action '...is essentially diocesan and is under the direct control of the bishops'.[177] As has already been seen, 'decentralisation' was regarded by Mussolini as offering the best guarantee of greater ecclesiastical control and therefore reduced lay influence in Catholic Action at both a national and local level.

---

[171] See, for example, the unsigned article 'Italia e Vaticano: una soluzione necessaria', in *Il Messagero*, 9 July 1931. It is clear from A.C.S., S.P.D. C.R., f. 251/R, '*Il Messagero*', sf. 2, that this article at least was 'planted' by Grandi.

[172] De Vecchi, *Memorie*, no. 17.

[173] Martini, *Studi sulla Questione Romana*, p. 143.

[174] Ibid., pp. 158–9.   [175] Ibid.

[176] Ibid., where Martini says that they took a total of eleven days.

[177] For the text of the September Accords, see Appendix III.

However, when the new Statutes of January 1932 are compared with those of ten years earlier, it is clear that the agreement of September 1931 in no way altered the organisational structure of Italian Catholic Action:[178] the movement continued to function in exactly the same way as before, that is under the strong leadership of the lay-dominated Giunta Centrale in Rome.[179] Not until September 1939, after the death of Pius XI and the election of Cardinal Pacelli as his successor, was any radical change made to the power structure of Catholic Action.[180] Only then was the national lay leadership of the organisation totally subordinated to the authority of a commission of Cardinals.

The vexed question of the *popolari* inside Catholic Action was also dealt with in Clause 1 of the agreement. Preceding the ritual reaffirmation that the movement was above and beyond party politics, it was stated that 'No one who has previously belonged to parties hostile to the Regime may be appointed as an officer of the movement.'[181] This was the most important element in the agreement as far as Mussolini was concerned, and the renewed instructions to the police to investigate the political antecedents of the members of Catholic Action, issued by the Ministry of the Interior on 1 September, suggest that at this stage the Regime was determined that the ban on the *popolari* should be enforced.[182]

The replies to this circular, and the information published in the diocesan column of the *Bollettino Ufficiale* in the following months, also suggest that in many areas the bishops took advantage of the process of reconstituting the youth groups, which began immediately after the announcement of September Accords, and the reshuffling of diocesan boards, which followed the publication of the new Statutes, to remove some of the more politically compromised of their lay Catholic Action officials, very often replacing them with priests, and in some cases taking on the role of president of the *giunte* themselves.[183]

---

[178] For the text of the Statutes see *Bollettino Ufficiale*, 15 February 1932.

[179] It is sufficient to turn the pages of the *Bollettino Ufficiale* for the early 1930s to see that the Giunta Centrale continued to make major policy decisions and hand them down to the *giunte diocesane* for implementation in the usual way. It is also very significant that the 'Circolare della Segretaria di Stato circa L'Azione Cattolica', of 31 July 1931 says: '...as far as Canon Law is concerned, the position of Catholic Action has in no way been changed'.

[180] See Chapter 7, p. 191.

[181] *L'Osservatore Romano*, 3 September 1931, 'Gli Accordi per L'Azione Cattolica'.

[182] This was a reminder to the Prefects of the need to reply to an earlier circular of 10 June requesting detailed information on the past and present political behaviour of members and officials of Catholic Action. The text of the circular is to be found in A.C.S., D.G.P.S., G.I., b. 146, 'Azione Cattolica', sf. I. The replies to this and the previous circular are to be found in ibid., bb. 95–125. It was presumably on these and other police reports that *Il Lavoro Fascista* based the articles about the *popolare* presence inside Catholic Action which it published between 7 and 16 July 1931.

[183] See the column entitled 'Giunte Diocesane Ricostituite' in the *Bollettino Ufficiale* for late 1931 and the first seven months of 1932.

On the other hand, a comparison of the many lists of members of diocesan *giunte* which appeared in the *Bollettino* in 1930 and 1931 with those reconstituted in late 1931 and early to mid-1932, demonstrates that in the majority of cases the whole diocesan *giunta* was confirmed in office. This means that in 1932 ex-*popolare* M.P.s like Callisto Giavazzi remained on the diocesan *giunta* of Bergamo – along with another controversial former leader of the local P.P.I., Don Clienze Bortolotti – Teodoro Bobbio on that of Alba, G. B. Bivaschi on that of Udine and Italo Rosa on the diocesan *giunta* of Padua.[184] In Florence, the Apostolic Administrator reappointed two local *popolare* leaders – Marchisone and Torricelli – who were later confirmed in office by the new archbishop, Elia Della Costa, despite the Prefect's objections.[185] From Milan the Prefect reported that Cardinal Schuster had re-appointed five *popolari* to the diocesan board,[186] and further examples of this widespread tendency to ignore the ban can be cited.

The assumption on the part of authors of some recent studies of the period that as a result of the September Accords the *popolare* influences were eliminated from Catholic Action is not, therefore, borne out by the documented facts.[187] Complaints, albeit fewer of them, about the activities of the *popolari* continued to arrive on Mussolini's desk long after September 1931.[188]

As far as the Giunta Centrale of Catholic Action was concerned, not a single member was removed from his or her post as a consequence of the 1931 crisis or its resolution: indeed the composition of the national governing body of Catholic Action remained unchanged for several years to come. The first change was the resignation of Righetti as President of F.U.C.I. in 1934,[189] Mons. Montini (who was not a member of the Giunta Centrale) having been forced to resign as Chaplain-General of the Catholic students' organisation the year before.[190] Even then, the influence of these two leading Catholic anti-Fascists was simply transferred to the Movimento Laureato, to which Righetti devoted himself in the early 1930s.

---

[184] For the pre-crisis composition of the Bergamo *giunta* see the *Bollettino Ufficiale*, 1 April 1931, p. 273; for that of Alba see ibid., 1 March 1931, p. 94; for Udine, ibid., 15 March 1931; and for Padua, ibid., 15 May 1930. On 31 October 1931, the *Bollettino Ufficiale*, p. 436, announced that the *giunta* of Alba had been confirmed in office, and those of Bergamo, Padua and Udine were confirmed according to the *Bollettino Ufficiale* of 31 December 1931, p. 479.

[185] A.C.S., D.G.P.S., G.I., b. 104, 'Firenze', 'Assoc. Cattol.' reports from the Prefect of 13 November 1931 and 24 April 1932.

[186] Ibid., b. 113, 'Milano', 'Ass. Catt. Scioglimento', report from the Prefect of 23 June 1932.

[187] See De Felice, IV, p. 269, where he says: 'As far as the leaders [of Catholic Action] were concerned, the explicit ban on former members of "parties hostile to the Regime" meant the elimination, at least for the moment, of the most politically active and able elements.' See also Spataro, *I Democratici Cristiani*, p. 131.

[188] De Vecchi, *Memorie*, no. 17, and Martini, *Studi sulla Questione Romana*, p. 172.

[189] Marcucci-Fanello, *Storia della F.U.C.I.*, p. 150.

[190] Webster, *The Cross and the Fasces*, p. 140.

Despite the confident predictions of the Fascist press, neither of their particular *bêtes noires*, Pizzardo or Dalla Torre, was sacrificed by Pius XI as the price of reconciliation. Much to the annoyance of the Fascist authorities, Pizzardo remained the presiding genius of Catholic Action until the changes of 1939, and Dalla Torre continued to exercise a powerful influence on the organisation until his resignation from the editorship of the Vatican newspaper in 1957. It was in fact Giurati and Scorza who paid the price of their intransigent opposition to Catholic Action, being removed from the Direttorio in the 'Changing of the Guard' of December 1931.[191] As Cardinal Pacelli and Ciriaci repeated ad nauseam, in terms of the leadership of Catholic Action, 'nothing has changed'.[192]

The future of the *sezioni professionali* was guaranteed by Clause 2 of the September Accords, but with the solemn injunction that: 'Catholic Action has never had plans to constitute professional or trade union organisations, nor does it seek functions of a trade union nature.'[193] Some contemporary observers interpreted this as a restriction of the functions of the *sezioni professionali*,[194] and therefore as a defeat for the Church, but I.C.A.S. had encouraged quasi-trade union activities before the crisis of 1931, and was to do so again after a decent interval. Clause 2 went on to state that the purpose of the *sezioni* was to ensure that '...the legally constituted trade union organisations conform more and more to the principle of class collaboration, and to the social and political objectives which, in a Catholic country, the corporative system seeks to achieve'.[195]

Once again, this must only be counted as a victory for the Church and Catholic Action as is clear from the deafening silence of *Il Lavoro Fascista*,[196] for the Regime was thus accepting the very thing which *Il Lavoro Fascista* in its polemics of March, April and May had rejected as intolerable and inadmissible in the Fascist, totalitarian state: the right of the Church to pass judgement on its social and economic policies and the right of Catholic Action, by means of the *sezioni professionali*, to make its influence felt inside the Fascist trade unions.

---

[191] According to De Begnac, *Palazzo Venezia*, p. 440, Scorza '...resigned from office before he could be dismissed. His "severed" head thus appeased the pontifical wrath'.

[192] *Bollettino Uffliciale*, 15 October 1931, 'Adunanza della Giunta Centrale dell'A.C.'. See also the letter of the Cardinal Secretary of State to the Italian bishops, 19 September 1931, in which Pacelli states, 'To avoid any doubts I must add that no changes have taken place in the existing General Presidency.' This is to be found in A.C.S., D.G.P.S., G.I., b. 146, 'Azione Cattolica', sf. I.

[193] *L'Osservatore Romano*, 3rd September 1931, 'Gli Accordi per L'Azione Cattolica'.

[194] *The Times*, for example, in its report of 3 September 1931, said that the settlement was '...distinctly to the advantage of the Italian Government', and claimed that the *sezioni professionali* had lost the power to *negotiate* labour contracts, a power which they had never held!

[195] *L'Osservatore Romano*, 3 September 1931, 'Gli Accordi per L'Azione Cattolica'.

[196] The newspaper of Fascist trade unionism published the text of the settlement on 3 September without a single comment!

As far as youth groups were concerned, apart from a change of name to Associazioni Giovanili dell' Azione Cattolica, and the insistence on the use of the Italian Tricolour rather than the 'foreign' papal flag by these groups,[197] their scope and structure remained unchanged. The ban in Clause 3 on the sponsorship of sporting or athletic activities by the Catholic youth groups was nothing more than a restatement of the policy which Catholic Action had been forced to accept in 1927–8 when the Catholic Boy Scouts and the Catholic Sporting Federations had been disbanded by the Regime. In addition, the Catholic youth groups were allowed to resume possession of those cinemas, theatres and recreation halls which were such a potent attraction to new members despite Mussolini's demands that they be handed over to the Balilla.

For its part of the bargain, the Party revoked its declaration of incompatibility between membership of its organisation and those of Catholic Action on 15 September, and the reconstitution of Catholic youth groups then followed very quickly.[198] By the Summer of 1932, the operation had been completed in most dioceses and in some cases there was a marked increase in membership,[199] despite the instructions of the new Party Secretary, Starace, that all children in private (Catholic) schools should be obliged to join the Balilla.[200]

Despite the expressions of approval and relief with which both the Fascist and the Catholic press greeted the announcement of the September Accords, it took some time for the effects of the 1931 crisis to dissipate themselves. In Milan, the heartland of Catholic anti-Fascism, serious misgivings about the nature of the settlement were voiced in some Catholic circles,[201] and as late as January 1932, strong resentment against the Regime was still to be found amongst members of the Archdiocesan Curia.[202] The clergy of other areas of northern Italy continued to harbour feelings of mistrust and suspicion towards Fascism in the months following the reconciliation, most notably in Vicenza where the bishop warned against over-optimistic hopes of an early rapprochement between the clergy and the Regime in a letter to his old enemy, the Fascist Federale.[203]

---

[197] Martini, *Studi sulla Questione Romana*, etc p. 167.

[198] A clear picture of the speed with which this was accomplished emerges from A.C.S., D.G.P.S., G.I., bb. 95–125, in the files entitled 'Ass. Giov. Catt.', 'Scioglimento' and/or 'Ricostituzione'.

[199] For example, ibid., b. 120, 'Roma', 'Ass. Giov. Catt. (1931–33)', report from the Prefect of 21 January 1932 which says that whereas only 82 Catholic youth groups were dissolved in May 1931, there were now over 100 operating.

[200] Tannenbaum, *Fascism in Italy*, p. 137.

[201] A.C.S., S.P.D., P.N.F., S.P.P., b. 7, 'Milano', report of the Milan Political Police, 15 September 1931.　　　　　[202] Ibid., report of 24 January 1932.

[203] See *Avanti!*, 14 November 1931, 'Come il Vescovo di Vicenza scrive al segretario federale di quella provincia': 'What is clear is that the lower clergy are not at all satisfied with the recent agreement which has naturally left the situation and the countryside, particularly, unchanged.'

The southern clergy were predictably more enthusiastic about the reconciliation between the Church and the State, as the numerous letters and
telegrams of congratulations which Mussolini received clearly demonstrate.[204]

The Fascist rank and file, for their part, were generally satisfied with
Mussolini's handling of the 1931 dispute, regarding the agreement
reached in September as confirmation of the strength of the Regime. There
were, however, the inevitable exceptions who interpreted it as yet another
surrender of power to the Church.[205] When the time arrived to celebrate
the third anniversary of the *Conciliazione*, the reconciliation between the
Church and the Fascism had been completed at a national level, and this
process was consolidated by Mussolini's long-awaited visit to the Pope on
11 February 1932.[206] This meeting between the two men who had been
both the chief architects of the *Conciliazione* and the chief protagonists in
the 1931 crisis was characterised by a remarkable degree of warmth and
understanding,[207] and put the final seal on a relationship of harmony and
peaceful co-existence, that 'marriage of convenience' that was to endure
until the eruption of a new dispute between the Church and the Regime
in 1938.

[204] A.C.S., S.P.D., C.R. 6/97/R, 'Questione Romana', 'Accordo col Vaticano, 1931'.
[205] See, for example, ibid., P.N.F., S.P.P., b. 4, 'Macerata', report of the Prefect for September
1931, where he says, 'Only a few intransigent elements seem to have desired less
moderation on the part of Fascism', and b. 6, 'Milano', report of 16 February 1932.
[206] Ibid.
[207] For an account of the visit, see Corsetti, 'Dalla preconciliazione ai Patti Laterano', p. 222,
'Colloquio col Papa, ore 11 del giorno 11 Febb. 1932, in Vaticano'. Mussolini was
particularly moved by the Pope's kind remarks about his brother Arnaldo, who had died
a few weeks before. But even this meeting was not without its unfortunate repercussions,
for Mussolini complained that his visit had not received sufficient attention in the Vatican
press, see De Vecchi, *Memorie*, no. 17.

CHAPTER 7

Conclusion and epilogue

The disputes between the Church and the Fascist Regime in the period 1929–32 were not caused by anything so trivial as differences in interpreting the meaning of the Lateran Pacts, unless, that is, one considers that the conflict over Catholic Action was generated by a difference of opinion over the meaning of Article 43 – and no one, on either side, seems to have suggested this at the time. Any real, practical problems of *interpreting* and executing the Pacts were resolved by the Joint Implementation Commission, the most obvious example being the thorny question of implementing the clauses of the Concordat relating to matrimony.

The conflicts in this period were about much more serious, substantial and intractable matters, more about each side's interpretation of the overall import and implications of the *Conciliazione* for the future balance of power between them. Mussolini, for his part, regarded the Lateran Pacts as not only having resolved the 'Roman Question' and having reconciled the Church and the Italian State, but by implication he believed that in both a legal and political sense, the Church had been subordinated or even subjected to the State. This much is confirmed by his remarks about the Church being 'neither free nor sovereign in the Fascist State'.

Having manoeuvred the Church into publicly supporting the 'Plebiscite' of 1929, he believed that it was now irrevocably committed to his Regime – as he explained to his brother Arnaldo during the crisis of 1931, 'We intended that the Church should become a pillar of the Regime. We never thought for a moment that the Regime would become the servant of the Church!'[1] But Pius XI was determined to keep his distance from Fascism, as was clearly demonstrated by the Vatican's reaction to Cardinal Schuster's speech of February 1930. When that naive prince of the Church made his notorious remarks about the Pope and Fascism,[2] after Turati's visit to the Vatican, *L'Osservatore Romano* quickly rushed into print to repudiate the statement.[3] And, as we have already seen, one of the major

---

[1] As quoted in Guspini, *L'Orecchio del Regime*, p. 108.
[2] See Chapter 3, p. 60.   [3] *L'Osservatore Romano*, 29 March 1930, 'Una Rettifica'.

reasons for Pius XI's obduracy during the 1931 crisis, and an essential object of his encyclical *Non Abbiamo Bisogno*, was to prove the Church's independence of Italian Fascism.[4]

In similar fashion, Mussolini did not take very seriously the sovereign, independent and neutral status which he had granted to the Vatican in the Lateran Pacts. Indeed, his 'throwaway line' in the speech of 13 May 1929, that '...we have not resurrected the temporal power of the Popes, we have buried it',[5] takes on a new and sinister meaning: with little or no genuine religious feeling, and with barely any more understanding of the historical role of the Papacy, he persisted in believing that the Vatican was an essentially Italian institution, and all the more so now as a result of the *Conciliazione*. Ignoring its fundamental character of universality, he fondly imagined that it would actively support the objectives of Italian Fascist foreign policy; a misconception which seems to have been shared by Grandi.

Mussolini's disappointment was, therefore, very real and bitter when it became abundantly clear that the Vatican would not allow itself to be entangled in his international ambitions. This dimension of the relationship between the Vatican and the Regime would probably have remained a minor, unimportant irritant but for the fact that some of the more glaring and clamorous manifestations of the Vatican's international independence of Fascist Italy happened to take place in the Spring of 1931, when tensions were beginning to build up between the Church and the Regime inside of Italy. The events in Yugoslavia and elsewhere thus exacerbated an already critical situation.

The Vatican's reaction to the events in Spain in the Spring of 1931 also brought home to Mussolini the political pragmatism of Pius XI and his collaborators. Faced by the fall of the Spanish Monarchy, and inevitable establishment of a liberal, democratic republic that was almost certainly going to introduce a wide range of secularising, ecclesiastical legislation, the Vatican did not lift a finger to save Alphonso XIII. There was not, in any case, very much the Vatican could do to help that unfortunate and unwise monarch. Some of the local clergy did publicly regret the passing of the Monarchy, as Cardinal Segura's inflammatory speech of May 1931 demonstrates, but the Vatican refused to support him. This kind of policy divergence between a national hierarchy and the Vatican was far from unusual during the reign of Pius XI, the most notable previous example being the Vatican's repudiation of the support given by some French bishops for the anti-republican and semi-Fascist organisation, Action Française.[6] But Mussolini does not seem to have grasped the significance of that and similar cases.

---

[4] See Chapter 6, p. 160.   [5] *O.O.*, Vol. XXIV, p. 74.
[6] Falconi, *The Popes in the Twentieth Century*, pp. 198–9.

The Vatican's response to the Spanish situation was extremely realistic and entirely predictable. It sought, as it had always done since the end of the First World War, to come to terms with the new regime, in order to protect the essential interests of Spanish Catholicism. After the publication of the draft of the republican constitution containing so many attacks on the privileges and immunities of the Spanish Church, the Vatican still strained every muscle in an attempt to maintain good relations with the Spanish Republic, and therefore to reach a compromise with it on the religious question.[7] And it continued this policy long after the Spanish Primate's speech and the resulting spate of Church burnings.[8]

Strange though it may seem, all this came as a blinding revelation to Mussolini, for despite all the evidence to the contrary – the Vatican's rapprochement with France in the 1920s, its extraordinary efforts as late as December 1928 to reach an accommodation with atheistic, bolshevik Russia,[9] and its consistent policy of generally seeking good relations with regimes of many different political hues – he had failed to perceive that though the Vatican under Pius XI undoubtedly preferred authoritarian regimes, it would not tie itself blindly and irrevocably to them. Mussolini's thoughts on the Spanish situation of 1931, if they are to be taken at face value, are evidence of a remarkable chapter in his political education, demonstrating that he had at last grasped the essence of Vatican policy:

His Majesty the Catholic King of Spain, has received no support from the Catholics. This is a fact. What are the reasons? They are in fact historical; the Church does not have a clear policy on the question of political institutions, except in a very theoretical way; in the final analysis it judges all institutions by their behaviour towards the Church.[10]

But if Mussolini acquired a new and more accurate perception of the underlying motives of Vatican policy, and if that contributed to a stiffening of his resolve in the disputes with the Church during 1931, there is no evidence that Vatican policy changed in the same way. It has been argued by the author of a recent study of Italo-Vatican relations in the 1930s that the events in Spain, together with the religious persecutions that were going on at that time in Soviet Russia and in Mexico, led to Pius XI '...placing his faith in Italian Fascism'.[11] That statement is true up to a point, i.e., after the resolution of the 1931 crisis, the Pope endeavoured to maintain good relations with the Italian Fascist Regime, *inside* Italy. Such a policy was perfectly consistent and in accord with the Vatican's overall policy towards governments and, therefore, involved no change in direction. But the author's further claim that the events in both Spain and Italy in 1931 had the effect of henceforth tying Vatican international policy more

---

[7] Rhodes, *The Vatican in the Age of the Dictators*, pp. 117–21.
[8] Ibid.   [9] Ibid., p. 139.
[10] As quoted in De Felice, IV, pp. 824–5.   [11] Kent, *The Pope and the Duce*, p. 139.

closely to Italian, Fascist foreign policy interests[12] is simply not borne out by the facts. In this area of the relationship between the Vatican and the Fascist Regime there was also no change. The Vatican did nothing to alter the anti-Italian stand of the Croat and Slovene clergy, and, as we have already seen, it continued to pursue its policy of reaching an agreement with the Belgrade Government. After 1931, the Vatican also pushed forward its policy of educating native, colonial peoples and elevating them to both the priesthood and the episcopacy,[13] a policy that ran counter to Mussolini's increasingly imperialistic and racialisitc ambitions in the 1930s. Though the bulk of the Italian clergy and laity gave enthusiastic, patriotic support to the imperial conquest of Ethiopia in 1935–6, and in some cases justified it on the grounds that it was bringing Christianity and Civilisation to 'barbarians', the Vatican remained publicly aloof.[14] To this extent, at least, Mussolini's expectations of the long-term political benefits of the *Conciliazione* were not realised.

Mussolini was not alone in having his expectations of the *Conciliazione* disappointed in the period 1929–32, for the hopes and expectations which Pius XI nurtured in February 1929 were also proved to be largely illusory by subsequent events. Trusting as he did in the sincerity and integrity of Mussolini's religious policy the Pope believed that the *Conciliazione* provided all the necessary pre-condition for a 'Christian restoration of society' in Italy. In this he was at one with those Clerico-Fascist, lay politicians who had rallied to Mussolini in the early and mid-1920s in the belief that the rise of Fascism offered an unrepeatable opportunity to bring about a restoration of that Catholic, clerical and confessional state that had existed under the *ancien Régime*.[15]

Given the deep-rooted anti-clericalism of early Fascism, the ruthless opportunism of Mussolini's religious policy and the tenacious, totalitarian ambitions of the Fascist Regime, Pius XI's hopes were doomed to failure. Mussolini was no more willing to accept clerical domination of Fascist policy in domestic affairs than Pius XI was willing to allow Vatican international policy to be subordinated to Italian foreign policy interests. Yet the Pope can be excused for making this mistaken judgement in 1929: by then, precisely as a result of Mussolini's religious policy, the standing

---

[12] Ibid., p. 120.

[13] See Neill, *A History of Christian Missions*, p. 524.

[14] This did not, however, prevent the Vatican from working behind the scenes, to save the 'Hoare-Laval Pact', in the hope of achieving a solution of the Abyssinian Crisis that would have been favourable to Mussolini: see the annual report of 1934 from the British Minister to the Holy See in Hachey (ed.), *Anglo-Vatican Relations*, pp. 292–5. Even this, however, was motivated by its desire to help maintain good relations between France and Italy.

[15] For an example of this aspect of Clerico-Fascist thought, see the letter from Filippo Crispolti to A. Gennari of 19 December 1928, as reproduced in Sorrentino, *La Conciliazione*, p. 97; see also Webster, *The Cross and the Fasces*, pp. 89–90.

of the Church in Italy had been transformed, and its social influence had been considerably increased. Seven years of Fascist rule had already brought about the restoration of the key elements of a Catholic, confessional state – the re-introduction of religion into primary and secondary schools, the restitution of ecclesiastical property, the re-establishment of the legal immunities of the clergy and the banning of ex-communicated priests from public employment and a marriage law which effectively transferred jurisdiction from the State to the Church and made the introduction of divorce virtually impossible. In addition, by means of Article 1 of the Concordat, the Church had succeeded in re-establishing what was for all practical purposes its old power of censorship within the City of Rome.

Pius XI understandably believed that the Fascist Regime would be prepared to go further along this road, that in particular it would be willing to turn itself into the 'secular arm' of the Vatican in the battle against Protestant propaganda and proselytism in Italy. Like the Clerico-Fascists, the Vatican saw the battle against the Protestant threat as a natural point of convergence between the Church and the Fascist Regime.[16] Since many of the Protestant churches in Italy were in large part inspired, financed and directed from abroad, and in view of the fact that others were heavily compromised by masonic connections, it seemed logical that a nationalistic, anti-masonic Fascist Regime would join in common cause with the Catholic Church against them. But if the Vatican was anxious not to be too closely identified with the Fascist Regime in the eyes of world opinion, then, by the same token, the Regime had no desire to be seen as a supine tool of Roman Catholicism, especially by its many Anglo-Saxon admirers.

Despite the Regime's stubborn resistance to demands to curb the Protestant minorities, and its general reluctance to do the Church's bidding as far as issues of public morality were concerned, the Vatican cannot be blamed if in March 1931 it failed to take heed of a strong warning signal, that is Arpinati's very public expression of irritation over the complaints about those matters. With hindsight, that incident can be seen as an important turning-point in relations between the Church and the Regime, if not as the beginning of the 1931 crisis itself. But barely six months before, in September 1930, Mussolini had after all acceded to the Vatican's unnecessary and unjustified demand for the abolition of the Feast of the 20th of September. Mussolini's craven repudiation of this part of Italy's risorgimental heritage was yet another extreme concession to Catholic pressure, giving rise to the impression in Vatican circles that nothing could now impede the onward march of the clerical, confessional state. Not surprisingly, therefore, the crisis of 1931 came as a brutal and shattering shock in the Vatican, and Pius XI's response to that crisis was strongly

---

[16] For an example of the Clerico-Fascist attitude towards the Protestants after 1929, see Martire, *La Conciliazione*, pp. 279–81.

determined by a profound sense of betrayal, ensuring that the dispute would be bitter and protracted.

What the crisis of 1931 proved to Pius XI were the limits to clericalisation and confessionalism under the Fascist Regime, even if it had been under that same Regime that the foundations for a clerical, confessional state had been laid in the Lateran Pacts. Only after the fall of Fascism, and under the aegis of a Catholic 'ruling class' – i.e., the Christian Democratic Party – was the dream of a clerical, confessional state to be realised in the late 1940s, the 1950s and early 1960s.

As significant a factor as the Pope's aggrandising and clericalising policy towards Fascism in the causes of conflict between the Church and the Regime in the period 1929–32, and therefore in the causes of the 1931 crisis was the instrument he chose to implement that policy, Catholic Action. It seems a fair assumption that Mussolini allowed Catholic Action to survive in 1929 because he believed that he could destroy it at a later, more propitious date. But for so many of Mussolini's followers, the survival of Catholic Action after 1929 was an intolerable, unacceptable anomaly and weakness in the structure of the Fascist State. For that reason they were determined to remove this last remaining obstacle to the realisation of the totalitarian dream. In the short term, however, Mussolini could do little more than keep Catholic Action within the strait-jacket that he believed the Concordat imposed upon it – hence his telegram to the Prefects of June 1929, and subsequent police surveillance of it.

The Fascist press campaigns against Catholic Action, and the other measures which Mussolini adopted against it during the 'creeping' crisis of 1929–30 were intended as a warning against clerical pretensions, an attempt to teach Catholic Action and the Church their true place in post-*Conciliazione*, Fascist Italy. But that attempt was a demonstrable failure, and by the Spring of 1931, the growth in Catholic Action membership and the aggressive expansion of its activities were exciting the anger of the leaders and members of the Fascist Party's rival organisations, thus posing in an acute and pressing form the problem of Catholic Action. Two particular wings of Catholic Action, the *sezioni professionali* and the youth groups seemed to present a threat, as perhaps never before, to the totalitarian goals of Fascism in the two major areas of national life – the economy and education – where the Regime had still not fully established its control.

In the case of the economy, it was not merely the *sezioni professionali*, but also the wider question of Catholic attitudes to the much-vaunted but largely embryonic 'Corporate State' which worried the Fascists. However little substance the 'Corporate State' had in reality, it was of course seen by the Fascists as their most original contribution to the development of solutions of the 'Social Question'. When virtually all other major political and economic issues were 'taboo', discussions and debates in the Fascist press and in the Fascist movement generally about the theory and practice of Corporatism remained relatively free. The fact that Catholic Social Thought could justifiably claim to have developed corporate theories rather earlier than Fascism was an inconvenient fact which some Fascist writers naturally glossed over. Moreover, in the period 1929–32, certain authoritative Catholic statements did not fail to point out the essential *differences* between Catholic and Fascist corporatist theory. In particular, Padre Balduzzi in his little *opusculo*, and Pius XI in his important encyclical *Quadragesimo Anno* clearly stated their reservations about Fascist corporatist practice. This half-hearted and ambiguous official Catholic attitude to the 'Corporate State' inevitably aroused the deepest of suspicions in Fascist circles.

The most serious Catholic reservation touched Fascist Corporatism in its most essential feature, the State monopoly of trade union organisation. The existence, therefore, of a small, limited, but clearly growing Catholic presence in the labour field – the *sezioni professionali* – and its pretentious activities in that fields were viewed by Fascist trade union leaders as a potential threat to their monopoly, as a concealed attempt at revanchism on the part of former leaders of the Catholic trade union organisation C.I.L. In the context of the palpably serious effects which the 'Great Depression' was having on the Italian economy in early 1931, the exaltation of Catholic Social Teaching during the celebrations for *Rerum Novarum* was also seen as an attempt to offer a viable alternative to Fascist Corporatism. At a time when the Regime seemed rather less solid than it had been for some time, the possibility that the *sezioni* might be falling into hands of the *popolari*, and could thus form the nuclei of a resurrected Catholic trade union movement, could not be ruled out. Hence the special animosity which *Il Lavoro Fascista* nurtured towards Catholic Action and, consequently, the leading role which that newspaper played in the 1931 crisis.

The completion of the process of 'fascistisation' in the educational and youth fields was also a logical and necessary step if Fascism was to perpetuate itself through the formation of its own ruling class. On the eve of the *Conciliazione* in 1929, the Italian educational system had barely felt the effects of 'fascistisation'. Gentile's educational reforms of 1924 had not been especially 'Fascist' in either spirit or purpose, and since then little else had been done other than to incorporate the teaching profession into the Fascist trade unions. Moreover, many Fascists educationalists had interpreted the re-introduction of religious instruction into the secondary schools, as laid down by Article 36 of the Concordat of 1929, as a step backwards, as a diminution of Fascist influence already established there.

This assessment by Fascist educationalists of the impact of the *Conciliazione* on the educational system lends credence to the view of several historians that the numerous measures carried out in the educational field in the period 1929–32 were largely motivated by a determination to combat increased Catholic influences. Apart from any other consideration, these measures were carried out by the new Minister of Education appointed in September 1929, Balbino Giuliano, who appears to have been distinctly less pro-Catholic than his predecessors, Pietro Fedele. A similar anxiety, this time about the alarming growth of the rival Catholic youth organisations, was clearly one of the prime considerations lying behind the measures which Giurati and Scorza introduced after October 1931 to strengthen and extend the youth organisations of the Party.

Even if these innovations in the youth and educational fields were rather more piecemeal, and rather less spectacular, than either Starace's creation of a single, party youth organisation, the Gioventù Italiana del Littorio in 1937,[17] or Giuseppe Bottai's comprehensive Carta della Scuola of 1939,[18] it can be argued that together they constituted a more important contribution to the 'fascistisation' of Italian education and youth. If this is true, then it suggests that the *Conciliazione* had a powerful influence on the development of the Fascist Regime.

At the root of all Fascist suspicions of Catholic Action was a nagging anxiety about the activities and influence of the thousands of *popolari* who remained in the avowedly 'apolitical' Catholic organisations after the demise of the P.P.I. in 1927. Despite that defeat, the *popolare* experience between 1919 and 1927 had already demonstrated the ability of the Catholic Movement to provide Italy with a new ruling class. The subsequent failure of the P.P.I. to establish some effective form of organisation in exile far from being a weakness, ought in fact to be recognised as the great strength and advantage of the *popolari* over the other anti-Fascist parties. The fact that 99 per cent of the P.P.I. apparatus, M.P.s, party officials and members, remained behind in Italy, but, more importantly, that they enjoyed the protection of the Church from the worst features of Fascist police repression, and that in Catholic Action they continued to be able to meet and even exercise their influence, ensured that they remained a formidable threat to the Fascist Regime in the period 1929–32. The Communists and the Giellisti[19] might be more active and more daring in their campaign against Fascism, but hardly more effective than the *popolari* in the long term. And in the short term, in the event of Fascism entering into crisis due to the deteriorating economic situation, the *popolari* possessed in Catholic Action a perfect springboard for a bid for power, and with the Vatican as guarantor, they offered the only acceptable alternative to

---

[17] A translation of the Decree Law instituting the G.I.L. is to be found in *Mediterranean Fascism*, ed. Delzell, pp. 143–5.

[18] For an analysis of the Carta della Scuola, see Tannenbaum, *Fascism in Italy*, p. 188.

[19] I.e., the members of the anti-Fascist Giustizia e Libertà organisation.

Fascism as far as the old political establishment was concerned. Judged in this light, Fascist suspicion towards Catholic Action was entirely justified.

As was demonstrated by his righteous rejection of Fascist claims in *Non Abbiamo Bisogno*, Pius XI seriously under-estimated both the numerical strength and the influence of the *popolari* inside of Catholic Action. Convinced that his reforms of Catholic Action in the early 1920s had returned it to the straight and narrow, that is to total dependence upon the bishops and the clergy, he trusted absolutely in his ability to enforce the obedience of the *popolari* and keep them out of trouble. But Pius XI proved incapable of suppressing the anti-Fascist enthusiasm and the activities of the *popolare* elements in Italy, a role which Mussolini expected of him after the *Conciliazione*, and one on which the whole of the Vatican's policy towards Fascism depended. There is, therefore, a real sense in which it can be said that the crisis of 1931 was partly the result of a revolt of the Catholic rank and file against the leadership, of *popolare* militants and other Catholic Action activists against the bishops and even against the Pope himself.

Mussolini and the Fascist leaders were clearly aware of the potentially mortal threat which the *popolari* inside Catholic Action posed to their Regime, and in 1931 they believed that they had either to destroy Catholic Action entirely or purge it of its *popolare* influences, if they were to eliminate that threat. This Mussolini tried to do with the dissolution of the Catholic youth groups in May 1931, because it was in the youth groups, more than in any other branch of Catholic Action, that the *popolari* were so numerous and their influence so pervasive.[20] Had Mussolini succeeded in closing down the Catholic youth groups permanently in May 1931, he would have effectively destroyed Catholic Action, for without the continued supply of trained cadres coming from below, the adult organisations of Catholic Action would have quickly withered and died. And, of course, the pernicious influence of the *popolari* on the rising generations of Italian Catholic youth would have been almost entirely eliminated.

The activities of the *popolari* inside Catholic Action were given fuller rein after September 1929, following the resignation and replacement of Luigi Colombo as its national President. With Colombo also went the one effective restraining influence on the aggressive activities of Catholic Action in the labour and youth fields, for if his successor, Augusto Ciriaci, really did attempt to restrain these activities, he lacked the necessary political 'clout' in the Vatican which Colombo had enjoyed by virtue of his friendship with Pius XI. Even though Colombo had had an early but

---

[20] The replies from the Prefects to D.G.P.S. circular 442/23217 of 12 December 1931, which requested information on the political sympathies of Catholic Action leaders, to be found in A.C.S., D.G.P.S., G.I., bb. 95–120, under the heading 'Associazioni Cattoliche', demonstrate this conclusively.

short-lived involvement in the P.P.I., and even if his role as President of Catholic Action prevented him from publicly identifying himself with the political activities of the Clerico-Fascists in the early and mid-1920s, it seems impossible to escape the conclusion that all of his political sympathies lay with Clerico-Fascism. His attitude towards the Regime as expressed in the 1920s, and his numerous friends and acquaintances among the Clerico-Fascists, most notably his fellow-Milanese, Stefano Cavazzoni, demonstrate this irrefutably.

The significance of Colombo's exit from the presidency of Catholic Action must therefore be seen in the wider context of the general decline, not to say virtual extinction, of Clerico-Fascist influences in both Catholic and Fascist circles which had taken place by September 1929. Within Catholic Action itself, many of the Clerico-Fascists who had been placed in key positions at a diocesan level in the mid-1920s, had been replaced by early 1929. With the progressive improvement in relations with the Regime, and particularly after the signing of the Lateran Pacts, it seemed to many of the bishops that the Clerico-Fascists were no longer needed as a guarantee of the political reliability of Catholic Action. In addition, many of those same bishops had long resented the role of the Clerico-Fascists as mediators between the Church and the Regime. Much the same was true of the Vatican's attitude towards the Clerico-Fascists: whilst the Clerico-Fascists were undoubtedly of great tactical value to Pius XI in his pursuit of an understanding with the Regime in the 1920s, their autonomous political activities did not fit into his overall strategy of an apolitical Catholic movement, utterly obedient to his commands. In March 1928, the Clerico-Fascists finally lost all sympathy and support in the Vatican, when Pius XI publicly criticised the C.N.I. national congress for its religious policy, and for its failure to ask for an audience with him when it had been received by Mussolini.[21]

Once the *Conciliazione* had been achieved, the attitude of both the Vatican and the Regime was that the Clerico-Fascists had had their day, and that they no longer served any very useful function. Thus, neither side lifted a finger to help the remaining two Clerico-Fascist newspapers – *Il Momento* of Turin and *Il Corriere d'Italia* of Rome – as they drowned in a sea of debts in 1929. Mussolini adopted an attitude of even more cynical indifference towards the Clerico-Fascists, enlisting their aid in the electoral propaganda for the 'Plebiscite' of 1929, but at the same time drastically reducing their representation in the Fascist Chamber elected by it. Furthermore, Mussolini removed the last remaining Clerico-Fascist influence in his Government, Paolo Mattei-Gentili, in his Cabinet reshuffle of September 1929. There can be no doubt that had he remained in office he would have exerted all of his influence to prevent the development of the 1931 crisis.

[21] See above, Chapter 3, p. 59 n. 60.

The effective demise of Clerico-Fascism as a political force in 1929 removed that 'bridge' between Catholicism and Fascism which had served both sides so well during the years of the rapprochement. Whilst we can only speculate as to the role that the Clerico-Fascists would have played during the crisis of 1931, we can be fairly sure that they would have at least attempted to exercise a moderating influence on both sides.

It has been suggested that Cardinal Gasparri was dropped as Secretary of State because he was too 'soft' on Fascism, but this is only a partial explanation of the change, for his replacement, Pacelli, was equally if not more conciliatory in his attitude towards the Regime, as his policy during the 1931 crisis amply demonstrates. As far as Pius XI was concerned, with the realisation of the *Conciliazione*, Gasparri too had served his turn, having guided the Vatican, over the sixteen-year period since his first appointment as Secretary of State by Benedict XV, towards a reconciliation with the Italian State. Pius XI now wished to be master in his own house: he had become impatient, if not jealous, of the power and influence which Gasparri had built up during that long tenure of office. Hence the appointment of the younger, less experienced and rather less influential Cardinal Pacelli. Caught in the grip of his two adventurous subordinates, Pizzardo in charge of Catholic Action and Borgoncini-Duca in control of the Nunciature to Italy, there was little likelihood that Pacelli would fail to do his master's bidding. Like Grandi in his new post of Minister of Foreign Affairs, Pacelli was largely excluded from matters concerning relations between the Church and the Regime. In Pacelli's case, however, this exclusion had rather more serious repercussions during the Spring and Summer of 1931.

Taken together, the leadership changes within the Fascist Regime in this period proved to have an equally important impact on the development of the crisis of 1931 as those on the Catholic side. Those which resulted from the ministerial reshuffle of September 1929, however, were rather less serious in their effects than the replacement of Turati by Giurati as Party Secretary just over a year later. The entry into the Cabinet of Grandi and Giuliano, whilst it can in some measure be regarded as a lessening of pro-clerical influence, with some significance for the future of relations between the Vatican and the Regime, was not on the other hand accompanied by the removal of that major architect of the *Conciliazione*, Alfredo Rocco, even if his Clerico-Fascist deputy, Mattei-Gentili, was dropped in 1929. Yet Rocco's contribution to the development of relations between the Church and the Regime in this period, and especially the role, if any, which he played in the disputes of 1929–30, and in the crisis of 1931, remain a mystery. There is simply no documentary evidence of the influence which he might have exercised in the field of Church and State relations. At the most, it could be inferred, from his departure from Government in the ministerial reshuffle of 1932, that he may have displeased Mussolini by adopting a moderate stance during the events of the previous year.

The party changes of October 1930 are much more susceptible to a clear-cut interpretation; indeed, they indicate that a definite about turn was already taking place in Mussolini's religious policy some considerable time *before* the outbreak of the 1931 crisis. Paradoxically, it seems likely that Turati's visit to the Pope in February 1930, the event which put an end to the disputes of 1929–30 and ensured a public peace between the Vatican and the Regime until the beginning of March 1931, was the real turning-point in the development of Mussolini's attitude towards the Church. Turati's initiative certainly seems finally to have alienated Mussolini's failing trust in his chief lieutenant, which suggests that the Duce had already made up his mind to take a tougher stand against Catholic 'aggression'. But faced by Turati's *fait accompli*, Mussolini was out manoeuvred, and until he could find a satisfactory replacement for Turati he was unable to enforce a tougher policy against the Church. This would help to explain why he was forced to swallow the bitter pill, and, contrary to his instincts, accept the abolition of the Feast of the 20th of September. But a month later, he had found a satisfactory replacement for Turati. The appointment of Giurati, and of Carlo Scorza, provided Mussolini with the agents he needed in the execution of his new policy towards the Church. The Duce now positively encouraged a resumption of the totalitarian offensive in the youth field, and, as a result, in their campaigns against Catholic youth, Giurati and Scorza came within an ace of success in May 1931.

According to one biographer of Mussolini: 'As we have already stated, between 1932 and 1943, the Regime began its period of decline.'[22] This is a grossly over-simplified, not to say simplistic, way of characterising the fortunes of the Regime in the periods 1922–32 and 1932–43, the former as one of steady rise and the latter of an equally steady decline. In fact, the fortunes of the Regime fluctuated constantly during the course of the Fascist period: there were high as well as low points in the period 1932–43 – e.g., the Abyssinian War of 1935–6 – and low points as well as high ones in the decade 1922–32 – the Matteotti Crisis of 1924–5 being an obvious example. In addition, the years 1930–2 must surely also be considered as a 'low'; by the Spring of 1931 both the objective reality of the effects of the 'Great Depression' and the more subjective reality of all those predictions in foreign newspapers and anti-Fascist circles of the imminent fall of Mussolini suggest that the Regime was facing its gravest crisis of confidence since the Matteotti affair.

[22] De Felice, IV, p. 304.

Inevitably the effects of the 'Great Depression' had a direct and crucial bearing on both the development and the outcome of the crisis of 1931. Given the outburst of Catholic, anti-Fascist activity in the Spring of 1931, not to mention the *Rerum Novarum* celebrations, the dispute with the Church cannot be separated from the other difficulties facing the Regime at this time. Whilst Mussolini's difficulties were obviously exaggerated by both foreign observers and anti-Fascist opponents, the outcome of the dispute with the Church was bound to be seen as a test of Mussolini's strength. The challenge from Catholic Action had to be crushed, sharply and publicly, in a form that would demonstrate beyond any shadow of a doubt, to friend and foe alike, the undiminished power of the Regime and its ability to survive. The dissolution of the Catholic youth organisations in May 1931 was intended to serve exactly this purpose.

The Pope's response to the dissolution, the encyclical *Non Abbiamo Bisogno*, was an equally necessary attempt to assert the independence of the Holy See from the Fascist Regime. Pius XI was temperamentally incapable of going to the negotiating table without a similar show of strength. Honour having been saved on both sides, it was now possible to talk. Though there were suggestions in the foreign press[23] and in anti-Fascist circles of the danger of a more serious rupture, of an out-and-out ideological war between the Vatican and Italian Fascism, given the opportunistic motives on both sides such a conflict was inconceivable. For the Vatican it would have put at risk the enormous benefits of the *Conciliazione* and signalled the utter bankruptcy of Pius XI's policy towards Fascism, and, in his turn, Mussolini was not prepared to contemplate the prolongation of the conflict, however enthusiastic Giurati, Scorza and the anti-clerical wing of Fascism might have been. For Mussolini, too, it would have meant putting at risk the enormous domestic benefits and foreign prestige which he had earned by signing the Lateran Pacts. Furthermore, the re-establishment of peace on the religious front was essential if the Regime was to cope successfully with the worsening economic situation. The September Accords were, therefore, bound to be a compromise, releasing both sides from a conflict which neither wanted and at the same time preserving their essential interests.

The September Accords and, in a broader sense, the long-term consequences of the crisis of 1931, have been the subject of remarkably differing interpretations by both contemporary observers and later historians alike. No less a person than Palmiro Togliatti, writing in *Stato Operaio* in September 1931, saw the recently concluded Accords as a victory for the Pope, '...on all the essential points'.[24] Yet his fellow anti-Fascist, Luigi

---

[23] See, for example, *Le Soir*, 15 July 1931, 'L'Eglise e le Fascisme: vers le rupture?'.
[24] *Stato Operaio*, 15 September 1931, p. 373, 'Le Vie Proletariense'.

Sturzo, regarded it very differently: '...the new agreement represents the complete triumph of the Fascist State over the Church'.[25] Equally divergent have been the opinions of historians writing after the event: whereas one authoritative historian of Catholic Action has summed up the significance of the September Accords as '...Mussolini at Canossa',[26] another has interpreted them as a capitulation, by means of which Catholic Action was '...confined to the shadow of the sanctuaries and the sacresties'.[27] And the author of the most recent, and probably the most detailed, account hitherto of the 1931 crisis, Renzo De Felice, has written that 'In reality, it is an historically indisputable fact that the agreement constituted a defeat for the Church.'[28]

But, in reality, neither the Church nor the Regime was either victorious or vanquished. In terms of the juridical status quo established by the Lateran Pacts, both sides managed to maintain their respective positions, but in terms of the aims and objectives of the Regime on the morrow of the dissolution of the Catholic youth organisations in May 1931, it is an undeniable fact that the Regime was forced to make the greatest concessions in order to reach an agreement. Mussolini failed to eliminate either the youth organisations or the *sezioni professionali*, without which Catholic Action had no future as a powerful, influential force in Italian society. In the words of another contemporary observer of these events: 'The obvious restrictions on the activities and scope of Catholic Action...have tended to obscure the essential fact that what was at stake was the existence of Catholic Action and its independence of the secular power, and on both these points the Pope obtained satisfaction.'[29]

Restrictions there were, though, as we have seen, they were more apparent than real, either because, as in the case of the ban on the *popolari*, they were difficult to enforce, or, as in the case of the ban on sporting and trade union activities, they were simply reiterations of the existing, accepted policy and practice. And, of course, these reiterations were for public consumption, a face-saving formula for Mussolini's benefit. The real restriction that the September Accords imposed on Catholic Action after 1931 was more general, a tendency to be less aggressive, less confident, less public and more prudent, more discreet in all its activities. Nevertheless, the mere survival of Catholic Action with its youth and labour groups intact meant the defeat, yet again, of Fascist efforts to establish a truly totalitarian state. A political regime which tolerated the continued existence of an alien organisation like Catholic Action in its midst can hardly be called a

[25] As quoted in De Felice, IV, p. 304.
[26] Magri, *L'Azione Cattolica in Italia*, Vol. II, p. 73.
[27] Civardi, *Breve Compendio di Storia*, p. 454.
[28] De Felice, IV, p. 271.
[29] Binchy, *Church and State*, p. 539; Webster, *The Cross and the Fasces*, p. 112, is of the same opinion, as is Scoppola, *La Chiesa e il Fascismo*, pp. 265–6.

totalitarian state in the real meaning of that term. One need look no further than Nazi Germany, where the Concordat of 1933 was brutally ignored by Hitler and the once powerful network of Catholic adult and youth organisations was almost completely destroyed,[30] to see the fate which awaited the Catholic Church and the Catholic movement in a genuinely totalitarian state. In this sense, therefore, it was the Fascist anti-clericals, and the 'hardliners' like Giurati and Scorza who were defeated in September 1931, forced to submit to the inexorable logic of Mussolini's religious policy.

By the same token, the outcome of the 1931 crisis also constituted a decisive defeat for the *popolari*, and for Catholic anti-Fascism in general. Those Catholic anti-Fascists who had seen in Catholic Action a convenient launching pad for the overthrow or at least the replacement of a Fascist Regime in decline were taught a sharp lesson. Through his handling of the 1931 crisis, Mussolini demonstrated that the Regime could not and would not tolerate such a threat to its existence. The dissolution of the Catholic youth groups, and the other police measures taken against anti-Fascist activity in general in the Spring and Summer of 1931, served to indicate to friend and foe alike that the grave economic problems facing the Regime had not robbed it of either the will or the ability to defend itself against its enemies. Indeed, viewed in a broader perspective, the crisis of 1931 proved beneficial to Mussolini, demonstrating to the world the essential strength and stability of the Regime.[31] His handling of the crisis not only provided a brief, violent but controlled outlet for the anti-Catholic feelings which had been building up inside the Fascist movement and silenced the Fascist critics of his religious policy, it also discouraged further challenges from his opponents. It also, incidentally, demonstrates the total control exercised by Mussolini over the religious policy of the Regime, unhindered now by interference from other Fascist leaders and, even less, conditioned by debates in the Grand Council of Fascism. And at the same time, the eventual reconciliation with the Vatican showed that Fascism had not, after all, lost the confidence of its conservative supporters. All those anti-Fascists in exile who had naively hoped that the Vatican would be forced to break with Fascism and pass into the anti-Fascist camp were to be bitterly disappointed by the September Accords.[32] It is difficult to escape the conclusion, therefore, that the Fascist Regime emerged from the crisis of 1931 stronger than before, and better able to deal with the political effects of the grave economic problems that continued to face it.

[30] Lewy, *The Catholic Church and Nazi Germany*, pp. 130–3.
[31] See Grandi's report on reactions to the Accords at the League of Nations in *D.D.I.*, 7, Vol. X (proofs), 4 September 1931.
[32] For an analysis of the reactions of the anti-Fascist parties in exile to the crisis of 1931 and its resolution, see Zunino, *La Questione Cattolica*, pp. 328–31.

Of all the exiled anti-Fascists, it was of course the *popolari* who were most disappointed by the September Accords.[33] Whilst the *popolari* had not shared the extravagant expectation of other anti-Fascists – they knew the Vatican too well to imagine that it would commit itself wholeheartedly to the anti-Fascist cause any more than it had committed itself wholeheartedly to Fascism – they had nevertheless hoped that the disputes with the Church would weaken and isolate Fascism.[34] But it was in fact the *popolari* in exile who found themselves more isolated and impotent than ever in the aftermath of the 1931 crisis. Whereas during the Spring and Summer the Pope's spirited defence of Catholic Action, and in particular his condemnation of Fascism in *Non Abbiamo Bisogno*, had suddenly and miraculously converted many anti-Fascists from their traditional anti-clericalism, after the reconciliations in September that anti-clericalism inevitably returned with a renewed bitterness which was sharply directed against the *popolari*. In effect, Sturzo and his friends were back to the position in which they had found themselves in February 1929, despised and ostracised by the rest of the anti-Fascist movement. In any case, the tiny P.P.I. in exile had already been weakened in August 1931 by the death of Giuseppe Donati. When two years later Francesco Ferrari also died, the tragic story of the *popolari* in exile at last came to an end.

The September Accords also had the effect of isolating and weakening Catholic anti-Fascism inside Italy. The groups of *popolari*, both inside and outside of the Catholic organisations, clearly went onto the defensive after September 1931, for in the years that immediately followed there were very many fewer police complaints or warnings against their activities. The only group whose activities do not appear to have been seriously affected was that of Piero Malvestiti and his friends who carried on their clandestine struggle for a further eighteen months after the 'nuova conciliazione'. The arrest of the leaders of the Movimento Guelfo in March 1933, and their trial and conviction by the Special Tribunal a year later, was naturally a cause of considerable embarrassment to the Vatican.[35] In contrast to other assorted anti-Fascists who were tried with them, the *guelfisti* were given stiff sentences as a warning to other Catholics who might follow their

---

[33] In September 1931, Francesco Ferrari wrote to the Padre Rosa in these terms: '...if I were to tell you that the recent agreement between the Holy See and the Fascist Government has deeply grieved me, then I would not be expressing strongly enough the anguish of spirit which I experienced when I read the *Agenzia Stefani* communique announcing the "nuova conciliazione"': *Luigi Sturzo: Scritti Inediti*, ed. Piva, Vol. II, p. 357.

[34] See Ferrari's report, as Secretary of the P.P.I. in exile, to the International Conference of Christian Democratic Parties held in Brussels in July 1931 as reproduced in ibid., p. 329.

[35] For an account of the trial, see C. Brezzi, 'Il Gruppo Guelfo tra Gerarchie ecclesiastica e regime Fascista', in Scoppola and Traniello (eds.), *I Cattolici tra Fascismo e Democrazia*, pp. 260–72.

example.[36] Not until 1937, when another clandestine organisation – the Movimento dei Cattolici Communisti – was founded by members of Rome Catholic Action, or, perhaps more realistically, not until 1942 when the old *popolare* ruling group began to reform itself around its 'historic' leader De Gasperi, did Catholic anti-Fascism take on a new lease of life and begin to prepare actively for the post-Fascist future.[37]

The defeat of Catholic anti-Fascism was, however, only a temporary setback, what really mattered was that Catholic Action had survived Fascist attempts to destroy it and that a certain *popolare* presence, albeit muted, also remained inside the organisation. Indeed, it would be no exaggeration to say that the survival of Catholic Action, and especially of its youth and labour groups, proved absolutely vital to the reconstitution of a Catholic ruling class in Italy. In the case of the labour organisations – the *sezioni professionali* – their continued existence was only bought at a price. After 1931, Catholic Action could no longer permit itself the luxury of even the mildest criticism of Fascist Corporatism and the Pope too was careful never to repeat the critical comments which he had made of the theory and practice of Fascist trade unionism in *Quadragesimo Anno*. The explanation for this, the most visible change in Catholic Action policy after the 1931 crisis, is to be found in Clause 2 of the September Accords which implicitly pledged the Catholic organisations to accept and support the 'existing system' of the Fascist 'Corporate State'. Furthermore, Catholic intellectuals outside of Catholic Action, especially on the teaching staff of the Catholic University of Milan, were to give increasingly vocal and unqualified support to the 'Corporate State' during the 1930s.[38] In this way, the crisis of 1931 had a direct impact on the development of Catholic Action, and had the effect of creating at least the appearance of greater convergence between Catholicism and Fascism on social and labour questions.

But the *sezioni professionali* had survived and they were thus able to maintain a Catholic presence, however shadowy, in the labour field throughout the rest of the Fascist period. In common with other branches of Catholic Action, the *sezioni* and their parent organisation I.C.A.S. quickly resumed their normal pattern of activities after the dust had settled in September 1931.[39] By 1935 the police were warning of the renewed and

---

[36] And probably also because neither the Vatican nor the *guelfisti* themselves were prepared to ask Mussolini for mercy: ibid., pp. 264–6.

[37] See C. Brezzi, 'L'Antifascismo Cattolico, in *La Resistenza Italiana*, pp. 134–6.

[38] For an analysis of the support given by Gemelli and his colleagues to the corporatist, imperialist and racialist policies of Fascism in the 1930s, see Ranfagni, *I Clerico-fascisti*, especially chaps. 4, 5 and 6.

[39] In May 1932, after nearly a year's absence, I.C.A.S. resumed its column in the *Bollettino Ufficiale* with the usual articles on labour contracts, emigration, etc.

relentless growth of the *sezioni* in the big cities,[40] and the *sezioni* continued to grow during the late 1930s.[41]

After the fall of the Regime in 1943 and the reconstitution of the free trade union movement in Italy, the *sezioni* came into their own. Faced with the problem of protecting the faith of Catholic workers and combating Socialist and Communist influences in the unitary confederation established in 1944 by the Pact of Rome, the leaders of Catholic Action found the answer in the model of the *sezioni* which had for two decades acted as a Catholic 'ginger' group inside another hostile environment – the Fascist trade unions. The *sezioni* thus provided the nuclei of a new Catholic organisation in the labour field – the Associazoni Cristiane dei Lavoratori Italiani (A.C.L.I.).[42] And in their turn, the A.C.L.I. were to form the basis of the new Catholic trade union confederation – the Confederazione Italiana dei Sindicati Lavoratori (C.I.S.L.) – which was born of the Cold War split in the Italian labour movement of 1947. In this way, the *sezioni* performed an important historical function, constituting one of the major, living threads of continuity between the *sindacati bianchi* of the *popolare* era and the new Catholic trade unionism of the post-Second-World-War period.

Even more important than the survival of the *sezioni*, was that of the Catholic youth groups, for it was inside these organisations, and in particular inside F.U.C.I. and the graduate Movimento Laureato, that the new cadres of the post-Second World-War Catholic political class were to emerge in the late 1930s and early 1940s.[43]

On the face of it, the Catholic youth organisations in the 1930s did not provide an ideal breeding ground for a new generation of Christian Democrats. In order to avoid giving the Regime pretexts for further attacks on the Pope's 'favourites', the ecclesiastical authorities themselves imposed restrictions upon the activities of the youth groups; there was thus a general tendency to concentrate on religious exercises and observances and to neglect such things as the study of Catholic Social Teaching. Moreover, the pride and confidence which had been the hallmarks of the Catholic youth organisations in the period 1929–1932 gave way to timidity and caution, attitudes which were encouraged by official pronouncements.[44]

As Fascism went from triumph to triumph in the mid-1930s, the flame

---

[40] See, for example, the report from the Rome Political Police on the growth of the *sezioni maestre, impiegate e lavoratrici* in A.C.S., D.G.P.S., G.I., b. 146, 'Azione Cattolica', sf. III, 9 September 1933.

[41] Civardi, *Breve Compendio di Storia*, chap. 9.

[42] For an account of the origins of the A.C.L.I. see C. Pasini, 'Le A.C.L.I. nel periodo dell'unita sindacale', in Scoppola and Traniello, *I Cattolici tra Fascismo e Democrazia*, pp. 415–50.

[43] The best account of this very complex process is to be found in Moro, *La formazione della classe dirigente Cattolica*.

[44] See, for example, the article entitled 'Perchè non vi sono più le grandi, le solenni manifestazioni dei cattolici italiani', in *Bollettini Ufficiale*, September–October 1932.

of Christian Democracy, the true political consciousness of Italian Catholics, burned very dimly indeed inside the organisations of Catholic Action. With the passing of the years, the influence of the *popolari* inevitably waned, especially amongst the young who had not lived through the experience of *popolarism* in the 1920s. As active, committed anti-Fascism declined, so 'aFascism', a rather apathetic, agnostic tendency towards unenthusiastic, outward conformity to Fascism, became the common attitude amongst many Catholics.[45] But it was precisely the continued presence of a few *popolari* which prevented 'aFascism', or even worse the 'national Catholic' mentality which was generated by the success of Mussolini's 'Christian crusades' in Abyssinia and Spain and cultivated by Clerico-Fascists like Egilberto Martire from becoming universal in Catholic Action.[46]

These residual, *popolare* influences were nowhere stronger than in F.U.C.I. and Movimento Laureato. It was in these organisations, under the guidance of Spataro, Montini and Righetti, that Catholic social and political traditions were kept alive and that the Catholic political class of the future was formed, and none of this escaped the attention of the more perceptive of the Fascist authorities. In July 1935, the Prefect of Treviso warned of the dangers which Catholic Action once more posed to Fascism, a warning which eventually reached Mussolini himself: 'Catholic Action...is without doubt the centre of a vast, tenacious but camouflaged activity which, through the F.U.C.I., is training the leadership cadres who will guide Catholic groups ready for any eventuality.'[47] But in the Summer of 1935, Mussolini had more important matters to think about and so he chose to ignore this and other warnings for a few years to come.[48] In the meantime, F.U.C.I. and Movimento Laureato quietly went ahead with the task of training the new Catholic elite – men like G. B. Scaglia, Emilio Colombo, Guido Gonella, Giulio Andreotti, Aldo Moro and Paolo Taviani.[49] In 1943 this new generation of Catholic leaders was to emerge from Catholic Action and to join forces with *guelfisti* and the old *popolari* to found a new Catholic party, the Democrazia Cristiana. And, of course, these are the men who have dominated the counsels of that Party, and therefore Italian politics, ever since.

[45] Moro, 'Afascismo e antifascismo'.
[46] For an account of Martire's journalistic support of Mussolini's foreign policy in the *Rassegna Romana* from 1928 to 1938, see Sorrentino, *La Conciliazione*, chap. 2.
[47] A.C.S., D.G.P.S., G.I., b. 146, 'Azione cattolica', sf. 2 (green), 'Movimento Laureato', 9 July 1935.
[48] In May 1934, for example, the Milan Political Police made another very accurate prediction: 'As a result of all this, and of the work of some parish priests, Catholic Action now has thousands of members. We are not, admittedly, dealing with a political party, but we are dealing with a mass organisation that could in a few hours become the most powerful and effective political party in Italy': ibid., 10 May 1935.
[49] It is indicative of the consistency of this new Catholic elite that in 1942 Andreotti, Moro, Scaglia and Taviani all sat on the Consiglio Direttivo of Catholic Action: ibid., b. 151, 'F.U.C.I.', letter from the Prefect of Rome, 29 March 1942.

It is clear, therefore, that from the point of view of Catholic Action, the crisis of 1931 and the September Accords which followed it did not constitute quite the disaster that some authors have suggested. Nor from the Fascist point of view could the September Accords be described as a triumph, for they had failed to remove what the Regime regarded as the underlying cause of the disputes with the Vatican – Catholic Action itself. Its continued existence in a regime with totalitarian pretensions would always be a source of potential friction with the Church. As Francesco Ferrari predicted in July 1931, any reconciliation between the Vatican and the Regime could only be a political compromise, a truce which sooner or later would be broken as those totalitarian tendencies actively reasserted themselves.[50] And Ferrari's prophecy was to be fulfilled by the events of 1938–9; having survived the crisis of 1931, Catholic Action faced a new and even greater threat to its existence seven years later when Italian Fascism entered upon a new phase of totalitarian development, and as a result relations between the Church and the Regime once more entered into crisis.

Though the September Accords of 1931 did not ultimately provide a definitive solution of the problem of Catholic Action, the new relationship which they inaugurated lasted for seven years. This relatively long period of harmonious relations between the Vatican and the Regime is attributable to a number of factors, not least of which was the way in which the crisis of 1931 had dissipated those false hopes and expectations which had been the cause of so many previous disputes. It is worth repeating at this point, that after the crisis of 1931 Mussolini no longer hoped for or sought the kind of Vatican support for his foreign policy which he had attempted to obtain after February 1929, and that for his part Pius XI nurtured few illusions about the Church's ability to 'clericalise' the Fascist Regime.[51]

The resolution of the crisis also involved the decisive defeat of those groups on each side – the *popolari* and the other Catholic anti-Fascists, and the Fascist anti-clericals and hardliners – whose activites in the Spring and Summer of 1931 had helped to upset the delicately balanced relationship between the Church and the Regime which had been established by the *Conciliazione*. After September 1931, the Regime felt itself to be stronger, was believed by both supporters and opponents to be stronger and was in real terms stronger in relation to the anti-Fascist forces, Catholics included, which had been mounting challenges to it in the previous twelve-month period. Being more confident, Mussolini was also, consequently, less concerned about the *popolare*, anti-Fascist influences in Catholic Action which were in any case considerably diminished after the period of

---

[50] *Luigi Sturzo: Scritti Inediti*, ed. Piva Vol. II, p. 330.
[51] There is evidence, however, that in the 1930s the leaders of Catholic Action were still trying to 'clericalise' the Regime from the outside: see Rogari, 'Come la Chiesa', p. 146.

reconstitution and reorganisation that followed the September Accords. And Catholic Action as a whole was deliberately less public and visible in its activities in the years after the 'nuova conciliazione' and thereby less likely to arouse Fascist suspicion and hostility.

The Vatican, too, could no longer entertain any serious doubts about the strength and durability of the Regime after Mussolini's handling of the 1931 crisis. At the same time, Mussolini was also reminded of the powerful moral authority and influence of the Holy See, and of Pius XI's determination to use it in the defence of Catholic Action. If the balance of power between the Church and the Regime had been disturbed in the critical months of April and May by the Fascist attacks on Catholic Action, and in particular by the dissolution of the youth groups, then it was re-established in July by the encyclical *Non Abbiamo Bisogno*. As was revealed by Padre Tacchi-Venturi in his rather melodramatic account of the meeting with Mussolini in which he conveyed the Pope's threat to utter a further, general condemnation of Fascism,[52] after the publication of the encyclical the protagonists had the choice of either negotiating a peace or embarking on all-out, total war. But the Pope and the Duce knew that the latter eventuality would have catastrophic consequences for both sides. Mussolini, for all his bravado, could not contemplate risking the damaging effects that continued conflict with the Church would have on the popularity of the Regime at a time when it was still grappling with the economic crisis.[53] It was the recognition that they had had too much to lose from a prolongation and worsening of the dispute and very much to gain by a reconciliation which drove Pius XI and Mussolini to a compromise agreement in September 1931 and encouraged them to maintain it for seven long years.

Apart from the desire to preserve the enormous benefits of the Lateran Pacts, which would almost certainly have been placed in jeopardy by further conflict, the Vatican had other compelling reasons to make the September Accords work and maintain good relations with the Regime after 1931. The 1920s closed with not only a continuation of the anti-clerical war against the Church in Mexico, but also with a renewal of the persecution of religion in the Soviet Union, and the 1930s opened with the rapid rise of general anti-clerical violence in Spain. By the middle of the new decade Pius XI had become more and more obsessed with the danger of Communism and the fearful threat which it posed to religion in general and Catholicism in particular.[54] In addition, the Pope was

---

[52] The text of Tacchi-Venturi's report to the Pope on the meeting is reproduced in Scoppola, *La Chiesa e il Fascismo*, pp. 276–9.

[53] I.e., the major effects of the Great Depression in Italy did not begin to abate until early in 1933, see De Felice, IV, pp. 58–63.

[54] Though, oddly enough, he did not publish his encyclical on the subject – *Divini Redemptoris* – until 1937.

intensely concerned about the social and moral effects of the Great Depression.[55]

In the midst of this turbulent, tormented and almost apocalyptic world, from the view point of the Vatican Fascist Italy seemed to be a haven of hope, peace and tranquillity and a bulwark against Communism; it also appeared to be relatively unscathed by the Great Depression. Moreover, Fascist social and economic policy, not to mention police repression, discouraged the evils which to the Church seemed inevitably to follow modernisation and urbanisation – sexual liberty, a loosening of family ties, divorce and abortion – and positively encouraged large families and the traditional role of women.[56] Given this 'ideological convergence' between the Vatican and Italian Fascism, it is perhaps not surprising that in the 1930s the Church in Italy, and especially Catholic Action, was very active in its role as part of the 'block of consensus' under-pinning the Fascist Regime. Thus, whereas Catholic Action had given only qualified support to the Fascist list in the 'Plebiscite' of 1929, when that electoral operation was repeated in 1934, the *Bollettino Ufficiale* unashamedly urged the membership: 'go to the polls and give your vote for the government of the Hon. Mussolini'.[57] Similarly, the official organ of Catholic Action published analyses of the policy of 'ruralisation' and the 'demographic battle' which were but echoes of the official propaganda of the Regime.[58] And though there were some reservations in the Catholic camp about the morality of a war of conquest, Catholic Action at any rate had no such scruples about supporting the invasion of Abyssinia.[59] The convergence was also evident in the field of foreign policy where from 1936 onwards, Mussolini was to give tangible aid to Catholicism by his intervention in Spain, and moreover until as late as early 1938, the Vatican could even hope that Fascist Italy would act as a counterweight to another menace that had arisen in Europe – neo-paganism in Nazi Germany.[60]

These, then, were the powerful motives which impelled both the Church and the Regime towards compromise, towards a 'marriage of convenience' that was to last until renewed disputes in 1938–9 brought about an irretrievable breakdown in their relationship.

[55] He published two encyclicals on the effects of the Great Depression – *Nuova Impendet* in October 1931 and *Caritate Christi Compulsi* in September 1932.

[56] And all this was enshrined in the Rocco Penal Code of 1931.

[57] *Bollettino Ufficiale*, 1934, nos. 1–2.

[58] Ibid., 1935, no. 3, p. 65, 'Il Pericolo della Morte delle Nazioni', and 1936, no. 3, 'La Civiltà arriva verso il Tramonto'.   [59] Ibid., 1935, nos. 9–10, 'L'ora della Patria'.

[60] Kent, *The Pope and the Duce*, p. 180, writes: 'For the Holy See, the Franco-Italian rapprochement of 1935 represented the ideal diplomatic organisation of Europe, uniting European Catholicism, as it did, initially against the anti-clerical Nazis and ultimately against the anti-Christian Bolsheviks.' This ideal state of affairs was, of course, shipwrecked by the Abyssinian War, but Italy continued to maintain good relations with both Austria and Hungary, giving rise to hopes in the Vatican that Mussolini would lead a block of Catholic 'neutrals'. This hope was proved illusory by Austrian Anschluss in March 1938.

The crisis of 1938–9 between the Church and the Fascist Regime was in large part one of the domestic, Italian consequences of the increasingly close ties which Mussolini developed with Nazi Germany in the mid-1930s.[61] In retrospect, probably the most important milestone in the development of relationship between the Führer and the Duce was the latter's visit to Berlin. Mussolini returned from Berlin deeply impressed with the ruthless efficiency and military might of Nazi Germany, and deeply dissatisfied with the shortcomings of his own 'totalitarian' regime. He determined to emulate Hitler's achievement and put some 'steel' into the Italians. So began yet another chapter in the history of Fascist attempts to construct the 'totalitarian state', the Racial Laws of 1938 being the first major fruit of this new policy.[62] Having already fought an unsuccessful battle against Nazi German 'paganism' in 1937,[63] Pius XI watched with mounting apprehension as the relationship between Mussolini and Hitler developed further in 1938, marked by the Italian sell-out over the Austrian Anschluss in March and by the Führer's visit to the Eternal City in May. The announcement, at the end of the Summer, of the introduction of racial legislation was, therefore, the last straw as far as the Pope was concerned.

But the domestic effects of the Italian alliance with Nazi Germany were not the only causes of conflict between the Pope and the Duce in the Summer of 1938, for over the previous six months tension had been building up between Catholic Action and the Fascist Party. As one contemporary observer has pointed out, 'In fact, the attacks on Catholic Action had begun before the racialist issue was heard of.'[64] The root cause of this renewal of Fascist hostility towards Catholic Action was, predictably, an upsurge in the membership and activities of the Catholic organisations which Fascism in its new totalitarian mood was no longer prepared to tolerate.

As we have seen, in the mid-1930s, Fascist officials were already becoming alarmed about Catholic Action's new lease of life and they were not slow to send warning signals to their superiors in Rome. Indeed, so rapidly was Catholic Action membership growing again that it would seem that in the Summer of 1935 another crisis, of 1931 proportions, was only averted due to the need to avoid damaging national unity in the face of the impending invasion of Abyssinia. And over the next few years, Catholic Action continued to expand its activities, especially in a field of endeavour which the Regime regarded as being its own, that of recreation. As the author of a recent study of the Dopolavoro has acknowledged, that Fascist

---

[61] There is as yet no very specific study of the crisis of 1938–9, the best available account is to be found in Binchy, *Church and State*.

[62] The view is taken here that the introduction of the Racial Laws were more the direct result of Nazi German influences than the consequence of the Italian conquest of Abyssinia.

[63] Lewy, *The Catholic Church and Nazi Germany*, chap. 6.

[64] Binchy, *Church and State*, p. 532.

organisation was at its weakest in strongly Catholic areas.[65] Perhaps the most alarming development in the eyes of the Fascist authorities was Catholic activity in the world of the cinema. Such was the success of Catholic Action there that in 1939 the Ministry of Popular Culture took steps to restrict it: as Cannistraro argues, 'The Catholic challenge to Fascist cultural dominance must have been very serious indeed to provoke such drastic counter measures.'[66]

In September 1936, Cardinal Pacelli himself found it necessary to write to the Italian Ambassador to the Holy See denying Fascist claims that Catholic Action was involved in political activities,[67] and at the beginning of 1938, in response to further allegations of this kind, the Secretary of State wrote to Mussolini reminding him that the Italian bishops, clergy and laity, and Catholic Action itself, had publicly and repeatedly demonstrated their patriotism by their unqualified support for the Abyssinian War.[68]

Despite all of Pacelli's efforts, the war of attrition between the Fascists and Catholic Action rumbled on through the Spring and Summer of 1938.[69] On 20 August, Tacchi-Venturi managed to patch up an agreement with Achille Starace, the Party Secretary, by re-affirming the validity of the 1931 September Accords.[70] But this was not the end of the matter, the attacks on Catholic Action resumed in the Autumn, exacerbated now by the growing rift between the Vatican and the Regime over the Racial Laws.[71] By Christmas, relations between the Church and the Regime were at their lowest ebb since July 1931. Only the death of Pius XI in February 1939, and the election of Pacelli as his successor a month later, resolved the dispute.[72]

Given Pacelli's 'soft' approach to Fascism during the crisis of 1931, the blow which he delivered to Catholic Action in April 1939 could have come

---

[65] De Grazia, *The Culture of Consent: The Mass Organisation of Leisure in Fascist Italy*, p. 14.

[66] Cannistraro, *La Fabbrica del consenso*, p. 317.

[67] A.C.S., S.P.D., C.R. VII/17, 'Questione Romana', 'Azione Cattolica', 23 September 1936.

[68] Ibid., 5 January 1938.

[69] *Ciano's Diary, 1937–38*, trans. Mayor, pp. 134–50, and Binchy, *Church and State*, pp. 531–5.   [70] Ibid., p. 535.

[71] Apart from the general condemnation of racialism by the Pope and other Catholic authorities, the Vatican had a specific complaint against the Racial Laws of 1938 in that, by prohibiting marriages between Jews and Gentiles, they infringed the marriage clauses of the Concordat; see Scoppola, *La Chiesa e il Fascismo*, pp. 316–26.

[72] It was for a long time a widespread belief in Catholic circles in Italy that Pius XI was about to denounce the Concordat in a speech to be given on the tenth anniversary of the signing of the Lateran Pacts, i.e., on 11 February 1939. The Pope, of course, died on 10 February and thus was unable to give it. When the contents of the speech were eventually published, by John XXIII exactly twenty years later, it became immediately clear that even on his deathbed Pius XI was unwilling to abandon the fruits of the *Conciliazione*, the speech being merely a bitter attack on the ways in which the Regime misinterpreted or ignored the Pope's speeches about Nazi Germany. For the text of the speech, see Scoppola, *La Chiesa e il Fascismo*, pp. 334–40, 'Un Discorso di Pio XI non pronunciato'.

as no surprise to anyone. In order to appease Mussolini and stave off the threat of further measures against Catholic Action,[73] Pizzardo (now a cardinal) was removed from the direction of the movement, the lay *giunta centrale* and presidency were abolished and supreme control was transferred to a commission of three Italian cardinal archbishops.[74] Mussolini had at last obtained what he had been seeking in 1931, the virtual elimination of the lay element in the leadership of Catholic Action and its virtual dismantling as a national organisation. But in view of the new totalitarian phase into which Fascism had moved in the late 1930s, it is very doubtful whether even this drastic re-organisation of Catholic Action would have satisfied Mussolini and the Fascists in the long term. Catholic Action was probably only saved from complete extinction by Italy's entry into the War in 1940, when the imperative need for national unity ruled out a further quarrel with the Church, and by the chain of subsequent military disasters which led to the fall of the Regime in July 1943.

In the not so long term, the crisis of 1938–9 had the effect of loosening the last remaining ties between the Church and the Fascist Regime. Despite all of Pius XII's conciliatory gestures, Mussolini had more or less turned his back on the Church, and under the increasing influence of Nazi Germany he relapsed into the red-necked anti-clericalism and atheism of his political childhood and adolescence.[75] Pius XII tried desperately to prevent Italy's entry into the War on the side of Hitler in May 1940, and thereafter the Vatican increasingly took its distance from Italian Fascism. In September 1943, it made the final break by refusing to recognise the Fascist Social Republic established by Mussolini in northern Italy under the tutelage of the German Occupying forces.

In the final analysis, it is clear that the common, underlying cause of the disputes of 1929–32 between the Vatican and the Regime was a fundamental, philosophical incompatibility between Catholicism and Fascism. Whenever Church and State relations reached a really low point in this period, as in the New Year of 1930 and in the Summer of 1931, this fundamental, philosophical conflict revealed itself, and was made explicit in the public pronouncements of both sides. From 1927 onwards, as Fascism pressed its totalitarian claims against the few remaining organisations of the Catholic movement, Catholic Action and its youth groups, Pius XI was made aware of the ideological consistency and conviction of the Fascist Regime. He discovered that Fascism was not as permeable and suggestible a conservative political force as he, the Clerico-

[73] Delzell, *I Nemici di Mussolini*, p. 102.
[74] Binchy, *Church and State*, pp. 536–7.
[75] *Ciano's Diary, 1939–45*, ed. with an introd. by Muggeridge, pp. 26, 39–40, 186 and 248–9, illustrates Mussolini's rapid and complete alienation from the Vatican during the course of 1939 and 1940.

Fascists and, for that matter, the Liberal supporters of the Regime had thought it to be. On the contrary, in the period 1929–32 Fascism showed that it possessed a central core of fundamental ideas that were as much if not more in conflict with the guiding principles of Catholicism as those of nineteenth-century Liberalism.

The Fascist doctrine central to this conflict was, of course, that of totalitarianism, or, in the terminology of Pius XI, 'statolatry'. The disputes over youth and education, over the conflicting claims of the Church, the Family and the State in this sphere; the arguments over the autonomy and activities of Catholic Action; and the bitter polemics over the Fascist Oath all stemmed from the same source: the incompatibility between the Catholic concept of the prior sovereignty of the Church over the State, and the Fascist doctrine of the omnipotent, totalitarian state.

The disputes of 1929–32 also brought out into the open the Catholic Church's natural abhorrence of the cult of violence and militarism, especially in the context of the emphasis of the Balilla on physical education and the increasing time devoted to pre-military training in the secondary schools and in the universities. Pius XI's strictures about these matters in *Rapresentanti in Terra* and the condemnation in *L'Osservatore Romano* of the Fascist youth organisations' encouragement to hate one's enemy, were inspired by the same fundamental principles which had moved him to condemn Action Française in 1926, and which ultimately led him to oppose the introduction of racialism into Italy in 1938.

If it was these questions of fundamental principle that were largely responsible for the disputes which disturbed Church and State relations in this period, then it is equally true that it was only the blatant compromising or shelving of principles which permitted the settlement of those disputes and a return to normal relations. For his part, Pius XI had already acquired the habit of compromising his principles during the negotiations for the Lateran Pacts when he acquiesced in Fascism's dissolution of some of the Catholic youth organisations and its restriction of the activities of those which were allowed to survive. Again, despite his formal protest against the cult of violence, war and the hatred of enemies, he did nothing further to oppose the inculcation of these virtues into Italian youth by the Fascist Regime.[76] And having made so much fuss about the moral propriety of the Fascist Oath in his encyclical in July 1931, the Pope then dropped the matter in September in order to achieve a reconciliation with Mussolini and his Regime.[77]

---

[76] Nor did the Vatican condemn the logical culmination of those policies, i.e., Italian aggression against Abyssinia in 1935.

[77] As Scoppola, *La Chiesa e il Fascismo*, p. 266, points out: 'There was in fact no mention of the Fascist Oath in the September Accords, even though this had been explicitly censured by the Pope in his encyclical of July 5 [1931].'

Pius XI's addiction to compromises, to backing down on what he had previously declared in the most solemn and public way to be matters of fundamental moral principle, stayed with him until his death. Having attacked racial anti-semitism *en principe* in 1938, and then having fought a rear-guard action to prevent the introduction of a ban on marriages between Jews and Gentiles, which in itself constituted a flagrant breach of the Concordat, the Pope gave way along the whole front in January 1939.[78] He did so in order to save the Concordat as a whole; a calculated, sensible move perhaps, but one which sacrificed both principle and Italian Jews on the altar of expediency.

The tendency to compromise principles was just as strong on the Fascist side; Mussolini was every bit as much addicted to this, even if his compromises and concessions were better camouflaged by face-saving formulas and Fascist rhetoric. As Togliatti pointed out in 1929, the whole concept of the *Conciliazione*, and therefore the main thrust of the Duce's religious policy, was a massive sacrifice of principle: 'As far as the State was concerned, it is undoubtedly true that this has capitulated on the ideological plane...The process of liquidating the ideology of Nationalism and Fascism itself has now begun.'[79] As far as Fascist ideology was concerned, Togliatti was hopelessly over optimistic, but the essence of his remarks was true enough. With the introduction of religious instruction into the schools, and the concordatory guarantees given to Catholic Action and its dependent organisations, the dream of the totalitarian state was irretrievably compromised. When Mussolini attempted to rectify this state of affairs during the disputes of 1929–30 and 1931 he failed and was forced to compromise yet again.

When he made one more attempt in 1938–9 to subjugate the Church to the Fascist State he came within an ace of success. But the outbreak of the War made it too late to undo the effects of the *Conciliazione*. Mussolini found himself trapped in the consequences of his own opportunism, deserted and betrayed by those institutions, the Church, the Monarchy and the Armed Forces, with whom he had been forced to compromise in order to establish his Regime.

It is frequently asserted that the Church and the Fascist Regime managed to co-exist and collaborate because they were similar in their underlying phiolosophy and in their internal power structure, in short, because they were both totalitarian organisations. In fact, nothing could be further from the truth: their conflicting totalitarian claims to the loyalty of Italian Catholics ensured that they only lived together uneasily and with great difficulty, especially in the period 1929–32. But as well as being leaders of great obstinacy and intransigence, Pius XI and Mussolini were also great

[78] It should be said in mitigation that by this time Pius XI was on his deathbed.
[79] As quoted in Togliatti, *L'Opera di De Gasperi'*, p. 186.

realists and opportunists, for if Mussolini has been stigmatised frequently and rightly as an opportunist then Pius XI cannot escape the same judgement. If in the period 1929–32 the Pope and the Duce managed to arrive at a *modus vivendi*, at a form of peaceful co-existence that was to last for the next six years, then it was precisely because they were both opportunists.

The Law of Guarantees of 1871*

Section I. Prerogatives of the Pontiff and of the Holy See.

1. The person of the Supreme Pontiff is sacred and inviolable
2. Any attempt against the person of the Supreme Pontiff, or any provocation to commit the same, shall be punished with the same penalties as are established by law for a similar attempt or provocation against the person of the King...
3. The Italian Government shall render to the Supreme Pontiff in the territories of the Kingdom, the honours which are due to royal rank, and shall maintain the privileges of honour which are paid to him by Catholic Sovereigns...
4. The annual donation of 3,225,000 lire in favour of the Holy See is maintained...for the diverse ecclesiastical wants of the Holy See, for ordinary and extraordinary repairs to and for the custody of the apostolic palaces and their dependencies; for all allowances, gratuities and pensions to the guards...and to all persons attached to the Pontifical Court, and for eventual expenditure; as well as for the ordinary repairs and custody of the museums and library thereto annexed, and for allowances, stipends, and pensions to persons employed for that purpose...
5. The Supreme Pontiff shall...have free enjoyment of the apostolic palaces of the Vatican and the Lateran...as also of the villa of Castel Gandolfo...
6. During the vacancy of the Pontifical See, no judicial or political authority shall...offer any impediment or limitation to the personal liberty of the Cardinals. The Government shall take proper measures in order that the assemblies of the Conclave and the Oecumenical Councils be not disturbed by any external violence...
12. The Supreme Pontiff shall be at liberty to correspond with the Episcopate and with the whole Catholic world, without any interference on the part of the Italian Government. To this effect he shall be free to

* *The Times*, 15 May 1871

establish in the Vatican, or in any other of his residences, postal and telegraphic offices, and to employ therein persons of his choice...

Section II. Relations of Church and State

14. Every special restriction of the right of assemblage of members of the Catholic clergy is hereby annulled.

15. ...Bishops shall not be required to take oath of allegiance to the King. The higher and lesser benefices shall be conferred solely upon citizens of the Kingdom, with the exception of such benefices as are situate in the city of Rome and in the suburban sees...

16. The *exequatur* and the *placet* of the Crown and every other form of Government warrant for the publication and execution of acts emanating from ecclesiastical authorities are hereby abolished...

17. No complaint or appeal from acts issued by the ecclesiastical authorities, in matters spiritual or disciplinary, shall be allowed, no compulsory execution, however, shall be acknowledged or granted to the acts aforesaid...

18. Provision shall be made by a further enactment for the reorganization, the conservation, and the administration of ecclesiastical property throughout the Kingdom...

The Lateran Pacts of 1929*

THE TREATY

In the name of the Most Holy Trinity, considering:

That the Holy See and Italy have recognized the advisability of eliminating every reason for enmity by settling in a permanent way their relations according to justice and to the dignity of the two High Contracting Parties and that, permanently assuring to the Holy See a state of right and fact that will guarantee to it absolute independence for the exercise of its high mission in the world, will enable the Holy See to recognize as definitely and irrevocably settled the 'Roman Question' which arose in 1870 with the annexation of Rome to the Kingdom of Italy under the dynasty of the House of Savoy;

that, to assure to the Holy See absolute and visible independence and an indisputable sovereignty even in the international world, it has been deemed necessary to create, by special arrangements, the 'Vatican City,' recognising to the Holy See the full property, exclusive dominion and sovereign jurisdiction over the said City.

His Holiness the Supreme Pontiff Pius XI and His Majesty Victor Emmanuel III, King of Italy, have decided to make a Treaty, and for this purpose they have nominated two plenipotentiaries, that is, on His Holiness's side, His Most Reverend Eminence the Cardinal Pietro Gasparri, his Secretary of State, and on His Majesty's side, His Excellency the Knight Benito Mussolini, Prime Minister and Head of the Goverment, who, having exchanged their full powers and having found them in good and due form, have agreed as per the following articles:

ART. 1.—Italy recognises and re-affirms the principle contained in the first article of the Constitution of the Kingdom of Italy, March 4th, 1848, by which the Holy Catholic Apostolic and Roman Religion is the only State religion.

ART. 2.—Italy recognizes the sovereignty of the Holy See in the

* From the translation in *Italy Today*, May 1929

international world as an inherent attribute of its nature, according to its tradition and to the necessities of its mission in the world.

ART. 3.—Italy recognises to the Holy See the full property, exclusive dominion and sovereign jurisdiction over the Vatican as at present constituted, with all its dependencies and dotations, thus creating the Vatican City for the special purposes and with the provisions contained in the present Treaty. The boundaries of the said City are indicated in the map which forms the first appendix to the present Treaty, of which it is an integral part. It remains however understood that Piazza San Pietro, although forming part of the Vatican City, will continue normally to be open to the public and subject to the police powers of the Italian authorities, which will cease at the steps of the Basilica, although this remains open to public worship; therefore they will refrain from mounting those steps and entering the Basilica, unless invited by the competent authority. When the Holy See for special ceremonies decides to close temporarily the Piazza S. Pietro to the free transit of the public, the Italian authorities, unless invited, will withdraw behind the outside lines of the Bernini colonnade and of their extension.

ART. 4.—The sovereignty and exclusive jurisdiction that Italy recognizes to the Holy See over the Vatican City means that in the said City there will be no interference whatsoever from the Italian Government, and that there will be no other authority save that of the Holy See.

ART. 5.—For the execution of what has been decreed in the preceding article, the territory constituting the Vatican City will be freed by the Italian Government from all liens and from actual occupiers, before the coming into effect of the present Treaty. The Holy See will arrange to close all access by erecting walls round all open parts, except on Piazza S. Pietro. It is however understood that as regards the properties existing there owned by religious bodies and institutions, the Holy See will negotiate directly without the intervention of the Italian State.

ART. 6.—Italy will arrange, with the competent authorities, for an adequate supply of water to the Vatican City, in perpetuity. She will also provide for a connection with the State Railways by building a railway station within the Vatican City, on the spot marked on the annexed map, and by allowing the transit of Vatican-owned carriages on the Italian railways.

She will also arrange for the connection, even directly with other States, of the telegraphic, telephonic, wireless, broadcasting and postal services of the Vatican City.

She will moreover settle the co-ordination of all other public services.

All these works will be executed at the expense of the Italian State within one year from the coming into effect of the present Treaty.

The Holy See will organise at its own expense all existing entrances at the Vatican, and all others that it may decide to open in future. Arrangements will be made between the Holy See, and the Italian State, for the circulation on Italian territory of vehicles and aircraft belonging to the Vatican City.

ART. 7.—The Italian Government binds itself to forbid new buildings within the zone round the Vatican City which may overlook the same, and partially to demolish those already existing at Porta Cavalleggeri and along Via Aurelia and Viale Vaticano.

In accordance with international rules, aircraft of any kind are forbidden to fly over the Vatican territory.

In Piazza Rusticucci and within the zones near the colonnade, to which the extra-territoriality mentioned in Art. 15 does not extend, all alterations in the streets or buildings that may interest the Vatican City will be made by mutual agreement.

ART. 8.—Italy, considering the person of the Supreme Pontiff as sacred and inviolable, will punish any attempt against him, or the incitement to commit such, with the same penalties decreed for attempts against the person of the King, or incitement to commit such. Public insults and offences made on Italian territory against the person of the Supreme Pontiff by speech, act or writing will be punished like insults and offences against the person of the King.

ART. 9.—In accordance with international law all persons permanently resident in the Vatican City are subject to the sovereignty of the Holy See. Such domicile is not forfeited by a temporary residence in another place, unless accompanied by the relinquishment of a residence within the said City or by other circumstances proving such relinquishment. On ceasing to be subject to the Holy See the aforesaid persons will be considered in Italy as Italian subjects, unless according to Italian law they are of another nationality, and independently from the circumstances of fact previously mentioned.

When the said persons are on Italian territory, but under the sovereignty of the Holy See, they will be subject to the rules of Italian law, unless they are of another nationality, in which case the laws of their State will apply; this applies in matters concerning personal law, when these are not regulated by rules emanating from the Holy See.

ART. 10.—Church dignitaries and persons belonging to the Papal Court inscribed in a list mutually arranged between the two High Contracting Parties even if not Vatican subjects, are always and in any case, as regards Italy, exempt from military service, from being jurors, and from service of a personal character.

This rule applies also to the regular Civil Servants declared indispensable to the Holy See, working permanently and with a fixed salary in the offices of the Holy See, and to the Departments and offices further mentioned in

Arts. 13, 14, 15 and 16 existing outside the Vatican City. These officials will be included in another list to be arranged as above, that will be prepared yearly by the Holy See.

Ecclesiastics who from the nature of their office take part in the issue of the acts of the Holy See outside the Vatican City, will not be subject in relation to these to any hindrance, investigation or trouble from the Italian authorities. All foreigners holding an ecclesiastical office in Rome will enjoy the same personal guarantees due to Italian citizens according to the laws of the Kingdom.

ART. 11.—The Controlling Bodies of the Catholic Church are exempt from any interference from the Italian State (save in respect of Italian laws concerning acquisitions made by moral bodies), and also from conversion in case of real estate.

ART. 12.—Italy recognises to the Holy See the right of Legation both active and passive according to the usual practice of international law. The Envoys of foreign governments to the Holy See will continue to enjoy throughout the kingdom all the privileges and immunities that are due to international Agents according to international law, and their residences may continue to remain on Italian territory and to enjoy all immunities granted to them according to international law, even if the States have no diplomatic relations with Italy. It is understood that Italy will guarantee complete freedom always and in all circumstances to the correspondence between all States, including belligerents, and the Holy See, and vice-versa, and also free access to the Apostolic See to the bishops of the whole world.

The two High Contracting Parties bind themselves to establish normal diplomatic relations by accrediting an Italian Ambassador to the Holy See, and an Apostolic Nuncio to Italy, who will be the Dean of the Diplomatic Corps according to the customary procedure as recognised by the Congress of Vienna in the Convention of June 9th, 1815.

In consequence of the acknowleded sovereignty, and without prejudice to what is stated in Art. 19, the diplomats of the Holy See and couriers sent in the name of the Supreme Pontiff will enjoy on Italian territory, even in war time, the same privileges due to the diplomats and official couriers of other foreign Governments, according to the rules of international law.

ART. 13.—Italy recognises to the Holy See the full property of the Patriarchial Basilicas of St. John Lateran, of Santa Maria Maggiore and of St. Paul, with all the annexed buildings. The State transfers to the Holy See the free management and administration of the said Basilica of St. Paul and of its annexed monastery, paying also to the Holy See an amount corresponding to the sums yearly allotted in the budget of the Ministry of Education for the said Basilica.

It is further understood that the Holy See enjoys full possession of the dependent building of St. Callixtus near Sta. Maria in Trastevere.

ART. 14.—Italy recognises to the Holy See the full possession of the Pontifical Palace of Castel Gandolfo with all the dotations, annexes and dependencies such as are already in possession of the Holy See, and also binds itself to hand over in full possession within six months of the coming into effect of the present Treaty, the Villa Barberini in Castel Gandolfo, with all its dotations, annexes and dependencies.

In order to integrate the property of the estates situated on the North side of the Colle Gianicolo owned by the Holy Congregation of Propaganda Fide and other ecclesiastical institutions, and facing the Vatican Palaces, the State undertakes to transfer to the Holy See or to the bodies that it may designate, the properties owned by the State or by private individuals in the said zone. The properties owned by the said Congregation and by other Institutes, and those to be transferred are shown in the annexed map.

Moreover, Italy transfers to the Holy See, in full and free possession, the ex-conventual buildings in Rome annexed to the Basilica of the Holy Twelve Apostles and to the Churches of St. Andrea della Valle and of San Carlo ai Catinari with all their annexes and dependencies to be handed over free of tenants within one year of the coming into effect of this Treaty.

ART. 15.—The estates mentioned in Art. 13 and in the first two paragraphs of Art. 14, together with the palaces of the Dataria, of the Cancelleria, of Propaganda Fide in Piazza di Spagna, the Palace of the Holy Office and its dependencies, that of the Convertendi (now the Congregation for the Oriental Church) in Piazza Scossacavalli, the Palace of the Vicariato and all other buildings in which the Holy See may decide in the future to instal other Departments, although being part of Italian territory, will enjoy the immunities recognized by international law to the domiciles of the diplomatic agents of foreign countries.

The same immunities will be applied also to the other churches, even outside Rome, during the time in which, without opening them to the public, services are being celebrated within them in the presence of the Supreme Pontiff.

ART. 16.—The properties mentioned in the three preceding articles, and also those used by the following Pontifical institutions: the Gregorian University, the Biblical, Oriental, and Archaeological Institutes, the Russian Seminary, the Lombard College, the two palaces of St. Apollinaris, and the Retreat House for Clergy of SS. John and Paul, shall never be subject to any lien, or be expropriated for any public utility, unless with the consent of the Holy See, and will be exempt from all taxation either ordinary or extraordinary, due either to the State or to any other body.

It appertains to the Holy See to administer freely all the properties mentioned in this article, and in the three preceding ones, without any need of authorisation or consent from Italian governmental, provincial or municipal authorities, which can have full confidence in the high artistic traditions to which the Catholic Church can lay claim.

ART. 17.—All salaries of any kind, due by the Holy See, by the other central bodies of the Catholic Church, and by the Institutions directly administered by the Holy See even outside Rome, to dignitaries, clerks and officials, even when temporary, will be exempt on Italian territory, from January 1st, 1929, from any taxation imposed either by the State or by any other body.

ART. 18.—The artistic and scientific treasures now in the Vatican City and in the Lateran Palace will remain on show to students and visitors, although the Holy See will have full liberty to regulate the access of the public.

ART. 19.—The diplomats and envoys of the Holy See, the diplomats and envoys of foreign Governments to the Holy See, and the dignitaries of the Church coming from abroad to the Vatican City and in possession of pass-ports from the State from which they are coming, visés by the pontifical representatives abroad, will be allowed access to the said City through Italian territory without any further formality. The same applies to the said persons, who, in possession of a regular pontifical pass-port, will go abroad from the Vatican City.

ART. 20.—All goods coming from abroad and sent to the Vatican City, or to institutes or offices of the Holy See, situated outside it, will always be admitted from any point of the Italian frontier, or any port of the kingdom, to transit across Italian territory with full exemption from all customs or 'octroi' duties.

ART. 21.—All the Cardinals will enjoy in Italy the honours due to the Princes of the blood royal; those resident in Rome, even outside the Vatican City, are to all effects subjects of the same.

During any vacancy of the Pontifical See, Italy will take particular care that the free transit and access of the Cardinals to the Vatican through Italian territory is not hindered, and that no obstacle or limitation is put to their personal liberty. Italy will also take care that on her territory round the Vatican City no acts will be committed such as to trouble in any way the meetings of the Conclave. The same rules will be applied to the Conclaves that may eventually be held outside the Vatican City, and also to any Councils presided over by the Supreme Pontiff or by his Legates, and to the Bishops summoned to participate in them.

ART. 22.—At the request of the Holy See or through any delegated authority that the Holy See may appoint either for individual cases, or in a permanent manner, Italy will arrange on her territory for the punishment of crimes committed in the Vatican City, except when the author of the crime has taken refuge on Italian territory, in which case proceedings will be taken directly against him according to Italian law. The Holy See will deliver to the Italian State all persons who may take refuge in the Vatican City when accused of acts, committed on Italian territory, which are considered as criminal by the laws of both States. The same procedure will be followed in the case of persons accused of crimes, who may have taken refuge on the properties declared as immune in Art. 15, unless the Heads of such properties prefer to invite the Italian agents to enter them to proceed to the arrest.

ART. 23.—For the execution in the kingdom of the sentences passed by the tribunals of the Vatican City the rules of international law will apply. On the other hand, all sentences and decisions passed by ecclesiastical authorities, and officially communicated to the civil authorities, concerning ecclesiastical or religious persons on spiritual or disciplinary matters, will forthwith have full judicial sanction throughout Italy, as well as all civil effects.

ART. 24.—The Holy See, considering the sovereignty due to it even in the international world, declares that it intends to remain and will remain outside the temporal rivalries between other States and outside the international congresses set up with that object, unless the contending parties make common appeal to its mission of peace, while in every case it reserves the right to use its moral and spiritual powers. In consequence of this the territory of the Vatican City will always and in every case be considered as neutral and inviolable.

ART. 25.—A special convention signed together with the present Treaty and which will constitute the fourth annex to it as an integrant part, settles the liquidation of the Holy See's credits towards Italy.

ART. 26.—The Holy See considers that with the agreements signed to-day it receives sufficient guarantees for the due liberty and independence of the spiritual government of the dioceses of Rome and of the Catholic Church in Italy and the whole world; it declares the 'Roman Question' definitely settled and therefore eliminated, and recognizes the Kingdom of Italy under the Dynasty of the House of Savoy with Rome as capital of the Italian State.

In its turn Italy recognises the State of the Vatican City under the sovereignty of the Supreme Pontiff.

The law No. 214 of May 13th, 1871, is abrogated, as well as any other act contrary to the present Treaty.

ART. 27.—The present Treaty will be submitted to the approval of the Supreme Pontiff and of the King of Italy not later than four months from its signature, and will take effect at the moment of the exchange of the ratification.

> Rome, 11th February, 1929
>> (Signed)   Pietro Cardinale Gasparri
>>   Benito Mussolini

THE CONCORDAT

In the name of the Most Holy Trinity,
considering:

That from the beginning of the negotiations between the Holy See and Italy to settle the 'Roman Question', the Holy See itself proposed that the Treaty dealing with the said Question was to be accompanied, as a necessary complement, by a Concordat intended to regulate the conditions of religion and of the Church in Italy;

That to-day the Treaty for the settlement of the 'Roman Question' has been concluded and signed;

His Holiness the Supreme Pontiff Pius XI and his Majesty Victor Emmanuel III, King of Italy, have decided to make a Concordat, and for this purpose they have nominated the same plenipotentiaries as for the stipulation of the Treaty, that is, on His Holiness's side, His Most Reverend Eminence the Cardinal Pietro Gasparri, His Secretary of State, and on His Majesty's side His Excellency the Knight Benito Mussolini, Prime Minister and Head of the Government, who, having exchanged their full powers and having found them in good and due form, have agreed as per the following articles:

ART. 1.—Italy, as per Art. 1 of the Treaty, guarantees to the Catholic Church the free exercise of the spiritual power, the free and public exercise of worship, and also of its jurisdiction on religious matters in conformity to the rules of this Concordat; when necessary, it guarantees to all ecclesiastics, for the acts of their spiritual ministry, the support of its authorities. In consideration of the sacred character of the Eternal City, epsicopal See of the Supreme Pontiff, centre of the Catholic world and goal of pilgrimages, the Italian Government will take care to prevent in Rome anything that might clash with that character.

ART. 2.—The Holy See shall communicate and correspond freely with the bishops, the clergy and the whole Catholic world without any interference from the Italian Government. In the same way, for all that concerns their pastoral ministry, the bishops can communicate and correspond freely with their clergy and with all the faithful. The Holy See, as well as the bishops can freely publish and also affix inside or outside the doors of the buildings dedicated to worship or to the offices of their ministry, all instructions, orders, pastoral letters, diocesan bulletins and other communications concerning the spiritual government of their flock, that they may deem within the limits of their competency. These publications and notices and generally speaking all the acts and documents referring to the spiritual government of the faithful will not be subject to fiscal dues. The above publications in regard to the Holy See can be made in any language and those of the bishops in Italian or Latin, but beside the Italian text the ecclesiastical authority can add a translation in other languages. The ecclesiastical authorities can have collections taken at the entrance of and inside the churches or other buildings belonging to them without any interference from civil authorities.

ART 3.—All theological students, scholastics in their last two years previous to their courses in theology who intend taking orders, and the novices of religious houses can, on request, delay year by year the fulfilling of their military service until their 26th year of age. Clerics ordained *in sacris* and those who have taken vows, are exempt from military service, except in case of a general mobilisation. In such a case priests pass into the Armed Forces of the State, but they retain the ecclesiastical dress in order to carry on their sacred ministry under the ecclesiastical jurisdiction of the military Ordinary as per Art 14. All other clerics and members of religious orders are in preference drafted into the auxiliary military corps. Nevertheless, even in case of a general mobilisation, all priests having the care of souls are exempt from answering the summons. As such are considered all bishops, parish priests and their assistants, vicars and all priests permanently in charge of churches open to the public.

ART. 4.—All clerics and members of religious orders are exempt from jury service.

ART. 5.—No ecclesiastic can be appointed to, or remain in any post or office of the Italian State or of any public body under its jurisdiction, without the *nihil obstat* (permission) of the Ordinary of the diocese. The withdrawal of the *nihil obstat* deprives the ecclesiastic of the capacity to continue to hold the appointment or position previously assumed. In any case no apostate or censored clergy can be appointed or kept in any teaching position, office or employment in which they would be in direct contact with the public.

ART. 6.—All salaries and other emoluments enjoyed by ecclesiastics in virtue of their office are exempt from seizure to the same extent as the salaries and emoluments of State employees.

ART. 7.—Ecclesiastics cannot be compelled by magistrates or other authorities to supply information concerning persons or matters with which they have become acquainted through their holy ministry.

ART. 8.—In the case of an ecclesiastic being charged before a magistrate with any penal offence, the Public Prosecutor must immediately inform the bishop of the diocese in whose territory he exercises jurisdiction; he must also transmit immediately to the bishop the result of the preliminary investigation and, when it takes place, also the sentence ending the trial, both in the first instance and on appeal. In case of arrest the ecclesiastic or religious is treated with the respect due to his state and to his hierarchical rank. When an ecclesiastic or member of a religious order is sentenced, the terms of imprisonment is spent, where possible, apart from ordinary criminals, unless the competent Ordinary has reduced the condemned man to the rank of a layman.

ART. 9.—As a rule, all buildings open to worship are exempt from requisition and occupation. If serious public necessities should require the occupation of a building open to the public, the authority that proceeds to the occupation must previously make arrangements with the Ordinary, unless reasons of absolute urgency prevent it. In such a case the acting authority must inform the Ordinary at once. Except in cases of urgent necessity, police forces in the execution of their duties cannot enter buildings open to worship, unless previous notice has been given to the ecclesiastical authorities.

ART. 10.—No building open to worship can be demolished for any reason, unless previously agreed upon with the competent ecclesiastical authority.

ART. 11.—The State recognizes all holidays of obligation prescribed by the Church, which are the following: all Sundays, New Year's Day, the Epiphany (January 6th), St. Joseph's Day (March 19th), Ascension Day, Corpus Christi, S.S. Peter and Paul's Day (29th June), the Assumption of the Blessed Virgin (August 15th), All Saints's Day (November 1st), the Immaculate Conception (December 8th), and Christmas Day (December 25th).

ART. 12.—On all Sundays and holidays of obligation, in Capitular Churches the celebrant of the Conventual Mass will sing a prayer for the prosperity of the King of Italy and of the Italian State, according to the rules of sacred liturgy.

ART. 13.—The Italian Government will forward to the Holy See the complete list of ecclesiastics appointed for the spiritual direction of the military forces of the State, as soon as it has been officially approved. The selection of the ecclesiastics to whom the supervision of the service of spiritual assistance is entrusted (Military Ordinary, Vicars and Inspectors) will be made in confidence to the Italian Government by the Holy See. If the Italian Government has any reason for objecting to the selection, it will notify the Holy See, which will proceed to make another appointment. The military Ordinary will have the rank of an archbishop. The military chaplains are nominated by the competent authority of the Italian State, on the designation of the military Ordinary.

ART. 14.—The Italian land, sea and air forces enjoy, regarding religious duties, all privileges and dispensations approved by the Canon Law. The military chaplains, in regard to the troops, have parish competence. They exercise their sacred ministry under the jurisdiction of the military Ordinary assisted by his own Curia. The military Ordinary has jurisdiction even over the religious personnel, masculine and feminine, employed in Military hospitals.

ART 15.—The military archbishop will be attached to the Chapter of the Pantheon Church in Rome, constituting with it the clergy to whom the religious services of the said basilica is entrusted. This clergy is authorised to arrange for all religious services, even outside Rome, which in accordance with ecclesiastical rules may be required by the State or the Royal Household. The Holy See consents to confer on all the Canons members of the Pantheon Chapter the dignity of protonotaries *ad instar durante munere*. Each one will be nominated by the Cardinal Vicar of Rome, on presentation by His Majesty the King of Italy, after the confidential indication of the candidate. The Holy See reserves to itself the power to transfer the present staff to another Church.

ART. 16.—The High Contracting Parties will proceed with mutual accord, by means of mixed commissions, to a revision of the territory of the dioceses, so as to make them, if possible, co-terminous with that of the provinces of the Kingdom. It is agreed that the Holy See will institute the diocese of Zara, and that no part of the territory under the sovereignty of the Kingdom of Italy will depend upon a bishop whose see is in a territory subject to the sovereignty of another State; and that no diocese of the Kingdom will include zones of territory subject to the sovereignty of another State. The same principle will be observed for all parishes, existing or to be made, in zones near the frontiers of the State. All alterations that it may be necessary to make in the future in the frontiers of a diocese after the previously mentioned arrangement, will be decided by the Holy See in consultation with the Italian Government and in conformity with the above mentioned rules, except such small alterations as may be for spiritual objects.

ART. 17.—The reduction of the dioceses that will result from the application of the preceding article will be effected little by little as the said dioceses fall vacant. It is understood that this reduction will not imply the suppression either of the titles or of the Chapters of the diocesec, that will be preserved although they will be so grouped as to make the diocesan centre correspond with the chief town of the province. The above mentioned reductions will leave untouched all the economic resources of the dioceses and of all other ecclesiastical bodies existing in the same, including the amounts paid at present by the Italian State.

ART. 18—If, by order of the ecclesiastical authority, it becomes necessary to group together, temporarily or permanently, several parishes, either entrusting them to one rector assisted by one or more vice-rectors, or collecting together several priests in the same presbytery, the State will maintain unaltered the financial treatment due to the said parishes.

ART. 19.—The appointment of archbishops and bishops pertains to the Holy See. Before proceeding to nominate an archbishop, a diocesan bishop, or a coadjutor *cum jure successionis*, the Holy See will notify to the Italian Government the name of the selected ecclesiastic in order to ascertain whether the said Government has any political reasons for objecting to the nomination. All arrangements concerning this will be made with the greatest possible speed and every reserve, so as to keep secret the name of the candidate until the nomination is made.

ART. 20.—All bishops, before taking possession of their diocese, will take an oath of fealty to the Head of the State, according to the following formula: 'Before God and His Holy Gospel I swear and promise as is fitting in a Bishop, fealty to the Italian State. I swear and promise to respect, and to make respected by my clergy the King and the Government established according to the constitutional laws of the State. Further, I swear and promise not to take part in any agreement, nor to be present at any meeting, which may injure the Italian State and public order, and that I will not permit my clergy to do so. Desirous of promoting the welfare and the interests of the Italian State I will seek to avoid any course that may injure it.'

ART. 21.—The provision of the ecclesiastical benefices pertains to the ecclesiastical authority. The appointment of priests to be invested with parish benefices must be communicated privately by the competent ecclesiastical authority to the Italian Government, and cannot take effect until thirty days after the communication. In the meantime the Italian Government, if serious reasons are opposed to the appointment, will privately inform the ecclesiastical authority, when, if agreement cannot be reached, it will refer the case to the Holy See. If serious reasons make the permanent tenure of an ecclesiastic in a parochial benefice undesirable, the Italian Government will notify these reasons to the Ordinary, who, in mutual agreement with the Government, will take the appropriate measures within three months. In case of divergency between the Ordinary and the Government, the Holy See will entrust the solution of the question to two ecclesiastics chosen by itself, who, in agreement with two delegates of the Italian Government, will arrive at a definite decision.

ART. 22.—Ecclesiastics who are not Italian subjects cannot be invested with benefices existing in Italy. The occupiers of dioceses and parishes must also speak the Italian language. If necessary, they may be assisted by co-adjutors who, besides Italian, understand and speak also the language in use in the district, so as to give religious assistance to the faithful in their own language, according to the rules of the Church.

ART. 23.—The rules laid down in Arts. 16, 17, 19, 20, 21 and 22 do not apply to Rome and the suburbicarian dioceses. It is also understood that should the Holy See proceed to a new arrangement of the said dioceses the amounts at present paid by the Italian Government either as stipends or to other ecclesiastical institutions will remain unaltered.

ART. 24.—The *exequatur*, the royal *placet*, and all other imperial or royal appointments to ecclesiastical benefices or offices are abolished, except in the cases laid down in Art 29, letter (g).

ART. 25.—The Italian State renounces the sovereign prerogative of the Royal Patronage over major and minor benefices. The 'regalia' on major and minor benefices is abolished. The 'pensionable third' in the provinces of the ex-kingdom of the two Sicilies is also abolished. The State and the administrations dependent in it, cease to be responsible for any financial obligation.

ART. 26.—The appointment of ecclesiastics to major or minor benefices or of those who may temporarily represent the vacant see or benefice, takes effect from the date of the ecclesiastical nomination, and must be officially communicated to the Government. The administration and the enjoyment of the income during the vacancy is settled in accordance with the rules of Canon Law. In case of bad administration the Italian State, after coming to an agreement with the ecclesiastical authority, may proceed to the seizure of the temporalities of the benefice, handing over the net income to the nominee, or, lacking him, to the benefice itself.

ART. 27.—The Basilicas of the Holy House in Loreto, of St. Francis in Assisi and of St. Anthony in Padua, with all buildings and workshops dependent, except those of a purely lay character, will be handed over to the Holy See and their management will wholly pertain to the said See. All other bodies of any nature directly controlled in Italy by the Holy See, including colleges for missionaries, will equally be free from any State interference or conversion. None the less all Italian laws regarding acquisitions by moral bodies remain in force.

Regarding the possessions owned at the present by the said Sanctuaries, a mixed Commission will proceed to their division, taking into consideration the rights of their parties and the endowments necessary to the said purely lay institutions.

The unrestricted control of the ecclesiastical authority will take the place of the civil administration existing in all other Sanctuaries, without prejudice to the division of possessions contemplated in the preceding article, where this is the case.

ART. 28.—To tranquilize consciences, the Holy See will grant full forgiveness to all those who, in consequence of the Italian laws against ecclesiastical patrimony, find themselves in possession of ecclesiastical properties. With this object the Holy See will give the necessary instructions to the Ordinaries.

ART. 29.—The Italian State will revise its legislation, in so far as it refers to ecclesiastical matters, so as to reform and complete it, putting it into harmony with the principles the treaty stipulated with the Holy See and this Concordat.

The following have been agreed upon between the two High Contracting Parties:

(*a*) While the juridical personality of the ecclesiastical bodies recognized up to the present by the Italian laws (Holy See, dioceses, chapters, seminaries, parishes, etc.) remains unaltered, such personality will be recognized also for churches open to public worship, that do not possess it already, including those previously owned by suppressed ecclesiastical bodies, in which case they will enjoy the income that at present the Maintenance Fund assigns to each of them. Except when prescribed in Art. 27, the Boards of Administration, wherever they exist and whatever their name, even if composed totally or mainly of laymen, may not interfere in regard to divine worship, and the appointment of their members must be made in consultation with the ecclesiastical authorities.

(*b*) Juridical personality will be recognized to the religious associations, with or without vows, approved by the Holy See, that have their principal residence in the kingdom, and are represented there, juridically and materially by persons who are Italian subjects domiciled in Italy. Juridical personality will also be recognized to Italian religious provinces within the limits of the territory of the State and its Colonies, as well as to associations having their mother-house abroad, as long as they fulfil the same conditions. Juridical personality will also be recognized to religious Houses when by the special rules of their Orders the capacity of acquiring and owning property is guaranteed to them. Moreover juridical personality will be recognized in the case of residences of Generals of religious orders and to the head offices of foreign religious associations. All Associations and religious Houses, which already have juridical personality, will retain it. All legal acts regarding the transfer of properties already owned by the associations, from their present nominal owners, will be exempt from any duty or tax.

(*c*) All confraternities having purely or mainly religious aims are not subject to any further definition of aims, and will depend upon ecclesiastical authority for their direction and administration.

(*d*) Religious foundations of every kind are admitted, so long as they correspond with the religious needs of the population and do not cause any financial burden to the State. This rule applies also to foundations already existing *de facto*.

(*e*) In the civil administration of the ecclesiastical patrimony arising from the confiscation laws, the boards of administration will be composed as to one half by members nominated by the ecclesiastical authority. The same applies to the religious foundations of the new provinces.

(*f*) All action taken up to now by ecclesiastical or religious bodies not in conformity with civil laws, may be recognized and legalized on the request of the Ordinary within three years from the coming into effect of this Concordat.

(*g*) The Italian State renounces the privileges of ecclesiastical jurisdictional exemption of the Palatine clergy throughout Italy, except for such clergy appointed to the churches of the Santa Sindone in Turin, of Superga, of the Sudario in Rome, and of the chapels appertaining to the residential palaces of the Sovereigns and of the Royal Princes, while all other nominations and appointments to benefices and offices will be ruled by the preceding articles.

A special commission will assign to each Palatine basilica or church an adequate endowment according to the rules laid down for the sanctuaries in Art. 27.

(*h*) Leaving unaltered all fiscal privileges already granted by the Italian laws to ecclesiastical institutions, all institutions with a strictly religious aim are put on an equality, for fiscal purposes, with those having a benevolent or educational scope. The special 30 per cent. tax imposed by Art. 18 of the law August 15th, 1867, No. 3848, the concomital quota of articles 31 of the law July 7th, 1866, No. 3036, and 20 of law August 15th, 1867, No. 3848, are abolished, as well as the tax on the transfer of usufruct of the goods constituting the endowment of benefices and other ecclesiastical bodies, as per Art. 1 of the Royal Decree, December 30th, 1923, No. 3270; so that in future no special tribute can be imposed upon the possessions of the Church. The 'professional' tax and the 'patent' tax instituted by the Royal Decree, No. 2538, of November 15th, 1923, in place of the suppressed tax on shops and re-selling, will not be imposed on priests in respect of the exercise of their clerical mission, nor any other similar tax.

(*i*) The wearing of ecclesiastical or religious dress by seculars, or by clerics or religious to whom this has been forbidden by a permanent decision of the competent ecclesiastical authority (which in such case should be officially communicated to the Italian Government), is forbidden and punished with the same penalties as are inflicted for the illegal wearing of military uniforms.

ART. 30.—The administration, both ordinary and extraordinary, of the properties owned by any ecclesiastical institutions or religious association is carried on under the supervision and control of the competent Church authorities, excluding any interference from the Italian State, and without any obligation to subject to conversion any estate or building.

The Italian State recognizes to all ecclesiastical institutions and religious associations the capacity of acquiring possessions within the limits of the civil law ruling acquisitions by moral bodies.

The Italian State, until new agreements ordain otherwise, will continue to make up the deficiencies in the incomes of the ecclesiastical benefices in the incomes of the ecclesiastical benefices with sums corresponding to an amount not inferior to the real value fixed by the laws now in vigour. In consideration of this, the patrimonial administration of the said benefices, in regard to all acts and contracts outside ordinary administration, will take place with the concurrence of the Italian State, and in the case of a vacancy the delivery of the possessions will be made in the presence of a representative of the Government, and an official report will be made of the fact. The episcopal stipends of the suburbicarian dioceses and the endowments of the Chapters and parishes of Rome and of the said dioceses will not be subject to the above conditions.

As regards the above, the amount of the incomes that are paid to the recipients of the benefices out of the said stipends and endowments will appear from a statement rendered yearly under his own responsibility by the suburbicarian bishop for the dioceses, and by the Cardinal Vicar for the city of Rome.

ART. 31.—The erection of new ecclesiastical bodies or religious associations will be made by the ecclesiastical authority according to the rules of Canon Law. Their recognition for civil effects will be granted by the civil authorities.

ART. 32.—The recognitions and authorizations contemplated by the present Concordat and by the Treaty will take place according to the rules of civil law, which will have to be put in harmony with the prescriptions of the Concordat and of the Treaty.

ART. 33.—The charge of the Catacombs existing in the subsoil of Rome and in other parts of the Kingdom is reserved to the Holy See, with the onus of custody, upkeep and preservation. The Holy See can therefore, while observing the laws of the State and the rights of third parties, proceed to the needful excavations and to the transfer of the holy bodies.

ART. 34.—The Italian State wishing to restore to the institution of matrimony, which is the basis of the family, the dignity it deserves considering the Catholic tradition of the nation, recognises the civil effects of the sacrament of marriage as laid down by Canon Law. The publication of the banns must be carried out, not only in the parish church but also by the municipality. Immediately after the ceremony the parish priest will explain to the married couple the civil effects of marriage, reading to them the articles of the civil code concerning the rights and the duties of husband and wife, and he will draw up the marriage certificate, a complete copy of which must be forwarded within five days to the Commune, in order that it may be entered in the registers of the Civil Status.

All causes concerning nullity of marriage and dispensations from marriages celebrated but not consummated, are reserved to the authority of the ecclesiastical courts. The decisions and verdicts, when they have been made absolute, shall be reported to the Supreme Court of the Segnatura which will verify whether the rules of Canon Law in regard to the competency of the judge, the summoning and legal defence or the contumacy of the parties concerned, have been complied with. The said decisions and final verdicts with the decrees of the Supreme Court of the

Segnatura shall be transmitted to the Court of Appeal of the appropriate district, which with an Order of the Council of Judges will pronounce them effective for civil purposes and will order them to be duly noted in the registers of the Civil Status in the margin of the certificate of marriage.

As regards all cases of personal separation the Holy See is willing that they should be decided by the authority of the civil courts.

ART. 35.—All secondary schools, conducted under ecclesiastical or religious supervision, shall continue to submit themselves to the State examinations, all candidates whether from the above schools or from government institutions being treated on an absolute equality.

ART. 36.—Italy considers the teaching of Christian doctrine in accordance with Catholic tradition, as both the basis and the crown of public education. It therefore agrees that the religious teaching now given in the public elementary schools shall be extended to the secondary schools, in accordance with a programme to be drawn up between the Holy See and the State. Such teaching shall be given by masters and professors, whether priests or religious, approved by ecclesiastical authority, and even by lay masters and professors, who, for this purpose, shall be provided with certificates of capacity from the Ordinary of the diocese. The revocation of such a certificate by the Ordinary forthwith deprives the teacher of his right to teach. For such religious instruction in public schools text books may only be used that have been approved by ecclesiastical authority.

ART. 37.—The directors of the State associations for physical training, for pre-military instruction, for Avanguardisti and for Balilla, in order to allow the youth entrusted to them to take part in religious instruction and services, will arrange their time-tables for Sundays and holidays of obligation in such a way as not to interfere with the performance of religious duties.

In the same way all directors of public schools will make similar arrangements for their pupils on all holidays of obligation.

ART. 38.—The nomination of the professors of the Catholic University of the Sacred Heart and of the dependent Istituo di Magistero Maria Immacolata, are subject to the *Nihil Obstat* of the Holy See, in order to ensure that there is nothing to take exception to from the point of view of faith or morals.

ART. 39.—All universities, greater or lesser seminaries, whether diocesan, inter-diocesan or regional, academies, colleges and other Catholic institutions for the formation and education of ecclesiastics will continue to be subject solely to the Holy See, without any interference from the educational authorities of the Kingdom.

ART. 40.—The degrees in sacred theology conferred by the Faculty approved by the Holy See will be recognized by the Italian State. It will also recognise diplomas conferred by the schools of paleography, of Archives and of diplomatic documents organised in connection with the library and record office of the Vatican City.

ART. 41.—Italy authorises the use within the Kingdom and in her Colonies of pontifical titles of knighthood after registration of the brevet on production of the original and at the written request of the recipient of the honour.

ART. 42.—Italy will permit the recognition, by means of a Royal Decree, of titles of nobility conferred by the Supreme Pontiff even since 1870, and of all those that may be conferred in future.

In certain cases the authorization in Italy will not be liable to the payment of fees.

ART. 43.—The Italian State recognises the organisations forming part of the Italian Catholic Action, in so far as, in accordance with the injunctions of the Holy See, they maintain their activity wholly apart from every political party and under the immediate control of the hierarchy of the Church for the diffusion and practice of Catholic principles. The Holy See takes the opportunity of the drawing up of the present Concordat to renew to all ecclesiastics and religious throughout Italy the prohibition to be members of, or take part in, any political party.

ART. 44.—If, in the future, any difficulties should arise concerning the interpretation of the present Concordat, the Holy See and Italy will proceed by way of mutual understanding to a friendly solution.

ART. 45.—The present Concordat will be applied after the exchange of ratifications contemporaneously with the Treaty stipulated between the same High Parties which eliminated the 'Roman Question'.

With the coming into force of the present Concordat all the dispositions of previous Concordats of the former Austrian laws and all laws, regulations and decrees of the Italian States shall cease to be applied in Italy. All Austrian laws and all laws, regulations and decrees of the existing Italian State in so far as they are in conflict with the dispositions of the present Concordat are to be considered abrogated as soon as the present Concordat comes into force.

In order to carry out the execution of the present Concordat a Commission shall be set up, immediately after the signing of the same, consisting of persons nominated by both the contracting parties.

Rome, February 11th, 1929.

(Signed)   Peter Card. Gasparri
                           Benito Mussolini

THE FINANCIAL CONVENTION.

Considering that the Holy See and Italy, in consequence of the stipulation of the Treaty with which the 'Roman Question' has been permanently solved, have deemed it necessary to regulate in a separate convention, forming an integral part of the Treaty, their financial relations; that the Supreme Pontiff, considering on one side the enormous damages suffered by the Apostolic See by the loss of St. Peter's Patrimony, consisting of the ancient Pontifical States, and of the possessions of ecclesiastical institutions, and on the other the ever increasing needs of the Church if only in the city of Rome, and at the same time taking into consideration the financial position of the State and the economic conditions of the Italian people, especially after the war, has decided to limit his request for an indemnity to the strictest necessary amount, asking for a sum, partly in cash and partly in Consols, which is greatly inferior in value to that which the State would have had to pay up to now to the Holy See, if only in fulfilment of the undertaking contained in the law of May 13th, 1871; that the Italian State duly appreciating the fatherly sentiments of the Supreme Pontiff, has considered it to be its duty to agree to the request for the payment of such an amount; the two High Parties, represented by the same plenipotentiaries, have agreed:

ART. 1.—Italy pledges herself to pay to the Holy See, at the exchange of the ratifications of the Treaty, the sum of Italian Lire 750,000,000 (seven hundred and fifty million; equals about £8,152,000) in cash, and to deliver at the same time sufficient 5 per cent Italian Consols, bearer bonds, of the nominal value of Italian Lire 1,000,000,000 (one milliard; equals about £10,869,000), with first interest falling due on June 30th, 1929.

ART. 2.—The Holy See agrees to accept the said amounts as a final settlement of its financial relations with Italy caused by the events of 1870.

ART. 3.—All acts necessary for the execution of the Treaty, of the present Convention and of the Concordat will be exempt from any tax.

Rome, February 11th, 1929.

    (Signed)   Peter Cardinal Gasparri
                             Benito Mussolini

The September Accords, 1931*

(1) The Azione Cattolica Italiana is essentially diocesan and is strictly dependent upon the Bishops, who choose the directors, both ecclesiastical and lay. There cannot in future be chosen as directors men who belonged in the past to parties hostile to the regime. In harmony with its ends of a religious and spiritual order, the Azione Cattolica does not interfere in any way in politics, and in the external forms of its organisations holds itself aloof from everything that is proper to and traditional in political parties. The flag of the local associations of the Azione Cattolica will be the national flag.

(2) The Azione Cattolica does not include in its programme the constitution of professional associations and trade unions; consequently it does not set before itself any tasks of a trade union order. Its internal professional sections, already now existing and governed by the law of April 3, 1926, are formed for exclusively spiritual and religious purposes, and they propose further to contribute to the result that the trade unions juridically recognised may respond ever better to the principle of collaboration between the classes and to the social and national ends which, in a Catholic country, the State with its existing organisations proposes to attain.

(3) The youths' clubs dependent upon the Azione Cattolica will be called 'Catholic Action Youths' Association'. These associations will be allowed to have membership tickets and badges corresponding strictly to their religious purpose; they will not have for the various associations any flag other than the national flag and their own religious standards. The local associations will refrain from pursuing any activity whatever of an athletic or sporting character, and will limit themselves solely to occupations of a recreative or an educational nature with a religious purpose.

* From the translation in *Italy Today*, May 1931

A note on archival and other sources

Broadly speaking, there is rather less documentary material on the subject of this study available from Catholic sources than there is from the Italian State. The Vatican authorities do not permit access to papers in the Secret Archives which date from after 1903 (the death of Leo XIII), thus excluding all material from the period under consideration. A part of this regrettable gap has been filled by the work of two historians who, by virtue of their ecclesiastical status, have been exempted from the general prohibition: Mons. Maccarone's publication of the diary of Prince Francesco Pacelli provides a unique, blow-by-blow account of the negotiations which produced the Lateran Pacts of 1929 by the Vatican's chief negotiator,[1] and Padre Angelo Martini whose work *Studi sulla Questione Romana e la Conciliazione* reproduces documents from the Vatican Archives, unavailable elsewhere, relating to the negotiations which brought the crisis of 1931 to an end.[2] In addition the *Documenti Diplomatici Italiani* proved to be absolutely indispensable for the whole period and for 1931 in particular.[3]

As well as having to cope with the handicap of not being allowed access to the Vatican Archives, the historian of this period also faces the problem of having only a very limited amount of biographical material, most of it of dubious value, on the leading Vatican personalities involved in the events described – Pius XI, Cardinals Gasparri and Pacelli, Monsignori Borgoncini-Duca and Pizzardo, and Padre Tacchi-Venturi.[4]

---

[1] F. Pacelli, *Diario*, ed. Maccarone.

[2] Martini, *Studi sulla Questione Romana*: Biggini, *Storia inedita della Conciliazione*, reproduces extracts of documents not cited in either the *Diario* or in Martini.

[3] D.D.I.

[4] The most useful profile of Pius XI is that by Falconi in *The Popes in the Twentieth Century*, pp. 151–233. Less useful is Spadolini, *Il Cardinale Gasparri e la Questione Romana con alcuni brani inediti delle sue memorie*, which, as the title suggests, it has little to say about Gasparri after 1929. Taliani, *La Vita di Cardinale Gasparri*, is not very illuminating either, nor is another pious work, Piolanti, *Il Cardinale Pietro Gasparri*. Falconi's section on Pius XII (Eugenio Pacelli) says next to nothing about Pacelli's early years as Secretary of State, and the numerous, pious popular biographies dedicated to him are not worth mentioning here. For Francesco Borgoncini-Duca, first Papal Nuncio to Italy, there is only the entry

It also proved impossible to obtain permission to view the archives of the Catholic Action Headquarters in Rome, though this would not appear to constitute any great loss since assurances were given by the Librarian of Catholic Action that the bulk of its papers were transferred to the Secret Archives in the Vatican during the crisis of 1931, and that what remained was of little value. On the other hand, the Catholic Action Library contains a collection of contemporary Catholic periodicals, unavailable elsewhere, which proved to be of enormous use in building up a picture of the activities and organisation of Catholic Action in this period.

As it happened, the lack of material from the Vatican and Catholic Action Archives was more than offset by the wealth of documentation held by two other archives in Rome – the Archive of *La Civiltà Cattolica* and the Archivo Centrale dello Stato. As far as the archives of the Jesuit journal are concerned, the most important section comprises the papers of Padre Enrico Rosa, editor of the journal in the 1920s and 1930s, and a close personal friend of Pius XI. As his papers demonstrate, Rosa played an important, behind-the-scenes, policy-making role in Catholic Action; it was he, for example, who drafted the statutes of its dependent organisation I.C.A.S. In addition, this collection is notable for the number of letters addressed to Rosa on all manner of subjects by the *popolare* leader in exile, Francesco Ferrari.

In the Archivio Centrale della Stato, the Central State Archives in Rome, the files of the Ministero dell'Interno, and particularly those of the police section – the Direzione Generale della Pubblica Sicurezza – provide a wealth of information about Catholic Action policy and activity in all its branches and at every organisational level – national headquarters in Rome, diocesan *giunte* and even parochial groups.[5] As a result of frequent nationwide police investigations of the Catholic organisations between 1927 and 1932, the Regime was in possession of a more accurate and up-to-date picture of the numerical strength and organisational effective-

in *Dizionario Biografico degli Italiani*, Vol. I, p. 783 (the author was refused permission to consult Borgoncini-Duca's file in A.C.S., C.P.C., on the grounds that close relatives of the recently dead prelate were still living). For Giuseppe Pizzardo there is a file of extremely critical, and sometimes downright scurrilous, reports in A.C.S., S.C.P., b. 44, f. 2, 'Mons Pizzardo'. For Padre Pietro Tacchi-Venturi see Castellani, *P. Pietro Tacchi-Venturi S.I.*

5 A.C.S., D.G.P.S., G.I., bb. 95–132; these *buste* contain files on Catholic organisations, on Protestant Churches and the 'Trimestrali' or quarterly reports from the Prefects on the state of their provinces which frequently include comments on the attitude of the clergy to the Regime. *Busta* 146 is of central importance for it contains material on Catholic Action as a national organisation. An additional source of information on the clergy and the bishops is the Fondo per il Culto which was brought under the control of the Ministry of the Interior in 1932; the Serie IV, 'Vescovi', section of these files contains the personal dossiers of all the Italian bishops appointed after the *Conciliazione*. (Since the research for this book was carried out, the Ministry of the Interior files have been largely recatalogued with the result that *busta* numbers used here do not always correspond to the system currently in use in the Archivio Centrale.)

ness of Catholic Action than was either the Giunta Centrale of that body or the Vatican Secretariat of State. And the accuracy of police information on the Catholic organisations is borne out by recent studies of the functioning of Catholic Action at a local level during the Fascist period.

Perhaps even more remarkable than this, was the fact that through its spies in the Vatican, the Regime was regularly supplied with the most detailed, up-to-the-minute and expertly informed reports on the politics of the Vatican itself; on the balance of power between its leading personalities and on the state of opinion there on matters regarding the Church's relations with Fascism.[6] The accuracy of this constant stream of information is very often verifiable by another source – the reports to the Foreign Office of the British envoys to the Vatican and the Quirinale.[7]

[6] There is still a great deal of uncertainty as to the exact identity of the Fascist spies in the Vatican, though we can at least be fairly certain that there was more than one. The favourite candidate at the end of the Second World War was Mons. Enrici Pucci who, as a correspondent for the Clerico-Fascist newspaper *Il Corriere d'Italia*, wrote the articles urging Sturzo to resign in the Summer of 1923. There are references in the police files to Pucci being 'il Nostro Informatore di Palazzo' (our Palace informant), and on these grounds his name was included in the 'Elenco dei confidenti dell'O.V.A.R.A.' (list of secret police agents): see the *Gazzetta Ufficiale*, 2 July 1946. But Pucci was eventually cleared by the Purge Commission: see the *Gazzetta Ufficiale*, 2 December 1946. A rather more highly placed person on whom much suspicion has fallen is Mons. Umberto Benigni, the leader of the 'Integralist' faction in the Vatican whose campaign against the 'modernists' in the reign of Pius X included an attack on Cardinal Gasparri. Benigni was at first violently anti-Fascist but then swung to the Fascist side in the late 1920s. Scoppola, *La Chiesa e il Fascismo*, p. 146 claims that he spied for the Fascists, as does Holmes, *The Triumph of the Holy See*, p. 285, but neither offers any supporting evidence, nor is there any such evidence in the police files. An even more highly placed ecclesiastic, Mons. Carlo Caccia-Dominioni, Maestro di Camera to Pius XI, had strong Milanese Clerico-Fascist connections, and it seems likely that he supplied Mussolini with more than just the report on Turati's visit to the Vatican in February 1930 (see Chapter 5, p. 131). According to Cesare De Vecchi, 'Mussolini il Vero', in *Il Tempo*, 3 March 1960, the person who supplied the reports on the secret, 'summit' meetings of the various branches of Catholic Action, which took place in Rome in May 1931 and were used as a pretext for the dissolution of the Catholic youth organisations, '...was one of the eight members of the Giunta Centrale of Catholic Action'. That body had in fact *nine* members, of whom only two – the Marchesa Patrizi Montoro and Conte Statella of Naples – had Clerico-Fascist connections that might suggest they spied for the Regime (one former *popolare* M.P., a partisan source admittedly, has claimed that the Clerico-Fascists had regularly spied on their fellow Catholics for the police: see Spataro, *I Democratici Cristiani*, p. 185). There undoubtedly were several police spies in the Vatican judging by the differing styles and the differing quality and quantity of information to be found in the police files. The reports on the meetings and activities of Catholic Action in A.C.S., D.G.P.S., G.I., b. 146, were clearly written by a highly placed, well-informed observer with a sophisticated understanding of the Vatican, of the Church in Italy and, above all, of the Catholic movement, suggesting that it was either Caccia-Dominioni, Benigni or one of the latter's disciples. Pucci is unlikely to have had either the access to information or the sophisticated knowledge which went into these reports – he was essentially a Roman parish priest who eked out his living with a little journalism. On the other hand, it is just possible that he compiled the profiles of Vatican personalities to be found in A.C.S., M.P.P.; they are largely speculative, salacious and lacking in solid fact. We shall probably never know for certain who the Fascist spies in the Vatican were, but whoever they were they served their masters very well. [7] These are to be found in the Foreign Office section of the P.R.O.

Finally, in view of the fact that it was impossible to gain access to the Vatican Archives, it is perhaps ironical that we nevertheless know more about the role of Vatican personalities – Pacelli, Borgoncini-Duca and Pizzardo – during the 1931 crisis than we do about their counterparts in the Regime – Grandi, Giurati, De Vecchi and Scorza. For De Vecchi, we do at least have his memoirs which, though they reflect the bombast and vanity of the man, are also a mine of essential information on personalities, and events in the period 1929–32,[8] and for Giurati a short memoir which unfortunately says nothing about his role in the crisis of 1931.[9] As for the others, who were equally closely involved with Mussolini in the handling of the dispute with the Vatican, we have nothing except a few, odd references in other people's memoirs.[10]

[8] Published posthumously by his son, Giorgio De Vecchi, in *Il Tempo*, January–March 1960, under the title 'Mussolini il Vero'.
[9] Giurati, 'La Parabola di Mussolini'.
[10] For example, Tamaro, *Venti anni di Storia*, Vol. II, pp. 450–3, and De Begnac, *Palazzo Venezia*, pp. 700–50.

Bibliography

This bibliography is arranged as follows:

Primary source material
Archival sources
Printed primary sources
Newspaper and periodical sources
Almanacs, dictionaries, encyclopedias, yearbooks, etc.

Secondary source material
Published books and articles
Unpublished papers, theses and dissertations

PRIMARY SOURCE MATERIAL

ARCHIVAL SOURCES

See the list of abbreviations and Appendix IV.

PRINTED PRIMARY SOURCES

Atti dei congressi del P.P.I., ed. F. Malgeri, Brescia, 1969
Atti della Commissione Mista Dei Delegati Della Santa Sede e Del Governo Italiano per Predisporre l'Esecuzione del Concordato (11 Aprile–25 Novembre 1929) e altri documenti conessi, ed. P. Ciprotti, Milan, 1968
Atti Parlamentari del Regno d'Italia, Camera dei Deputati/Camera dei Senatori
Ciano's Diary, 1937–38, trans. A. Mayor, London, 1952
Ciano's Diary, 1939–45, ed. with an introd. by M. Muggeridge, London and Toronto, 1947
Discorsi di Pio XI, Vol. II, 1929–33, Turin, 1960
I Documenti Diplomatici Italiani, Settima Serie (1922–35), Rome, 1952–00
Giuseppe Donati, Scritti Politici, Vol. II, ed. with an introd. by G. Rossini, Rome, 1965
Dossier Conciliazione, ed. with an introd. by E. Cavaterra, Milan, 1971
Mediterranean Fascism, 1919–45, ed. with an introd. by Charles F. Delzell, New York, 1971
Memorie, memoirs of C. M. De Vecchi, published posthumously in *Il Tempo*, January–March 1960
Ministero dell'Economia Nazionale, Compendio di Statistica Elettorale Politica, 1919, 1921 and 1924, Rome, 1929
A. Mussolini: Scritti e Discorsi, Vol. III, ed. with an introd. by B. Mussolini, Rome, 1932

B. *Mussolini: Corrispondenza Inedita*, ed. D. Susmel, Milan, 1972
Opera Omnia di Benito Mussolini, 36 vols., ed. E. and D. Susmel, Florence, 1951–63
F. Pacelli, *Diario della Conciliazione*, ed. M. Maccarone, Vatican City, 1959
The Papal Encyclicals in their Historical Context ed. with an introd. by Anne
    Freemantle, New York, 1956
La Polemica per l'Azione Cattolica (L'Osservatore Romano), Vatican City, 1931
Luigi Sturzo: Scritti Inediti, 2 vols. ed. with an introd. by F. Piva, Rome, 1975

NEWSPAPER AND PERIODICAL SOURCES

The following have been consulted for the whole or part of the 1929–32
period.

DAILY NEWSPAPERS
L'Avvenire d'Italia (Catholic, Bologna)
Il Corriere d'Italia (Clerico-Fascist, Rome)
Il Corriere della Sera (Liberal, later Fascist, Milan)
La Gioventù Fascista (organ of Fascist Youth, Rome)
L'Impero (organ of the extreme anti-clerical Settimelli, Rome)
L'Italia (Catholic, Milan)
Il Lavoro Fascista (organ of the Fascist trade unions, Rome)
Il Momento (Clerico-Fascist, Turin)
L'Osservatore Romano (official Vatican organ, Vatican City)
Il Popolo d'Italia (official Fascist organ, Milan)
Il Popolo di Roma (Liberal, later Fascist, Rome)
La Stampa (Liberal, later Fascist, Turin)
The Times
La Tribuna (edited by the ex-nationalist, Forges D'Avanzati, Rome)
L'Unità Cattolica (Catholic, Florence)

PERIODICALS
L'Azione Fucina (organ of the F.U.C.I., Rome)
Bollettino Diocesano di Padova (Catholic, Padua)
Bollettino Ufficiale dell'Azione Cattolica Italiana (official organ of Catholic Action)
Camicia Rossa (independent Fascist youth organ, Rome)
La Civiltà Cattolica (organ of the Jesuits, Rome)
Critica Fascista (edited by Giuseppe Bottai, Rome)
Educazione Fascista (originally edited by G. Gentile, Rome)
Fides: Rivista Mensile dell'Opera Pontificia per la Preservazione della Fede (edited by
    I. Giordani, Vatican City)
Foglio d'Ordini (Official organ of the P.N.F.)
Gazzetta Ufficiale del Regno (della Repubblica after 1946) (official government gazette)
Gerarchia (officially edited by Benito Mussolini)
Italy Today (anti-Fascist news-sheet published in Britain)
Libro e Moschetto (official organ of the G.U.F., Rome)
Pegaso (literary journal)
Res Publica (published by Ferrari, 1931–3, Brussels)
Rivista Internazionale di Scienze Sociali e Politiche (publication of the Catholic
    University of Milan)
Rivista Pedagogica (educational journal)

Lo Stato Operaio (official publication of the Italian Communist Party in exile)
The Tablet (English Catholic journal)
L'Universale (publication of Fascist anti-clericals, 1931–5, Florence)
Vita e Pensiero (publication of the Catholic University of Milan)

ALMANACS, DICTIONARIES, ENCYCLOPEDIAS AND YEARBOOKS, ETC.

Almanacco Italiano, published annually in Florence
Annali dell'Italia Cattolica, published annually in Milan
Annuario delle Banche Cattoliche, published annually in Milan
Annuario LXXVI della Gioventù Cattolica, published annually in Rome
Annuario Pontificio, published annually in the Vatican City
Annuario della Stampa Italiana, published annually in Rome
Chi è?, Rome, 1929
Dizionario Biografico degli Italiani, A–C, Rome, 1964
Dizionario degli'Italiani d'Oggi, Rome, 1931
Encyclopedia Biografica Italiana – Ministri, Senatori e Deputati, 42nd series, 3 vols., Rome, 1941
Manuale Hoepli, Milan, 1967 (contains the text of the *Codice Rocco*)
Manuale dei Senatori del Regno XXVIII legislatura, Rome, 1930

SECONDARY SOURCE MATERIAL

PUBLISHED BOOKS AND ARTICLES

L. Ambrosoli, 'Stefano Jacini Junior', in *Humanitas*, VIII, no. 4, April 1973
G. Anichini, *Cinquant'anni di Vita della F.U.C.I.*, Rome, 1947
Anon., *Modernismo, Fascismo e Communismo: Aspetti della cultura dei Cattolici nell'900*, Bologna, 1972
     Pius X, the Popes and Catholic Action, Catholic Truth Society Pamphlet, London, 1930
M. Antonetti, 'La F.U.C.I. di Montini e Righetti di fronte ai patti lateranensi', in *Humanitas*, XXXIV, no. 1, Feb. 1979
A. Aquarone, *L'organizzazione dello stato totalitario*, Turin, 1965
A. Aquarone and M. Vernassa (eds.), *Il Regime Fascista*, Bologna, 1974
P. G. Balduzzi, *Brevi Note Illustrative della Carta del Lavoro*, Rome, 1929
P. Ballerini, *Il Movimento Cattolico a Firenze (1900–1919)*, Rome 1969
A. Baroni, *Igino Righetti*, Rome, 1948
P. Beccaria, 'L'Azione Cattolica a la norma concordataria', in *Quaderni di Iustizia*, XII, Studium, 1959
L. Bedeschi, *I Cattolici Ubbidienti*, Naples, 1962
     Giuseppe Donati, Rome 1945
P. Bellu, *I Cattolici alle Urne: Chiesa e Partecipazione politica in Italia dall'Unità al Patto Gentilone*, Cagliari, 1977
M. Bendiscioli, *Antifascismo e Resistenza: impostazioni storiografiche*, Rome, 1964
     'I Patti lateranensi: il Conflitto dopo la Conciliazione', in *Terzo Programma*, no. 2, June 1962
M. Bernabei, *Fascismo e Nazionalismo in Campania*, Rome, 1975
C. A. Biggini, *Storia inedita della Conciliazione*, Milan, 1942
D. A. Binchy, *Church and State in Fascist Italy*, 2nd impression, Oxford, 1970

P. Borzomati, *I Giovani Cattolici nel Mezzogiorno d'Italia dall'unita al 1948*, Rome, 1970

M. T. Brunori Di Siervo, 'L'Istituto Cattolico di Attività Sociali dalla nascita alla seconda guerra mondiale', *Storia Contemporanea*, XII, nos. 4–5, Oct. 1981.

P. V. Bucci, *Chiesa e Stato: Church and State Relations in Italy*, The Hague, 1969

E. Buonaiuti, *Pellegrino di Roma*, Rome, 1945

I. U. Camerini, *Il Partito Popolare dall'Aventino alla discesa nelle catacombe*, Rome, 1975

F. Canali, 'La Gioventù Cattolica a Parma durante l'episcopato di Mons. G. M. Conforti (1907–1931)', in *La Gioventù Cattolica dopo l'Unità*, Rome, 1972

G. Candeloro, *Il Movimento Cattolico in Italia*, Rome, 1953

P. V. Cannistraro, *La Fabbrica del consenso*, Bari, 1975

A. Caracciolo, *Teresio Olivelli*, Brescia, 1947

Elisa A. Carillo, 'Alcide De Gasperi and the Fascist Regime, 1924–29', in *Review of Politics*, XXVI, 1964

A. Caroleo, *Le Banche Cattoliche*, Milan, 1976

G. Carocci, *La Politica Estera dell'Italia Fascista*, Bari, 1969

A. Cassels, *Mussolini's Early Diplomacy*, Princeton, 1970

G. Castellani, *P. Pietro Tacchi-Venturi S.I.*, Milan, 1939

G. Castelli, *La Chiesa e il Fascismo*, Rome, 1951
Il Vaticano nei tentacoli del Fascismo, Rome, 1946

V. Castronovo and N. Tranfaglia, *La Stampa italiana dell'età Fascista*, Bari, 1980

A. M. Cavagna, *Pio XI e l'Azione Cattolica*, Rome, 1929

L. Cavazzoni (ed.), *Stefano Cavazzoni*, Milan, 1955

F. Charle-Roux, *Huit ans aux Vatican*, Paris, 1949

A. Cicchitti-Suriani, 'L'Opposizione italiana ai Patti Lateranensi (1929–31)' in *Nuova Antologia*, July 1952

L. Civardi, *Breve Compendio di Storia dell'Azione Cattolica Italiana*, Rome, 1956

J. C. Clancy, *Apostle for Our Time*, London, 1964

A. Coletti, *Il Divorzio in Italia*, 2nd edn, Rome, 1974

C. Confalonieri, *Pio XI visto da vicino*, Turin, 1957

L. Cornaggia-Medici, *Antesignani della Conciliazione*, Florence, 1936
Lettera aperta al Senatore Morello, Florence, 1933
Il Passato e il Presente della Questione Romana, Rome–Florence, 1930

A. Corsetti, 'Dalla preconciliazione ai Patti del Laterano: Note e documenti', in *Annuario 1968 della Biblioteca Civica di Massa*, Lucca, 1969

G. Dalla Torre, *L'Azione Cattolica e il Regime*, Rome, 1945
Memorie, Milan, 1965

A. Dal Pont, *Aula IV*, Rome, 1961

I. De Begnac, *Palazzo Venezia: Storia di un Regime*, Rome, 1950

L. De Bosis, *Storia della mia morte e ultimi scritti*, ed. with an introd. by G. Salvemini, Turin, 1948

J. De Fabregues, 'The Re-establishment of Relations between France and the Vatican' in *Journal of Contemporary History*, II, no. 4, 1967, pp. 163–82

R. De Felice, *Intervista sul Fascismo*, Bari, 1975
Mussolini il rivoluzionario, 1883–1920, Turin, 1965
Mussolini il Fascista, Vol. I, La conquista del potere, 1921–25, Turin, 1966
Mussolini il Fascista, Vol. II, L'organizzazione dello Stato Fascista, 1925–29, Turin, 1968
Mussolini il Duce, Vol. I, Gli anni del consenso, 1929–36, Turin, 1974
Storia degli ebrei italiani sotto il Fascismo, Bari, 1961

A. De Gasperi, *Lettere sul Concordato*, ed. M. Romana De Gasperi, Brescia, 1977

V. De Grazia, *The Culture of Consent: The Mass Organisation of Leisure in Fascist Italy*, Cambridge, 1982

C. Delzell, *I Nemici di Mussolini*, Turin, 1966

  The Papacy and Totalitarianism between the Two World Wars, New York, 1974

(ed.) *The Unification of Italy, 1859–61*, New York, 1965

G. De Montemayor, 'L'Azione Cattolica nel Concordato fra il Vaticano e L'Italia' in *Studi in onora di Federico Cammeo*, Padua, 1933

C. M. De Vecchi di Val Cismon, 'Mussolini Vero', in *Il Tempo*, January–March 1960

P. Di Lauro, *La Conciliazione Italo-Vaticana giudicata dall'Estero*, Rome, 1953

Dizionario Storico del Movimento Cattolico in Italia 2 vols., Vol. I, Turin, 1981

Dizionario dei termini storiografici, Bologna, 1969

C. d'Olivier Farran, 'The Sovereign Order of Malta in International Law', in *International Law Quarterly*, April 1954

G. De Rosa, 'L'Azione Cattolica e il "Regima" nella prospettive di F. L. Ferrari', in *Humanitas*, V, no. 5,

  I Conservatori Nazionali: Biografia di Carlo Santucci, Brescia, 1962

  Filippo Meda e l'età liberale, Florence, 1959

  'Una lettera inedita di Cardinale Gasparri sul Partito Popolare', in *Analisi e prospettivi*, no. 1, January–February 1959

  Luigi Sturzo, Turin, 1977

  Il Movimento cattolico in Italia: Dalla Restaurazione all'età giolittiana, Bari, 1966

  Il Partito Popolare Italiano, Bari, 1974

  Rufo Ruffo della Scaletta e Luigi Sturzo, Rome, 1961

  Storiellografia Anticlericale, Rome, 1963

A. De Stefani, *Baraonda Bancaria*, Milan, 1960

J. P. Diggins, *Mussolini and Fascism: The View from America*, Princeton, 1972

S. Z. Ehler and J. B. Morrall, *La Chiesa attraverso i secoli*, Milan, 1958

F. Engel-Janosi, *Il Vaticano tra nazionalismo e fascismo*, Florence, 1973

M. Falco, *The Legal Position of the Holy See before and after the Lateran Agreements*, Oxford, 1936

C. Falconi, *The Popes in the Twentieth Century: From Pius X to John XXIII*, London, 1967

A. Fappani, *Giorgio Montini*, Brescia, 1974

A. Fappani and G. Molinari, *Giovanni Battista Montini Giovane*, Turin, 1979

Fascismo e Antifascismo: Lezioni e testimonianze, 4th edn. 2 vols., Milan, 1974

Fascismo e Antifascismo a Padova negli anni venti e trenta, Padua, 1975

F. L. Ferrari, *L'Azione Cattolica e il Regime*, Florence, 1957

H. Finer, *Mussolini's Italy*, London, 1935

A. M. Fiocchi, *Enrico Rosa S.I.*, Rome, 1952

S. Fontana (ed.), *Il fascismo e le autonomie locali*, Bologna, 1973

F. Fonzi, 'Documenti per le storia dei patti lateranensi: due relazioni di Domenico Barone del 1928' in *Rivista Storica della Chiesa in Italia*, XIX, 1965

  'S. Jacini Junior', in *Tre Cattolici Liberali*, Milan, 1972

H. Fornari, *Mussolini's Gadfly*, Nashville, 1971

G. Fusco, *Storia segreta della Conciliazione*, Milan, 1967

T. Gallarati-Scotti, 'Stefano Jacini Junior', in *Il Risorgimento*, IV, no. 3, 1955

Robert L. Gannon, *The Cardinal Spellman Story*, London, 1963

B. Gariglio, *Cattolici Democratici e Clerico-fascisti a Torino, 1922–27*, Bologna, 1976

A. Garosci, *Il Seconde Risorgimento*, Rome, 1955

  Storia dei fuorusciti, Bari, 1953

A. Giannini, *Il Cammino della Conciliazione*, Milan, 1946
  I Gerarchi di Mussolini, Novara, 1973
I. Giordani, *Celestino Endrici: Un grande pastore*, Trento, 1966
  I Protestanti alla conquista d'Italia, Milan, 1931
  La Rivolta Cattolica, Rome, 1945
G. Giurati, 'La Parabola di Mussolini', in *La Settimana Incom Illustrata*, 21 February 1956
G. Gonella, *Piero Malvestiti nell'Antifascismo e nella Resistenza*, Milan, 1965
R. A. Graham, *Vatican Diplomacy: A Study of Church and State on the International Plane*, Princeton, 1959
G. Guderzo, *Cattolici e Fascisti a Pavia fra le Due Guerra*, Pavia, 1978
G. B. Guerri, *Giuseppe Bottai: un fascista critico*, Milan, 1976
U. Guspini, *L'Orecchio del Regime*, Milan, 1973
E. Hachey (ed.), *Anglo-Vatican Relations*, Boston, 1972
E. E. Y. Hales, *The Catholic Church in the Modern World*, London, 1958
S. William Halperin, *The Separation of Church and State in Italian Thought from Cavour to Mussolini*, Chicago, 1937
A. Hamilton, *The Appeal of Fascism*, London, 1971
A. C. Helmreich (ed.), *A Free Church in a Free State? The Catholic Church in Italy, Germany and France, 1864–1914*, Boston, 1964
D. Holmes, *The Triumph of the Holy See*, London, 1978
G. Hourdin, *La Stampa Cattolica*, Catania, 1947
P. Hughes, *Pope Pius XI*, New York, 1937
E. P. Howard, *Il Partito Popolare Italiano*, Florence, 1957
How the Roman Question was Settled, Catholic Truth Society Pamphlet, London, 1929
'Ignotus', *Stato Fascista, Chiesa e Scuola*, Rome, 1931
A. Iraci, *Arpinati Oppositore di Mussolini*, Rome, 1970
S. Jacini (pseud. 'Dott. G. Tonelli'), 'Die Lateranvertrage und ihre Auswirkungen auf Italianische Katholicismus', in *Hochland* (Munich) October 1933
R. Jacuzio, *Commento alla Nuova legislazione in materia ecclesiastica*, Rome, 1932
A. C. Jemolo, *Chiesa e Stato in Italia negli ultimi cento anni*, 3rd edn. Turin, 1963
  'Pio XI e il Fascismo', in *Il Ponte*, XIX, no. 6, January 1963
Peter C. Kent, *The Pope and the Duce: The International Impact of the Lateran Agreements*, London and Basingstoke, 1981
G. Lewy, *The Catholic Church and Nazi Germany*, London, 1964
G. Licata, *Il Giornalismo Cattolico Italiano*, Rome, 1964
C. J. Lowe and F. Marzari, *Italian Foreign Policy, 1870–1940*, London and Boston, 1975
L. Luzzatti, *Elezioni Politiche e Leggi Elettorali in Italia*, Rome, 1968
A. Lyttelton, *The Seizure of Power: Fascism in Italy, 1919–29*, London, 1973
  (ed.), *Italian Fascisms from Pareto to Gentile*, London, 1973
H. H. Macartney and P. Cremona, *Italian Foreign and Colonial Policy, 1914–37*, 2nd edn, New York, 1972
R. MacGregor-Hastie, *Pope Paul VI*, London, 1964
D. Mack Smith, *Italy – A Modern History*, Ann Arbor and London, 1959
  Mussolini, London, 1982
  Mussolini's Roman Empire, London and New York, 1976
F. Magri, *Angelo Mauri*, Milan, 1957
  L'Azione Cattolica in Italia, 2 vols., Rome, 1963
A. Majo, *La Stampa quotidiana cattolica Milanese – il caso de 'L'Italia'*, Milan, 1974

F. Malgeri (ed.), *Luigi Sturzo nella Storia d'Italia*, Rome, 1973
   Storia del Movimento Cattolico in Italia, 6 vols., Rome, 1980–
P. Malvestiti, *La Parte Guelfa in Europa*, Milan, 1945
L. Mangoni, *L'Interventismo della Cultura*, Bari, 1974
D. Marchesini, 'Romanità e la Scuola di Misticismo fascista', in *Quaderni di Storia*,
   IV, 1976, pp. 55–73
G. Marcucci-Fanello, *Storia della F.U.C.I.*, Rome, 1971
F. Margiotta-Broglio, *L'Italia e la Santa Sede dalla Grande Guerra alle Conciliazione*,
   Bari, 1966
   (ed.), *La Chiesa del Concordato; anatomia di una diocesi*, Vol. I, Bologna, 1977
A. Martini, *Studi sulla Questione Romana e la Conciliazione*, Rome, 1963
E. Martire, *La Conciliazione*, Rome, 1969
F. Meda, *I Cattolici e la Guerra*, Milan, 1928
G. Miglioli, *Con Roma e con Mosca*, Cremona, 1945
A. Milano, *Storia degli ebrei in Italia*, Turin, 1963
S. Minerbi, 'The Italian Activity to Recover the "Cenacolo"', in *Risorgimento*, II,
   1980
M. Missiroli, *Date a Cesare*, Rome, 1929
   'Il Conflitto dopo la Conciliazione', in *Storia Illustrata*, August 1966
M. Missori, *Governi, alte cariche dello Stato e prefetti del Regno*, Rome, 1973
J. M. Molony, *The Emergence of Political Catholicism in Italy*, London, 1977
F. Monicelli, 'La leggenda politica di P. Tacchi-Venturi', in *Settimana Incom Illustrata*,
   31 March 1966
I. Montanelli, *Padri della Patria: De Vecchi di Val Cismon*, Milan, 1949
A. Monticone (ed.), *Cattolici e Fascisti in Umbria (1922–45)*, Bologna, 1978
R. Moro, 'Afascismo e antifascismo nei movimenti intellettuali dell'Azione Cattolica
   dopo il '31', in *Storia Contemporanea*, VI, no. 4, 1975, pp. 733–801
   La Formazione della classe dirigente Cattolica, 1929–37, Bologna, 1979
R. Murri, *L'Uliva di Santena*, Milan, 1932
S. Neill, *A History of Christian Missions*, Harmondsworth, 1964
S. Negri and A. Lazzarini, *Uomini e Giornali*, Florence, 1954
A. C. O'Brien, 'L'Osservatore Romano and Fascism: The Beginning of a New Era',
   in *Journal of Church and State*, Spring 1971
S. N. Onofrio, *I Giornali bolognesi del Ventennio Fascista*, Bologna, 1972
P. Orano, *De Vecchi di Val Cismon*, Milan, 1939
V. E. Orlando, *I Miei Rapporti di Governo con la Santa Sede*, 2nd edn, Milan, 1944
N. Padellaro, *Portrait of Pius XII*, London, 1956
H. W. Paul, *The Second Ralliement: The Rapprochement between the Church and the
   State in France in the Twentieth Century*, Washington, 1967
P. Pecorari (ed.), *Chiesa, Azione Cattolica e Fascismo nell'Italia Settentrionale durante
   il Pontificato di Pio XI (1922–39)*, Bologna, 1979
A. Pellicani, *Il Papa di Tutti*, Milan, 1966
M. Piacentini, *I Culti Amessi nello Stato Italiano*, Milan, 1934
A. Piolanti, *Il Cardinale Pietro Gasparri*, Rome, 1960
E. Poulat, *Catholicisme, Democratie et Socialisme*, Paris, 1977
   Integrisme et Catholicisme Integrale, Paris, 1969
E. Pucci, *La Pace del Laterano*, Rome, 1929
G. Quazza (ed.), *Fascismo e Società Italiana*, Turin, 1973
A. Randall, *Vatican Assignment*, London, 1956
   'The Vatican and European Politics, 1922–45', in *The Ampleforth Journal*,
   Summer 1973

C. Ranfagni, *I Clerico-fascisti: i giornali dell'Università Cattolica negli anni del Regime*, Florence, 1975

G. Rapelli, 'Azione Cattolica e i Sindacati bianchi di fronte al Fascismo', in *Quaderni di Cultura e Storia Sociale*, III (New Series), 3 March 1954

'Rastignac' (pseud. of V. Morello), *Il Conflitto dopo la Conciliazione*, Milan, 1932

M. Reineri, *Il Movimento Cattolico in Italia dall'Unità al 1948*, Turin, 1975

La Resistenza Italiana: Dall'Opposizione al Fascismo alla Lotta Popolare, Rome, 1975

E. Reut-Nicolussi, *The Tyrol under the Axe of Fascism*, London, 1930

A. Rhodes, *The Vatican in the Age of the Dictators, 1922–1945*, London, 1973

A. Riccardi, *Roma 'Città Sacra'?'* Milan, 1979

B. Ricci, *Duello col Papa*, Rome, 1931

L. Riva Sanseverino, *Il Movimento Sindacale Cristano del 1850–1939*, Rome, 1950

F. Rizzi, 'Sturzo in esilio: Popolari e forze antifasciste dal 1924 al 1940', in *Luigi Sturzo nella Storia d'Italia*, Rome, 1973

E. M. Robertson, *Mussolini as Empire-Builder: Europe and Africa, 1922–36*, London, 1977

S. Rogari, 'Come la Chiesa si difese da Mussolini', in *Nuova Antologia*, MMCXXV, 1978

F. Rosengarten, *The Italian Anti-Fascist Press, 1919–45*, Cleveland, 1968

E. Rossi, *Il Manganello e l'aspersorio*, Florence, 1959

M. Rossi (ed.), *La Toscana nel Regime Fascista*, Vol. I, Rome, 1965

G. Rossini, 'Banche Cattoliche sotto il Fascismo', in *Nuovo Osservatore*, VII, nos. 56–7, Nov.–Dec. 1966

Il Movimento Cattolico nel Periodo Fascista, Rome, 1966

G. Rumi, 'Chiesa Ambrosiana e Fascismo', in *Dallo Stato di Milano alla Lombardia contemporanea* (Autori Vari), Vol. I, Milan, 1980

D. I. Rusinow, *Italy's Austrian Heritage (1919–46)*, Oxford, 1969

G. Sabbatucci (ed.), *La Crisi Italiana del Primo Dopoguerra*, Rome–Bari, 1976

L. Salvatorelli, *La Chiesa e il Mondo*, Rome, 1948

La Politica della Santa Sede dopo la Guerra, Milan, 1937

E. Santarelli, *Storia del Movimento e del Regime Fascista*, Vol. I, Rome 1967

R. Sarti (ed.), *The Axe Within: Italian Fascism in Action*, New York, 1974

G. Sciaccaluga, *Camillo Corsanego*, Rome, 1969

P. Scoppola, *La Chiesa e il Fascismo: documenti e interpretazioni*, Bari, 1971

Chiesa e Stato nella Storia d'Italia, Bari, 1967

Dal neoguelfismo alla democrazia Cristiana, Rome, 1957

La proposta politica di De Gasperi, Bologna, 1977

P. Scoppola and F. Traniello (eds.), *I Cattolici tra Fascismo e Democrazia*, Bologna, 1975

D. Secco Suardo, *I Cattolici Intransigenti*, Brescia, 1962

G. Seldes, *The Vatican, Yesterday, Today and Tomorrow*, London, 1937

R. Sencourt, *The Genius of the Vatican*, London, 1936

C. Seton-Watson, *Italy from Liberalism to Fascism 1870–1925*, London, 1967

E. Settimelli, *Aclericalismo: Parole Chiare*, Rome, 1929

Preti Adagio, Florence, 1931

Svaticanamento, Florence, 1931

R. Sgarbanti, *Ritratto politico di Giovanni Grosoli*, Rome, 1959

M. Sica, 'Storia dell'associazione Scouts Cattolici Italiani', in *Estote Parole*, XXI, nos. 108–9, 1966

D. Sorrentino, *La Conciliazione e il 'Fascismo Cattolico': i tempi e la figura di Egilberto Martire*, Brescia, 1980

G. Spadolini, *Le Due Rome: Chiesa e Stato fra '800 e '900*, 3rd edn, Florence, 1975
   Giolitti e i Cattolici, 1901–14 2nd edn, Florence, 1960
   (ed.) *Il Cardinale Gasparri e la Questione Romana, con alcuni brani inediti delle sue memorie*, Florence, 1972
G. Spataro, *I Democratici Cristiani dalla Dittatura alla Repubblica*, Rome, 1968
G. Talamo (ed.), *La Lunga Via per Roma*, Rome, 1970
F. Taliani, *La Vita di Cardinale Gasparri*, Milan, 1939
B. Talluri, 'La Civiltà Cattolica e il Fascismo: 1922–24', in *Studi Senesi*, LXXVIII (5th series), Fasc. 2
A. Tamaro, *Venti anni di Storia: 1922–43*, 2 vols., Rome, 1945
E. Tannenbaum, *Fascism in Italy: Society and Culture, 1922–45*, London, 1972
W. Teeling, *The Pope in Politics*, London, 1937
P. Togliatti, *L'Opera di De Gasperi*, Florence, 1958
M. Toscano, *Le Minoranze Etniche nella Politica e nel diritto internazionale*, Novara, 1931
S. Tramontin, 'La crisi del 1931 nella documentazione veneta', in *Rivista Storica della Chiesa*, XXVII, July–December 1974.
   Cattolici, Popolari e Fascisti nel Veneto, Rome, 1975
Trent'anni di Storia Italiana (1915–45), Turin, 1961
N. Tripodi, *Patti Lateranensi e Fascismo*, Bologna, 1959
A. Turati, *Fuori dell'ombra della mia vita: Dieci anni nel solco del Fascismo*, ed. with an introd. by A. Fappani, Brescia, 1973
L. Ubaldi, *Maria Rimoldi*, Rome, 1969
L. Valiani, G. Bianchi and E. Ragionieri, *Azionisti Cattolici e Communisti nella Resistenza*, Milan, 1972
K. O. Von Aretin, *The Papacy and the Modern World*, London, 1970
F. P. Walters, *A History of the League of Nations*, 2 vols. London, 1952
Richard A. Webster, *The Cross and the Fasces: Christian Democracy and Fascism in Italy*, Stanford, 1960
E. Wiskemann, *Europe of the Dictators, 1919–45*, London, 1966
G. B. Zilio, *Un Condottiere d'anime – Mons. Fernando Rodolfi Vescovo di Vicenza*, Vicenza, 1969
P. G. Zunino, *La Questione Cattolica nella Sinistra Italiana*, Bologna, 1973

UNPUBLISHED PAPERS, THESES AND DISSERTATIONS

F. Agostini, 'Il Movimento Giovanile Cattolico Padovano, 1919–32', doctoral thesis for the University of Padua, 1972–3
A. R. Jervolino, 'Lo Scioglimento dei Circoli della Gioventù Cattolica Italiana nel 1931', Catholic Action Study Circle, Rome, 16 February 1956
P. Scoppola, 'The State and the Church in the Fascist Period in Italy 1922–43', paper given at Cambridgeshire College of Arts and Technology, 4 November 1979

Index